40 YEARS OF BRITISH TELEVISION

Jane Harbord & Jeff Wright

BⓉXTREE

First published in 1992 by
Boxtree Limited
21 Broadwall, London SE1 9PL

Text © copyright Topical Television Limited 1992

ISBN 1 85283 409 9

13579108642

Designed and typeset by Blackjacks

Front cover painting by Tim Bernhard

Printed and bound in Great Britain

A CIP catalogue for this book is available from the British Library.

Acknowledgments

The authors would like to thank the following people and organisations for their help and cooperation in the research, development, writing and editing of this book.

Mike Hills, the managing editor of *TV Times*, and Brian Thomas, managing editor of *Radio Times*, for permission to reproduce some of their invaluable and nostalgic pages of television history.

Martin Jackson, group publisher of *Broadcast*, for access to their library.
Barry MacDonald and his staff at the ITC library for their help and guidance.

BARB for permission to reproduce TV audience research figures and for helping to fill in gaps in the published record.

Tony Mucklow for picture research. Tim Bernhard for not only his front cover painting but also for the loan of his collection of television memorabilia. Jon Keeble of ITC and Miranda Pollock of the BBC Picture Library for their enthusiastic help with picture research.

Mike Fuller, Peter Hayton, Chris Riley and Tarne Sinclair for additional research.

Val Wheeler for her keyboard skills and good humour, and, particularly, Diana Saggers for her forbearance and equanimity. And on a personal note, to Mark and Hilary for their patience, support and understanding.

And finally to Barry Took whose TV Replay spot on **TV Weekly** was the inspiration for this book.

Introduction by Barry Took

You may reasonably expect **40 Years of British Television** to start at the beginning of the 1950s – or in 1946 when TV returned after the War. Or perhaps even when BBC TV first broadcast. However the authors have chosen 1955 as the beginning of modern television – this was the year the BBC monopoly was broken with the arrival of ITV and when programme makers began to compete for the public's interest. A birth, an explosion of talent, ideas, stars and series was promised – as the TV infant started to cry for attention. Some believe it has grown into a monster – but whatever your view, TV has become Britain's number one leisure pursuit and primary source of information. This book is like a glimpse into its family album.

Television before 1955 had contained very little of note – at least that I can remember. It was still very much the 'little brother' of radio and was watched by only a tiny minority. What's more, at that time the TV day was very short: an hour of programmes in the afternoon aimed at women, children's television between 5.00 and 6.00 pm and then close down until 7.30 when the service resumed with the news and weather. After an evening of plays, variety and talks, close down came at 10.30 with the news 'in sound only'.

The early fifties included my own first TV appearance – in 1952 at the Television Theatre on Shepherd's Bush Green. It was in a Carroll Levis Discovery Show – an early version of Opportunity Knocks – which was produced by Bill Ward, a man with a very long career in TV production that continued into the nineties with Sir Harry Secombe's Highway.

Barry Took – a young discovery

However, before 1955 I didn't watch much TV at all, being too poor to pay 79 guineas – about eight weeks' wages for the average man – for a set. I did occasionally see my parents tiny Cossor set and remember how dull the programmes, and the picture, were. Eventually, though, with regular work in a West End review, I splashed out on a 14-inch screen, walnut-veneered Pye to watch the cricket presented by the Sportsview Unit with commentary by Brian Johnston.

Evening television was lost to me as I was working in the theatre, but I do remember children's television. Stamped on my mind is All Your Own with Huw Wheldon hectoring talented, if nervous, child performers like a sergeant major with a row of new recruits. I also recall Humphrey Lestocq with the bad-tempered puppet Mr Turnip; Annette Mills with the well-behaved Muffin the Mule and his friends Peregrine the Penguin and Willy the Worm dancing around on her piano top. George Cansdale struggling with uncooperative small furry animals in Pet's Corner and Armand and Michaela Dennis taking us with them on their adventures to the African plains in On Safari. All very safe and very cosy.

A new category of 'star' was created – 'TV personalities'. People like TV cook Philip Harben and the gardener Fred Streeter had a new kind of fame thrust upon them. McDonald Hobley, Sylvia Peters and Mary Malcolm were to become the faces of the BBC as the cultured and unruffled announcers who acted as hosts and hostesses for the evening's viewing.

From the 22nd September 1955 British TV audiences began to have a choice in viewing. At first only the London region viewers could watch the new Independent Television, but over the next six years other areas joined the ITV network and the choice of channels was extended to the vast majority of viewers. So what did we choose to watch?

That's what this book is all about – our TV favourites. If you dip in at random you'll find fascinating facts and information – some questions answered and some questions posed too.

What is it about Rolf Harris, Sir Harry Secombe and Leo McKern that has made them among the few to appear as regulars for over 40 years? Why are there so many famous bar-tenders on British TV? (Roy Barraclough may have some ideas – long before coming The Street's Alec Gilroy he pulled pints for Rigsby in Rising Damp.) I trod the same route myself, polishing glasses in Associated-Rediffusion's first chat show called Late Extra in 1959.

Some of these glimpses are frustrating – knowing that Cliff Richard played a 'meatily dramatic' role as a villain in a 1968 TV programme isn't quite enough – we want to see it (particularly the 'deeply emotional love scenes'), and I'd love to know why Carla Lane has created two sets of Boswells for TV: one of the two 'Liver Birds' parents were called Boswell – as well as the tribe from Bread. There must be a story there somewhere.

You'll see people's lives develop through these pages too. Peter Sissons may never have taken the presenter's chair of shows such as Question Time but for a machine gun attack on him and his ITN crew in Biafra in 1968; the scars marked the end of his days as a foreign correspondent. When Michael Aspel was the subject of This Is Your Life in 1980, he little knew how accurate the show's title was to prove seven years later.

There is also plenty of fascination for trivia fans. It's hard to believe that there were only ever 26 episodes of Andy Pandy – repeated over and over to children with short memories. Morecambe and Wise starred in The Sweeney (in 1978) – a return deal for John Thaw's appearance in their Christmas show.

Trivia maybe – but these thousands of snapshots of TV life are anything but trivial. Social historians, TV pundits and star-watchers will all have their own particular kind of field-day – and each of us can build up our own picture of the life and times of Britain.

I work regularly with Jane Harbord and Jeff Wright producing the 'TV Replay' slot in **TV Weekly**. You'll enjoy, as I do, their encyclopaedic knowledge of the ins and outs of TV people and programmes. They have a healthy disrespect for the pretensions and pomposity of the medium and put it all into amusing perspective. Open the box and take your pick!

Barry York

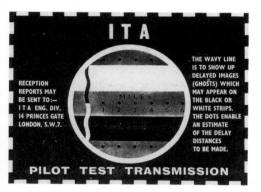

The 'Other Side' Arrives

At the time of the Coronation there was growing pressure for a second television service. Commercial TV was at first set back by reports of the coverage of the Coronation in America, where sponsors' messages kept interrupting the service in Westminster Abbey. But it was conceded that sponsorship wasn't the only way for advertisers to use TV. A White Paper was issued in late 1953 by the conservative government who were keen to see the BBC monopoly broken. The Television Bill was given the royal assent in July 1954 and the Independent Television Authority was formed.

Independent Television's arrival was not a great revolution in programming. It was said at the time that ITV was trying to be more like the BBC than the BBC itself. The first night was introduced by Leslie Mitchell, who 19 years earlier had

presented the opening of BBC TV. This was followed by speeches from the Mansion House in the City of London, then **Variety was shown** – a programme featuring an array of stars, most of whom were familiar faces from BBC variety shows: Shirley Abicair, Harry Secombe, Billy Cotton and Derek Roy to name but a few. After some extracts from safe classic plays and a boxing contest, Leslie Mitchell was back with Lady Pamela Berry, looking at London's latest fashions from the Mayfair Hotel. The night ended with the national anthem.

This was the new channel that was predicted to be: 'a planned and premeditated orgy of vulgarity', a 'tuppenny Punch and Judy show', and a 'Caliban emerging from his slimy cavern'. Lord Reith, the founding father of the BBC, compared the coming of advertising to the screen on a level with the introduction of smallpox and Black Death (Bubonic Plague) to England.

The viewers, however, loved the 'planned vulgarity'. In homes with televisions that could get both ITV and BBC, viewers were glued to ITV (known at the time as CTV, ITA, Channel 9 or simply the other side). In December 1955 84 per cent of viewers tuned into **Sunday Night At the London Palladium**.

Associated-Rediffusion provided the programmes for the five weekdays. ATV took over at the weekend for viewers in London and the home counties. They

were joined by ABC in the Midlands, after five months, and Granada in the north later in 1956. It wasn't until 1962 that the ITV network was completed.

The BBC Fights Back

The BBC had been providing Britain's growing number of viewers with a cosy TV service since 1946 before ITV burst onto the scene in September.

It may have seen itself as the senior service: 'the BBC is the oldest service in the world, but it is not run for, or by, greybeards – we are not venerable, but we do feel experienced,' the Director General wrote in *Radio Times*. Sir George Barnes, Director of Television Broadcasting, took a page to sell the national service in an article that was clearly attacking the regional system of ITV: 'BBC Covers The Country, it's not a boast it's true; 92 out of a 100 homes can watch BBC'. He ended by restating the BBC's independence and hinting at the

INTRODUCTION

pressures of pleasing advertisers. 'This service is paid for by the viewers, it owes no allegiance to anyone else.'

The coming of ITV meant more TV hours per day. The BBC expanded from 41 hours a week to 50. Programmes would start earlier in the evening at 7 pm and go on to 11 pm. In the next six months there were 28 light entertainment series, 31 plays, more sport, concerts and opera, more afternoon programmes for women and for children westerns on Fridays. The 'Talks Department' would bring: **Zoo Quest**, **The Brains Trust**, **Commonwealth Magazine** and **Animal, Vegetable and Mineral**.

The year saw the BBC bring in a crop of new programmes that would be successful in countering the loss of its monopoly.

The Grove Family, its weekly 15 minute soap opera, arrived in January – its success took the BBC by surprise. The popular press was full of stories of the cast and family affairs, and the BBC received a vast postbag from viewers believing it was a real family. It was a mirror of the sort of family the BBC saw as its TV audience – comfortable, respectable and suburban.

Dixon of Dock Green, Ted Willis' archetypal London bobby began pounding his beat. Jack Warner's character first appeared in a film called **The Blue Lamp** – unfortunately he was shot by a young tearaway played by Dirk Bogard. It was quite a reincarnation. Dixon ran for 21 years with Warner, by then 80 years old, leaving most of the action to the rest of the cast. It was a series in which the law

was seen to regularly triumph and depicted Dixon's friendly relations on the 'manor' with law abiders and law breakers. It created a safe image of what a policeman should be; ironically something which the real police force have always had trouble keeping up with.

This Is Your Life was established as one of TV's bankers. Eamonn Andrews brought the programme over from the US. The first programme's victim was supposed to be footballer Stanley Mathews, but it was leaked to the press and a last replacement was found – Eamonn himself. The same trick was played on him in the seventies, after Thames TV had taken over the show, when David Nixon turned the tables.

The first **Benny Hill Show** was broadcast from the TV Theatre at Shepherd's Bush. His straight man was Jeremy Hawke and guest stars were Alma Cogan and Beryl Reid. The first show was a flop, but it was with the second that he found success with his famed multi–character impersonations and set pieces satirising other TV shows.

Children also saw new friends arrive. **Andy Pandy** in **Watch With Mother** on Tuesdays was joined by **Picture Book** on Mondays with Patricia Driscoll, later to be Maid Marion in **Robin Hood**, and on Fridays **The Woodentops**. This completed the Watch with Mother week with **The Flower Pot Men** on Wednesday and **Rag Tag and Bobtail** on Thursday. This pattern was repeated until the late sixties.

Time for the Commercial Break

At 8.12 pm on the night of the 22nd September 1955, Jack Jackson, the host of **Variety**, *ITV's first-night show, said: "...and here's the moment you have all been waiting for; it's time for the natural break."*

A 90 second Gibbs SR toothpaste advert was the first commercial. Its producer called it "an illustrated lecture." The next day one critic wrote: 'I feel neither depraved or uplifted... I've already forgotten the name of the toothpaste.' The Times called the ads 'Comic little interruptions.' The Daily Worker headline said 'Too much marge and toothpaste' and The Observer added there wasn't enough vulgarity and attack in the ads. A visiting critic from The New York Times said the commercials were 'a paragon of British understatement and restraint.'

On ITV's opening night only 170,000 TV sets were equipped to pick up the channel in the London area, and of those a mere 100,000 tuned in. A quarter of viewers stayed loyal to the BBC. Eleven per cent didn't even switch on! Far less than had been hoped for and promised to the advertisers who paid a 50 per cent premium to appear on that first night. They were charged about £1,500 a minute for the honour. Demand was so strong to get one of the 23 slots available that night, that a ballot was held and Gibbs SR was picked out of a hat to be the first shown. There is a familiar ring to the products advertised on that first day; Cadbury's Drinking Chocolate, Dunlop tyres, Woman magazine, Lux, Surf, Ford, Shredded Wheat, Brillo...

Commercial breaks or 'natural breaks' as they were called, were severely governed. No religion, no politics, good taste at all times – two committees vetted ads in script and finished form. There was even a debate as to whether toilet rolls should only be seen wrapped rather than 'running free'. Natural breaks – the term 'natural' was never tested or defined – were restricted to six minuted per hour and there had to be a two minute interval between any state occasion, church service, formal royal ceremony or any appearance by a member of the royal family and an advertisement.

INTRODUCTION

Associated TeleVision

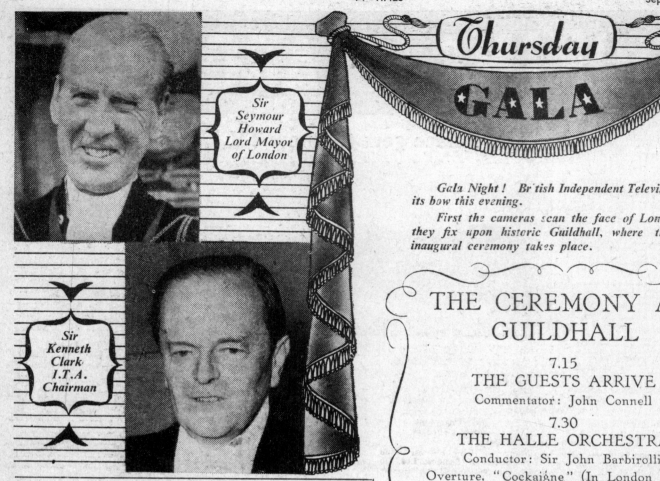

Sir Seymour Howard Lord Mayor of London

Sir Kenneth Clark I.T.A. Chairman

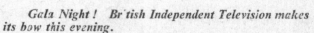

Thursday GALA

Gala Night ! British Independent Television makes its bow this evening.

First the cameras scan the face of London ; then they fix upon historic Guildhall, where the official inaugural ceremony takes place.

THE CEREMONY AT GUILDHALL

7.15
THE GUESTS ARRIVE
Commentator : John Connell

7.30
THE HALLE ORCHESTRA
Conductor : Sir John Barbirolli
Overture, "Cockaigne" (In London Town)
by Sir Edward Elgar

The National Anthem

7.45
INAUGURAL SPEECHES
by
The Rt. Hon. The Lord Mayor of London,
Sir Seymour Howard
The Postmaster-General,
Dr. the Rt. Hon. Charles Hill, M.P.
The Chairman of the Independent Television
Authority, Sir Kenneth Clark

8.0　　VARIETY

A sparkling show, "Channel Nine," from ABC's television theatre. Appearing in Channel Nine are some of the stars who will be regularly featured in Independent Television's variety programmes.

Introduced by **Jack Jackson**, they include :—

Shirley Abicair	**Elizabeth Allan**
Daphne Batchelor	**Billy Cotton**
Reg Dixon	**Lucille Graham**
Hughie Green	**John Hanson**
Sheila Mathews	**Michael Miles**
Bessie Rogers	**Shirley Norman**
Leslie Randall	**Derek Roy**
Joy Shelton	**Harry Secombe**
Leslie Welch	**Kip Van Nash**
Theda Sisters	**The George Carden Dancers**

Production by Bill Ward.

Sept 22 OPENING

Dr. Charles Hill Postmaster General

Sir Robert Fraser I.T.A. Director General

8.40　DRAMA

Robert Morley introduces:—

An excerpt from:

THE IMPORTANCE OF BEING EARNEST
by Oscar Wilde.

Lady Bracknel.................Dame Edith Evans
Gwendoline...................Margaret Leighton
John Worthing................Sir John Gielgud

Directed by Quentin Lawrence.

BAKER'S DOZEN
by "Saki" (H. H. Munro).

Mrs. Carewe.....................Pamela Brown
The Major.......................Alec Guinness
Mrs. Payley-Paget.................Faith Brook

Directed by Desmond Davis.

An excerpt from:

PRIVATE LIVES
by Noel Coward.

Amanda...........................Kay Hammond
Elyot............................John Clements

Directed by Robert Hamer.

The sequences from "The Importance of Being Earnest" and "Baker's Dozen" were produced by Towers of London Ltd., in association with H. M. Tennent, Ltd. The sequence from "Private Lives" was produced by Associated-Rediffusion, Ltd.

9.10　PROFESSIONAL BOXING

Jack Solomons presents
Terence Murphy v. Lew Lazar

in a 12-round contest at 11 st. 6 lb. for the Southern Area Middleweight Championship, from Shoreditch Town Hall. Commentators : Len Harvey and Tony Van den Bergh.

Produced by Keith Rogers.

10.0　NEWS AND NEWSREEL

Newsreel presents outstanding events of recent days.

10.15　GALA NIGHT AT THE MAYFAIR

Opening Night Gala at the Mayfair Hotel, London.

Leslie Mitchell introduces some of the guests.

London's leading fashion houses present their latest creations ; the models introduced by **Lady Pamela** Berry, with a commentary by **Mary Hill**.

Arranged in co-operation with the Incorporated Society of London Fashion Designers.

10.30　STAR CABARET

With music by **Billy Ternant** and his Orchestra.

Directed by Kenneth Carter and Bill Perry.

10.50　PREVIEW

A glimpse of some of the programmes to come on Independent Television during the coming months.

11.0　EPILOGUE

The National Anthem and close-down.

Today's programmes produced by Associated-Rediffusion, Ltd., and Associated Broadcasting Company, Ltd.

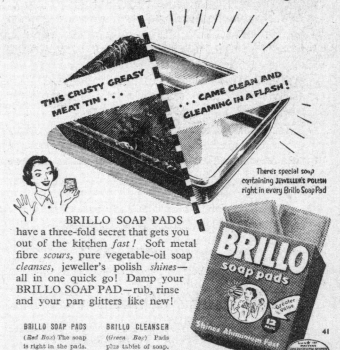

1955

TOP TWENTY
Percentage of audience (London)

1	Sunday Palladium	ITV	84
2	Theatre Royal	ITV	79
3	I Love Lucy	ITV	79
4	Dragnet	ITV	78
5	Take Your Pick	ITV	78
6	Robin Hood	ITV	73
7	Figure Skating	ITV	72
8	People Are Funny	ITV	71
9	Saturday Showtime	ITV	71
10	Stage One	ITV	71
11	Double Your Money	ITV	70
12	Gun Law	ITV	69
13	Love and Kisses	ITV	69
14	Highland Fling	BBC	68
15	Boxing	BBC	66
16	Movie Magazine	ITV	66
17	Jack Jackson Show	ITV	65
18	TV Playhouse	ITV	64
19	Fairbanks Presents	ITV	63
20	Gerry's Inn	ITV	62

• No 1 – Stars were singer Dickie Valentine and Patacou, France's First Lady of Cabaret. The compere was Tommy Trinder.

• No 7 – Men and women's UK Figure Skating Championship finals live from Streatham Ice Rink.

• No 9 – Saturday's Variety Showcase Wakey! Wakey! was fun and frolics with master showman Billy Cotton and his band.

• No 16 – John Fitzgerald introduced Movie Magazine news with film clips.

ITV Hits the Top

ITV became a household name with its three major hits – **Sunday Night at the London Palladium, Take Your Pick** and **Double Your Money**.

Sunday Night at the London Palladium (1) enticed top showbiz guests to appear and introduced US game show **Beat the Clock** to UK audiences. Its first Sunday Night, presented by Tommy Trinder, featured singers Gracie Fields and Guy Mitchell. The Palladium became a national institution with one vicar switching the time of his evening service so his congregation could catch the show.

Take Your Pick (5) was ITV's first Friday night game show. Quiz inquisitor Michael Miles picked contestants from the studio audience to ask them three simple general knowledge questions. He then gave them a key to a locked box, where they might find a dried prune or a star prize. But before reaching that stage they could win five shillings if they avoided saying Yes or No for a minute while being bombarded with questions or bullied into selling back their key to possibly avoid winning the booby prize.

Double Your Money (11) was, with Take Your Pick, one of ITV's core shows. Both never left the charts in their 13-year run. Hughie Green, like Michael Miles, brought his quiz show from Radio Luxembourg to ITV.

On Monday nights contestants were given a choice of 42 subjects and if they answered correctly, doubled their money up to £32. They could then go on the Treasure Trail with a top prize of £1,000.

People Are Funny (8), hosted by Derek Roy, hit the headlines. It was a very early UK import of a US game show format and the forerunner of a host of embarrassment factor shows like **Candid Camera, Game For a Laugh, Beadle's About** and **People Do the Funniest Things**. Practical jokes and minor ordeals were played on contestants after which they won a prize. One woman was told to smash up china under a cloth, it was then revealed it was her own china. It was condemned as cruel, tasteless and exploitative – although the people winning the prizes, the audience and the waiting list of volunteers didn't agree. However, it was the first programme to be censured by the ITA – they thought it too cruel. Rather than tone it down, ATV, its producers, took it off.

TV TIMES, September 18, 1959 Volume 16   No 203   SOUTHERN EDITION   FOURPENCE

TV TIMES
SEPT 20–SEPT 26 ITV PROGRAMMES PAGES 32-45

HUGHIE GREEN
Double Your Money
Monday, 8.35 pm

MICHAEL MILES
Take Your Pick
Friday, 8 pm

General Election: The week's party political broadcast and ITV news round-ups

NEAR MISSES

• **Fabian of Scotland Yard**, starring Bruce Seton as ex-Flying Squad officer Detective Superintendent Robert Fabian, was the BBC's first crime series. Some of Fabian's real-life cases were used as plots for the half-hour series. The real-life Fabian turned up on ITV in 1956 as the Guardian of the Questions in **The $64,000 Question** quiz.

• **Colonel March of Scotland Yard** was ITV's first home-grown police series starring Boris Karloff as the Head of the Queer Complaints Department. The one–eyed detective turned his good eye towards solving cases that had proved too much for ordinary coppers.

• **What's My Line?**, the first US import of a Goodson and Todmann show, was Britain's first successful game show. Hosted by Eammon Andrews, the regular panelists – Lady Isobel Barnet, Barbara Kelly, Gilbert Harding and David Nixon – had to guess what the contestants did for a living. Goodson and Todmann created some of the biggest TV quiz and game shows including **The Price Is Right** and **Blockbusters**.

• Roy Rogers, the singing King of the Cowboys, appeared in a modern western. All the traditional goodies and baddies were there, gunfights, rustlers and hold-ups, but then a jeep would drive into shot

Boris Karloff staring as 'Colonel March of Scotland Yard'.

carrying the Sheriff. Dale Evans, his wife, Trigger, Buttercup and Bullet the dog helped Roy beat the baddies.

• **The Adventures of Robin Hood** starring Richard Green – made for children in a tiny studio in Walton on Thames – became a family favourite. More than 140 episodes were made with TV stars popping up in Robin's band of Merry Men or on the wicked Sheriff's side including Jane Asher, Paul

Eddington, Richard O'Sullivan, Leo McKern and Billie Whitelaw. The end credit music was a hit record for American singer Dick James.

• Ex-RAF pilot Peter Dimmock presented **Sportview**, the BBC's mid-week sports roundup programme. Dimmock became Head of Outside Broadcasts while still presenting the programme which started the annual Sports Personality of the Year Award.

1955

Sooty was a well-established star of BBC, having made his first appearance with Harry Corbett in 1952 on **Talent Night**, when he starred in a series of award winning commercials for OXO.

"Murray Mints – the too good to hurry mints" was voted the top TV ad by a Gallup Poll. Its catchy tune was hummed on buses, tubes and trains.

Took's
TV Teasers

1 Who was TV's 'Mr Pastry'?

2 What was the children's television programme presented by Huw Wheldon called?

3 Who was Andy Pandy and Teddy's little doll friend on Watch With Mother?

TV advertisers regularly took space in magazines to promote mini-programmes or long commercials – some lasting for up to three minutes. TV cook Philip Harben did a rich Christmas cake recipe for *Woman's Own* on TV.

A YEAR IN THE SOAPS

Morning Soap's Short Run

In ITV's first week on air it launched Britain's first 15-minute daily soap opera, **Sixpenny Corner**, which was centred on the trials and tribulations of newlyweds Bill and Sally Norton. The true-to-life story was set in a dilapidated garage, managed by Bill, in a town called Springwood.

Starring Howard Pays and Patricia Dainton – who appeared alongside Lucille Ball on the front cover of the *TV Times'* first edition – the morning soap's airing was short-lived. A cash crisis forced ITV to axe its morning programmes after a few weeks. Sixpenny Corner was transferred to an evening slot, but was cut after ten months in June '56.

A youthful Rolf Harris (*below*), crayon in hand, appeared on **Small Time** which was screened in ITV's first week on air. Harris (then 25) is just one of three TV regulars still appearing in the nineties, along with Harry Secombe, who starred in the opening night variety show, and Leo McKern who played a baddie in the first Robin Hood adventure.

12.0 NEWS
Followed by Programme Parade.
12.10 IT'S AN IDEA Each week someone will tell you about a useful idea that they have had and demonstrate how to carry it out. This week Jeanne Kent shows, in the simplest way, how to make a lampshade.
12.15 SMALL TIME Big Black Crayon Rolf Harris and Jean Ford in a programme of stories and pictures. The young audience are invited to help Rolf Harris in drawing pictures with their "big black crayon."
12.30 Time signal : close down till 5.0

Rolf Harris

A Mr Plantagenet Somerset Fry became an overnight celebrity after appearing on Double Your Money. The Oxford post-graduate was the first contestant to enter the 'Treasure Trail'. He even had to ask a fellow student to act as his 'press officer' to keep Fleet Street at bay. However, he was not game enough to risk his money on the £1,000 question and quit the quiz when he reached £512.

TEASER ANSWERS

1 Richard Hearne was famous for his Mr Pastry character with droopy grey moustache, black string tie and bowler hat. He received an OBE in 1970, the year he died.
2 All Your Own – a TV regular in the fifties where children with special talents came on to show them off.
3 Looby Lou settled into the basket at the end of each programme. Only 26 episodes were made and the BBC just kept repeating them.

American TV Hits Britain

Shows with an American flavour proved popular in the fifties. In 1956 five shows made it to the top 20 as well as four British series based on American game-show formats.

Dragnet (5) 'The story you are about to see is true, only the names have been changed to protect the innocent' was the classic introduction to this cop show with a documentary feel. Jack Webb starred as Sgt Joe Friday in the first American cop show to be screened in Britain. Webb created, starred, wrote and produced the dramas of life in the Los Angeles Police Department – 300 were made from 1951 to 1959.

Assignment Foreign Legion (10) starred Merle Oberon as a roving foreign correspondent working in North Africa. The series was shot in Algeria and Morocco 'with the full cooperation of the French Foreign Legion', but not the nationalist freedom fighters. Skirmishes meant that the filming had to be completed at Beaconsfield Studios in peaceful Buckinghamshire.

Gun Law (14) or **Gunsmoke** as it was originally called, with James Arness as Matt Dillon the Marshall of Dodge City, Kansas, was the first adult western

In this scene from tonight's "Dragnet" Sgt. Joe Friday (Jack Webb) and Officer Frank Smith (Ben Alexander) stand over young Bruce Abbot (Jimmy Ogg)

8.30 DRAGNET
This is the first of the "Dragnet" series, in which the events you are about to see are true.
　　　　THE BIG ESCAPE
　　　　　by James Moser.
　Produced and directed by **Jack Webb.**
Sergeant Joe Friday..................Jack Webb
Officer Frank Smith.................Ben Alexander
Max Tyler.........................Harlan Warde
Dorothy Tyler...................Elizabeth Fraser
Dr. Hall..........................Vic Perrin
Captain Diddion....................Art Gilmore
George Grayson.................Emerson Treacy
Larry Thompson................Bill Boyett
In this episode the man remanded in custody on a charge of robbery breaks out of jail, and we are shown the methods used by the American police force to track him down.

running on American television. It ran for 20 years with more than 500 episodes. Dennis Weaver was the limping deputy Chester and Miss Kitty of the Long Branch Saloon (Amand Blake) provided the feminine touch.

Frontier Doctor (15) dealt with the adventures of Doctor Bill Baxter (Rex Allen) as a 'tough young medico who goes about his mission of tending the sick in the turbulent days of the land rush in the western territories'.

Douglas Fairbanks Presents (17) was another transatlantic hit, but this long running series was made in Britain. Commissioned by NBC in the States, the series was shown all over the world. The half-hour dramas had a theme of average people caught in unusual situations. Fairbanks only starred in some of the 117 episodes made between 1953 and 1957.

> The Liberace story was serialised in the TV Times – fans who missed episodes could order a copy of his biography for 2s 6d.

Took's TV Teasers

1 Who was the future Conservative MP who introduced Highlight ?

2 Who was a newsreader for ITN and later became a Conservative MP ?

3 Who was the first Prime Minister to make a TV ministerial broadcast ?

1956

TOP TWENTY
Percentage of audience (London)

1	The Gang Show	ITV	81
2	Armchair Theatre	ITV	79
3	Take Your Pick	ITV	76
4	Sunday Palladium	ITV	75
5	Dragnet	ITV	75
6	Val Parnell's Startime	ITV	75
7	Secret Mission	ITV	74
8	TV Playhouse	ITV	74
9	Fireside Theatre	ITV	73
10	Foreign Legion	ITV	73
11	Theatre Royal	ITV	73
12	Before Your Very Eyes	ITV	71
13	The 64,000 Question	ITV	71
14	Gun Law	ITV	71
15	Frontier Doctor	ITV	70
16	Close Up	ITV	69
17	Fairbanks Presents	ITV	69
18	Two For the Money	ITV	68
19	Robin Hood	ITV	68
20	Double Your Money	ITV	68

• No 1 – Presented by Jack Hylton on Thursday nights in September, The Crazy Gang were Nervo and Knox, Naughton and Gold and Bud Flannagan, but his partner Chesney Allen and Monsewer Eddie Grey were absent.

• No 2 – The top drama starred Ronald Lewis and Margaretta Scott in The Hollow Crown about a king coming home after a coup.

• No 7 – A series of true wartime stories about the Special Operations Executive (SOE) and the Resistance.

1956

TVnews

1956

- The BBC celebrated its tenth year back on air since the war with a 90-minute gala show called **We Are Your Servants**.
- Granada TV started broadcasting in the north. At first its franchise only covered five week days with ABC doing the weekends.
- A series of sponsored programmes were ruffling feathers at the ITA. John Betjeman introduced **Discovering Britain** – a series of motoring films highlighting Britain's heritage for which Shell Petrol bought the whole of a three minute commercial break. But events overtook the ITA's worries – the fuel shortage following the Suez crisis banned all advertising of petrol.
- The first experimental colour TV broadcasts were made in November from the Alexandra Palace studios. They continued with different systems until 1969 when the German PAL (Phased Alternation Line) provided colour TV for all of Britain.
- A **TV Playhouse** called **Teddy Gang** caused a rumpus. The programme was listed in *TV Times* as 'a story of today, of Teddy Boys and Teddy Girls and their grim fight against organised society... it is the story of Nick who has murdered to get power.' The subject matter of teenage violence fuelled further newspaper headlines on the problem of youth and teenage violence.

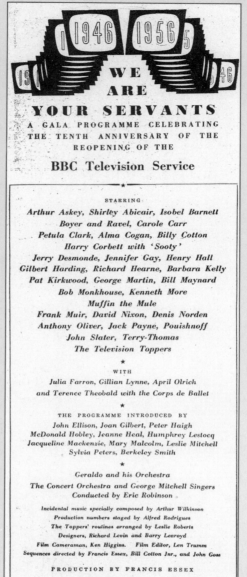

- Flash London motor dealer, Raymond Way, was the first person to have a TV in the back of his Rolls Royce. The specially mounted and ventilated nine inch set had a hydraulic aerial that adjusted for BBC and ITV.

- *The New York Post's* TV Editor, Jay Nelson, praised British television during a UK visit, but slammed American TV saying: 'Much of the programming is junk, our commercials are intrusive, vulgar and frequently painful to watch'.

TEASER ANSWERS

1   Geoffrey Johnson Smith introduced the early evening ten minute magazine programme which was seen as the prototype for Tonight.
2   Christopher Chataway, who went on to be the government minister responsible for broadcasting.
3   Sir Anthony Eden in April. He had taken over from Churchill the previous year and had never given a TV interview or made a ministerial broadcast in his long political career.

Hello and Goodbye to the Armstrongs

One Family was ITV's answer to **The Groves**. The family in this case, the Armstrongs, even had the same number of kids, two boys and two girls. Dad, played by Patrick Holt, had just quit his job in a furniture shop to set up on his own. Mum, Joyce Heron, was a bit scatter-brained, but well-meaning.

Grandpa, played by veteran actor Gordon Harker, 'was a Boer War veteran with a VC, a pet parrot called Kaiser Bill and a collection of military mementos in a chalet in the garden.' At the foot of the cast list was Arthur Lowe as Mr Boswick.

The author, R F Delderfield, wrote the daily serial working from his little cottage in Budleigh Salterton, Devon; he promised to make the family as real as possible, not just a TV family. They were so real that they even had a 'daily'; Mrs Hook 'is a lovable cockney with her hair in a bun and turban who, although she could earn 3s 6d a week more elsewhere, says: "I prefer to work for the 'appy Armstrongs."' The sheer unrelenting grind of producing a daily soap must have been far too much for Delderfield because the 'appy Armstrongs only lasted for 18 weeks.

FIRST NIGHTS

Hancock's Half Hour, written by Simpson and Galton moved from radio to TV in June. Tony Hancock played the dreamer living with Sid James at 23 Railway Cuttings, East Cheam.

Hancock later went solo and made **The Blood Donor**, **The Bowmans** and **The Radio Ham**.

Billy Cotton's **Wakey! Wakey!** was also another transfer from radio in May, featuring Alan Breeze and Doreen Stephens. Renamed **The Billy Cotton Band Show** it was one of BBC's Saturday night bankers until Cotton died in 1969.

The Eurovision Song Contest was broadcast for the first time in Britain, but there was no UK entry. It was held in Lugano, Switzerland and won by the Swiss with 'Refrain' sung by Lyss Assia.

What the Papers Say with Brian Inglis started its criticism of the British press. Guest presenters have included Michael Parkinson, Mike Scott and Bill Grundy with many of Fleet Street's finest attacking their fellow hacks.

This Week, ITV's longest running current affairs programme, started in January. Presented by Leslie Mitchell, it was basically a topical news magazine. Now it is an investigative single topic programme.

The Adventures of Sir Lancelot introduced the story of Queen Guinevere's Champion. The successful 30 half-hour adventures were repeated until the late sixties. William Russell also had staying power – he turned up in **Coronation Street** in 1992 as Rita Fairclough's suitor.

Jimmy Edwards played the headmaster of seedy Chislebury Boys School in **Whack-O!** – keeping parents, inspectors and creditors at arms length.

TV Crisis

The 1956 Suez conflict created a TV crisis when Prime Minister Sir Anthony Eden, furious that air-time was given to those opposing the invasion, threatened Government-controlled broadcasting. It had the opposite effect however of dissolving the '14 day rule' which had prevented TV talks, discussions or coverage of any parliamentary business upto two weeks before it was due to be discussed in the House.

ITV also had a crisis – lack of cash. Early investors had been hopelessly over-optimistic. Associated-Rediffusion lost

£2.7 million in its first year and major backer Associated Newspapers wanted out. The *Daily Mirror* supported a new share issue which saved ATV from bankruptcy. However investors sticking with ITV did see huge returns – in the case of ATV a one shilling share was worth £11 just three years later.

Kingsway Corner was probably the most basic TV programme ever made by Associated-Rediffusion. Interviewers Kent Walton and Muriel Young literally grabbed people passing the company's London studio for 30 minutes of live TV.

• Grumpy **What's My Line?** panellist Gilbert Harding was promoting Sky Tour holidays for £27 16s 6d – all in.

American Comedy Hits Britain

Top American Comedy show **I Love Lucy** arrived on ITV. Starring Lucille Ball – a multi-millionairess who was the first woman star to produce her own series – and Desi Arnaz living in a New York apartment with William Frawley and Vivian Vance playing their landlords. Ball and Arnaz made a pilot in 1950 and since 1951 the show had been a raging success.

Another much-loved show, based on the formula of established stars playing themselves in a fictionalised series was **The Burns and Allen Show** which ran for seven years notching up 139 stories. Starring the well-known film and theatrical pair – George Burns, playing the straight man to Gracie Allen's hair-brained schemes. In some episodes the plot took on a bizarre twist as Burns watched the show on *his* TV and wondered how his wife would get out of her latest madcap scheme.

Joan Davis, dubbed the Queen of Television, starred in **I Married Joan**. Playing the part of a scatty wife, Joan always complicated the life of her husband, Judge Bradley Stevens played by Jim Backus – who was famous as the voice of the cartoon character Mr Magoo.

The Jack Benny Show, halfway between a sitcom and variety show, also starred Eddie Anderson as Benny's butler Rochester. Viewers saw a tight-fisted Benny taking shopping trips, holidays and being stopped by a robber – 'Your money or your life?' to which Benny replied 'I'm thinking, I'm thinking.'

Topper was a fantasy sitcom based on a house haunted by its previous owners – a couple who were tragically killed in a skiing accident. Leo Carroll starred as banker Cosmo Topper – the only person who could see the couple and their martini-drinking St Bernard.

1956

1957

TOP TWENTY
Homes [millions]

1	Take Your Pick	ITV	3.25
2	Sunday Palladium	ITV	3.23
3	Criss Cross Quiz	ITV	3.22
4	The Army Game	ITV	3.21
5	TV Playhouse	ITV	3.20
6	Prince of Wales Show	ITV	3.14
7	O.S.S.	ITV	3.12
8	Double Your Money	ITV	3.09
9	Salute To Showbusiness	ITV	3.05
10	Armchair Theatre	ITV	3.01
11	Arthur Askey Show	ITV	3.01
12	Emergency Ward Ten	ITV	3.01
13	Spot the Tune	ITV	3.00
14	Murder Bag	ITV	2.97
15	Life With the Lyons	ITV	2.94
16	Jack Jackson Show	ITV	2.94
17	Caroll Levis Discoveries	ITV	2.94
18	This Week	ITV	2.83
19	Alfred Marks Time	ITV	2.81
20	Tell the Truth	ITV	2.78

• No 2 – Stars in the top Palladium were Americans Paul Anka singing his hit *Diana*, and film star Janet Blair. Alfred Marks compered.

• No 5 – The top drama was Pick Up Girl starring Andre Morrell and Janet Munro in a play about juvenile delinquency.

• No 9 – This was a celebration of ITV's second birthday. A two hour tribute of drama, variety, comedy and song.

1957

Quiz Prize Record

Criss Cross Quiz (3), hosted by Jeremy Hawke, started in June 1957 and was basically noughts and crosses with questions chosen from 98 categories. Every right answer was worth £20 and if you kept winning you kept collecting the money. At the time there was no prize limit and one contestant walked away with £2,360. Jeremy Hawke left the quiz in 1962 but the quiz continued to roll until 1967.

The Army Game (4) was ITV's first big comedy hit. The show, set in a transit and surplus ordnance depot at Nether Hopping with Hut 29 housing a bunch of failed soldiers, struck a chord with millions of ex-servicemen. Sgt Major Bullimore, William Hartnell, tried to make soldiers out of dropouts like Alfie Bass as Excused Boots Bisley, Michael Medwin as the con-man Corporal Springer and the CO Major Upshot-Bagley, Geoffrey Sumner, who was more interested in his pigs than army life. It ran for five years with a total of 153 episodes.

O.S.S. (7) was an early example of ATV's mid-Atlantic TV policy. Set in wartime Europe the true stories followed the work of the Office of Strategic Services, the forerunner of America's CIA. Ron Randell starred as Major Hawthorne with Lionel Murton as his controller. The strong US flavour meant good sales in the US as well as ratings success in Britain.

Emergency Ward Ten (12) was ITV's first hit soap opera. Oxbridge Hospital was the setting for the lives and loves of doctors and nurses. The main character was played by Jill Browne who starred as Nurse Carol Young for eight years. Many stars passed through the hospital including heart-throbs Desmond Carrington, Charles Tingwell and John Alderton and patients Albert Finney, Ian Hendry and Joanna Lumley. About 1,200 actors were used in the programme's ten year run.

Life With the Lyons (15) The TV version of the long running radio family comedy starring Ben Lyon, his wife Bebe Daniels and their children Barbara and Richard. Molly Weir played their maid.

'...and later this evening'

Sylvia Peters helped BBC TV to celebrate its 21st birthday in 1957. She joined stars like Leslie Mitchell, the first TV programme announcer in 1936, McDonald Hobley and Eamonn Andrews at the National Radio Show. Peters became the nation's sweetheart when she joined the BBC ten years earlier as a staff announcer – a job that is now virtually extinct.

Announcers also had to fill when something went wrong, which it did regularly in the days of live TV.

The BBC was embarrassed by Peters' glamourous image – she had many a run-in with BBC bosses over her low-cut dresses. She left the BBC after 11 years to freelance and was a regular on Southern TV's **Houseparty**.

FIRST NIGHTS

With **Shadow Squad** came more free-lance crime fighters starring Peter Williams as Don Carter and George Moon as his cheerful cockney side kick Ginger Smart. The two ex-flying squad detectives resigned so that they could drive over 30mph, beat up suspects and not have to worry about issuing cautions. The series was originally made by Associated-Rediffusion, but switched to Granada TV which made 175 episodes.

The Sky At Night is the longest running science programme in the world and

TV news

• Scottish TV joined the ITV network. *The Scotsman* called the opening night 'a spectacle sumptuously mounted, the most brilliant collection of Scots artists ever to amalgamate their talents in a single production.' Its owner, Lord Thomson, was pleased as well. He later called his ITV franchise 'a licence to print money'.
• **Panorama's** 1st of April edition carried a story about the successful spaghetti harvest in Switzerland. Amazingly hundreds of viewers asked where they could buy the plants!
• The Queen made her first TV broadcast – a recorded speech for her subjects in Canada. She also made her first live Christmas Day broadcast on TV and radio.
• Prince Phillip also took to the screen presenting **Round the World In Forty Minutes** for children's TV and then **The Restless Sphere** for the International Geophysical Year.
• Schools television service started on ITV in May with **Looking and Seeing**. The BBC followed suit in September.
• TV's shutdown period, also known as Toddler's Truce, between 6pm and 7pm, ended in 1957. The off-air period was introduced to allow mums to put kiddies to bed with no distractions, but ITV wanted the extra hours to sell more air time and grab early evening viewers.

Patrick Moore is also the longest running presenter of a single programme. He has turned into one of TV's most impersonated people and his stature has increased literally since the space shots of the sixties and seventies brought him to a wider audience.

Pinky and Perky – the puppet creations of Jan and Vlasta Dalibor – were not just for children's hour, they were guest on the **Palladium**, **Royal Variety** and many other TV shows. Actors Jimmy Thompson and John Slater were their straight men and, with their funny falsetto voices, their records were hits.

Fury, the **Black Beauty** of the fifties, starred Bobby Diamond as an orphan who comes to live on a ranch and befriends a horse. Peter Graves was the other male lead, later he starred in **Mission Impossible**. Over 100 adventures were made of the horse with telepathic powers.

Six Five Special on Saturday evenings was the first BBC pop music programme.

TONIGHT
Look around with
Cliff Michelmore
Sport—Music—People
Cinema—Theatre—Travel
WITH
Derek Hart
Geoffrey Johnson Smith
AND THIS WEEK
Rory McEwen
Produced by
DONALD BAVERSTOCK
NOW AT 6.45
CLIFF MICHELMORE

Took's TV TEASERS

1 Which American soldier was based at Fort Baxter, Kansas?
2 Which fat schoolboy did Gerald Campion play?
3 What was the name of George Dixon's son-in-law in Dixon of Dock Green?

Pete Murray and Josephine Douglas introduced fifties pop stars like Chris Barber and His Jazz Band, The Dallas Boys, Michael Holliday and Don Lang and The Frantic Five were the resident band. Another co-presenter was ex-heavyweight boxer Freddie Mills. (*Pictured at the base of the page are Jon Pertwee and a very young Adam Faith in a skiffle session.*)

Tonight has a supreme status as *the* current affairs programme to beat all current affairs programmes. In theory, the mix of serious journalism and light features all ending with a topical calypso shouldn't have worked, but the highly experienced team of print journalists and TV professionals like Cliff Michelmore, Kenneth Allsop, Alan Whicker and Fyfe Robinson gave the live programme an edge that has seldom been matched.

1957

Terry Scott in
SCOTT FREE
★
WITH
Norman Vaughan
Henry Longhurst
Marcia Ashton
Peter Swanwick
June Rodney
AND
Wallas Eaton
Original music and
arrangements by Bruce Campbell
Orchestra directed by Eric Robinson
Script by Lew Schwartz
Designer, Guy Sheppard
Produced by
HARRY CARLISLE
at 8.0

1957

• **Scott Free** was Terry Scott's first starring comedy series. With Norman Vaughan he played an out of work actor who is sent by his agent to be an entertainment officer in the seaside town of Bogmouth. Many of the plots for the sitcom were based on Terry's experiences in seaside rep.

• **Theatre Flash** came 'direct from the stage of the The Old Vic Theatre'. The BBC in one of its live relays from current theatrical hits, presented an extract from A Midsummer Night's Dream with Frankie Howerd playing Bottom.

• **The Perry Como Show** was a popular long running imported variety show from the US starring the Italian/American crooner. His easy-going style was the prototype which many British stars copied. The one hour show was sponsored by Kraft in the States and had to have the various sponsors messages cut.

• **Joan and Leslie** were the husband and wife team the Randalls, although Joan remained Joan Reynolds in an American-style comedy where stars more or less played themselves. Co-starring were Harry Towb and Noel Dyson. The Randalls went on to a rewarding career advertising Fairy Snow washing powder. They spent nine years 'forcing grey out and forcing white in'.

The Grove Family

For no apparent reason the BBC's first successful soap was axed in June. **The Groves**, a 20-minute weekly saga about a respectable working class family, was the **Eastenders/Coronation Street** of its day. Fleet Street just could not get enough Grove stories. Edward Evans played the builder dad, mum was Ruth Dunning, and the star of the show was grumpy gran Nancie Roberts. The children were Christopher Beeny as Lenny, Margaret Downs as Daphne, Peter Bryant as Jack and Sheila Sweet as Pat the pin-up girl of the serial.

The BBC's lack of foresight and a row with writers Michael and Roland Pertwee who were tired out after three years writing, led to the soap's demise.

Robin Day was back from holiday. That week he was newscasting for ITN and presenting **Impact** *'a hard hitting interview on a matter of the moment.' TV Times said 'He is not one of those who has made a career out of rudeness. True, his questions are often uncomfortable and his manner aggressive, but his bluntness is used to get results'.*

The music sheet for Shell petrol's latest commercial *(right)* was printed for those who wanted to sing-along-a-shell.

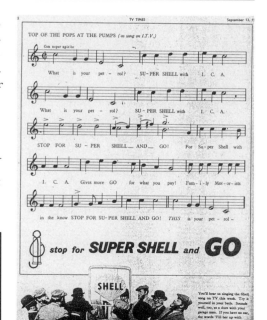

TEASER ANSWERS

1   Sergeant Ernest G Bilko in The Phil Silvers Show.
2   Billy Bunter of Greyfriars School. A popular series based on the famous Frank Richards books.
3   Detective Sergeant Andy Crawford, played by Peter Byrne – who was to turn up many years later playing Ma Boswell's boyfriend in Bread.

Game Shows Win the Rating Prizes

Six game shows gained places in the year's hit parade with Dotto winning the star prize as the most watched show.

Dotto, a quiz based on the children's game of joining the dots up to form a face, started in 1958 with Robert Gladwell. Jimmy Hanley was the next host, then Shaw Taylor with his first big hit on TV. And there was none of todays high tech computer graphics – a gang of technicians were behind the scenes joining the dots by hand.

Twenty One (6) hit the headlines in 1958. Bernard Davies, a bit part actor, won a record £5,580 – enough in those days to buy him a house and a car.

Two contestants sat in soundproof boxes and answered tough general knowledge questions asked by Chris Howland. The first to 21 points won the money. Twenty One was dropped by Granada after a contestant claimed he was given 'definite leads' to answers.

Spot the Tune (7) was hosted by Jackie Rae with Marion Ryan. Contestants with an ear for music could win large cash prizes and compete for the jackpot prize if they recognised a few bars of music and pressed the buzzer. As **Name That Tune** the format was seen again in the seventies and late eighties.

Make Up Your Mind (20) was a primitive fifties version of **The Price Is Right**. David Jacobs asked studio challengers to decide whether a valuable object or a sum of money was worth more.

Many other game shows failed to reach the Top 20 in 1958 including **Tell the Truth** a celebrity panel game hosted by McDonald Hobley, **I've Got a Secret**, in which celebrities guessed viewers' secrets, **Turnaround** hosted by Roy Ward Dixon, **Criss Cross Quiz** with Jeremy Hawke and **Make Me Laugh**, a panel game starring The Crazy Gang.

Took's TV Teasers

1 How did a contestant beat the panel in What's My Line ?

2 Which science fiction series that had half the nation hiding behind the settee ?

3 Who was Lenny the Lion's master ?

1958

TOP TWENTY
Homes [millions]

1	Dotto	ITV	4.90
2	Wagon Train	ITV	4.76
3	Sunday Palladium	ITV	4.83
4	The Army Game	ITV	4.65
5	TV Playhouse	ITV	4.57
6	Twenty One	ITV	4.56
7	Spot the Tune	ITV	4.56
8	Take Your Pick	ITV	4.53
9	Double Your Money	ITV	4.49
10	Murder Bag	ITV	4.23
11	Playhouse 90	ITV	4.11
12	Val Parnell's Star Time	ITV	4.00
13	Jack Hylton Presents	ITV	3.90
14	Professional Boxing	ITV	3.89
15	Saturday Spectacular	ITV	3.86
16	Play of the Week	ITV	3.83
17	Emergency Ward Ten	ITV	3.82
18	Armchair Theatre	ITV	3.75
19	Women In Love	ITV	3.74
20	Make Up Your Mind	ITV	3.71

• No 3 – Bruce Forsyth took over as host of the Palladium Show and Eartha Kitt was the top of the bill.

• No 5 – An IRA drama featuring the young Patrick McGoohan and Richard Harris as two Irish brothers.

• No 16 – Sir Laurence Olivier made his debut in a TV Play – Ibsen's John Gabriel Borkman.

• No 18 – Presented Thora Hird and Dennis Price in the Witching Hour where a crackpot witch arrives to cure an author.

1958

How the West Won Viewers

Wagon Train was the top western of the year. This was the continuing story of a wagon train heading west bossed by Major Adams played by Ward Bond, with Robert Horton as Flint McCullough the scout. Each week a guest star had a story built around them and they would then disappear from the trek. John Wayne, Ronald Reagan and Rhonda Fleming were just three of the many pioneers in the five-year search for a new life in California.

But nine-year-old Anthony Brown of Burton Trent wasn't happy. 'Ugh! Kissing. Even Wagon Train has KISS-ING in it now. It spoils everything.'

Westerns were popular with both viewers and schedulers – one was screened every night in February that year. On Monday: **Grey Ghost and Sheriff of Cochise**, Tuesday: **Zane Grey Theatre**, Wednesday: **Rin Tin Tin**, Thursday: **The Cisco Kid**, Friday: **Gun Law** and at the weekend: **Wyatt Earp** and **Hawkeye and the Last of the Mohicans**. And that was just on ITV. The BBC had **Boots and Saddles** and **Wells Fargo**.

ITV hit back at critics that said there were too many American shows. They said that only 12% of programmes came from abroad and they spent only 5% of their programme budget on foreign shows.

SOUTHERN EDITION | TV TIMES | Sept 10 • Sept 16 | BRUCE FORSYTH IS BACK IN CHARGE | VAL PARNELL'S SUNDAY NIGHT AT THE LONDON PALLADIUM 8.25 | THIS WEEK'S STAR BOB HOPE

FIRST NIGHTS

1958

This year saw six long-running programmes start on BBC.

Monitor with Huw Wheldon was the first in February. During its ten-year run Wheldon, in a somewhat headmasterly fashion, steered the Sunday night flagship arts programme.

Your Life In Their Hands brought the world of medicine and surgery into grisly close-up.

Scottish culture was introduced to the rest of Britain in May with **The White Heather Club**. Singers included Robin Hall, Andy Stewart and Jimmy Macgregor.

The Black and White Minstrel Show arrived in June. The George Mitchell Singers were suitably blacked up as nineteenth century American minstrels with The Television Toppers, female dancers as their partners. It ran for 20 years until its caricature of blacks became too embarrassing to sustain any longer.

Saturday afternoons were never the same after **Grandstand** started in October. Peter Dimmock was its first presenter. David Coleman, Frank Bough and Des

Lynam also anchored the afternoon's sporting excitement over the years.

In the same month **Blue Peter** arrived hosted by ex-beauty queen Leila Williams and Christopher Trace.

And ITV offered a couple of less than memorable crime series.
Dial 999 starred Robert Beatty as a Canadian policeman Mike Maguire, who was seconded to Scotland Yard to help clear London's streets of crime.
The Invisible Man was loosely based on the H G Wells' novel. It was billed as 'featuring the invisible star'. The programme's listing never revealed the actor that played Pete Brady.

The Forsyth Saga

September saw **Sunday Night At the London Palladium** come back with a new compere – Bruce Forsyth. For him, at the age of 30, after years grafting in the lower echelons of show business, this was stardom!

Since 1947 Forsyth had been doing the rounds of seaside concert parties, troop entertainment, the Windmill Theatre and then touring with his wife in a duet 'Forsyth and Calvert'.

He recalled his first job: 'I had my first booking for £5 per week at Bilston in Staffordshire, billed as 'Forsyth M.A. (Mighty Atom)', singing and dancing and playing the fool. Alas the people of Bilston were not impressed and all I got was 13s 4d.' That was at the age of 14!

Famous for his catchphrase 'I'm in charge', Forsyth stayed with the Palladium for four years. In one show he was literally in charge – an industrial dispute meant that he was the sole performer! Didn't he do well?

TEASER ANSWERS

1   Eamonn Andrews, the host, turned over a card each time the guest answered one of the panel's questions with a no. When ten nos were reached they won a certificate.
2   Quatermass and the Pit was the third in the series of Quatermass horrors. The Pit was a large hole being dug for an office block in London where they found... ?
3   Terry Hall had thought of Lenny while watching a lazy lion at Blackpool Zoo.

TV news

- Actor Gareth Jones collapsed and died while starring in **Underground** in November. The live play, about a group of passengers trapped in the London Underground after an explosion, continued with actors ad-libbing around his part.
- Research revealed that £300,000 had been spent on laxative products, advertised on TV, but only £180,000 outlaid on bread and bakery commercials.
- Paul Robeson came to Britain. The singer and civil rights activist had been restricted to working in the USA as his passport had been withdrawn. A US Supreme Court ruling returned his passport and he then began a world tour.
- Granada TV covered the Rochdale by-election and broke the ban on TV programmes commenting on politics at the time of elections.
- The American Ampex company brought video recording to Britain. The BBC used it first in a trailer for **Tale of Two Cities** in October.
- Actor Alistair Sim sued H J Heinz to stop them running a commercial with 'his' voice. It was really the voice of actor Ron Moody, impersonating Sim. Mr Justice McNair refused to grant an injunction and the ad continued.

- Commercial TV came to the south with Southern TV and Television West and Wales began broadcasting from Cardiff and Bristol. *(see picture)*
- An unusual commercial break ended the year. On New Year's Eve, Sir Isidore Gluckstein, chairman of food manufacturers J Lyons, booked a two minute break to talk to employees and customers nationwide.
- The Queen's State Opening of Parliament was broadcast for the first time in a joint BBC/ITV production. Richard Dimbleby and Robin Day were the commentators on their respective channels as TV cameras saw inside the Palace of Westminster for the first time.

A YEAR IN THE SOAPS

Starr and Company

Starr and Company was the BBC's attempt to get back some of the viewers being lost to ITV's soap, **Emergency Ward Ten**.

Set in the town of Sullbridge on the south coast, the soap followed the comings and goings of a company that made buoys. It went out live on Mondays and Thursdays at 7.30pm against ITV quiz shows. But it was only moderately successful and sunk after 77 episodes.

It was four years before the BBC tried another soap – the dramas of a women's magazine called **Compact**.

NEAR MISSES

- ITV's **The Jubilee Show** which attempted to copy the BBC's **The Good Old Days** hit, came to the screens every Monday for half an hour. The Good Old Days, outlasted it and ran for 30 years in total with Leonard Sachs as its memorable chairman.
- **Val Parnell's Star Time** was another show case series from the theatrical impresario and managing director of Associated Television. Gracie Fields, Arthur Haynes, Jewell and Warriss, Eartha Kitt, Lionel Blair and Rosemary Squires were among the stars to feature in the Thursday night variety slot.
- **Bernard Delfont Presents** was more variety from another of TV's Mr Bigs. When Val Parnell's Palladium Show was off the air in the summer, he presented a show from the Prince of Wales Theatre. In August there was **The Charlie Drake Show** with The King Brothers, Maxine Daniels and Ron Parry for viewers' delight.

The Six Five Special ended, being replaced by **Dig This!** *on Saturday night.*

A woman's work was never done, even on TV. This bargain vacuum cleaner *(far left)* 'as advertised on TV' with a free hair dryer or spray gun, cost £6 16s 6d (£6.82).

Also advertised on ITV *(left)* was this bargain beaker from Bourn-vita.

1958

1959

TOP TWENTY
Homes [millions]

1	Wagon Train	ITV	6.13
2	Take Your Pick	ITV	5.98
3	Sunday Palladium	ITV	5.95
4	The Army Game	ITV	5.72
5	Double Your Money	ITV	5.60
6	Concentration	ITV	5.59
7	Emergency Ward Ten	ITV	5.51
8	Dotto	ITV	5.50
9	Arthur Haynes Show	ITV	5.39
10	Armchair Theatre	ITV	5.38
11	Play of the Week	ITV	5.30
12	Knight Errant 1959	ITV	5.25
13	Probation Officer	ITV	5.19
14	No Hiding Place	ITV	5.16
15	Saturday Spectacular	ITV	5.07
16	TV Playhouse	ITV	5.03
17	Hippodrome	ITV	4.94
18	Spot the Tune	ITV	4.92
19	The Larkins	ITV	4.87
20	Blackpool Circus	ITV	4.86

• No 3 – Harry Secombe was the star of this edition.

• No 6 – David Gell was the host, it was described as not a quiz, nor a panel game but an intriguing test of memory and observation.

• No 12 – This was a 20th-century Sir Lancelot starring hunky John Turner as the gallant righter of wrongs.

• No 15 – The variety show starred comedy duo Jimmy Jewel and Ben Warriss with guest star Yana.

1959

Lockhart Changes Again

No Hiding Place (14) was first screened on Wednesday 12th September. The previous week its star copper, Chief Detective Superintendent Lockhart, played by Raymond Francis, had been looking for an escaped criminal in **Crime Sheet**.

It was the third name change for Lockhart who started life two years earlier in **Murder Bag**, which changed because it limited its stories to murders. Harry Baxter was Lockhart's right-hand man, with Eric Lander doing the leg work for over 140 episodes. Then Sgt. Russell (Johnny Briggs) took over for another 70. Francis carried and used a silver snuff box, given to him by actor Kenneth More, which turned into his trademark. Lockhart and No Hiding Place became a TV institution and the stirring title music became a hit record. It lasted until 1967 with over 230, usually solved, crime stories with very little violence and few car chases.

Probation Officer (13) was an early drama-documentary following the case load of an inner London office. Praised for its research, the series was shown to a select committee in the House of Commons, during the passage of the Criminal Justice Bill – as an accurate account of the work of the Service. Launched in September 1959 with 13 one-hour episodes, it stayed until 1962. It starred John Paul, an ex-Ward Ten doctor, Honor Blackman, although she only lasted one series, and David Davies a Welsh ex-policeman, as the chief probation officer.

Blackpool Tower Circus (20) was just one of four circuses to make the charts that year. It starred clown Charlie Carrolli with 'all the laughter and thrills of the circus ring.' **The Circus Comes to Town** from Belle Vue Manchester in September was followed the next week by the **Moscow State Circus**. And **Hippodrome**, a studio-based variety show had a circus theme.

The Original Larkins

The Larkins, with David Kossoff as Alf and the lady with the loudest voice on TV, Peggy Mount as Ada, was a massive cockney comedy hit in the fifties and early sixties. It had very humble origins – the writer, Fred Robinson, an ex-chippie from Hackney, developed the characters for his local amateur dramatic society. ATV producer Bill Ward, thought it the funniest script he'd ever seen, but it over-ran its 30 minute slot by 15 minutes. And that was the way it went out – uncut, a unique privilege for a new sitcom.

It was first tried out in six off-peak slots on Saturday nights in Autumn 1958. The TV critic of the *Daily Mail* said it was the best comedy series created by British television. Six series were made altogether, the last in 1964 when Alf and Ada had taken over a transport cafe.

TV news

- Britain's Pearl Carr and Teddy Johnson came second in the Eurovision Song Contest with 'Sing Little Birdie'. During the next 34 years Britain finished second 14 times.
- More than half of British homes had a television set. Sets then cost about £80 – the equivalent of around £700 today. Renting was a cheaper option at 8s 4d (42 pence) a week. A licence cost £4.
- **Play of the Weeks** twice hit the headlines. The Bridge at St Luis Rey had nearly reached its exciting climax when ITV took a commercial break. Parliament and the Press complained ITV was being 'too commercial' and had spoiled the play. Following the row the rules on what was a 'natural break' were tightened up. The Skin of Our Teeth – a much publicised drama starring Vivien Leigh in her TV debut – was only watched by a tenth of the homes expected to tune-in – some advertisers received their money back.
- Sutherland's Paste withdrew its TV commercial from Granada TV, in protest that the national anthem wasn't played after close-down.
- President Dwight D Eisenhower and Prime Minister Harold Macmillan broke into the TV schedules for an 'informal talk' live from Number Ten.
- Television covered the general election for the first time. Both channels held studio discussions, analysis and nationwide outside broadcast link-ups. Late night anchormen were Richard Dimbleby at the BBC and Ian Trethowan and Brian Connell at ITV.

Singer Marty Wilde married Joyce Baker, one of the Vernon Girls, the backing group from his pop show **Boy Meets Girl** where they first met. The rest of the Vernon Girls sang in the choir at the wedding and singer Mike Preston was the best man.

BOY (Marty Wilde) MEETS GIRLS Saturday, 6.30

NEAR MISSES

- Musical comedy show **Keep In Step** starred Phil Silvers, in his Sergeant Bilko guise with his two henchmen, corporals Barbella and Henshaw. Although it was made in the USA, it co-starred British actress Diana Dors.
- **Skyport**, starred George Moon, Lisa Gastoni and Gerald Harper, and was centred on an airport. Moon, who had just finished the series **Shadow Squad**, played travel courier Ginger Smart who was involved each week with airport security and international crime. Italian actress Lisa Gastoni was also to be seen as a glamorous assistant in the **Four Just Men**.
- **Home Front** looked back to 1939 and the twentieth anniversary of the outbreak of the Second World War. Tommy Trinder introduced memories of 'fire hoses, gas masks, stretcher, sandbags, sirens and unquenchable spirit' and clips from wartime propaganda films.

- **Jack Hylton's Monday Show** was another star showcase. Hylton was a show business impresario, like Bernard Delfont and Val Parnell, who turned his success in theatre into producing successful TV shows. His springtime hits in the Monday slot were **Alfred Marks Time** and the **Anne Shelton Show**.
- **Ticket For Tomorrow** was Richard Briers' first leading part in a TV play, set in Edwardian Manchester, it portrayed the problems of a youthful marriage.

1959

*Radio favourite **Semprini** came to TV. The pianist played what he called the 'old ones, loved ones, neglected ones' – all the classics.*

'KEEP IN STEP'
ALSO STARRING ARE
Diana Dors and Sidney Chaplin

Sidney Chaplin

Harvey Lembeck, Phil Silvers, Allen Melvin

Took's TV TEASERS

1 Who had a hit with the song from Champion the Wonder Horse?

2 Who were the first presenters of Blue Peter?

3 Name the pirate captain in The Buccaneers?

The Arthur Haynes Show

After years in show business, Arthur Haynes achieved TV fame in 1956 with his infamous silent character Oscar Pennyfeather, a thick-skinned social menace and know-all. Nicholas Parsons watched a monitor and voiced-over Oscar's thoughts – live! Arthur's considerable talents were reinforced by an equally talented support group. With actors like Dermot Kelly, Freddie Frinton, Patricia Hayes, Rita Webb, Jack Douglas and with scripts by Johnnie Speight, he couldn't go wrong.

In 1964 Arthur's shady ex-serviceman character hit the headlines when some real old soldiers complained about him wearing the wrong medals, from the First World War, not the Second World War. ATV said sorry and the decorations were changed! In 1966 Arthur signed up for another three series but, sadly, only one was made. He died in December of that year and TV lost one of its major talents.

1959

Ward Comebacks

Long serving staff members Jill Browne and Frederick Bartman returned to **Emergency Ward Ten** at Oxbridge Hospital after a sabbatical. Browne, Nurse Carol Young, and Bartman, the young dashing Dr Simon Forrester, did not admit it but they were probably fed up with life on the Ward and needed a break. Browne was run down and took a long holiday. After a Mediterranean cruise she took parts in **William Tell**, **Dial 999** and **Murder Bag**. Bartman 'just wanted to stretch his legs' – 'I always intended to come back,' he said.

The soap became a movie that year – excitingly called Emergency Ward Ten. Its special premiere was given to the Royal College of Surgeons and went on general release in 1960.

Face To Face, a simple interview programme, set a standard in television that producers have failed to emulate since. John Freeman, the *New Statesman* editor, talked to guests live in an unobtrusive way although he was rarely on camera. Viewers just watched a close up of the guest as they opened up in a way not seen on TV before.

Interpol Calling and more worldwide crime-busting. Charles Korvin starred as Inspector Paul Duval at the Paris headquarters of the International Police Organisation.

The Four Just Men, based on an Edgar Wallace novel, were four freelance crime fighters played by Jack Hawkins, Dan Dailey, Richard Conte and Vittorio De Sica. Based in London, New York, Paris and Rome, each actor starred in his own episode with a sexy lady assistant, apart from Jack Hawkins, who had a gentleman's gentleman played by a crusty, bearded Scot.

Juke Box Jury was a pop show for the growing teenage audience. David Jacobs was chairman of the Jury, usually made up of a pop star, another disc jockey, a producer and someone else. Susan Stranks, introduced as a 'typical teenager' later found fame on children's TV with **Magpie**.

Lassie, the TV's star collie, was reported to be earning $100,000 dollars – then about £30,000 – a year for TV and film work. She lived on a 160 acre estate near Hollywood with her own air conditioned kennel and the best food that money could buy. Her trainer claimed she wasn't pampered! The Lassie TV viewers was watching in 1959 was the second one. The original – her mother – had retired after 11 years.

TEASER ANSWERS

1   Frankie Lane. He later had a hit later with another cowboy TV series Rawhide.
2   Christopher Trace and Leila Williams, a former Miss Great Britain.
3   Captain Dan Tempest of the galleon Sultana, played by Robert Shaw.

By Royal Command

The Royal Command Variety Performance (1) was an annual charity show in the music hall days when Vesta Tilley and Sir Harry Lauder trod the boards and performed for King George V. Fifty eight acts obeyed the royal command in 1960, from Max Bygraves to Yana. Sammy Davis Jnr made his British TV debut in the show at the Victoria Palace.

Television's influence grew over the years with scenes from TV shows being played on stage. In 1963 **Steptoe and Son** with Harry H Corbett and Wilfred Brambell did an item (in which they coined the term 'Buck House' as a new name for the Palace) where they were doing some door-knocking, looking for scrap and castoffs.

The programme was notorious for over-running with every star stretching their spot as far as possible. The first shows were over three hours long – that's been reduced but it still must be quite an endurance test for the Royal Box party. And it is probably why the Queen shared out the tickets and sent the Queen Mother every other year.

Wagon Train (5) lost its trainmaster, Ward Bond, who died suddenly of a heart attack in Dallas, Texas. Actor John McIntire stepped into the role to keep the Train rolling for another two years.

The Army Game (6) saw some changes in Hut 29. Sgt Snudge and Private Bisley had left and back came the dreaded CSM Bullimore played by William Hartnell with Geoffrey Sumner as Major Upshot-Bagley – two of the show's original cast. A new recruit was Private Chubby Catchpole played by Dick Emery.

Don Arroll Takes Over From Bruce

Sunday Night At the London Palladium came back for its autumn season in September with Bruce Forsyth as compere, but within two weeks there was a new name on the bill. A virtually unknown comic called Don Arroll replaced Forsyth as the new host.

In reality Arroll had been around for years. At 31 he had spent his adult life in the business whether it was doing impersonations of Stan Laurel, or a circus clown in America or a stand-up comic with a roomful of bizarre props. He spent many frustrating years working in music halls all over the country before his big break at the Palladium. However, his stardom only lasted a year as Forsyth returned in September 1961 and Arroll gradually disappeared from TV.

During the lunch-hour BBC viewers across the UK were treated to their programmes in Welsh. It was not only part of the BBC's obligation to a minority language but also an alternative to closing down in between morning and afternoon schools programmes. ITV, by the way, didn't open up at all until 1.00 pm.

Took's TV Teasers

1 Who were the two pilots in Whirlybirds ?

2 What was the full title of Panorama ?

3 What were the booby prizes on Crackerjack ?

1960

TOP TWENTY
Homes [millions]

1	Royal Variety	ITV	8.06
2	Armchair Theatre	ITV	7.70
3	Take Your Pick	ITV	7.46
4	No Hiding Place	ITV	7.18
5	Wagon Train	ITV	7.18
6	Army Game	ITV	7.15
7	Bootsie and Snudge	ITV	7.12
8	Sunday Palladium	ITV	7.04
9	The Larkins	ITV	6.99
10	Arthur Haynes Show	ITV	6.89
11	Bernard Delfont's Show	ITV	6.81
12	Knight Errant Ltd	ITV	6.58
13	Double Your Money	ITV	6.51
14	TV Playhouse	ITV	6.40
15	Emergency Ward Ten	ITV	6.37
16	Hippodrome	ITV	6.37
17	Dickie Henderson	ITV	6.18
18	Concentration	ITV	6.17
19	Candid Camera	ITV	6.17
20	Moscow State Circus	ITV	6.08

• No 2 – The Cupboard concerned the disappearance of a wife and landlady. Donald Pleasance played the husband under suspicion.

• No 14 – Jill Bennett played a suffragette in the Edwardian costume drama with Barry Foster and Patrick Barr.

• No 16 – Hippodrome starred singer Michael Holliday and international stars of circus and vaudeville. Hosted by Paul Carpenter.

1960

FIRST NIGHTS

All Our Yesterdays with James Cameron – aided by newsreel clips – looked back 25 years to events of 1935 when Stanley Baldwin was Prime Minister, Italy invaded Abyssinia and Ted Drake scored seven goals for Arsenal. Brian Inglis took over after a year and carried the programme for 600 editions until 1973.

It was a good year for cowboys and Indians with: **Cimarron City** starring George Montgomery cleaning up a frontier town... **Bronco** with Ty Hardin as an ex-Confederate officer cleaning up another bit of the West. Bronco shared its title with a brand of toilet roll and was the source of many schoolboy jokes... **Rawhide** made a star of Clint Eastwood and followed the adventures of cowboys driving cattle to Kansas... **Bonanza** was the family saga of the Cartwright family; Ben, Adam, Hoss and Little Joe living on the Ponderosa Ranch near Virginia City... **Riverboat** was a western with a difference, here the cowboys floated down the Mississippi with Burt Reynolds at the wheel... In **Whiplash** the 'cowboys' found themselves in the Australian outback with Peter Graves running a stagecoach line – there was not an Indian in sight!

MAIGRET

No one knows what William Brown does when each month he goes to Cannes and disappears for several days. One day, however, he returns with a knife in his back...

Left: Paul Eddington as Harry Brown, and Rupert Davies as the Inspector

AT 8.45

8.45
MAIGRET
A crime series from the novels of Georges Simenon
starring
RUPERT DAVIES
as Inspector Maigret
with
EWEN SOLON
as Lucas
Liberty Bar
Dramatised by Margot Bennett
Guest stars,
RENEE HOUSTON
PAUL EDDINGTON
Directed by Andrew Osborn
Cast in order of appearance:
Gina..............DIANA BEAUMONT
Madame Martine
.............BLANCHE FETHERGILL
Inspector Maigret....RUPERT DAVIES
Inspector Boutigues...JOHN GAYRELL
Ja Ja...............RENEE HOUSTON
Sylvie..............ANNETTE CARELL
Yan................COLIN DOUGLAS
Giovani............DAVID LANDER
Police Officer.....MARTIN STENDALE
Male Secretary.......JOHN KIDD
Harry Brown.......PAUL EDDINGTON
Female Secretary...ANNA CHURCHER
Hotel Clerk...........ERIC CHITTY
Albert............DAVID GRAHAM
Flower Seller.......IRENE PRADOR
Music composed by Ron Grainer
Film cameraman, Bryan Langley
Film editor, Ken Bilton
Script editor, Giles Cooper
Executive producer, ANDREW OSBORN
Associate, Bill Luckwell
A BBC recording produced in association with Winwell Productions Ltd.
See page 23

Maigret, with Rupert Davies, lit his pipe for the first time.

Candid Camera arrived hosted by Bob Monkhouse who also smoked a pipe in the first show.

Police Surgeon starred Ian Hendry in the series that was to evolve into **The Avengers** the following year.

77 Sunset Strip, with Efrem Zimbalist Jnr and Ed Byrnes as Kookie the hair-combing teenage heart-throb, was a private eye series set in Hollywood.

1960

NEAR MISSES

• **Deadline Midnight** was the exciting life of Fleet Street dramatised with the help of the editor of the *Daily Express*. Peter Vaughan and Jeremy Young starred as the hard-bitten hacks. One viewer wrote to the *TV Times* praising the series. 'I once worked in a hotel that was suddenly bombarded with reporters following up a local crime and the action in Deadline Midnight was just like the real event. It made me realise how true to life in every detail ITV is'.

• **Spycatcher** was an army intelligence interrogator Colonel Oreste Pinto played by Bernard Archer. Another series of spy-catching and counter-intelligence, but this time done in uniform without the aid of an American side-kick.

• **The Land of Song** was the Welsh language Sunday evening religious programme produced by TWW which starred Ivor Emmanuel. Even though it was all in Welsh it proved popular throughout the UK.

• **The Strange World of Gurney Slade** starred Anthony Newley in a bizarre series. It was very abstract and had Newley dancing with a vacuum cleaner, talking to dogs, but mostly to himself as he wandered around London in a kind of Newley in Wonderland. It made the charts at first, but it proved too much for sixties' viewers and ratings plummeted. It was shunted off to a late night slot and replaced by **77 Sunset Strip**.

AD NEWS

• ITV passed £1 million a week in advertising revenue and there were complaints from Labour MPs that there were far too many commercial breaks.

• Soap powder and household cleansers were the most advertised products in ITV's first five years. But washing powders that claimed to wash whiter than white were banned by the ITA. Lines like 'Daz washes whitest of all' and 'Persil washes whitest' were cut.

• A *Daily Express* survey revealed that only 23% of women kept watching when the commercials came on, 30% claimed they were knitting or sewing, 19% did household chores and 13% were cooking.

• The music from the 'You're never alone with a Strand' cigarette ad – 'The Lonely Man Theme' – became a hit record, but the commercial was a total flop. People associated the ad and the cigarette with loneliness.

30th July 1960 and topping the bill on 'Saturday Spectacular' was Cliff Richard. Even then a big star, Cliff allowed himself just £10 a week spending money and admitted he often had £8 left by Friday. He added, "My fans have made it clear they don't want me to marry. So I've firmly decided not to marry before I'm 25."

The **Tonight** programme's line-up read like a Who's Who of television in December 1960, when the programme was in its heyday. Even the assistant editor, Alisdair Milne, was to become a BBC Director General.

TEASER ANSWERS

1 P T Moore and Chuck Martin – Craig Hill and Kenneth Tobey – were ex-American Air Force charter pilots operating a Bell helicopter and doing some crime-fighting on the side.

2 Panorama – The Window On the World presented by Richard Dimbeby.

3 Eamonn Andrews asked general knowledge questions in the 'Double Or Drop' quiz item. If the contestants got it wrong they 'won' a cabbage – three cabbages and they were knocked out.

40 YEARS OF BRITISH TELEVISION
25

Danger Man Jets In

Danger Man Patrick McGoohan was Bond before Bond – it wasn't until 1962 that Dr No came to the cinema screen. McGoohan turned down the role of Bond – the rest and Sean Connery is history. The adventure series was panned by the critics. *Television Today* said: 'Patrick McGoohan came over as a handsome exciting lead, but the characters were cardboard, the direction jerky and bitty,

the script banal; why pick a bad one to start the series with?'

But 71 adventures were made and shown over the next eight years, repeated here and around the world. Foreign locations – Paris and New York among others – gave the series a glamorous jet-set feel.

By 1962 it could be watched from Finland to New Zealand, via Algeria, Iran and Thailand and many other stops along the way. It topped the ratings when first shown in the States.

TVnews

- Television licences passed the ten million mark for the first time. Since ITV began in 1955 the number had doubled.
- The Grand National was televised for the first time and the Rome Olympics were the first Games to be seen live via the Eurovision link.
- More than 300 million people world-wide watched Princess Margaret marry Anthony Armstrong-Jones.
- The BBC opened its new TV Centre at White City. The BBC then employed 17,000 people.
- Nan Winton was the first woman to read BBC's national news.
- The Queen's Christmas Day broadcast was pre-recorded for the first time.

Haven't Prices Changed!

Shirley Bassey, a big star in 1960, spent all of £200 on glittering frocks in which to top the bill at the Palladium. She could also afford a £12,000 house, a £2,000 black diamond mink coat, an £800 black velvet mink jacket, a £500 champagne mink stole, a string of pearls, her portrait in oils....

1960

A YEAR IN THE SOAPS

Wedding on the Ward

In **Emergency Ward Ten** Dr John Rennie was having problems getting close to Nurse White. This was particularly apt for actors Richard Thorp and Maureen Moore, who were engaged at the time. The producer said there would be no flirting in the programme, but the script said that Maureen should flirt with nearly everyone except Richard. Script or not the couple did marry in real life.

Richard Thorp was something of a heart-throb on Ward Ten, a slim good looking doctor raising the pulses of lady patients, nurses and women viewers. He turned up in 1982 in **Emmerdale Farm** as Alan Turner, the estate manager that everyone disliked.

Tony Hancock says . . .

"HAS **YOUR** TUBE GONE AGAIN?"

Telesurance

14 WINDMILL STREET, LONDON, W.1.
Please send me without obligation full details of the TELESURANCE Tube only scheme

Name ....

Address ....

....

....

TV.38

"Mine has. Half-way through *Rawhide.* This bloke pulled out his gun just as the arrow hit him. His legs went one way, his head went the other, he let out a gasp of agony and disappeared out of the bottom of the screen. I thought, 'allo, either the adverts are coming on, or my tube's gone. Fortunately I was lucky. My tube had gone. Well, I've insured it. It can go every night as far as I'm concerned, it doesn't cost me a bean. It's the best day's work I ever did. Ah! This is the life. Laying on the floor in front of the telly, a packet of crisps in one hand, a bottle of Spanish Burgundy in the other, and a new tube coming round just in time for *Emergency—Ward 10.* What more can a chap want?"

Hancock again. This time with the dreaded words for any 1960's viewer, 'The tube's gone!' The tube was, and is, the heart of a television – the glass contraption with the screen at the front and electronics at the back. Expensive to replace and often short-lived, the 'tube' was guaranteed to 'go' at weekends and Christmas.

1961

TOP TWENTY
Homes [millions]

1	Royal Variety Show	ITV	8.48
2	No Hiding Place	ITV	7.73
3	Sunday Night At the Palladium	ITV	7.68
4	Coronation Street	ITV	7.49
5	The Army Game	ITV	7.34
6	Probation Officer	ITV	7.18
7	Russ Conway Show	ITV	6.93
8	The Dickie Henderson Show	ITV	6.93
9	Take Your Pick	ITV	6.90
10	Double Your Money	ITV	6.90
11	Armchair Theatre	ITV	6.85
12	Emergency Ward Ten	ITV	6.79
13	Echo Four-Two	ITV	6.77
14	British Song Contest	ITV	6.69
15	Arthur Haynes Show	ITV	6.61
16	Harpers West One	ITV	6.57
17	Circus Comes To Town	ITV	6.56
18	Knight Errant Limited	ITV	6.55
19	Somerset Maugham	ITV	6.54
20	Bootsie and Snudge	ITV	6.51

• No 1 – Star billing went to George Burns, Sammy Davis Jnr and Maurice Chevalier.

• No 14 – The contest was broadcast over five successive nights and viewers voted on 20 songs.

• No 17 – The town was Manchester and it was the Belle Vue Circus.

1961

Top Spot For Russ

The Russ Conway Show (7) was his first series for ITV and it went straight to number one in January. Russ had made his name on **The Billy Cotton Band Show** and was one of Britain's biggest pop stars with his simple piano style and tunes like 'Side Saddle', 'Roulette' and 'China Tea'.

Echo Four-Two (13) was another spin off hit. This was son of **No Hiding Place**. Detective Sergeant Harry Baxter, Eric Lander, Chief Superintendent Lockhart's right-hand man, had won promotion to D.I. and his own series.

Harpers West One (16) was 'shopping with the lid off', according to the blurb: 'all the life and loves of a big London department store. The characters are real, the carpets are plush, the atmosphere is authentic. Yes, madam, you'll enjoy buying at Harpers – that's our slogan.'

Bootsie and Snudge (20) was the result of Granada TV getting two hits for the price of one. Two of the best characters in **The Army Game**, Excused Boots Bisley and Sgt Major Snudge, were demobbed from the series and in civvy street found jobs in a gentlemen's club. Bootsie as the below stairs general factotum and Snudge as the snobbish majordomo with Richard Dornin and Clive Dunn as an ancient waiter.

NEAR MISSES

• Jimmy Edwards starred in a showcase series called **Seven Faces of Jim**. It was written by Frank Muir and Dennis Norden and gave him the chance to extend his range of comic characters.

• **Our House** was a series of comedy plays based around a large house divided into bed sitters. 'Carry On...' stars like Hattie Jacques, Charles Hawtrey, Joan Sims and Bernard Bresslaw were cast regulars.

• **Ghost Squad** was more under-cover agents at work with an international brief. Donald Wolfit starred as the boss and Michael Quinn, an American actor brought in to boost programme sales in the States, as Nick Craig.

• **Boyd QC**, played by Michael Denison as Richard Boyd a leading barrister, was a series illustrating the many facets of British justice. A real Queen's Counsel said that any young man wanting a career at the Bar could not do better than to model himself on Boyd QC.

• **Three Live Wires** made a sitcom out of TV repairmen. Stars included Michael Medwin and Derek Guyler. Guest stars were imported as the team went around London 'repairing' the televisions of the famous.

• **Twenty Questions** was the radio show pinched by TV. The chairman was long-time BBC announcer Stewart McPherson and regular panelists guessing the words were: Isobel Barnett, Frankie Howerd and Muriel Young.

BBC tv RadioTimes and SOUND 5D

The Seven Faces of Jim
THURSDAY TELEVISION

A YEAR IN THE SOAPS

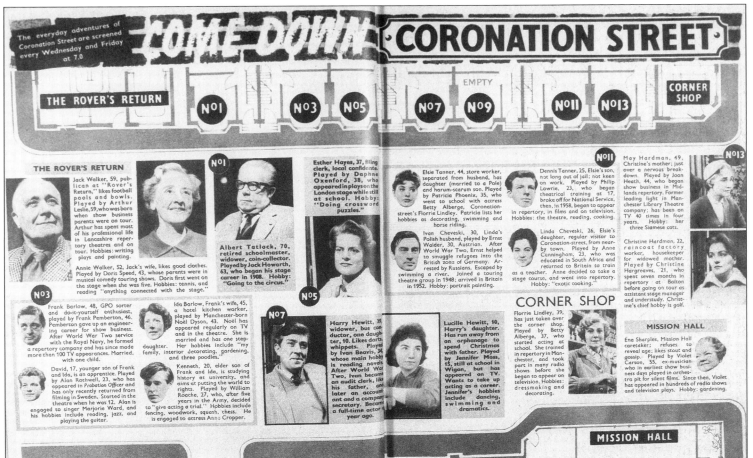

1961

The Street Arrives

TV history was made with the entry of **Coronation Street** at number four. What had begun as a 13-week try-out in December 1960 turned into a television phenomenon. It first appeared in the charts in March, by October it was number one. Over the next 30 years it has never been out of the charts. *TV Times* devoted a two-page spread to introduce us to The Street. The highlights of that first year were: Ken Barlow had an affair with a librarian, his mother died under the wheels of a bus, Elsie Tanner became a grandma and Leonard Swindley caught Ena Sharples drinking milk stout. Only two characters have survived since 1961: Ken Barlow played by William Roache and Emily Bishop, nee Nugent, played by Eileen Derbyshire.

• **Home Tonight** was a soap that didn't last. The story of the sea-side Sutton family, with 'new faces' David Hemmings and Patricia Brake, only lasted eight weeks (40 episodes) in the Autumn of '61.

In 1961 Eric Morecambe moved from London to a grand new £8,000 house 25 miles into the country. He was asked about the problems of getting to the studios and back. 'I don't mind the commuting,' he said 'it's the travelling that gets me down.'

The forerunner to colour TV - and all for 19s 6d, less than a pound in today's currency! Of course, the screen couldn't really create anything like real colour television, but disappointed customers could always get their money back.

Took's TV Teasers

1 Who was ITV's Wrestling commentator?

2 Name the two stars of Route 66.

3 Dorothy Provine starred in which American drama series?

FIRST NIGHTS

1961

The Avengers arrived with Ian Hendry as the star and Patrick Macnee as Steed only getting second billing. Hendry left after a year and Honor Blackman joined the cast as Catherine Gale PhD. Dressed in leather, she raised male temperatures and the ratings.

In 1965 Diana Rigg became Steed's next assistant Emma Peel. Linda Thorson was his last assistant when the series ended in 1969.

As well as **Coronation Street**, three other programmes from 1961 were still going strong over 30 years later: **Points of View** began with Robert Robinson airing the viewers' moans and praise for BBC programmes. Letters always seemed to begin 'Why oh why oh why...' It was later presented by Barry Took and Anne Robinson.

Songs of Praise is television's longest running religious programme. Church pews were uncharacteristically packed and lots of new hats appeared in shot.
Survival, Anglia TV's natural history programme began with a short series on the wildlife of London. It is now watched in more countries than any other British TV programme.

Ben Casey, an American hospital drama series, ran on ITV. It starred Vince Edwards as the surgeon with the hairiest arms in TV. **Dr Kildare** was his competitor on the BBC. Another US series, it starred heart-throb Richard Chamberlain as the young idealistic doc. Both series ran for five years.

The Morecambe and Wise Show was the start of Eric and Ernie"s phenomenal comedy success. This was their first star series since a failed showcase called **Running Wild** in 1954.

Supercar, the Andersons' first adventure puppet series, was launched.

The Dickie Henderson Show

This was the British version of a lot of American situation comedies. Take a showbiz star who more or less plays himself, build a family around him and write scripts that introduce a star guest each week. It was a winning formula for Lucille Ball, Dick Van Dyke, Jack Benny and George Burns and Gracie Allen. It certainly worked for Dickie Henderson, from 1959 to 1964 his show was a regular in the charts.

June Laverick played his wife, John Parson his son and Lionel Murton was his right-hand and straight man. Guest stars ranged from boxer Freddie Mills to comedian Ted Ray, from opera singer Adelle Leigh to footballer Billy Wright.

His dancing skill and agility were called on regularly. Falling off a horse, jumping from Brighton Pier and into a lake were scripted in just one series. His real son Matthew once asked him: "Why do you fall down so often on TV?" "That's what they pay me for" he replied.

Dickie was one of the many comics who took a turn at hosting **Sunday Night At the London Palladium**, during '65 and '66 and was a regular in the annual **Royal Variety Show** with his song and dance act.

Answer by Groucho Marx to critics of TV: "What do they expect... ten hours a day of T.S. Eliot?"

TEASER ANSWERS

1   Kent Walton the Canadian sports commentator covered wrestling from 1955 to 1989.
2   George Maharis and Martin Milner played Buz and Tod, two easy riders drifting across America in the Chevrolet Corvette.
3   Dorothy Provine played Pinky Pinkham in The Roaring Twenties a music and drama series set in the bootlegging days of Chicago.

- The BBC celebrated its 25th birthday. The world's first regular TV service, begun at Alexandra Palace, north London in 1936.
- The Duke of Edinburgh was deferentially chatted to by Richard Dimbleby on **Panorama**, the first royal television interview.
- Westward, Grampian and Border TV brought commercial TV to the south west of England, north of Scotland and the Scottish borders.

- Television actors went on strike in the Autumn. Many series were halted early and commercials not made. It also made a dent in the cash flow of the new ITV companies only just struggling on-air.
- The Allisons came second in the **Eurovision Song Contest** with 'Are You Sure'. This was the third year the Brits had finished second. In '59 Pearl Carr and Teddy Johnson just missed with 'Sing Little Birdie' and in '60 'Looking High High High' didn't look quite high enough for Bryan Jonson.

The Play's the Thing

For the first ten years of ITV there was always a single play to be found in the top programmes of the year. The drama strands had titles like: **Theatre Royal, TV Playhouse, Fireside Theatre, Play of the Week, Drama 62** and **Armchair Theatre**.

This year was no exception. Each week at least three ITV-produced dramas appeared. The most controversial was **When the Kissing Had To Stop**, about a left wing government elected in Britain and the takeover by a communist super power. It caused a political storm for what was inferred as its anti-Labour stance. In November ITV went overboard – the play of the week was **Electra**, by Sophocles, done in the original Greek!

The three plays featured in the year's top 20 were: **Dead Letter (6)**, a first TV play by Robert Storey which followed events after a Yorkshire funeral. **Lonesome Road (11)** by Giles Cooper, voted best playwright in 1961, was a neurotic drama starring Ronald Fraser as a man who follows a fellow commuter home and stays. And **Alida (17)** about a young man's obsession with the sculpted head of a girl and the murderous consequences of tracking her down.

Armchair Theatre, or 'Armpit Theatre' as it was dubbed for its plays of social realism, was the most successful play strand. It ran from 1956 to the mid 70s first with ABC and later with Thames TV.

The list of stars who appeared in 1962's plays is considerable. Some of the names still around are Frank Finlay, Michael Caine, George Cole, Ian McShane and Leo Mckern.

Compact Is Launched

In 1962 the BBC took on ITV's dominance of the soap operas with **Compact**. Carefully avoiding **Coronation Street**, it was scheduled for Tuesday and Thursday evening. It was a mannered and up-market drama of life at a glossy woman's magazine. With a strong female editor played by Jean Harvey surrounded by the love lives of her workforce.

It first appeared in the ratings in March, at number 16, but didn't stay long. The BBC hierarchy were uncomfortable with it and it ceased broadcasting in 1965. Meanwhile its writers and creators had moved to the Midlands with another idea. Hazel Adair and Peter Ling's names will long be remembered for their shaky credits at the end of **Crossroads**. As will Ronald Allen who played Compact's editor before moving on to manage the Crossroads motel as David Hunter.

Took's TV Teasers

1   What character did Clint Eastwood play in Rawhide ?

2   'Here's your starter for ten.' Which programme ?

3   Who was Muriel Young's feline friend ?

1962

TOP TWENTY
Homes [millions]

1	Royal Variety	BBC	9.25
2	Coronation Street	ITV	8.86
3	Miss World 1962	BBC	7.55
4	Sunday Palladium	ITV	7.43
5	European Cup Football	ITV	7.30
6	Armchair Theatre	ITV	7.28
7	Val Parnell	ITV	7.21
8	Crazy Gang Last Night	ITV	7.16
9	No Hiding Place	ITV	7.14
10	Bernard Delfont Show	ITV	7.14
11	Drama '62	ITV	7.08
12	Take Your Pick	ITV	6.96
13	Double Your Money	ITV	6.95
14	Maigret	BBC	6.94
15	One Step Beyond	ITV	6.75
16	Emergency Ward Ten	ITV	6.75
17	Play of the Week	ITV	6.75
18	Rawhide	ITV	6.67
19	Top Secret	ITV	6.59
20	Bruce Forsyth Show	ITV	6.59

• No 3 – Miss World entered the year's top 20 for the first time and stayed for the next 14 years.

• No 5 – Spurs v Benfica with Jimmy Greaves and Eusebio live from White Hart Lane.

• No 15 – An American series with John Newland re-enacting unexplained mysteries and the supernatural.

• No 19 – Best remembered for its hit theme tune 'Sucu Sucu' and for William Franklyn as a British agent in South America.

1962

1962

NEAR MISSES

• Quiz show **Abracadabra** was hosted by Canadian Roy Ward Dixon and wife Shirley. The basic idea was to answer a general knowledge question and pick a letter to complete a word to win up to £125. There was also a 'money pot' of coins that the contestant could dip into and win all they could hold.

• **Candid Camera**, the American show brought to Britain with Bob Monkhouse and Jonathan Routh, was the pioneer embarrassment show much imitated over the years with the hidden camera catching us out.

• **The Rag Trade**, another BBC comedy classic, was a team comedy based around the East End clothing industry. In the team were Peter Jones, Reg Varney, Barbara Windsor, and Sheila Hancock with Miriam Karlin as the shop steward with the catch phrase: 'Everybody out!'

• **The Odd Man** was a drama hit with something of a cult following. It starred Keith Barron as Detective Sergeant Swift and, later in the series, his posh boss Chief Inspector Rose played by William Mervyn. Two other hit series followed from the Inspector: **It's Dark Outside** and **Mr Rose**.

• **Mess Mates** starred Sam Kydd, Dermot Kelly and Archie Duncan and the tramp steamer Jersey Lily in a shipboard comedy.

• Windsor Davies took over as the star of **Probation Officer** sorting out the lives of juvenile delinquents.

• **The London versus Paris Twist Competition** was a bizarre item. It was hosted by David Frost. Imagine Frostie twisting to Chubby Checker's hit of '62, 'Let's Twist Again'.

• **Man of the World** starred American actor Craig Stevens as globe-trotting photo-journalist Mike Strait. As might be expected his assignments were more than photo-opportunities as he foiled varying degrees of murder and mayhem.

Norman Vaughan Grew On You

Norman Vaughan leapt to stardom in January 1962 when he took over from Bruce Forsyth as host of **Sunday Night At the London Palladium** after Bruce was ordered to rest. He was terrified: "I was paralysed with nerves with the thought of 20 million viewers watching

Regular advertisements at the back of the two TV magazines suggest that the British were obsessive builders of sheds, garages and greenhouses and the occasional coal bunker. Sheds for 11 guineas, a fireproof garage for £39 and a greenhouse from £16.

me." And it was from this nervousness that his near-legendary catch phrase 'swinging and dodgy' sprung. "It was just something to say at rehearsals and it caught on."

His fame led to a long running commercial for Cadbury's Roses chocolates. For five years he had roses growing all over him. He was 34 when he took over at the Palladium and had first appeared on TV in 1954. Norman did over 100 Sunday Nights and left the series in June 1965. Jimmy Tarbuck was the next host. But soon 'Whatever happened to Norman Vaughan?' stories began to appear. TV's instant fame was whipped away: no telly equals no success. He was in fact doing very nicely as a straight actor until 1972 when it was back to the TV studio with the **Golden Shot**. This time taking over from Bob Monkhouse as the host of the Sunday evening live game show. The 'darts' game show **Bullseye** was his next success in 1981, but this time not as presenter but as creator of the format, and that one was still on the 'ochie' over ten years later.

TV news

• With the opening of Channel TV and Wales West and North, the ITV network, begun in London only in 1955, was completed.

• The age of satellite television began with the launch of Telstar in the US and the first crude pictures were beamed across the Atlantic in July.

• The Pilkington Committee on the Future of Broadcasting reported and made 120 recommendations including a second channel for BBC, but not ITV as the Report was critical of commercial TV.

• An OMO washing powder commercial was voted the best commercial of the year by readers of the *Daily Mail*.

• Ulster TV experimented with adult education. **Midnight Oil** was a series of lectures from Queens University Belfast covering topics such as science, literature and law.

TEASER ANSWERS

1   He played Rowdy Yates who was Gil Favor's right hand man on the cattle drive.
2   University Challenge hosted by Bamber Gascoigne. It ran from '62 to '87.
3   Pussy Cat Willum was Muriel's puppet co-presenter on Small Time, the afternoon programme for young children.

FIRST NIGHTS

It was a vintage year for the BBC, four of its best ever programmes were premiered.

The **Z Cars** of Newtown police first appeared on the streets and Ford Zephyrs patrolled a fictionalised Liverpool. At the wheel were top actors Jeremy Kemp, James Ellis, Colin Welland and Brian Blessed (who couldn't drive).

Steptoe and Son began their rag and bone round with Hercules the horse through the streets of Shepherds Bush.

Dr Finlay's Casebook followed the life of a Scottish country practice in 1920s Tannochbrae.

That Was the Week That Was (TW3) was the show that kicked Auntie into the Swinging Sixties. David Frost introduced a team of sharp young men and Millicent Martin, and TV satire was born. Its comedy stung politicians, religion and every vested interest of the day. The 1964 election gave the BBC the excuse to take it off, and it never came back. It was all a bit too embarrassing for Auntie.

On the Braden Beat was ITV's long running consumer show. Bernard Braden took TV into new territory. It used satire to fight bureaucracy on behalf of the viewer. In 1968 he took the format to the BBC, where one of his researchers, Esther Rantzen, later carried on his style of consumer-led TV in **That's Life**.

Ken Russell's film **Elgar** was shown on **Monitor**. It was the first in his series on great composers that established his reputation.

Roger Moore brought **The Saint** to the TV screen. The Saint, aka Simon Templar, must be one of the only long running crime series that didn't have a girl Friday or side kick. Although he did seem to have a lovely leading lady each week. Honor Blackman, Lana Morris, Dawn Addams, Sylvia Syms and Shirley Eaton played opposite Moore. There were 114 adventures, ending in 1969. The series was one of British TV's most successful exports, estimated to have earned over £370 million, and much of that going to Moore who owned the rights to a third of them.

1962

May 20th 1962, one of variety's biggest names bowed out. The Crazy Gang, the celebrated comedy team formed in 1929, were given a top of the bill send off at 8.25 on a Sunday night.

Clint Eastwood, who played Rowdy Yates in **Rawhide** found himself on the wrong end of the law in 1962, when neighbours called the police to complain about his singing. It was not only bad and out of tune but also 3.00 am in the morning.

Remember the man with the gong on **Take Your Pick** ? Yes?... Dong!!
He was Alec Dane, a former singer and actor who became 'head gonger' and a national institution.

1963

TOP TWENTY
Homes [millions]

1	Royal Variety Show	ITV	10.4
2	Coronation Street	ITV	9.70
3	Steptoe and Son	BBC	8.79
4	Dr Finlay's Case Book	BBC	8.39
5	Drama 63	ITV	8.27
6	Miss World	BBC	8.25
7	They've Sold a Million	ITV	8.24
8	Max Bygraves Show	ITV	8.22
9	Take Your Pick	ITV	8.02
10	Val Parnell's Sunday Show	ITV	8.02
11	This Week	ITV	7.98
12	No Hiding Place	ITV	7.91
13	Armchair Theatre	ITV	7.88
14	Kennedy's Funeral	ITV	7.75
15	Here's Harry	BBC	7.74
16	The Odd Man	ITV	7.61
17	Dickie Henderson	BBC	7.59
18	Laughter USA	BBC	7.53
19	Juke Box Jury	BBC	7.50
20	The Larkins	ITV	7.47

• No 5 – The highest rating drama in '63 starred Mark Eden – later to play Alan Bradley in Coronation Street in 1989.

• No 6 – The winner was Carole Joan Crawford from Jamaica.

• No 13 – The play was The Higher They Fly – it went out a few days before Drama 63: Leave All Hope Behind and also starred Mark Eden!

1963

Royal Beatles

The Royal Variety Performance (1) topped the charts for the fourth consecutive year and the Beatles topped the bill. Nineteen sixty three was the year the Beatles hit the television big time. February saw their national television debut on **Thank Your Lucky Stars**. In October they made their first appearance on **Val Parnell's Sunday Night At the London Palladium (10)**.

A month later it was the Royal Variety Performance and the front cover of the *TV Times (see picture)*. The *TV Times* called them 'the show-business sensation of the year' and launched ReadaBeatla Week - a series of interviews conducted in the ITV studio's staff canteen while the Fab Four were tucking into their egg and chips.

The BBC had six Top 20 hits this year including **Dr Finlay's Casebook (4)**. The series had begun the previous year having been hastily put together to fill a

five-week gap in the schedules. By 1963 Dr Finlay and the residents of Arden House in Tannochbrae had become a Sunday night 'must' for eight million viewers. Bill Simpson, a local newsreader with Scottish TV in Glasgow, played the 'young' Doctor Finlay and Barbara Mullen was the trusty housekeeper Janet. Scottish Television remade the series nearly 20 years later with David Rintoul in the lead and Annette Crosbie as Janet.

FIRST NIGHTS

The Doctor and the Police Box

On the 23rd of November 1963, as the world was reeling from the death of President Kennedy in Dallas the previous day, millions of British viewers settled in front of their sets to watch the first episode of **Dr Who**.

William Hartnell played the first Doctor, a 750-year-old Time Lord with two hearts and, over the years, seven different faces – the others were those of Patrick Troughton, Jon Pertwee, Tom Baker, Peter Davison, Colin Baker and Sylvester McCoy. The Daleks made their debut later in December.

World In Action was launched by Granada TV. The hard-hitting current affairs series promised to give 'not simply the news but the full background story'. The first edition in January looked at the atomic arms race and showed Khrushchev and Kennedy at loggerheads.

Leslie Phillips became **Our Man At St Marks**, the Rev. Andrew Parker. He was a serious young vicar, new to the Parish, and each week saw him facing the 'routine problems of his position'. Anne Lawson was his girlfriend and Joan Hickson played his housekeeper. Later Donald Sinden took over the role.

The Plane Makers told of union disputes in an aircraft factory. Patrick Wymark played the bullying managing director John Wilder. In 1965 the action switched from the factory floor to the boardroom and the series became the **Power Game**.

ITV ran the first series of **Naked City**. Actor Paul Burke declared at the end of each episode: 'There are six million stories in the Naked City, this has been one of them.'

One viewer from Bognor wrote to the *TV Times* to complain about women news-readers: 'No women newscasters if you don't mind. They are entirely inadequate. They seem unfamiliar with their script, read with downcast eyes, never look up at the viewer and they gabble. Let the news rest in the very capable hands of men'!

NEAR MISSES

• Just bubbling under was usual Top 20 hit **Double Your Money** which this year saw fresh-faced 15-year-old Monica Rose, later to become hostess of the show, as a contestant. Monica, a junior accounts clerk from the East End, won £8 answering questions about famous women. Hughie Green was so impressed with her Cockney charm and chatter he brought her back as a hostess a year later.

• Herbert Lom starred as a Harley Street psychiatrist in **The Human Jungle**. One of his toughest cases was sorting out a young Joan Collins play-ing a girl found walking naked through London's underground.

• Tony Hancock was back, this time on ITV, but although the new series constantly hovered close to the top of the ratings, it wasn't a critical success.

LAST NIGHTS

Goodbye to **Take a Letter**, the chil-dren's crossword-puzzle quiz hosted by Bob Holness. Holness got the job in 1961 after arriving in the UK from South Africa. His background was theatre and radio – he had never seen television before let alone been inside a TV station. Each week at the end of the quiz the viewers would be thrown a question. There was a £5 prize. One week they had 980,000 entries – probably a record. After 20 years Holness returned to TV quiz shows with **Blockbusters**.

1963

Took's
TV TEASERS

1   Who was the announcer on Take Your Pick ?

2   Basil Brush first appeared on TV this year. Who invented him ?

3   Shirley Bassey starred in the Palladium Show. What was her hit song this year ?

1963

A YEAR IN THE SOAPS

Emergency —Ward 10

WITH

JILL BROWNE

DESMOND CARRINGTON

Dick Moone spends his first day on the medical wards and assists in a crisis of Elizabeth French's. Chris Anderson has a hectic day in the accident wing dealing with anything from a car smash to a man with a fish bone in his throat

CAST

Harold de la Roux	**John Barron**
Bob Coughlin	**Desmond Jordan**
Sister MacNab	**Dorothy Smith**
Edward Bryan	**Richard Bidlake**
Richard Moone	**John Alderton**
Lester Large	**John Carlisle**
Ann Webb	**Jean Trend**
Elizabeth French	**Valerie Sarruf**
Ken Barnes	**Nicholas Pennell**
Mrs. Maugham	**Elizabeth Wallace**
Bill Barron	**Kenneth Watson**
Carole Young	**Jill Browne**
Chris Anderson	**Desmond Carrington**

SCRIPT BY ROGER MARSHALL

A New Arrival in Ward Ten

It was good news for the sick and infirm of Oxbridge, a new doctor joined the staff of **Emergency Ward Ten**. Dr Richard Moone was a fresh-faced junior houseman, also known as John Alderton. He became very busy. First there was pretty nurse Sally Bowen and a frowned-on secret romance, a troop carrier over-turned stretching Casualty to the limit and the star of the Ward, Sister Carole Young, was taken ill and admitted to her own ward. What drama!

TV news

- The BBC ended its ban on mentioning politics, royalty, religion and sex in its comedy programmes.
- TV cigarette advertising was banned from children's programmes. All performers in cigarette commercials had to be 'clearly over the age of 21'.
- Millions watched on TV as Lee Harvey Oswald, the man charged with the assassination of President Kennedy, was shot dead in Dallas.
- **The Lovers**, an erotic play by Harold Pinter caused eyebrows to rise. Its makers Associated Rediffusion moved it to a later slot hoping 'for an audience which does not include the unmarried in the 18-23 age bracket'.
- A 34-year-old Alastair Burnet joined ITN as a political reporter.
- The first home video recorder was demonstrated at the BBC's Alexandra Palace. It was the opening of the **Nine O'Clock News** which was recorded and reshown later in the bulletin.

Queen of the Mods

At the beginning of the year Cathy McGowan was a lowly secretary earning £10 a week working in London. By the end of the year she was Queen of Mods and Princess of Pop, receiving 600 fan letters a week. The 19-year-old from Streatham was one of 600 hopefuls who answered an advertisement for a 'typical teenager' to act as an adviser on the Friday night pop show **Ready, Steady, Go!** She ended up as co-presenter with Keith Fordyce.

In the days when Oxfam was known by the grander title of The Oxford Committee for Famine Relief – the charity praised the generosity of ITV viewers to the regular Give At 7 charity slot. Their appeal raised £5,300.

Hancock fan, but –

About this new Hancock series. It's a bit off, isn't it? Where is the Hancock we all knew and loved? Where is the romantic philosopher, the middle-class intellectual snob with the ready wit and brilliant repartee?

All we get now is a twittering script that is like Bootsie and Snudge on an off day, which relies too much on farce and situation for easy laughs. My mates and I, all ardent Hancock fans, reckon that he is wasting his talents on trifles. We're all very disappointed in our hero.

Tim Heritage
London

TV Times
February 1963

Closedown for Ad-mags

Ad-mags had begun with ITV. They were 15-minute local programmes devoted to advertisements – yet remained outside the ten per cent quota for spot advertising. Each advertising magazine consisted of a series of advertisements featuring everything from shops to car showrooms. Each area had its own mag. There was *Elizabeth Allen Goes Shopping* in London, *What's In Store In the Midlands*, and *Shop In the South*, among others. But ad-mags were an anomaly – they were called programmes yet had to be clearly defined as advertising. In 1963 the legislators decided that the viewer might find endorsement of products *within* programmes confusing.

In August **Thank Your Lucky Stars** celebrated its 100th edition. Producer Phillip Jones said the show had featured every British recording star and most American ones – over 1,000 in all.

TEASER ANSWERS

1   Bob Danvers-Walker – famous as the voice on British newsreels during and after the War.
2   Howard Williams. They first appeared in an act called 'The Three Scampis'.
3   'I, Who Have Nothing' – in the charts for 20 weeks.

1964

TOP TWENTY
Homes [millions]

1	Steptoe and Son	BBC	9.71
2	Sunday Palladium	ITV	9.69
3	Coronation Street	ITV	9.43
4	Dick Powell Theatre	BBC	8.45
5	Take Your Pick	ITV	8.39
6	Royal Variety Show	BBC	8.37
7	No Hiding Place	ITV	8.22
8	Armchair Theatre	ITV	8.12
9	It's Tarbuck	ITV	8.08
10	Crane	ITV	7.96
11	Stars and Garters	ITV	7.84
12	Double Your Money	ITV	7.80
13	Emergency Ward Ten	ITV	7.80
14	Around the Beatles	ITV	7.61
15	Frank Ifield Show	ITV	7.57
16	The Avengers	ITV	7.54
17	Christmas Comedy	ITV	7.46
18	Miss World 1964	ITV	7.45
19	Max Bygraves Show	ITV	7.43
20	Love Story	ITV	7.33

• No 4 – Dick Powell was a Hollywood movie actor who introduced the series of one hour dramas.

• No 17 – All the faces of ITV in a play-cum-panto called Deep and Crisp and Stolen.

• No 18 – Won by Miss UK Ann Sydney – afterwards she began an acting career.

• No 20 – A long running series of single romances. One episode saw a young Ian McShane fall for Francesca Annis.

A Cockney Year

Steptoe & Son (1) was a comedy of truly classic status starring Harry H Corbett as Harold and Wilfred Brambell as the 'dirty old man'.

Written by Alan Simpson and Ray Galton, it began life as a one-off **Comedy Playhouse** called **The Offer** about a young London rag and bone man and his attempt to leave home. Harold was desperate to get on, but was held back by his conniving ageing father who always frustrated his attempts at self-betterment.

Steptoe ran for over ten years and 40 episodes and won award after award. The format was shown in the US as **Sandford and Son**, with an all black cast.

It is said that Harold Wilson owed his '64 election victory to a shift in the schedules of the series. Such was its pulling power on Thursday evenings some nine million homes tuned in, that Wilson feared it would keep voters at home and he pressurised the Beeb to put it on after the polls had closed.

Stars and Garters (11) was the other cockney TV hit of the year. A lively raucous East End pub sang along with stars and real pub entertainers, all set in the studios of Associated-Rediffusion. Kathy Kirby, Susan Maugham, Kim Cordell and Al Saxon were resident singers. Ray Martine was the host. The show brought him fame and he moved into a Mayfair home. But he was last seen working market stalls in the north of England.

Viewers commented on how immaculate and suave young ITN newscaster Peter Snow always looked. And his secret was revealed – he never went near a studio without a hairbrush, comb, clothes brush, tin of make-up, mirror and eyebrow brushes.

Took's TV Teasers

1 Zoo Time came from London Zoo. Who introduced it?

2 The Beverly Hillbillies comedy concerned a poor family who discovered an oil well. What was the family name?

3 Ready, Steady, Go with Keith Fordyce and Cathy McGowan had a catchphrase. What was it?

1964

1964

Pop Goes the Year

The men in suits and ties running television were waking up to the potential of the teenage audience. In 1964 every variety, comedy and entertainment show had to have a group on the bill. Like the Dave Clark Five on the **Palladium Show**, The Dave Clark Five on **The Arthur Haynes Show** and the Dave Clark Five on **Five O'clock Club**. Nearly every regional company also had its own pop show: **Beat the Border** from Border TV, **Now Hear This** at Ulster TV, **Dad You're a Square** in the Southern region and **Discs a Go Go** in Wales.

1964 began on the BBC with 'It's number one, it's **Top of the Pops**'. Those immortal words sprang out of the TV on New Year's Day. DJ Jimmy Savile introduced stars Dusty Springfield, The Hollies, Rolling Stones and, yes, The Dave Clark Five singing 'Glad All Over'.

Juke Box Jury continued its ratings success on Saturday evenings with David Jacobs and a panel of four stars deciding the likely fate of new releases. Will it 'hit' or will it 'miss'? **Lucky Stars** or **Thank Your Lucky Stars** was ITV's Saturday evening pop slot hosted by Brian Matthew. It also had its own jury in 'Spin a Disc' which made a West Midlands teenager, Janice Nicholls, and her catchphrase 'Oill give it foive', an unlikely TV star. Other TV chart hits that year were **The Pop Spot**, **They've Sold a Million** and showcases for singers in **Call In On Mark Wynter** and **The Billy Fury Show**.

BBC2 Launches

In April the BBC launched the third channel with a kangaroo, and a little joey in its pouch, called Hullabaloo and Custard. The problem was you needed a new telly and a new aerial to pick it up on the new ultra high frequency (UHF) band with 625 lines on the screen instead of the original 405 lines.

It had a disastrous first night. There was a power cut in most of West London and the screen was blank. The opening night was planned to come from Studio A at Alexandra Palace, where British TV began. It included Howard Keel in the musical **Kiss Me Kate**.

Its early successes were **Late Night Line Up** with Joan Bakewell and Tony Bilbow. **Match of the Day** began on BBC2. The first match covered was Arsenal versus Liverpool. **Playschool**, the harassed mum's favourite, guaranteed 15 minutes of quiet from the viewing toddlers.

Martha – Gone!

After May, things were never the same in the snug of the Rovers Return – Martha Longhurst was gone! Heartbroken viewers complained that Coronation Street scriptwriters were monsters for killing off Martha, Lynne Carol.

Regional Differences

The network charts indicate the nation's favourite shows week by week, but there were considerable differences in region and tastes. A look at the top tens for each region in November adds a total of 39 programmes to those that appeared in the national chart. **The Royal Variety Performance** was No 1 in Wales and the West, but didn't make it at all in the Midlands. The pop show, **Discs a Go Go**, made by Television West and Wales, made no headway in that area, but was No 6 in central Scotland. For north east Scotland, **Double Your Money** was first choice. Only Northern Ireland and East Anglia were turned on to Hughie Green, he never made it in the rest of the country. The humour of Benny Hill and Arthur Haynes amused Londoners, but failed to tickle any other region.

TEASER ANSWERS

1   Desmond Morris.
2   Clampett – with Buddy Ebsen as Pa and Irene Ryan as Granny.
3   It ran on Friday evenings and the catch phrase was 'The weekend starts here.'

TV news

- Wales West and North closed down. It was the first and only case of an ITV company going broke. The famous 'licence to print money' didn't extend to this region of Welsh Wales and it was taken over by Television West and Wales. All the other ITV companies survived the first franchise re-allocation that year. Lord Hill of the Independent Television Authority praised the companies' programmes, but appointed a 'viewers panel' to watch over ITV's future output. This was the last time that all TV companies would survive the franchise race.
- Dulux paint began their advertising campaign using Old English Sheepdogs. They were trained for the commercials by Barbara Woodhouse who became an unlikely TV star.
- The first live broadcast from the grounds of Buckingham Palace saw the Queen presenting new colours to the RAF as viewers got their first look at the Royals' back garden.

'I Remember You'

Frank Ifield was one of the leading solo pop singers of the early 60s who was eventually squeezed out by the groups. He had 15 records in the charts from 1960 to 1966 with four number ones along the way: 'I Remember You', 'Lovesick Blues', 'Wayward Wind and Confessin'.

Although he was born in Coventry, he grew up in Australia. He became the biggest recording star Down Under, and arrived back in Britain in 1959. In 1962 his record 'I Remember You' became the first disc to ever sell a million in the UK alone. His singing style owed as much to Country and Western as to the outback and appealed to both teenagers and mums and dads.

1964 saw him top the bill at the Palladium twice, star in a Christmas special called **Once a Jolly Swagman**,

and have his own show-case **The Frank Ifield Show (15).** The next year ahe had his own series, **Frank Ifield Sings**.

1964

A YEAR IN THE SOAPS

It is November 1964 and a 'Special Press Release' from ATV announces a new daily serial.

'CROSSROADS'

These are the principal characters in the cast of Midland ATV's new 25-minute daily serial 'Crossroads', which starts on November 2nd at 6.30pm.

The story is based on the lives of two sisters, living within a short drive of each other on the outskirts of a sprawling, still developing industrial city.

It is also the saga of the people who travel the Midland road, who stop overnight or sometimes longer – when their lives get entangled with those of the main characters.

The lives of millions of viewers would 'get entangled' with Crossroads over the next 24 years. The critics hated it. The public loved it. Even after its closure an active fan club survives swapping pirated video copies and longing for the halcyon days when it was on five nights a week.

The world mourned the murder of one the greatest stars of the TV western – Cochise, Little Joe's pinto horse in **Bonanza**. An intruder broke into the stable in Hollywood where the horse was kept and stabbed him. Little Joe, played by Michael Landon, was heartbroken.

1965

TOP TWENTY
Homes [millions]

1	Royal Variety Show	ITV	11.00
2	Coronation Street	ITV	9.66
3	Take Your Pick	ITV	8.80
4	Riviera Police	ITV	8.60
5	No Hiding Place	ITV	8.48
6	Double Your Money	ITV	8.35
7	This Week	ITV	8.35
8	Love Story	ITV	8.35
9	Crane	ITV	8.10
10	Emergency Ward Ten	ITV	8.01
11	The Power Game	ITV	8.00
12	Hello Dolly	ITV	8.00
13	Steptoe and Son	BBC	7.95
14	The Avengers	ITV	7.95
15	Music of Lennon and McCartney	ITV	7.90
16	It's Tarbuck	ITV	7.80
17	Miss World 1965	BBC	7.75
18	Here Comes the Pops	ITV	7.60
19	Blackmail	ITV	7.60
20	Professional Boxing	ITV	7.27

• No 12 – Preview of the Broadway hit opening in London's West End that week.

• No 15 – Also starring were Marianne Faithfull, Lulu, Cilla Black, Billy J Kramer and the Dakotas and Peter Sellers.

• No 17 – Miss UK won for the second year running with Lesley Langley.

• No 20 – Heavyweights Billy Walker of West Ham and Charlie Powell of California.

1965

Cops and Robbers

Top newcomer of the year was **Riviera Police (4)**, a glossy crime series set on the French Riviera. It had everything – four hunky policemen, hundreds of bikini-clad starlets, blue skies, a beautiful backdrop and big-time crime. The Cannes Film Festival and the murder of a rising star provided the plot for the first episode which guest-starred Anthony Valentine. Despite going in at Number One in its first week – helped by the fact it followed **Coronation Street** – the series proved that sun and sex do not necessarily equal staying power and it ended after 13 weeks.

It was a different story for **No Hiding Place (5)**. After six successful years Superintendent Lockhart and his team were suspended from duty in 1965. Fans, with and without helmets, protested and they were brought back to the Yard for two more years.

Amateur detective and part-time smuggler Richard **Crane (9)** also gave up the game in January 1965 after 39 episodes on the sun-drenched shores of Morocco. The episode to top the charts also starred Keith Barron much later to be found across the water on the Costa Del Sol in **Duty Free**.

Bottom of the cops in this year's top 20 but still being repeated somewhere in the world today was **The Avengers (14)** with Diana Rigg who starred as Steed's all-action partner Emma Peel in 83 episodes.

Tarbuck Sweeps In

Nineteen sixty five was a vintage year for Tarbie. It all started with **It's Tarbuck** in January. The Wednesday night showcase also co-starred the lovely Amanda Barrie – over 20 years later she turned up in **Coronation Street** as waitress Alma Sedgewick. The Merseyside comic rode into national fame on the wave of Beatlemania that seemed to sweep every talented scouser off the streets of Liverpool into the pop charts or onto the telly.

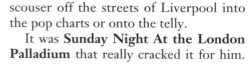

It was **Sunday Night At the London Palladium** that really cracked it for him. Virtually unknown, the 22-year-old comic and ex-Butlins redcoat walked on in October '63 and was such a hit that he made three rapid repeat guest spots.

And in September 1965 he walked out onto that stage again for **The New London Palladium Show** as the host of TV's most successful variety show following in the illustrious footsteps of Tommy Trinder, Bruce Forsyth and Norman Vaughan.

Like many comics, Jimmy became a professional TV host with shows like **Winner Takes All**, **The Frame Game, Tarbuck On Golf**, and the 'Live From ...' series – the last of which was **Live From the Palladium**.

A unique move out of **Coronation Street** in 1965. Leonard Swindley (played by Arthur Lowe) was such a favourite that he was given his own comedy series entitled **Pardon the Expression** which was set in a department store. Curiously one of Mr Swindley's staff was played by Betty Driver – who went into the Street herself four years later as the new barmaid Betty Turpin.

TVnews

- Mary Whitehouse launched the unofficial telly watchdogs – The National Viewers and Listeners Association and TV producers headed for cover.
- Cigarette and rolling tobacco, but not pipe tobacco, was banned from the commercial breaks.
- The schedules were swept aside for the funeral in January of Sir Winston Churchill, the biggest outside broadcast since the Coronation.
- ITV came to the Isle of Man with Border TV.
- ITV celebrated its tenth birthday. In 1955 it began with 188,000 homes able to watch. By 1965 it was over 12 million.
- The Homepride Flour Graders in their little bowler hats began picking the lumps out of self-raising flour in the long running commercial.

A YEAR IN THE SOAPS

1965

Newcomers United

Compact the BBC's twice weekly soap of life in a magazine finally ceased and gave way to two more attempts at taking on ITV's dominance with **Emergency Ward Ten** and **Coronation Street**.

The Newcomers followed a family who had moved out of London to a new town in East Anglia. Maggie Fitzgibbon starred as Vivien Cooper. Her husband Ellis was played by Alan Browning, he turned up in the Street years later as Alan Howard, another of Elsie's husbands. Wendy Richard, later **EastEnders**' Pauline, was the Coopers' cockney neighbour.

A braver departure in the soap opera stakes was **United!** This was all the excitement and action of Brentwich United football club. All sweaty socks and hunky men, although the BBC chiefs insisted they keep their shorts on at all times. The 'action' sequences were filmed at Stoke City's ground and would not have fooled an extremely short sighted soccer fan. Stephen Yardley played the goalkeeper and David Lodge the manager. Jimmy Hill was the soccer adviser for the series and it probably delayed his break into TV by years.

Secret Wedding

Coronation Street's David Barlow and Irma Ogden, played by Alan Rothwell and Sandra Gough, tried to get married in secret with a quiet wedding at the local Weatherfield Registry Office. But the secret leaked out – well it was on the front page of that week's *TV Times* – and the whole Street turned up at the reception. They took over the corner shop and later emigrated to Australia where, naturally, tragedy waited. David was killed in a car crash.

Also that year, Elsie Tanner went out with a shady character called Robert Maxwell, who promptly died – at the wheel of his Jaguar.

TV TIMES 6d

Coronation Street: Irma and David's wedding—on Wednesday

Took's TV TEASERS

1 What were the names of the three old ladies in the Snug bar at the Rovers ?

2 Who were the babies in the Flintstones ?

3 Who was Burke in Burke's Law ?

Peyton Place was the first major American soap to hit British TV and was probably the most successful ever. There were 514 episodes in all. It minted a

Follow the fortunes of Mia Farrow, as Allison Mackenzie, and Ryan O'Neal, as Rodney Harrington, in another episode of Peyton Place—see below

9.10 Peyton Place
STARRING
DOROTHY MALONE
WARNER ANDERSON
MIA FARROW
ED NELSON
CAST
Constance Mackenzie..Dorothy Malone
Mathew Swain........Warner Anderson
Dr. Michael Rossi.........Ed Nelson
Allison Mackenzie.......Mia Farrow
Dr. Robert Morton.......Kent Smith
Elliot Carson...........Tim O'Connor
Rodney Harrington......Ryan O'Neal
Betty Anderson......Barbara Parkins
Leslie Harrington......Paul Langton
Julie Anderson........Kasey Rogers
George Anderson.....Henry Beckman
Norman
  Harrington....Christopher Connell
Eli Carson...........Frank Ferguson
Dr. Bradley..........Charles Irving
For Elliot Carson, decisions must be made for his freedom to be regained. George Anderson rapidly approaches an emotional point-of-no-return, his wife and friends helpless to assist

9.40 It's Dark Outside
'We can't even begin to love everybody. We've just got to start with one person, and just see how it would feel if you honestly believed their life, their fear, their pain was yours. Really yours. So that you could eventually stop using the word 'I' altogether'
WILLIAM MERVYN
AND
JOHN STRATTON
VERONICA STRONG
ANTHONY AINLEY
IN
The Prevalence of Liars
BY MARC BRANDEL
WITH
MARY MORRIS
OLIVER REED
KATHLEEN MICHAEL
MICHAEL JOHNSON
Sebastian...............Oliver Reed
Pad.................Michael Johnson
Sheila Barrett..........Sheila Steafel
Claire Martin........Veronica Strong
Fred Blane...............John Stratton
Chief-Insp. Rose......William Mervyn

fortune for its producers and made stars of the leading characters. Ryan O'Neal, Mia Farrow, Barbara Parkin and Dorothy Malone were the biggest names in the glamorous and steamy soap.

Going For a Song made a star of Arthur Negus and turned antiques into a British obsession.

Public Eye, with Frank Marker, the first detective with a real dirty mac, was played with superb seediness by Alfred Burke.

The Smashing Sandie Shaw: 'On her own... One of the brightest new girls on the music scene.'

Call My Bluff was hosted originally by Robin Ray with Robert Morley and Frank Muir, plus bow-tie, as the two captains of the teams of showbiz stars trying to con each other with obscure words from the Oxford English Dictionary.

The World of Sport came to Saturday afternoons with Eamonn Andrews as the anchor man and reports from Jimmy Hill, Freddie Trueman, Peter Lorenzo, Ian Wooldridge and Wrestling with Kent Walton.

Stingray was the latest puppet series from Gerry and Sylvia Anderson to be launched. The underwater adventures of Troy Tempest and Marina were filmed in a fish tank in Slough.

Orlando was the children's spin-off from **Crane**. It took Sam Kydd's character Orlando O'Connor and turned him from a detective's right-hand man into – a detective.

The Power Game starred Patrick Wymark as hard-faced businessman Sir John Wilder moving into politics.

Jackanory, Jackanory, Jackanory, Jackanory, bom, bom – first spun its kiddies' tales for tiny tots.

• **Cinema** that Spring was introduced by Derek Grainger, but in September, Mike Scott took over the late-night review of what was on at the pictures that week. After many years off the box, as Director of Programmes at Granada TV, Mike came back to the TV screen in 1988 to host the morning talk show **The Time...the Place...**
• **Opportunity Knocks** ran through the summer, no stars knocked that year for Hughie.
• **Blackpool Night Out** was another summer variety spectacular, this one hosted by Mike and Bernie Winters. With seaside stars like Tommy Cooper, Vicky Carr, Jimmy Edwards and the statutory pop group for the kids, like Freddie and the Dreamers and The Beatles.
• **The World Tonight** had Michael Parkinson as the link man in this ambitious world-wide weekly current affairs show. They were 'covering the world from the world' in the days before instant satellite communications.

TEASER ANSWERS

1 Ena Sharples, Minnie Caldwell and Martha Longhurst were played by Violet Carson, Margot Bryant and Lynne Carol.
2 Pebbles was the daughter of Fred and Wilma Flintstone. Bamm Bamm was an orphan boy that Barney and Betty Rubble found on their doorstep.
3 Gene Barry starred as Captain Amos Burke, a very smooth and cultured Beverly Hills detective. The title of every of its 80 episodes began with the words 'Who Killed.....?'

Curtains Up – Variety Lives

There's no business like show business was certainly true in 1966. There were six variety shows in the year's top programmes.

A Royal Gala (3) was a two and a half hour show-case for ITV. Stars from **Coronation Street**, **Ward Ten**, **Double Your Money** and **Ready Steady Go** joined the usual crop of variety performers on the Palladium stage and entertained the Duke of Edinburgh.

Secombe and Friends (4) saw Harry Secombe being given the stage of the Palladium, a peak Sunday night slot and the chance to get a load of his mates on the telly. The Welsh seemed to dominate. Actors Richard Burton, Stanley Baker, Donald Houston and singer Geraint Evans ended up singing in the shower with Harry. More madness followed with Harry's fellow Goons Peter Sellers, Spike Milligan, Ray Ellington and writer Eric Sykes solving The Whistling Spy Enigma.

The London Palladium Show (5) certainly had variety in September with 'Roger Moore making a special guest appearance.' The star of **Bonanza**, Lorne Greene joined singers Kathy Kirby and Millicent Martin on the bill.

The Morecambe and Wise Show (15) with Eric and Ernie, revealed its music hall roots by introducing a 'turn'; a guest singer, musician or pop group in between their increasingly sophisticated television sketches. Sixties stars like Jackie Trent, The Settlers, The King Brothers and The Shadows provided the musical break.

Hippodrome (18) certainly mixed and matched, it had the Everly Brothers, Dusty Springfield and circus acts Les Volants, Ruppert Bears, El Gran Tonisko and the band of The Royal Air Force all on the same bill!

The Blackpool Show (19) was beside the seaside for summer Sunday nights with 'a glittering hour of comedy and music from the entertainment capital of the north – the stage of the ABC Theatre Blackpool' according to the *TV Times*. Tony Hancock hosted.

TV news

The biggest TV event of the year failed to appear in the top 20. Yes, '66 was the year of the World Cup. Four hundred million people watched it worldwide, but the UK audience was split. For the final, 26 million watched the BBC and listened to Kenneth Wolstenholme say: 'They think it's all over – it is now,' as Geoff Hurst scored. Only four million tuned into ITV's coverage introduced by Eamonn Andrews, claimed the BBC's researchers. The other research organisation, TAM, explained the final only reached number 13 in that week's top 20 because they only metered homes with a choice of channels. It wasn't until 1980, when audience research became a joint venture in BARB (Broadcasting Audience Research Board), that disputes over viewing figures were ended.

LAST NIGHTS

- **Ben Casey**, the US hospital drama starring Vince Edwards, ended its five year run.
- **Dr Kildare** with Richard Chamberlain and Raymond Massey also ceased to practice after 200 episodes.
But they both came back as head-to-head repeats in the 1970s.

1966

TOP TWENTY
Homes [millions]

1	Miss World 1966	BBC	9.80
2	Mrs Thursday	ITV	9.55
3	A Royal Gala	ITV	9.55
4	Secombe and Friends	ITV	9.45
5	The London Palladium Show	ITV	9.15
6	Coronation Street	ITV	9.05
7	Double Your Money	ITV	8.85
8	Take Your Pick	ITV	8.80
9	The Rat Catchers	ITV	8.50
10	No Hiding Place	ITV	8.45
11	The Avengers	ITV	8.40
12	Cinema	ITV	8.30
13	World Title Boxing	BBC	8.15
14	Dare I Weep, Dare I Moan	ITV	8.10
15	The Morecambe and Wise Show	ITV	8.00
16	Emergency Ward Ten	ITV	7.85
17	Gone Laughing Home	ITV	7.85
18	Hippodrome	ITV	7.85
19	The Blackpool Show	ITV	7.70
20	The Power Game	ITV	7.60

- No 1 – Won by Reita Faria a medical student from India.

- No 14 – Starred James Mason and Jill Bennett in a cold war spy film which was based on a John Le Carré story.

1966

1966

BBC Hits Back

After a dismal showing in the charts in previous years '66 saw some of the Beeb's greatest ever shows win big audiences.

The Likely Lads were Rodney Bewes as Bob and James Bolam as Terry. Written by Dick Clement and Ian La Frenais, it had a warm reality that many other situation comedies of the period lacked.

In 1973 the question **Whatever Happened To the Likely Lads?** was answered in another series. Just as successful as the original it found Bob married to Thelma, upwardly mobile and deeply embarrassed by his old drinking partner Terry.

Till Death Us Do Part with the wonderfully awful bigot Alf Garnett, starred Warren Mitchell, Dandy Nicholls as the downtrodden Else and Una Stubbs and Anthony Booth as daughter and son-in-law. Viewers loved Alf's tirades against Harold Wilson, immigrants, Catholics and loyalty to 'Her Majesty', West Ham FC and the Conservative Party.

In 1985, the writer Johnny Speight brought back Alf and Else as pensioners with **In Sickness and Health**.

David Frost had **The Frost Report** on subjects like women, crime, sin and authority. Sketches were written and acted by a team that went on to become **Monty Python's Flying Circus** – Cleese, Chapman, Idle, et al. The two Ronnies – Corbett and Barker – also formed an enduring partnership on The Report.

Softly, Softly, a spin-off from **Z Cars** saw detectives Watt and Barlow, Frank Windsor and Stratford Johns, leave for the southwest to set up a Regional Crime Squad.

Teaser Answers

1　He played Rodney Harrington, Mia Farrow was Allison McKenzie.
2　Jeff Tracy's sons were Scott, Virgil, Alan, Gordon and John who all worked for International Rescue.
3　Raymond Baxter was the first presenter of the magazine programme that looked at what was new in science and technology.

It was a big year for children's TV.

Hey, hey its **The Monkees**. American television's version of The Beatles was manufactured from four young men after hundreds of auditions. Micky Dolenz, Mike Nesmith, Davy Jones and Peter Tork took the group to world success.

Flipper was another adventure series in the long line of small boys and animal shows. This time a dolphin helped fight off the baddies.

Batman with a loud 'POW', 'BAM' and 'KERRUP' fought off the baddies and kept Gotham City safe. Adam West starred as the Caped Crusader.

How! was a simple format that simply explained the way things work. With Fred Dinenage, Jack Hargreaves and Bunty James among others. It came back in 1990 as **How 2**.

It's a Knockout, while not actually for kids, saw teams from UK towns playing oversized kids games in mock battle for points and glory. Best remembered for hosts Eddie 'Up and Under' Waring and laughing Stuart Hall.

For the grown-ups **The Money Programme** began on BBC2 looking at the world of big business and the pounds, shillings and pence in our piggy banks. And that 1966 pound is now worth two shillings and four pence – 11 pence in today's money.

Cathy Come Home, one of the Wednesday play series, was the disturbing drama of a homeless couple played by Ray Brooks and Carol White. It had such an impact that it was repeated within eight weeks and helped turn Shelter into a major charity and pressure group.

The top American comedian Woody Allen hosted the **Hippodrome** variety show. In one sketch he had to box with a kangaroo and was terrified – Woody lost on points.

The Real Mrs Thursday

Barry Bucknell the television DIY expert had a new book of tips on sale. *The ABC of Do It Yourself* cost 3s 6d (18p).

Awards

ITV stalwarts Michael Miles and Hughie Green received a joint award from the Variety Club for the long success of their game shows.
The Writers' Guild voted **Dr Finlay's Casebook** the best drama series with **Z Cars** as runner up. **Not Only, But Also** with Peter Cook and Dudley Moore won the best comedy series prize with **Steptoe and Son** in second place. **Danger Man** was honoured by Hollywood producers as the best produced TV programme of the year.

Sixty-eight-year-old Kathleen Harrison was the surprise star of the year. **Mrs Thursday** was the top series of '66 knocking regulars like the **Palladium Show** and **Coronation Street** off their customary top spots. The one hour comedy drama was built around a retired charwoman who had inherited millions of pounds and control of a multi-national company.

This was a late TV success for Kathleen who had carved out a long career in film and radio and is best remembered for the 'Huggett' series of films and radio hits. She was a favourite of writer Ted Willis, who had created Mrs Thursday specially for her and he claimed it took just 20 seconds or so to sell the idea to ATV. The millions of viewers and the resulting fame brought its own peculiar problems: "I can't go out shopping any more, it's embarrassing to be recognised and stopped all the time" said Kathleen.

A YEAR IN THE SOAPS

Weavers Green

Welcome to **Weavers Green**. This was TV's answer to the radio hit **The Archers** with a story line woven around an East Anglian country vet's practice – an Ambridge for sick animals. Alan Armstrong and Geoffrey Toms were the two vets, played by Grant Taylor and Eric Flynn as senior and junior partners.

Sadly the series suffered from a terminal attack of ITV politics and its makers, Anglia TV, were forced to take it off when big boys ATV wanted the slot for **Emergency Ward Ten** – even though it had proved a ratings success.

Two young regulars in the cast were Susan George and Kate O'Mara.

1966

1967

TOP TWENTY
Homes [millions]

1	Royal Variety	ITV	11.60
2	Miss World 1967	BBC	10.80
3	London Palladium	ITV	9.95
4	Coronation Street	ITV	9.45
5	Market In Honey Lane	ITV	8.85
6	Eurovision Song Contest	BBC	8.85
7	Take Your Pick	ITV	8.75
8	Morecambe and Wise	ITV	8.70
9	Mrs Thursday	ITV	8.60
10	Dr Finlay's Casebook	BBC	8.50
11	Secombe and Friends	ITV	8.30
12	Z Cars	ITV	8.20
13	This Is Petula Clark	BBC	8.15
14	World In Action	ITV	8.10
15	Double Your Money	ITV	8.05
16	The Avengers	ITV	8.00
17	Cinema	ITV	8.00
18	Professional Boxing	BBC	8.00
19	Death By Misadventure	ITV	8.00
20	International Ice Gala	BBC	8.00

• No 11 – The friends were John Cleese, Michael Bentine, Anita Harris and the choir of the First Battalion Welsh Guards.

• No 14 – The subject was Unidentified Flying Objects, investigating encounters of the third kind.

• No 19 – Granada TV investigated the causes of some of 20th Century's great disasters, like the R101 airship's loss in 1930.

1967

East Enders Market

Market In Honey Lane (5) was launched in April and within a week it had overtaken long-standing hits. 'We're not a southern Coronation Street,' its producers said, 'we're a series not a serial.' Each episode told a particular story of a character working or living in the London street market. It closed in March '69. For Honey Lane, ATV built a cockney street scene with shops, stalls and pub at their Elstree studio. Eighteen years later the BBC bought the studios and did the same – they called it **EastEnders**.

Sandie Shaw finally broke Britain's run of near misses on the **Eurovision Song Contest (6)** with 'Puppet On a String'. The song was already in the charts by the time Sandie headed off to Vienna without her shoes and it stayed there for another 18 weeks.

Morecambe and Wise (8) were the top comedy act of the year. In November their guests were Tom Jones, Millicent Martin and The Hollies. This was Eric and Ernie's last chart success with ITV. In 1968 they changed channels after 13 years and went to the BBC, and with a new scriptwriter, Eddie Braben, entered their golden period with their history-making Christmas shows.

The Bongs At Ten

In July, tucked away between **Coronation Street** and a cure for constipation is a real piece of TV news. Alastair Burnet with the **News At Ten** intro-

---

10.0 Alastair Burnet with the News at Ten

See pages 2-3

ALSO IN THE STUDIO
Andrew Gardner
Reginald Bosanquet   George Ffitch

A new style half-hour of up-to-the-minute news. ITN's experienced teams of correspondents, specialists and cameramen range the world to report the action and the argument

---

duced the first half hour news programme. The format was borrowed from the much more relaxed US TV style of news presentation and it went straight into the charts. Also appearing in that first week were George Fitch, Andrew Gardner and Reginald Bosanquet who were paired up with Alastair Burnet. It was also the first news to have a commercial break.

This turned out to be highly lucrative for the TV companies as advertisers fought to use a slot which, it was claimed, got all the 'best' viewers. The opening sequence of Big Ben's chimes – called 'the Bongs' is the second longest running signature tune after Coronation Street.

FIRST NIGHTS

The Golden Shot arrived in July, live on Saturday nights. The high tech game show had a blindfolded cameraman firing a crossbow at prizewinning targets. Viewers could participate from home, calling out 'up a bit, right a bit, fire' on the telephone. Jackie Rae was the first host, Bob Monkhouse took over and stayed for over 200 shows saying: 'Bernie the bolt, please' about 1,000 times. Norman Vaughan was the next host, followed by Charlie Williams. Bob came back in '75 to try and boost the flagging show but the Shot got the bullet that year.

The Prisoner with Patrick McGoohan was either loved or hated. Its devotees still meet once a year at the location of the series, Portmeirion in North Wales, and re-enact scenes. After the success of **Danger Man**, McGoohan was given his head. He was originator, executive producer, scriptwriter and director on

some of the episodes. John Drake was prisoner 'Number Six' in what could have been a fascist micro-state, a prison or just a state of mind. A load of tosh or a piece

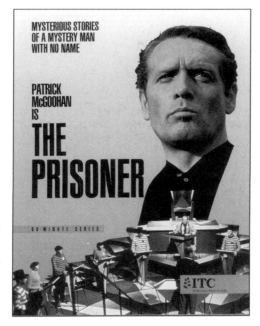

MYSTERIOUS STORIES OF A MYSTERY MAN WITH NO NAME

PATRICK McGOOHAN IS

THE PRISONER

60 MINUTE SERIES

ITC

of mould-breaking TV? History still hasn't decided.

Man In a Suitcase was another international crime-buster. McGill was an ex-CIA man, played by Richard Bradford, in another ATV series with an imported American star. Bradford said he was trying to show McGill as a real human being, not a superman. Thirty episodes were made and sold to the US.

A YEAR IN THE SOAPS

Wedding of the Year

Coronation Street's viewing figures leapt in September for Elsie Tanner's wedding. She was marrying Master Sgt Steve Tanner of the US Army who had been Elsie's war-time sweetheart.

TV Times published a special: 'On sale Thursday, price one shilling, the only official souvenir of the TV wedding of the year.'

The wedding preparations, ceremony and honeymoon flight took up the week's two episodes and were written by Jack Rosenthal. As usual the honeymoon didn't last long for Elsie, the marriage went wrong and they split up after a year.

1967

Took's TV Teasers

1 Who presented Animal Magic ?

2 Who was Dick Van Dyke's wife ?

3 Who played the wife in Meet the Wife ?

Frost Over Television

David Frost, always a busy man, was particularly busy in '67. He began the year with a series of **The Frost Programme** with Rediffusion in London.

• **Perry Mason**, ten years after he was first shown in the US, was still having his day in court and still winning big audiences. Raymond Burr starred in 271 episodes and each week destroyed the Los Angeles District Attorney with a brilliant defence.

• **The Eamonn Andrews Show** 'Live From London', but recorded earlier that evening at ABC's Teddington studio, ran for five years from 1964 with Eamonn sweating buckets over his 'famous, frank and funny guests'. It was the first real British attempt to repeat the success of American chat shows like Johnny Carson.

• Hughie Green said **Opportunity Knocks** to six acts every Saturday night for nearly six months. These had been whittled down from 8,000 auditions. Getting their big chance in '67 were acts like: Vivion and Collette, Haydock and Ashton Youth band, The Crackpots, Dave Olivier... but no name that seems to have made it to stardom.

• **All Gas and Gaiters** drew its comedy from the church. Derek Nimmo played the hapless curate to William Mervyn's bishop and Robertson Hare was the bumbling archdeacon, in what was a comic version of Trollope's *Barchester Chronicles*.

• **Sanctuary** was more TV religion, this time about nuns. 'The series is documentary fiction made with accuracy and reverence without being mushy' said its producer. It was The Sound of Music without the music, with a very pretty Joanna Dunham as the 'young high-spirited' Sister Benedict.

This 'late night miscellany' was on three nights a week, but was only seen in some ITV regions. In the spring he was back on the BBC for **Frost Over England**. This series of reports and sketches on aspects of British life starred Ronnie Barker, Ronnie Corbett and John Cleese and won the Golden Rose of Montreux for the best comedy series.

In September it was back to ITV and **The Frost Programme**, and the more serious edge to Frost as he grilled people in front of a studio audience. The phrase 'Trial By Television' was born. His exposure of a crooked insurance boss, Emil Savundra, was a moment of television history. At the same time he had pulled together a team of media stars called The London Television Consortium to bid for the ITV franchise in London at the weekends. The ITA were dazzled by his cast list and they won 'hands down'. London Weekend Television came on air the following August.

WILL THE REAL DAVID FROST STAND UP?

He has been described as dynamic, outspoken, unpredictable. Since he signed off his last Independent Television programme at 11.9 p.m. on February 3. 1967 he has travelled 45,000 miles and visited 14 countries. All his experiences, everything he saw, everything he heard since then have a bearing on *The Frost Programme*, which starts this week. For the first of three articles about the *Real David Frost* we naturally invited David Frost himself to write it. NOT that he wrote about himself. BUT he did write about his summer . . .

NEXT WEEK: Neil Shand, formerly of TV Times and now one of The Frost Programme team, takes a stable-mate's eye view of Boss Frost. The following week journalist Sally Vincent waits for David Frost—the man whose "working hours seem to be from dawn to dawn"

My 45,000 miles
by DAVID FROST

WILL you write an article, they said. What sort of article would you like, I asked. Up to you, perhaps something about what you have been doing since the end of the last series of *The Frost Programme*, they said.

Well, I spent two or three months at the B.B.C., I said. That wasn't quite what we meant, they said.

Look, the man went on, a trifle impatiently now, because I think, on the side, he also does most of the drawings for the cartoon page and wanted to be going off and doing one about a man and a girl shipwrecked on a desert island.

Look, he said, do you remember those essays you had to write at school on the first day of every autumn term? Oh yes, I said, you mean " How I spent my summer holidays." Got it in one, he said, and went off to draw his cartoons.

Not that I am the best person to get to write about holidays. I had not had one for four years until this summer, and then it was sandwiched between various stages of a trip round the world that was otherwise work most of the way.

Nevertheless I am a great believer in travel and the value of this trip, like any other, was the way it serves to turn upside down some of your thinking, and make you a good deal more objective about this country when you get back to it. (When I was commuting to the States a couple of years ago, the fashion photographer craze was at its height here, and it was most instructive the way it looked even dafter from New York than it did at close range.)

There are innumerable ways that any trip round the world, which includes a fair bit of time spent in Asia, must affect your views. Let me try and quote one small example. With the coming of colour magazines in assorted newspapers, one of the many sorts of article with which we are now all familiar is the highly-coloured—both in picture and word—article on food. We positively expect to see Clement Freud recommending 47 vegetables unobtainable anywhere outside one area of 40 sq. yd. in Soho, the Cradocks suggesting an adventure with Brussels sprouts, and Robert Carrier finding something new to do with a German Sausage.

My B.O.A.C. flight landed in Asia at the same time as the weekly consignment of Sunday newspapers from London, and I was soon sitting in an English diplomat's lounge, when his

Not only shortage of food but a chronic shortage of living space, too. A mud road in New Delhi transformed into a flood in 15 minutes

TVnews

• BBC2 began Europe's first full colour TV service in July with lots of green pictures of the Wimbledon Tennis Championships. The problem was a new colour TV set cost about £200 (£1,400 in the nineties!) and the licence fee was doubled at £10.

• The Crossroads motel was blown up – in the script – by a World War II unexploded bomb. This was the on-screen reason, for in reality ATV were moving the series to a new studio and took the opportunity to build new sets.

• Lord Hill, the chairman of the ITA, was plucked away by Prime Minister Harold Wilson to be chairman of the BBC. Wilson put in Hill, an ex-Tory minister, to rein-in the new wave of BBC executives that were getting up the Government's nose.

• Birds Eye fish fingers introduced Captain Birdseye to the commercials.

• **Our World** was a worldwide live satellite hook up by the BBC hosted by Cliff Michelmore, notable for The Beatles singing 'All You Need Is Love' with a studio full of all the top names in pop music.

• Associated Television (ATV) received the Queen's Award To Industry for outstanding export achievement. Its policy of bringing over American stars to appear in light entertainment shows or to star in drama series had proved extremely successful when selling programmes back to America.

• French actor Fernandel was sacked from the 'Do have a Dubonnet' campaign when it was revealed that he couldn't speak a word of English – not even 'Do have a Dubonnet.'

Sport – The Big Winner

Four big sporting occasions made it into the top 20 in this Olympic Year and the royal gala at No 1 was in aid of sport.

A Special Royal Performance (1), held before Her Majesty at the London Palladium, was a charity show to raise funds for the British Olympic team bound for Mexico City. The cast of the musical Sweet Charity, appropriately, featured and about £50,000 was raised.

The '68 Olympics were the first to be seen via satellite and the British star performers were boxer Chris Finnegan and hurdler David Hemery who both won gold.

The Grand National (4) appeared in the charts for the first time, Red Alligator won.

International Football (6) was the European Nation's Cup semi-final in which England were beaten 1 – 0 by Yugoslavia.

The Boat Race (7) was won by Cambridge, the first in a series of five wins.

The European Cup Final (16) featured Manchester United beating Benfica 4 – 1 after extra time at Wembley.

David Coleman was given his own midweek sports programme; **Sports Night With Coleman**. And on ITV, Dickie Davies took over as the Saturday afternoon anchorman on **World of Sport**.

Actress Sue Nicholls, who played Marilyn Gates, a waitress in **Crossroads,** sang a song on the programme which caused so much interest that it was released as a single. 'Where Will You Be When I Need You?' got to No 17 and stayed in the charts for eight weeks.

Comedy Tonight

Howerd's Hour (5) took the top comedy slot of the year. It was one of Frankie Howerd's rare TV specials. 'Frankie recalls an episode in the life of his great grandfather Howerd in the wild west.' Patrick Wymark played a gun-toting bandit and Hattie Jacques was the bar-room belle. Pop stars Sandie Shaw and Scott Walker were also guests along with the Big Ben Banjo Band.

Life With Cooper (8) was one of the comedian's regular series on ITV. This one followed his adventures taking up a hobby, applying for a passport and taking a holiday abroad all of which ended in chaos.

The Des O'Connor Show (15) was another regular series. In '68 he inherited Tommy Cooper's slot on Saturday nights with a mix of sketches, songs and guest stars.

Took's TV Teasers

1 Who was the charlady in Crossroads ?

2 Who were the original presenters on Magpie ?

3 Which antiques expert became a household name ?

1968

TOP TWENTY
Homes [millions]

1	A Special Royal Performance	ITV	10.55
2	Miss World 1968	BBC	10.05
3	Eurovision	BBC	9.45
4	The Grand National	BBC	9.25
5	Howerd's Hour	ITV	9.10
6	International Football	BBC	8.85
7	The Boat Race	BBC	8.80
8	Life With Cooper	ITV	8.75
9	Coronation Street	ITV	8.60
10	Frost On Sunday	ITV	8.45
11	Till Death Us Do Part	BBC	8.40
12	World In Action	ITV	8.20
13	Harlech Opening Night	ITV	8.10
14	Morecambe and Wise	BBC	8.10
15	Des O'Connor Show	ITV	8.05
16	European Cup Final	ITV	8.05
17	Piccadilly Palace	ITV	7.90
18	Sherlock Holmes	BBC	7.90
19	News At Ten	ITV	7.90
20	Father Dear Father	ITV	7.85

• No 3 – Cliff Richard singing 'Congratulations' came a close second to Spain's winner 'La La la'.

• No 13 – Starring Elizabeth Taylor and Richard Burton plus a long list of eminent Welsh performers.

• No 17 – A one-off variety show starring Millicent Martin and Bruce Forsyth.

• No 18 – Peter Cushing was the hero and Nigel Stock his partner Doctor Watson.

1968

FIRST NIGHTS

Dad's Army Falls In

1968

Dad's Army, British TV's greatest team comedy, first began its defence of Walmington on Sea against the invading Hun. Writers Jimmy Perry and David Croft re-created a Home Guard platoon defending a south coast town during the Second World War invasion scare. The local bank manager, butcher, undertaker and greengrocer paraded at the church hall for a weekly inspection. Arthur Lowe, John Le Mesurier, Clive Dunn, Arnold Ridley, Ian Lavender, James Beck, John Laurie – all were well established character actors who blended beautifully together and made the 1940s come alive.

Like all long running series it had its catch phrases and regular comic devices. Lavender's Private Pike was always 'a stupid boy', the Scot Frazer, always a pessimist, would claim 'we're doomed', the genteel sergeant was always polite on parade 'would you mind awfully, falling in?' Clive Dunn's ancient corporal was always a beat behind everyone else shouldering arms, and Godfrey was always desperate to find the little boys' room.

Please Sir, which has been called ITV's most successful comedy show, had an uncertain start. LWT was the new week-end station and in its early days of Autumn '68 had a few problems – not least collapsing viewing figures. Then in October a new comedy series began about a secondary modern school and 'grim 5c', a class of no-hopers and teenage delinquents. ITV regions outside London, alarmed at the loss of viewers, were not taking all of LWT's shows and Please Sir didn't get the launch it may have deserved. By the end of the first series in December it was a hit and re-scheduled for an immediate repeat after Christmas in all regions on Sunday afternoons. So, enter Bernard Hedges (played by John Alderton) a fresh-faced teacher out to save a class of delinquents and a TV station.

Nice Time gave the young Kenny Everett and a university lecturer from Warwick, Germaine Greer, their first break in TV. They joined Jonathan Routh in a half hour of controlled chaos.

TEASER ANSWERS

1   Amy Turtle, played by Ann George, who wasn't the best actress in the world but had a cult following for the ten years that she played the part of the Brummie busybody.

2   Susan Stranks, Tony Bastable and Pete Brady. Later presenters were Tommy Boyd, Mick Robertson, Douglas Rae and Jenny Hanley.

3   Arthur Negus, who first appeared on Going For a Song, which was hosted by Max Robertson.

TV news

Changes at ITV

- **Harlech Opening Night** was the on-screen indication of the big changes that ITV had been through in 1968. In came London Weekend Television, Yorkshire TV, Thames TV and Harlech TV. Out went Rediffusion, who as Associated-Rediffusion were the first ITV company to go on air in 1955, in London. ABC lost its weekend franchise in London and the Midlands and the north, Granada lost its bit of Yorkshire and TWW lost Wales and the west of England. The changes didn't affect viewers that much, but there were howls of protest at the loss of **Take Your Pick** and **Double Your Money**. ITV's first and most successful game shows, never out of the charts for 13 years, were victims of broadcasting politics.

- Bernard Braden swapped channels and began **Braden's Week** for the BBC.

- Morecambe and Wise also swapped sides to the BBC.

- But ITV pulled off a coup and poached one of the BBC's top double acts – **Pinky and Perky**, the puppet piglets.

- The system of measuring TV audiences was changed by ITV. A new company placed electronic meters in 2,650 homes and measured the viewing habits of 7,790 people minute by minute. This apparently small sample was said to be representative of the national viewing public.

- Cadbury's Milk Tray launched their 'all because the lady loves Milk Tray' campaign with actor Gary Myers acting out a series of dangerous stunts to deliver the box of chocolates.

- Peter Sissons, ITN's reporter covering the Nigerian civil war in Biafra, was machine gunned with his crew. ITN flew a London surgeon out to him, but the wound ended his days as a foreign correspondent and he became a studio presenter.

NEAR MISSES

Bring On the Girls

• The BBC gave four female singers their own light entertainment shows that year. **This Is Petula Clark**, featured our Pet and her recent hit 'The Other Man's Grass', a song about envy, not marijuana. Cilla Black's springtime pop hit was 'Step Inside Love' – her TV hit was simply called **Cilla**. Scotland exported **Moira Anderson Sings**, but there were no chart singles for her to plug, only her long tartan frocks. **Lulu's Back In Town**. Where she had been is not known, but she was singing 'I'm a Tiger'.

• **The Goon Show** came to ITV. In August Thames TV re-united the stars from BBC radio's classic 50s hit for a TV tale entitled A Tale of Men's Shirts. Spike Milligan, Harry Secombe and Peter Sellers were there with the addition of John Cleese to celebrate the show's 21st birthday.

• **Motorway** was a documentary series from Yorkshire TV which followed the progress of the 'Trans-Pennine Motorway' – the M62. In 1968 Britain had 561 miles of motorway (in 1992 there are 1,800) and a tax disc cost a driver £25.

Holiday Time

After Christmas the commercial breaks were full of holidays in the sun. Four of the top five biggest advertising spenders were holiday companies. A Butlins holiday would have cost £7.50 for a week of 'Butlin's Breakfast and Fun'. But the habit of two weeks guaranteed sunshine on the Costa Brava was catching on as Government financial restrictions were being eased.

• **The Forsyte Saga** hit the charts a year late. It had begun on BBC2 the previous year and although a critical hit, not many people could watch because they didn't have a telly that could pick up BBC2. The repeat on BBC1 made it appointment viewing in over seven million homes for 26 weeks. Susan Hampshire played Fleur, and baby clinics were flooded with girls called Fleur. Eric Porter became a TV hate figure as Soames Forsyte after raping Irene played by Nyree Dawn Porter.

• **Not in Front of the Children** starred Wendy Craig and Paul Daneman as Jennifer and Henry Corner in a family comedy written by Richard Waring. This was Wendy's first 'harassed mum' sitcom in which she dealt with the problems of living with growing children – a role she was to corner the market in.

• **George and the Dragon** were Sidney James as George Russell and Peggy Mount as Georgina Dragon. They worked as domestics in the stately home of a retired colonel played by John Le Mesurier. The series was directed by Shaun O'Riordan who had played Peggy's son Eddie in the hit comedy **The Larkins** nine years earlier.

• **Whicker's World** began and the much imitated Alan Whicker set off on his travels for Yorkshire TV.

• Jimmy Edwards hosted **The Auction Game**, a new game show devised by Bamber Gascoigne.

• **The Avengers** were back in the charts with a new series, but Steed had a new assistant – Emma Peel had gone. Diana Rigg had joined in 1965 and made over 50 episodes. The new girl in Patrick Macnee's life was Linda Thorson as Tara King who was to be the final Avengers' action girl for another 33 adventures until 1969 and the end of the eight year run.

It was congratulations to Cliff Richard who was making his TV drama debut. In April he played a suave young villain called Riley manipulated by a gang of crooks in A Matter of Diamonds. It was described as a meatily dramatic role with some deeply emotional love scenes. "The sort of character is nothing like me and it gives a performer plenty to work at," Cliff said.

A list of the 20 top spending advertisers for February show how little buying habits have changed.

1	Oxo
2	Milk Marketing Board
3	Weetabix
4	Heinz Soups
5	Daily Mirror
6	Vim
7	Mackintosh Quality Street
8	Daz
9	Stork Margarine
10	Ambrosia Milk Pudding
11	Maxwell House Coffee
12	Galaxy Milk Chocolate
13	Rowntrees After Eight
14	Guinness
15	McVitie & Price Digestive
16	Supersoft Hairspray
17	Sunblest Bread
18	Australian Immigration
19	Colgate UltraBrite
20	Egg Marketing Board

1968

A YEAR IN THE SOAPS

Driveway To Honey Lane

Programme makers had tried hospitals, garages, factories, football teams and lots of other backdrops for soap operas – now the idea was the adventures of a driving school. **Driveway** told the story of the day-to-day dramas of Major Alan Brock who uses his army gratuity to start a school of motoring. The tea time series went out twice a week on Tuesdays and Thursdays, but by episode 16 there were problems and Alan was trying to sell the business. He must have succeeded because the next Tuesday **Honey Lane** was in the Driveway slot.

Honey Lane was the cut down version of the hit drama series of the lives of those who worked in the East End street **Market in Honey Lane**. It had fallen on hard times and ATV were now trying to boost its popularity with a twice weekly format. But after several changes in its transmission time, which saw the cockney series run in the afternoons and late at night in different ITV areas, the market finally closed down in the following March after six months in the soap business.

1969

TOP TWENTY
Homes [millions]

1	Miss World 1969	BBC	10.55
2	Royal Variety	ITV	9.15
3	In Loving Memory	ITV	8.60
4	Coronation Street	ITV	8.35
5	Benny Hill Show	ITV	8.30
6	Max	ITV	8.25
7	The Dustbinmen	ITV	8.25
8	Mr Digby Darling	ITV	8.25
9	The Power Game	ITV	8.20
10	Till Death Us Do Part	BBC	8.15
11	Royal Family	BBC	8.05
12	Eurovision Song Contest	BBC	8.00
13	Please Sir	ITV	8.00
14	This Is Your Life	ITV	8.00
15	Two In Clover	ITV	7.75
16	Sportsnight With Coleman	BBC	7.75
17	The Best Things Of Life	ITV	7.75
18	Special Branch	ITV	7.70
19	News At Ten	ITV	7.65
20	Opportunity Knocks	ITV	7.55

• No 1 – Miss World 1969 was Miss Austria Eva Rueber Staier.

• No 12 – Lulu with 'Boom Bang-A-Bang' came joint first. It was a four-way draw with France, Spain and Holland.

• No 17 – This was a sitcom starring Harry H Corbett and June Whitfield, about a couple that had been engaged for 11 years.

Royal TV Stars

The Royal family became television stars in 1969 and they have probably been regretting it ever since. The investiture of the Prince of Wales at Caernarvon in July was the excuse for a year of the 'Royal Windsor TV Show'.

Royal Family (11) was the record-breaking documentary that followed the family through a year and viewers saw them off-duty and relaxed – just like any other family with a film crew in their front room. Richard Cawston and the BBC crew shot the film, he was rewarded with a personal honour from Her Majesty. ITV repeated the documentary and also had the rights to sell it abroad – it was seen in 112 countries. The programme was a watershed in Royal coverage. The film had been seen by royal advisers as a way of popularising the family at a time when public interest was waning. In retrospect, it may have created a demand for royal news that the family could never satisfy and taken away much of their mystery as a very special family.

Before the investiture, Prince Charles, the Prince of Wales, gave his first TV interview to Brian Connell of ITV and Cliff Michelmore from the BBC. The 20-year-old student talked about: 'his education, his views on Welsh nationalism, leisure interests and several other day to day aspects of his life.' Because it was shown simultaneously on both channels the interview was the most watched programme of the year.

Wynford Vaughan-Thomas, one of the best known voices in Britain, was on home territory to commentate at Caernarvon Castle. Coverage of the day's events took up four hours of the schedules on 1st July, with recorded highlights in the evening for another hour of the pageantry designed by his brother-in-law Lord Snowdon.

The Royal Variety Performance (2)

was also a special TV event – the first to be broadcast in colour. The Queen, wearing light blue, and the Duke of Edinburgh, in black and white, watched the usual line-up of stars like the colourful Danny La Rue, Cilla Black – also in blue – and Shari Lewis and her off-white puppet Lamb Chop..

Magpie published The ABC of Space *with Peter Fairley the TV space expert. 'T' was for TV in Space: 'The television camera which American Lunarnauts use on the Moon weighs seven and a quarter pounds and has four lenses. It can take pictures in near darkness and costs £200,000.'*

In Loving Memory (3) concerned the comings and goings – but mostly the goings – of an undertaker's business in a 1920s Lancashire mill town. As a comedy series it must be unique. It killed off its star in the first week (Jeremiah Unsworth played by Freddie Jones). His widow Ivy (Thora Hird) and dimwit nephew Billy (Christopher Beeny) took over t'shop and kept the business running, after a fashion.

There were a few worries about the subject matter of the comedy. Was it in bad taste? Can death be funny? Apparently it was and viewers didn't seem to have any reservations. Five series were made altogether. And with our Billy at last getting wed, In Loving Memory finally closed the lid in 1986.

The Dustbinmen (6) was a cult comedy hit of the year. But real-life binmen were not too happy with the series. Wareham and Purbeck Rural Council's dusties complained: 'We're sick and tired of being called "Heavy Brethin" or "Cheese and Egg" and other nicknames in the show.' A spokesman for Granada TV said that Lancashire dustmen had watched the pilot and loved it – and they were the show's advisers. But the production team did have trouble finding a depot willing to let them film the second series.

NEW SERIES THE DUSTBINMEN 8.30

BY JACK ROSENTHAL

BRYAN PRINGLE	
GRAHAM HABERFIELD	
JOHN WOODVINE	
TREVOR BANNISTER	
TIM WYLTON	

Enter the crew of Thunderbird Three, a Corporation dustcart wending its hilarious way through the streets of a Northern town.

The first episode of a six-programme series centres on the tribulations of Winston, played by Graham Haberfield. His mates dream of throttling him. His girl friend dreams of marrying him.

But all Winston dreams about is football. Then tragedy strikes . . .

Can his fellow dustmen lead him back to sanity? Worse still, can his girl-friend lead him to the altar?

Cheese and Egg	Bryan Pringle
Winston	Graham Haberfield
Bloody Delilah	John Woodvine
Heavy Breathing	Trevor Bannister
Eric	Tim Wylton
Naomi	Paula Wilcox
Bridesmaid	Stephanie Turner

MUSIC DEREK HILTON : DESIGNER DENIS PARKIN : DIRECTOR LES CHATFIELD : PRODUCER JACK ROSENTHAL
Granada Television Production
See page 8

Wylton, Pringle, Haberfield and Bannister—the litter people

A YEAR IN THE SOAPS

High Living For Castle Haven

Daytime TV took the plunge with two new soap operas..

From Yorkshire TV came **Castle Haven** – a large seaside Victorian house that had been converted into flats. 'It was a slice of life without the sugar' the producers said. 'Future generations will refer to Castle Haven when they wish to know what life was like in the seventies.' Unfortunately for future generations, the twice weekly soap only lasted two years and all the recordings have been wiped.

However, two of the residents did survive and go on to greater things. Gretchen Franklin to Ethel in **East-Enders** and Kathy Staff to **Last of the Summer Wine**.

High Living was the other tale about life in a block of flats. This time it was life in a Glasgow tower block. 'The dramatised stories concern the problems that develop among the people who are learning to live a little nearer the clouds,' said Scottish TV and they made over 200 of the 15-minute dramas.

- Europe's highest TV mast, the 1,265 foot high Emley Moor transmitter in Yorkshire, collapsed during a storm. Ice collecting on the supporting cables had done the damage and viewers in the new Yorkshire TV area lost ITV for several weeks.
- On 20th and 21st July TV schedules were swept aside for Apollo 11 and the moon landing. Michael Collins, Buzz Aldrin and Neil Armstrong were the crew and at 02.56 GMT the world watched Armstrong make his first small step. James Burke and Patrick Moore hosted the BBC coverage. On ITV David Frost injected a little showbiz into the coverage with Cilla Black, Lulu and Englebert Humperdinck filling-in just in case the viewers got bored.
- Colour TV came to both main channels (BBC1 and ITV) in November. However, only between one and two percent of homes had a colour TV at the time.
- TV licences for black and white went up to £6 – £11 for colour.
- The Post Master General, John Stonehouse, had the plate changed outside his office. As the government minister in charge of TV, he was now to be called the Minister of Posts and Telecommunications.

John Alderton, the teacher Bernard Hedges in **Please Sir**, went back to his old school, Kingston High School in Hull, and met his old English master. 'Talented... but his mind tended to wander' said his 1954 school report. His first school play was The Winslow Boy. In his second play he played a father of three boys and his teacher said he looked like a natural.

News At Ten mounted a special report on the Loch Ness Monster. With underwater cameras, sonar, time lapse cameras, divers and all the scientific gear they could find, they spent two weeks on location. At the end Richard Lindley signed off with: 'If you are there Nessie, all we can do is congratulate you on evading our attempts to find you.'

NEAR MISSES

- **The Virginian** was one of the few westerns left on TV. James Drury starred as the foreman of the Shilo Ranch and Doug McLure played Trampas, one of the hands. The theme of The Virginian was how the urban east was destroying the old west.
- **The Fossett Saga** wasn't a misprint for the **Forsyte Saga**, but was a comedy show starring Jimmy Edwards. He played a Victorian writer of penny dreadfuls with more than a hint of Sherlock Holmes in his character. With Sam Kydd as his manservant, they attempted to solve Gothic mysteries.
- **Callan** was more mystery-solving, but with deadly purpose. Edward Woodward played the hit-man in the very sordid world of espionage doing dirty jobs for British Secret Service. He had a conscience but not that deep, for Callan managed to go on operating for nearly six years and over 50 episodes. Lonely was his helper with a bad case of body odour played by Russell Hunter.
- **Who-Dun-It** was a series of murder mysteries set in the 1930s in the style of Agatha Christie. The viewers were challenged to solve the murder at the end of the second act when the detective would summarise the evidence before he went on to name the guilty party.
- **The Troubleshooters** followed on from the other oil industry hit **Mogul**. Ray Barrett was the jet-setting oil executive fixing mega-deals and keeping the black gold flowing. The Troubleshooters gained quite a reputation in the oil industry for the uncanny accuracy of its plots.

1969

Took's
TV TEASERS

1   Which pre-war radio detective made a TV comeback ?

2   In which comedy series did an Irish and Jewish tailor work ?

3   Singer Gerry Dorsey had his own show, what was it called ?

1969

Patrick Wymark

Patrick Wymark had been a TV regular for about ten years appearing in several TV plays until the part of John Wilder turned him into a TV star.

Gradually a 1963 series about an aircraft factory – **The Plane Makers** – became a story of board room battles and was re-named **The Power Game** with Wymark as the bullying entrepreneur. To millions of viewers Patrick Wymark was John Wilder, but like most actors he tried to keep clear of his character in real life.

'As far as I was concerned it was a job, of course I liked the man, but he was not me.' After five series he said goodbye to the now Sir John, who was by then running big corporations and challenging Government and Whitehall.

But the producers were anxious to bring back the character. By 1969 he was in the Foreign Office playing a diplomat and globe-trotting fixer. Thirteen more episodes were made but with the death of Wymark in 1970 the Power Game ended.

TV comedians revealed their previous careers to readers of *TV Times*:
• Jimmy Tarbuck – milkman, gardener's assistant, butcher's boy and then an apprentice hairdresser.
• Norman Wisdom – left school at 14 to be an errand boy, page boy, cabin boy then joined the army as a band boy.
• Sid James – went straight into showbiz aged ten, then truck driver, coal loader, boxer and ballroom dancer.
• Arthur Askey – worked as a £3 a week clerk for eight years before turning pro.
• Tommy Cooper – an apprentice shipwright in Southampton then the army in World War II.
• Max Bygraves – an apprentice carpenter then the RAF in the War.

Opportunity Knocks

For over 20 years Hughie Green had been plucking unknown performers from obscurity and turning some of them into stars. Hughie's clapometer and viewers' votes made many household names and stars like; Les Dawson, The Bachelors and Mary Hopkin. Hughie's last opportunity to showcase new talent came in March 1978.

The BBC tried the formula as: **Bob Says Opportunity Knocks** in 1987, with Bob Monkhouse stepping into Hughie's shoes and heavily on his toes – a complex court case ensued with a fight over the show's copyright.

TEASER ANSWERS

1 Paul Temple starred Francis Matthews as the elegant amateur detective who had first appeared in 1937.
2 Never Mind the Quality Feel the Width starred Joe Lynch as Patrick Kelly and John Bluthal as Manny Cohen. It was written by Harry Driver who had been a tailor himself.
3 The Englebert Humperdink Show. Gerry Dorsey was his original name when he began his TV career in 1960.

Monty Python's Flying Circus arrived along with the Spanish Inquisition, the Ministry of Silly Walks, a dead Norwegian blue parrot and spam. The team of Eric Idle, Michael Palin, John Cleese, Graham Chapman and Terry Jones had been maturing nicely on radio and TV writing scripts and performing as individuals or double acts. (A long running children's TV series **Do Not Adjust Your Set** was something of a pilot for some of the team.) Far from being an instant hit, its late night slot and quirky scheduling, and the antagonism of some BBC chiefs, could have left it dead in the water. But from the few after-the-pub fans who loved Python, it spread wider into mainstream TV viewing with its second and third series. With its fourth series in 1972 simply called **Monty Python** the run ended, although repeats on both the BBC channels have kept it fresh in viewers' minds.

Pot Black turned snooker from a little minority sport into one of TV's greatest pulls. The brain-wave of a BBC producer looking to exploit colour TV – perversely the signature tune was the 'Black and White Rag' – it was famous for one of TV's all-time gaffs: "For those watching in black and white, the pink's behind the brown," said a whispering commentator.

The Liver Birds starred Nerys Hughes as Sandra and Polly James as Beryl in the adventures of two Liverpool girls sharing a flat. Carla Lane's first hit, it lasted until 1978.

The Wheel of Fortune was Michael Miles' come-back show. **Take Your Pick** had been killed off the year before, now Michael imported another American format and dusted off his chums Bob Danvers Walker, Alec Dane and Harold Smart at the organ. Although the 'Yes-No' interlude was restricted to the show's warm-up in the studio.

Nationwide changed the teatimes of millions of viewers. Michael Barratt and Frank Bough were the best known anchormen for the BBC's regional link-up news and current affairs show that mixed the ludicrous with hard news.

New Life For 'Life'

This Is Your Life (4) which began in the US in 1952, was on the BBC until 1964. In 1969, Eamonn Andrews brought it back on Thames TV with Des O'Connor as the first surprise subject. Eamonn died in 1987 and the programme was expected to die with him, but it was such a tremendous ratings success that a replacement presenter was found in Michael Aspel and its success continued.

On the Buses (11) is perhaps LWT's biggest ever sitcom hit. Its route to the top 20 began in February 1969. Writers Chesney and Wolfe offered the idea to the BBC, but it was rejected as not being funny enough. Then Frank Muir of LWT jumped on board the bus and the rest is TV history. Reg Varney got star billing, but like many comedy hits it had a team of solid characters and actors. Its raw, aggressive, working class humour sustained it through 60 episodes, and it was voted top ITV show in the 1970 *Sun* awards. The team and the formula inevitably started to show signs of wear and tear and the series finally failed its MOT in April 1973.

Opportunity Knocks (18) was the all-winners final in March and featured: '...yodeller Bill Gore, the nine-year-old classical pianist Wolfgang Plagge and the Black Abbots, a vocal and instrumental group.' The drummer was Russ Abbot and the band were Hughie Green's winners that year.

A Family At War (19) was Granada TV's most expensive and longest running drama series to date. Twenty six episodes of the wartime saga were made, initially on a budget of £500,000 (in the nineties that's the budget for just one hour). The family were the Ashtons of Liverpool. The episode that made the year's chart was broadcast in November when the story had reached January 1941.

FIRST NIGHTS

Manhunt reconstructed war-time France and the story of three resistance fighters on the run from the Nazis. Each week Alfred Lynch, Cyd Hayman and Peter Barkworth just managed to escape from the nasty Germans played by Philip Madoc and Robert Hardy. As usual with period dramas, viewers spotted slips in historical accuracy: a real-life flying ace mentioned as operational was actually a PoW at the time, a German officer wore the wrong collar and Alfred Lynch's character said he had flown Spitfires, but the squadron he mentioned in reality flew only bombers.

The Six Wives of Henry VIII starred Keith Michell. BBC costume drama at its most lavish, it won awards for its sets, costumes and actors. Among the wives were Angela Pleasance, Annette Crosbie and Elvi Hale.

Doomwatch, a drama which was years before its time, discovered 'Green Issues' and threats to the environment. Its team of heroes had a roving commission to track down and punish any environmental offenders. John Paul and Robert Powell starred in the 'Greenpeace with teeth' series.

Up Pompeii! was Frankie Howerd's biggest TV hit. Based on the musical 'A Funny Thing Happened On the Way To the Forum' it was a cross between a Roman soap and a Carry On film. Howerd, as Lurcio the slave, narrated the bawdy stories in his familiar style, wearing a toga and sandals.

Took's TV Teasers

1 What was the name of the caretaker in Please Sir ?

2 In what series did John Stride play David Main ?

3 What was the name of the American animator in Monty Python ?

1970

TOP TWENTY
Homes [millions]

1	Miss World 1970	BBC	10.6
2	Benny Hill Show	ITV	9.3
3	Eurovision Song Contest	BBC	9.2
4	This Is Your Life	ITV	8.9
5	Coronation Street	ITV	8.9
6	News At Ten	ITV	8.7
7	Steptoe and Son	BBC	8.7
8	Royal Variety	BBC	8.5
9	Apollo 13 Splashdown	ITV	8.3
10	Kate	ITV	8.2
11	On the Buses	ITV	8.2
12	633 Squadron	BBC	8.2
13	News At Ten	ITV	8.2
14	Max	ITV	8.1
15	Morecambe and Wise Prizewinners	BBC	8.0
16	Please Sir!	ITV	8.0
17	The Dustbinmen	ITV	8.0
18	Opportunity Knocks	ITV	7.9
19	A Family At War	ITV	7.9
20	Callan	ITV	7.8

• No 3 – Mary Hopkin sang 'Knock Knock Who's There' and came second. The winner was Dana for Ireland with 'All Kinds of Everything'.

• No 9 – The world watched the damaged American spacecraft limp back from moon orbit with its crew James Lovell, John Swigert and Fred Haise.

• No 12 – A war movie about an RAF Mosquito squadron starring George Chakaris.

1970

A YEAR IN THE SOAPS

Elsie Gets Married Again

Elsie Tanner, Pat Phoenix, had another ring slipped on her finger. This time it belonged to Alan Howerd, played by Alan Browning. There was no fanfare this time, just the brief *TV Times* listing in July: 'The Street gets a surprise.' Alan and Elsie had crept away to the Weatherfield Registry Office for the ceremony and then it was back to the Rovers for a celebration drink. In real life the couple had a much more public showbiz wedding. But life reflected art and both marriages split up. Also Browning, who had played an alcoholic in the **Street**, was in reality an alcoholic and died of liver disease in 1979.

For the second year running Eric Morecambe and Ernie Wise won the BAFTA award for the best light entertainment programme.

1970

Rupert Davies, who played Maigret for many years, came back from France with a souvenir. He picked up one of the black Citroens used in the series for just £40 and set about restoring it to concourse condition.

• Channel TV celebrated the 25th anniversary of the liberation of the Channel Islands in 1945 with a documentary called the **Bitter Years** which looked at the experiences of the only part of the British Isles to be occupied by the Nazis in World War II.

• Hughie Green went to Butlins for **Opportunity Knocks** and remembered some of the TV stars who had been Butlins' redcoats: Dave Allen, Clinton Ford, Des O'Connor, Ted Rogers, Jimmy Tarbuck, Freddie Davies.

• Among the advertisements for well known British TV makers like Pye, Cossor, Ekco, Bush, Murphy and GEC, names like National Panasonic, Sony and Mitsubishi began to creep in, trade marks that would eventually overtake the British TV industry in sales and production.

TEASER ANSWERS
1   Norman Potter, played by Derek Guyler, was the caretaker of Fenn Street.
2   The Main Chance, in which he played a thrusting young solicitor.
3   Terry Gilliam who went on to be a leading movie director.

NEAR MISSES

• **The Lovers** saw Geoffrey desperately trying to get his evil way with Beryl; she repelled his every stratagem and attack, against the trend of those permissive times. Richard Beckinsale and Paula Wilcox starred in this major comedy success. As with many TV hits, the memory plays tricks on their longevity. Only two series were made – 13 shows in all in '70 and '71.

• **A Man Called Ironside** starred Raymond Burr as a San Francisco chief of detectives. In the opening pilot TV movie he was shot and confined to a wheelchair. But he kept on crime busting for another 180 episodes with Dan Golloway and Barbara Anderson as his aides.

• **Take Three Girls** was a drama series on the lives of three girls living in bed-sit land. It starred Lisa Goddard, Susan Jameson and Angela Down. The theme tune 'Late Flight' was a hit for the folk group Pentangle.

• **Girls About Town** starred Denise Coffey and Julie Stevens as bored housewives. The comedy took a very short step into feminist humour as the two women sought to assert themselves and find new excitement in their lives.

• **Doctor In the House** was one of the Doctor series: **Doctor At Sea**, **Doctor On the Go** and **Doctor At Large**. They were based on the Richard Gordon books and became one of LWT's biggest hits.

The run began in 1969 and ended five years later after 90 episodes and starred Barry Evans and George Layton as the young doctors.

• **For the Love of Ada**, starring the wonderful Irene Handl and Wilfred Pickles, proved that love, like youth, was wasted on the young. They were a pair of pensioners who met in a cemetery and fell in love. Complications ensued as their families were horrified at the thought of geriatric naughtiness.

John Alderton

John Alderton, teacher Bernard Hedges in **Please Sir!**, was celebrating in 1970. The awful pupils of class 5c were finally graduating (most of the actors playing them were well into their 20s by then). He married his TV fiancee Penny Wheeler, Jill Kerman, in a Christmas special edition and in real life married actress Pauline Collins. Alderton hoped that with 5c's graduation he would be able to wave goodbye to Bernard Hedges, but LWT had other plans. Rather than lose such a ratings success, they followed 5c into the world of work and created the **Fenn Street Gang**. A new class of kids was brought in at the school and LWT persuaded Alderton to do some guest spots as Hedges in the new series.

Try this for a TV time snack – Lumberjack Pie. The recipe called for spam, baked beans, instant mash and 5oz of cheese, only 18 pence a portion.

TV news

• The BBC ran a series of Louis Malle documentaries about India, which upset the Indian government who threatened the Beeb with censorship. The BBC closed its India office rather than submit.

• From reading it to making it – Ex-ITN newsreader Chris Chataway was appointed Minister of Posts and Telecommunications in the new Conservative Government.

• The BBC sold over 8,000 hours of programmes abroad and received £2.5 million back. **Dr Finlay's Casebook** was exported to Yugoslavia, **Civilisation** to Japan and **Monty Python** to Nigeria. Auntie was particularly successful in Australia; 21% of ABC's programmes were the BBC's.

• LWT bravely screened the late night series **Family Planning**. But it was only for the sophisticated viewers of London.

• George Cole in a saucy bedroom scene with Dawn Addams, sparked off protests about TV nudity in an **Armchair Theatre** play **A Room In Town**. It was a comedy about adultery and infidelity, but one viewer complained that there was nothing funny about adultery, 'I just cannot understand why actors and actresses take part in such sordid rubbish.'

• In the days of long hair for men, Mrs Westgate of Southampton complained to *TV Times* about the Cambridge team on **University Challenge**: 'I missed the introduction and could not be sure whether I was looking at boys and girls – or girls and boys. How nicely masculine the other team looked though.'

• **Coronation Street** celebrated its 1,000th episode and Granada TV announced that it was opening the Street to the public and joining the stately home set. It was opened over August Bank Holiday and the entrance fees went to charity.

• The Prime Minister Edward Heath featured in TV coverage of Cowes Week at the helm of his £7,000 glass fibre sloop Morning Cloud.

1970

1971

TOP TWENTY
Homes [millions]

1	Benny Hill Show	ITV	9.9
2	Miss World 1971	BBC	9.6
3	Boxing: Clay v Frazier	BBC	9.6
4	Royal Variety Performance	ITV	9.1
5	Bless This House	ITV	8.9
6	This Is Your Life	ITV	8.8
7	Speaking of Murder	ITV	8.7
8	A Family At War	ITV	8.6
9	Frankie Howerd	ITV	8.6
10	Coronation Street	ITV	8.5
11	Eurovision Song Contest	BBC	8.5
12	On the Buses	ITV	8.5
13	The Persuaders	ITV	8.5
14	Nearest and Dearest	ITV	8.3
15	Man At the Top	ITV	8.2
16	Carry On Christmas	ITV	8.1
17	For the Love of Ada	ITV	8.0
18	News At Ten	ITV	7.9
19	Dixon of Dock Green	BBC	7.8
20	Sports Night With Coleman	BBC	7.8

• No 2 – Won that year by Miss Brazil Lucia Tavares Petterle.

• No 3 – Joe Frazier beat Cassius Clay at Madison Square Garden to retain his World Heavyweight title.

• No 7 – A play starring John Gregson and Jill Bennett, a tale of jealousy in a domestic love triangle.

Carry On Sid

Sid James starred in two of the year's top rating shows.

Bless This House (5) was a classic in the tradition of formula family sitcoms. Take a mum and dad, add two bolshie teenage kids, a kitchen, bedroom and sitting room that must have a sofa, sprinkle with some aspects of sex, the generation gap and a lot of misunderstandings and you have a hit, in theory. The Abbott family was: Sid played by Sid James, Diana Coupland as Jean, Sally Geeson as daughter Sally and Robin Stuart, son Mike. In its first series it became an established hit and ran for another five years.

Sid was equally at home in **Carry On Christmas (16)**. Along with most of the movie Carry On team, and with Talbot Rothwell as writer, they re-worked 'A Christmas Carol'. Where Charles Dickens would have put Frankie Howerd in a lurex dress in his script, only the ghost of Christmas past would know.

The Persuaders (13) was the top crime series and TV's most expensive to date at £100,000 per episode. Tony Curtis and Roger Moore played two globe-trotting adventurers who fought crime where normal legal channels had failed. Not the two most expressive actors in the world, the stars seemed to romp through the 24 episodes with their tongues set firmly in their cheeks.

Man At the Top (15) picked up the life of Joe Lampton whom we had last seen in the film **Life At the Top**, with Laurence Harvey as the get-on-at-all-costs nasty piece of work. Kenneth Haigh became the man TV viewers loved to hate. Zena Walker played his long suffering wife.

BLESS THIS HOUSE at 6.45
SIDNEY JAMES
DIANA COUPLAND
ROBIN STEWART
SALLY GEESON in
The Generation Gap
BY VINCE POWELL AND HARRY DRIVER
with Gay Soper

Ladies and gentlemen: we give you the Abbott family. Just another group of people who find themselves – unfortunately, they sometimes think – related and, at the same time, divided by that ever-present generation gap. In the chair at the top of the table, there is Sid: father, breadwinner and a representative for a stationery firm. Sid's interests in life are alphabetical – Ale, Birds and Chelsea. He likes to think he is with it, but, in fact, he wouldn't know it if he saw it! Then there's Jean, Sid's wife, enjoying the constant battle of the sexes, particularly as she usually wins. Joining in, and often starting the confusion, are Sid and Jean's offspring, Mike and Sally.

Mike's just left college, but he's far too busy straightening out the affairs of the world to bother about finding a job. Sally's in her last year at grammar school and is Daddy's little girl—or so Daddy thinks . . .

The Abbot family live in a state of perpetual turmoil, varying between hysterical neutrality, punctuated with occasional moments of veiled hostility and open warfare. In short, an average family.

Sid Abbott — Sidney James
Jean Abbott — Diana Coupland
Mike Abbott — Robin Stewart
Sally Abbott — Sally Geeson
Angela — Gay Soper
DESIGNER NORMAN GARWOOD; DIRECTOR/PRODUCER WILLIAM G. STEWART
Thames Television Production

Meet the Abbott family: Robin Stewart, Sally Geeson and seated, Diana Coupland, Sidney James.

The Benny Hill Show

Benny Hill was television's most successful comedian. **The Benny Hill Show** began in 1955 and he was the first variety performer to make real use of television techniques rather than just doing his stage act on TV. It began to mixed reviews: 'Benny wasted most of his talents on worthless stuff'; 'The show was patchy and lacked cohesion'; 'Benny had little new to offer'. Who cares about critics – the viewers wanted more.

In 1970 he joined Thames TV for a series of one hour specials. As usual he wrote all the material, songs and sketches along with his now regular cast of 'extras', including 'Hill's Angels' – a group of lovelies that Benny spent a lot of time leering at and chasing. Henry McGee his long-standing straightman, Bob Todd, of the rubber face, and Jack Wright as the the thin little old codger, were his regular support with Jennie Lee Wright providing the glamour.

His top TV show was mirrored by a number one in the pop charts. 'Ernie – The Fastest Milk-man In the West' was the Christmas hit that year and was in the charts for 17 weeks.

In 1979 Thames re-edited his shows for the US where they were a huge success. For many Americans, Benny Hill was England.

But the sexual innuendo and sauciness of his comedy began to embarrass Thames TV. Although there was little sign of his popularity waning with viewers, the TV bosses felt the show was old-fashioned. In 1989 Thames refused to renew his contract and after 34 years his show came to an end. Benny died in April 1992 still loved by the viewers.

Actress Coral Atkins, who starred as Sheila Ashton in the series **A Family At War**, gave up acting to start a home for mentally disturbed children.

FIRST NIGHTS

Sale of the Century, with Nicholas Parsons, first came to the screen in the Anglia region in 1971. Later, on the network, it proved to be one of ITV's biggest game show hits.

Answer the question, win some money and bid for the discounted prizes... 'If you can't resist a bargain – you can't resist Sale of the Century .. A fridge for £3.75; a holiday for two for £15.' But it got a slap on the wrist from the ITA. The spoilsport TV watchdogs thought the quiz 'gloated over the high value of its prizes too much' and told them to tone it down. But can you tone down Nicholas Parsons? Then as now the nation was divided: like these letters from the *Daily Mirror*: 'Sale of the Century is an excellent programme, but Nicholas Parsons makes me squirm' wrote Vivienne Holmes of Northolt, but from Mrs Lacey of Caversham: 'I only watch to see and hear Nicholas Parsons. I just love that man.'

Sesame Street arrived from the US. It was rejected by the BBC as being of little educational value. But ITV didn't exactly snap it up, only three regions ran it for a trial 13 weeks up to Christmas. It has now

been helping millions of toddlers with their numbers and letters for over 20 years. It also launched Kermit the Frog and **The Muppets** into stardom with their creators Jim Henson and Frank Oz.

The Two Ronnies also began another marathon run, which ended in 1988. Ronnie Barker and Ronnie Corbett's names provided the title, their glasses gave it the logo. Their comedy was of the British sea-side tradition of double entendres, spoonerisms, wordplay and disguised bawdiness. The show started with the two behind desks reading joke news items and was followed by sketches, a guest singer, a big production number and ended back at the desk with the equivalent of the '...and finally' from **News At Ten**. And the immortal: 'It's goodbye from me... and it's goodbye from him.'

Michael Parkinson began his marathon chat show **Parkinson**. He became the longest running chat show host on British

TV, and didn't quit until 1982 after over 1,000 guests had been interviewed. Peter Ustinov was his favourite guest. His least favourite was Rod Hull's Emu who more than perturbed the imperturbable Parkie by attacking his naughty bits and wrestling him to the ground.

Bruce Forsyth and the Generation Game completed the trio of BBC long runners. With Anthea Redfern, who Bruce had met at a Miss Lovely Legs competition and who later became his second wife, they ran the updated version of **Beat the Clock** with puzzles, games and embarrassment for six years. Larry Grayson took over with Isla St Clair until the run ended in 1981. But Brucie hadn't finished with the Game, he brought it back ten years later.

1971

Big screen TV came early with new sensational Telerama: 'The big screen in your own home. Fantastic breakthrough in TV viewing. Enlarges picture by up to eight inches' said the ad.

A YEAR IN THE SOAPS

The Doctors Retire

Once again a BBC attempt to find the right formula for success with a twice weekly soap opera. After buoy making, magazines, football and new town families, how about medicine? **Dr Kildare**, **Ben Casey** and **Emergency Ward Ten** had shown that doctors pull audiences, so **The Doctors** was set in a busy north London group practice with Justine Lord, then described as 'the sexiest woman on TV', as Dr Liz McNeil. Top writers like Fay Weldon and Elaine Morgan produced story lines covering topics of current medical and social concern. It only lasted nine months.

Took's TV Teasers

1 Name The Goodies.

2 What was Beryl's pet name for Geoffrey in The Lovers ?

3 What was the late night Saturday ITV arts show ?

NEAR MISSES

Old Rocking Chair's Got Him

• Val Doonican, the nicest of TV stars, made rocking chairs, pullovers and Paddy McGinty's goat national institutions. This was Val's first ITV series after ten years with the BBC. His contract was for

1971

a million pounds over five years plus an airing for his show in the US. To bolster his American appeal a big American star would jump on a plane each week – do a guest spot in London with Val – then jump back on the plane again. But the audience figures were disappointing – the BBC had scheduled the crime series **Ironside** against it. Five years later, after a not very happy time with ITV, Val headed back to the Beeb where he stayed until 1986, when he finally laid up his rocking chair.

• **Budgie** was Adam Faith's big TV acting break. 'He plays a petty criminal whose dream is getting rich quick but he's a born loser. His wife has left him and his girlfriend's had a baby' ran the listing.

• **Dear Mother... Love Albert** saw Rodney Bewes leaving home and entering a bit of a fantasy world. But he found reality by getting engaged to Doreen Bissel, played by Liz Gebhart who was also the adoring Maureen in **Please Sir!**

• **The Comedians** established the TV careers of a lot of new comics. Tom O'Connor, Mike Reid, Jim Bowen and Charlie Williams are just some of the names that sprung from the joke-a-minute quick fire format.

• Hughie Green had **The Sky's the Limit**. Not a million miles from his axed show **Double Your Money** it had chirpy little Monica Rose and instead of winning money, contestants could win 21,000 miles of travel plus spending money.

• Cilla Black had her own show – in colour. The first in the series featured a sketch with Frankie Howerd and their version of Romeo and Juliet.

TV news

• The **Open University** began transmitting its TV programmes. Insomniacs and early risers could watch: Man's Religious Quest, Engineering Mechanics: Solids and Fluids and Mass Communications and Society, presented by a man in a kipper tie, with a Zappata moustache and very long hair for years as the courses were repeated and repeated.

• The BBC opened its Pebble Mill studios in Birmingham and used its foyer for **Pebble Mill At One**. Any writer, actor or pop star with something to plug was chatted to by the likes of Donny McLeod and Marion Foster.

• Rupert Murdoch's first sally into TV was halted by the IBA. He had ridden to the rescue of the ailing London Weekend Television because their new approach to TV, which had so pleased the IBA, had been losing them viewers and money since it launched in 1968. Murdoch was asked to choose between his stake in television and his newspapers. He chose newspapers – for a while.

• Princess Anne won the Sport's Personality of the Year Award for her horse riding successes. She was also the subject of a **Blue Peter Royal Safari** special following her working with Save the Children in Africa.

• Coca Cola launched the commercial I'd Like To Buy the World a Coke.

The song was released as the single 'I'd Like To Teach the World To Sing' by the New Seekers and went to number one.

• Sandra Gough, who played Irma Barlow in **Coronation Street**, was dropped from the series in December. She had played the part for over five years and said it was driving her mad.

• TV technicians at Yorkshire TV went on strike. Viewers tuning in for **News At Ten** saw nothing but a handwritten notice saying: 'Yorkshire TV have threatened to sack us. We are going on strike. Goodnight.'

• **News At Ten** passed its 1,000th edition in May, of those, 632 had been in the week's top 20.

• The ban on showing toilet bowls in commercials was finally lifted. Up to then the rule had been: '...a toilet cleanser may be shown on a bathroom window ledge or being above the actual toilet, but this should not reveal any part of the toilet itself.'

TEASER ANSWERS

1   Tim Brooke-Taylor, Bill Oddie and Graeme Garden.
2   Beryl, played by Paula Wilcox, called him 'Geoffrey Bobbles Bom Bom'.
3   Aquarius with its theme taken from the musical 'Hair', hosted by Humphrey Burton.

Right-Wingers Rule OK

There were three television bigots in close competition for the bad taste of the year award.

Albert Steptoe, in **Steptoe and Son (4)**, then in its tenth year, wasn't exactly renowned for his liberal views and was always embarrassing the more radical Harold with his sexism, racism and right wing politics.

Love Thy Neighbour (5) had Eddie Booth, played by Jack Smethurst as a suburban bigot who sees a black family move in next door. Rudolph Walker and Nina Baden-Semper were the Afro-Caribbean neighbours on the receiving end of Booth's overt racism. The community relations industry attacked the programme for reinforcing prejudice rather than undermining it with comedy. But the viewers loved it and they turned it into a regular number one hit for Thames TV which ran for four years.

In **Till Death Us Do Part (6)**, first seen in 1965, Alf Garnett was TV's archetypal opinionated monster. Again, Johnny Speight's words were supposed to expose prejudice and reactionary views with comedy – well that was the defence for Alf's tirades against 'coons', 'darkies', 'Jews', 'paddies'.... But it's no secret that for a lot of viewers the subtlety of that argument was lost – they just thought it was very funny.

Coronation Street (7) received a boost to its viewing figures with the wedding in April of Emily Nugent, Eileen Derbyshire, to Ernie Bishop, Stephen Hancock. Poor Emily, the Street's spinster, had had problems with affairs of the heart before, but she and Ernest would live happily ever after, that is until his death did them part – he was shot by robbers at Mike Baldwin's factory in 1978.

For **A Family At War (8)** the war is over. VE night has been celebrated, a new Labour Government elected, evacuees have returned to Liverpool and it's December 1945. In the last episode of the series, the Briggs and Ashton families were together on Christmas Day looking forward to a world at peace.

Marker, the Downbeat Detective

For ten TV years Alfred Burke was Frank Marker – **Public Eye**. Not for him the glamorous globe trotting and exotic locations of other crime fighters, no exotic assistant or trusty side-kick. And not for him the cosy relations with the local coppers. At the end of one series he was done for possession of stolen property and went to prison.

Burke was 46 when the series began in January 1965 and was chosen for the part because he didn't look like a private detective. Unlike most actors involved in a long run, Burke didn't knock the TV image that had brought him fame.

Marker took on his last and 87th case in 1975 – 'Unlucky For Some' – and hung up his dirty raincoat for good.

Alastair Burnet said goodbye to ITN after coverage of the US presidential elections. He joined the BBC's **Panorama** for two years, but later re-

1972

TOP TWENTY
Homes [millions]

1	Eurovision Song Contest	BBC	9.1
2	This Is Your Life	ITV	8.9
3	Miss World 1972	BBC	8.8
4	Steptoe and Son	BBC	8.4
5	Love Thy Neighbour	ITV	8.4
6	Till Death Us Do Part	BBC	8.3
7	Coronation Street	ITV	8.3
8	A Family At War	ITV	8.2
9	Public Eye	ITV	8.2
10	Opportunity Knocks	ITV	8.2
11	Benny Hill Show	ITV	8.1
12	On the Buses	ITV	8.1
13	The Strauss Family	ITV	8.1
14	Suspicion	ITV	8.1
15	Bless This House	ITV	8.1
16	News At Ten	ITV	7.9
17	The Persuaders	ITV	7.8
18	Football: England v West Germany	BBC	7.8
19	Nine O'Clock News	BBC	7.8
20	Carry On Christmas	ITV	7.7

• No 1 – The New Seekers came second with 'Beg, Steal Or Borrow'.

• No 13 – The story of the waltzing Johanns. Eric Woolfe and Stuart Wilson played father and son.

• No 14 – A series of plays on the theme of jealousy. This starred Ian Hendry and Alexandra Bastedo as a young wife taunting her middle aged husband.

1972

1972

Rainbow, ITV's most successful tiny tots TV show arrived. It emerged from a search for a British alternative to **Sesame Street** and was designed as instructive play for tots not able to go to playschool or playgroups. The first presenters were David Cook and Bungle the Bear, a sort of giant glove puppet but with a human being inside, and Zippy the Martian. Geoffrey Hayes and George, the pink Hippo, joined the team in 1974.

Shut That Door was not another prison yarn but was Larry Grayson's showcase where he asked the viewers to: 'make yourself at home for a gay evening... pull up a chair and let's unwrap that surprise package... with everyone doing their own thing.'

The Adventures of Black Beauty was one of the few children's programmes to ever get into the week's top 20, which it did in September after two episodes. Ted Willis took the characters from Anna Sewell's original books and wove some new characters into the story of the girl and her horse.

Judy Bowker was the original owner and Stacy Dorning took over in later series. 'Black Jet' played Black Beauty in the original series and he was also the original horse in the long-running Lloyd's Bank black horse commercials.

Mastermind began its mind-boggling run. It must be the only TV programme that ever made an executive chair into a star. 'I've started, so I'll finish...' became Magnus Magnusson's catch phrase and Fred Housego, a London cabbie, is the best-remembered winner. He became a minor TV celebrity and presenter after his win in 1977.

Colditz, the story of the German fortress turned into a prisoner of war camp, was one of the BBC's most successful drama series. British stiff upper lip officers were played by David McCallum, Jack Hedley and Christopher Neame and the nasty Nazi officers by Anthony Valentine and Bernard Hepton. Robert Wagner played an American prisoner who helped the escapees and the programme sales in the United States.

There's Trouble On t'Farm

Three new soap operas came to daytime television. **General Hospital**, an updated version of **Ward Ten**, **Harriet's Back In Town**, starring Pauline Yates as a newly divorced middle aged woman and **Emmerdale Farm**.

Emmerdale Farm, the sole survivor, was Yorkshire's answer to **The Archers** – a twice weekly story of the Sugden family and their farm in the Dales. After the first series Yorkshire TV were forced to abandon their location as the local residents were getting fed up with rubber neckers. They found another village which they desperately tried to keep secret, but Esholt is now a tourist attraction and thousands of visitors stop for a drink in the Woolpack, in real life the Commercial Inn. In the best soap tradition Emmerdale has had its murders, divorces, extra-marital sex, disasters and even the threat of a nuclear dump. Annie Sugden, played by Sheila Mercier, along with Frazer Hines, Joe Sugden, are the only two original cast members to take the Farm into its 20th season, although the word 'Farm' has been dropped to give the show a wider, more up-to-date appeal.

The success of the spin-off movie **On the Buses** led to a stampede of other TV sitcoms into the film studios. **Bless This House, Never Mind the Quality Feel the Width, Nearest and Dearest, The Garnett Saga, Dad's Army** and **Steptoe and Son** were just some of the 20 television series that were made into movies.

TEASER ANSWERS

1   They were in the road haulage business. The brothers were three sons who fought over their father's inheritance.
2   'Beckindale'.
3   John Craven's Newsround, the first news programme to be named after its presenter.

Daytime Dawns

On 19th January 1972 Christopher Chataway, the Minister of Posts and Telecommunications announced in Parliament that he would no longer exercise his powers under section 17 of the Television Act 1964. That meant the end of government controls on the hours TV was allowed to broadcast.

Probably not since the launch of ITV in 1955 have so many new shows hit the screen in one week. Nineteen new shows and 20 more hours of viewing time for housewives, children, pensioners, the sick, disabled and shift workers. The whole mix of TV was there; news and current affairs, soaps, quizzes, comedy, films, a cornucopia of telly goodies.

NEAR MISSES

Sitcoms of families in all shapes and sizes became hits this year.

• **My Wife Next Door** concerned a newly divorced couple who, unknown to each other, buy country cottages – next door to each other. John Alderton and Hannah Gordon starred as the couple with the same milkman.

• **And Mother Makes Three** starred Wendy Craig as the single parent struggling to bring up two teenage boys. Some of the scripts were co-written by Carla Lane, the writer of a later hit for Wendy; **Butterflies**, which again saw her struggling with two teenage sons.

• **Keep It In The Family** had problems with ageing parents rather than teenage sons. The Bannisters had *his* mother and *her* father living under the same roof – literally, for Jack Haigh, who played the old man, was forced into the attic by his son-in-law's mother, Joyce Grant.

• **My Good Woman** saw Leslie Crowther married to Sylvia Syms who was a whirlwind charity worker leaving her husband in the wake of her good works. Mother-in-law jokes were plentiful.

• Dora Bryan starred in **Dora** as another single parent bringing up her son. This time the hard-up widow is forced into a variety of schemes and jobs to raise money and laughs.

• **His and Hers** had Barbara Murray playing a jet-set executive wife whose

TVnews

• In February power cuts meant the telly went off in many homes and it was an early bedtime for viewers following the Heath Government's confrontation with the striking miners.

• The 'British Invasion of American TV', as the US media called it, began. Alistair Cooke's documentary series **America** was sold back to the US, Glenda Jackson's **Elizabeth R** won five US TV Emmy Awards. And **The Wives of Henry VIII** was shown twice on US networks.

• It was estimated that over one million people were not paying their TV licence and a national campaign was launched to find them and make them pay up.

• The Independent Television Authority – ITA – changed its name to the IBA – The Independent Broadcasting Authority – after the Government had given it responsibility for the new independent local radio stations.

• Marty Feldman won the Golden Rose of Montreux for a compilation of the best bits from his ATV series the **Marty Feldman Comedy Machine**.

• **24 Hours**, the BBC's long running current affairs programme was dropped after seven years and 1,695 editions, but to compensate, **Nationwide** was extended from three to five nights a week.

• The Munich Olympics, from which the BBC had planned to show 170 hours of sport covered by 16 commentators, was stormed by Arab Guerrillas and the coverage switched to watching the siege and gun battle which killed all the hostages and gunmen.

• Britain's first cable TV station opened in Greenwich covering 9,000 homes. In 1992 it was available to 1.5 million homes.

The Marty Feldman COMEDY MACHINE

Comedy reaches new hilarious horizons. Marty Feldman helped by Spike Milligan, Britain's most unique, zany and provocative laughter makers...with the bulbous eyed Marty in his most spectacular international television series.

THE MARTY FELDMAN COMEDY MACHINE is the most unusual machine of all time. It manufactures mirth as Marty pursues the illogical to its logical conclusion and Spike goons his way through one bizarre situation after another. They are aided by regulars Bob Todd and Hugh Paddick and world-famous guest stars include Groucho Marx, Orson Welles, Roger Moore and Godfrey Cambridge.

A SERIES OF ONE HOUR SHOWS PRODUCED IN COLOUR

PRODUCERS : LARRY GELBART/COLIN CLEWS
EXECUTIVE PRODUCER : GREG GARRISON
DIRECTOR : JOHN ROBINS

husband, Ronald Lewis, reverses roles and stays at home to be the househusband. But it wasn't that revolutionary, he was a freelance writer working at home even if he did put a pinny on now and again.

• **Father, Dear Father** starred Patrick Cargill as a single parent bringing up two teenage daughters – Natasha Pyne and Ann Holloway. Noel Dyson played nanny to the whole family.

1972

1973

TOP TWENTY
Homes [millions]

1	Eurovision Song Contest	BBC	9.8
2	Benny Hill Show	ITV	9.2
3	This Is Your Life	ITV	9.1
4	World Cup Football	ITV	9.0
5	Miss World	BBC	8.8
6	Love Thy Neighbour	ITV	8.6
7	Colditz	BBC	8.4
8	Coronation Street	ITV	8.3
9	Bless This House	ITV	8.2
10	My Good Woman	ITV	8.1
11	And Mother Makes Three	ITV	8.1
12	Public Eye	ITV	8.1
13	International Boxing	ITV	8.0
14	Special Branch	ITV	8.0
15	Cilla	BBC	7.9
16	Morecambe and Wise	BBC	7.9
17	Opportunity Knocks	ITV	7.9
18	Some Mothers Do 'Ave 'Em	BBC	7.9
19	Love Story	ITV	7.8
20	Van Der Valk	ITV	7.8

• No 1 – It's number two again for Cliff Richard singing 'Power To All Our Friends.'

• No 4 – In the World Cup qualifier England drew 1-1 with Poland at Wembley and failed to make the finals.

• No 5 – Miss USA Marjorie Wallace won.

• No 13 – Muhammad Ali fought Joe Bugner over 12 rounds in Las Vegas. He won.

Special Coppers

Special Branch (14) had been a regular top 20 entry in the cops and robbers category since it began in September '69. For women, dimple-chinned Patrick Mower as Haggerty was the main reason for the popularity of the series. By the third year Haggerty had gone and George Sewell, DCI Craven, was the new head of Scotland Yard's SB Division. However, viewers missed Mower and he came back to the series later in the year. This was the first production of the Thames TV off-shoot, Euston Films, makers of **The Sweeney** and **Minder**.

Some Mothers Do 'Ave 'Em (17) had Michael Crawford making his TV sitcom debut. On the face of it his accident prone Jonah of a character was way over the top, but it worked. With Michelle Dotrice as his long suffering partner, each episode featured a carefully choreographed disaster that put Crawford at risk, as he did all his own stunts. Falling through ceilings, hanging from speeding lorries and cars, hanging from a helicopter and dodging a falling factory chimney were just a few of the dangers he created and faced in the five year run.

Van Der Valk (20) was the Amsterdam detective played by Barry Foster and based on the Nicholas Freeling books.

Twenty one people wrote to *Radio Times* complaining about an item on the early evening news. Not violence, murder or political bias, but a piece about the engagement of Peter Sellers to actress Liza Minelli.

The first series began in 1972 just as Freeling killed off the hero in *A Long Silence*, but he lived on in TV. The second series began in August and went to the top of the week's top 20. He survived for another four years, then in 1991 was resurrected with Foster again playing the Dutch detective.

TVnews

• Trevor McDonald joined **News At Ten** from The BBC World Service. The Trinidad-born journalist said: "I think I'll be able to produce a different outlook on the news but I won't be specifically concerned with racial problems."

• The BBC switchboards were jammed in November when Uri Geller appeared on the **Dimbleby Talk-In** programme. While he demonstrated his psychokinetic powers on TV, viewers' cutlery had bent and broken clocks and watches had restarted.

• ORACLE – it stands for 'Optional Reception of Announcements by Coded Line Electronics' – began transmitting its teletext service in London. By using some of the spare lines on the TV screen to send coded messages, viewers could select up-to-the minute news and information. The BBC's service CEEFAX – 'See Facts' – arrived the following year.

• In November Princess Anne married Mark Phillips at Westminster Abbey. It was the first royal wedding to be transmitted in colour and there were about four million colour TV sets to watch it on. An estimated 500 million people watched the ceremony throughout the world.

• Mr Gerald Pasqua of Sussex booked a seven second commercial on Thames TV to sell his house. It cost £380, he received 30 calls and sold the house for £85,000.

• A fuel crisis created by the Arab-Israeli Six Day War brought in Government fuel saving measures. TV transmissions were closed down early at 10.20 pm. Nine months later there was a considerable increase in bookings at maternity clinics.

NEAR MISSES

• **Upstairs Downstairs** continued to follow the lives of the Bellamys of Eaton Square and their servants below stairs. Pauline Collins is found to be pregnant but Watkins the chauffeur, John Alderton, is denying any blame.

• Alan Whicker continued his globe-trotting with a series looking around the Pacific, **Whicker's South Seas**. From primitive islanders in the New Hebrides to sophisticated New Zealand. From the filthy rich to the positively poor. From the helicopter-riding deer hunters of South Island to the cats cradle weavers of Nauru. Whicker found them all.

• In January Thames TV staged **Miss TV Europe**. The girls had won competitions run by listings magazines – Zoe Spink was Miss TV Times. The winner was Sylvia Krystel, from Holland, a 20-year-old model 'whose burning ambition is to be an actress'. She went on to be the star of the soft-porn **Emmanuelle** movie series. Sylvia won a Mercedes sports car, £1,000, £1,000's worth of clothes and a holiday in Jamaica as prizes in the competition.

• **The Dick Emery Show** exploited not only the star's acting skills but also the skills of the BBC make-up department. All his familiar repertory of characters were there: Mandy the blousy blonde (who gave him his catch phrase: 'Ooh you are awful, but I like you'), Lampwick the old man in a cap, the skinhead, the toothsome vicar and the retired colonel. The long run and continued success of the show made him one of the richest men on TV.

• **Softly, Softly: Task Force** was back but minus Barlow, Stratford Johns. He had gone to the Home Office. DCS Watt, Frank Windsor, was now in charge with DCI Hawkins, Norman Bowler, as number two.

A documentary about Andy Warhol was attacked in the tabloid press: 'The Worst TV Shocker Ever'. David Bailey's film was hot news but the IBA held out against pressure to ban it and ran it at 10.30 pm.

WHO'LL BE MISS TV EUROPE?

1973

Five Years As Father

Patrick Cargill celebrated five years playing Patrick Glover in **Father Dear Father** then in its seventh series. He said: "You don't change a winning formula. It's the same mixture as before, we have the same cast, director, writers, camera crew as we've always had. Members of the public come up to me and say you look as if you are enjoying yourself, and indeed we all are."

There was more to celebrate that year; a moderately successful spin-off movie was released in the spring. But the celebrations were short-lived; 1973 was its fifth and final year. Two other series followed for Cargill; **Ooh La La** and **The Many Wives of Patrick**. Also the success of the Father series in Australia, persuaded Aussie TV to produce another seven episodes Down Under in 1977.

World of Sport experimented with highlights from American Football. Jimmy Hill said: "I don't think it compares with soccer for sheer thrills, but on an intellectual level it makes our national sport look a lot like a Sunday afternoon game of tiddly winks."

Took's TV Teasers

1 What does M*A*S*H stand for ?

2 What was the original title of Boss Cat ?

3 What characters did these American actors play: William Shatner, Leonard Nimoy and De Forrest Kelly ?

Crossroads Goes Nationwide

Crossroads was now completely networked on ITV but it had been a tough journey, ATV seriously considered taking it off after two years – they were so fed up with critical derision – but they didn't. In 1968 Thames TV in London did and for five months they suffered a torrent of protest, hate mail, phone calls and death threats until they relented and brought it back. Granada refused to show it at all for six years until 1970.

A Gallup Poll in 1971 and 1972, asked the question: 'Which is the best TV programme you have seen this year?' Number four on respondents' lists was Crossroads – number one was **Coronation Street**. But by 1973 Crossroads was number one! Now completely networked – which meant special announcements and programmes to bring all the regions into synchronisation – it was never to leave the top 20 until 1988.

• The scriptwriters of the Street gave Ken Barlow, William Roache, a new girlfriend. The lucky man got Joanna Lumley. She played Elaine Perkins and things got very serious, but due to many rows the couple parted after a few months.

1973

The BBC ran another series of **Comedy Playhouse**. Six new comedy formats were tried out. Among them were: John Cleese as an updated Sherlock Holmes; a TV unknown Gordon Peters in a story of a loser; Michael Robbins of **On the Buses** in a domestic sitcom and a comedy about three retired, late middle aged misfits called **Last of the Summer Wine**. Peter Sallis, Bill Owen and Michael Bates starred in the first series, as a mixture of senior citizens, philosophers and naughty boys. Liberated from their jobs they wandered the Yorkshire Dales and the town of Holmfirth and relived their childhoods.

More youthful experiences were relived when the question **Whatever Happened To the Likely Lads?** was brilliantly answered by writers Dick Clement and Ian Le Frenais. Terry, James Bolam, has been in the army and is now back home and unemployed. Bob, Rodney Bewes, is engaged to Thelma and is buying a new house on the estate. Bob's new class pretensions were clashing with his past and his old mate. Would their friendship survive? The series was a rare example of a sequel that was better than the original.

In **Too Long a Winter** a most unlikely TV star was created. Hannah Hauxwell was a semi-recluse who lived on the high Pennines barely making a subsistence living from her tiny farm. The documentary by Barry Cockroft mesmerised viewers not just with her plight but with her total composure and serenity.

New Faces began challenging Hughie Green's role as TV talent spotter. Derek Hobson introduced the acts. The panellists, the real stars, judged, and upset acts and viewers with their frank comments; one critic said it was TV's version of the Roman games where the acts were thrown to the lions, and that it was the unacceptable face of talent shows. Tony Hatch and Micky Most were the regular hard men on the panel. In its first season it discovered Victoria Wood, Malandra Burrows and Les Dennis, but the all-winners final was won by Tony Maiden a singing comic. On **TV Weekly** in 1991 Les Dennis wondered whatever happened to Tony? He was tracked down to a bar on the Costa Brava entertaining holiday makers with his impressions. Lenny Henry, Jim Davidson and Marti Caine, who brought the show back in 1989, as host, were three other discoveries from New Faces.

TEASER ANSWERS

1. Mobile Army Surgical Hospital.
2. In Britain it was billed as Boss Cat because the original title Top Cat was a brand of cat food which the BBC didn't want to promote.
3. In Star Trek they were Captain Kirk, Spock and Dr McCoy.

Television Awards Itself

The British Screen Awards (7) were hosted by Petula Clark and Eamonn Andrews. This was the annual Society of Film and Television Arts (later the British Academy of Film and Television Arts – BAFTA) awards presented by Princess Anne 'accompanied by her husband Captain Mark Phillips'. Some of the TV names that won that year were: Stanley Baxter for the **Stanley Baxter Big Picture Show**; **Porridge** was the best comedy series; Lee Remick, best actress for **Jennie**; and Peter Barkworth, best actor, for **Crown Matrimonial**.

And Mother Makes Five (9) was the follow-up to Wendy Craig's **And Mother Makes Three**. Now mother has remarried to David, Richard Coleman, and he has a daughter: three plus two equals five with a second place in the charts in the first week of the expanded family series.

No, Honestly (15) was written by husband and wife team Terence Brady and Charlotte Bingham, it starred husband and wife John Alderton and Pauline Collins as the about-to-be-married and then married couple. He played the straight man to her eccentricities. A later series starred Liza Goddard and Donal Donnelly in **Yes, Honestly**. The theme tune was a hit for singer/composer Lynsey De Paul rising to number seven in the charts.

Within These Walls (17) starred Googie Withers as the new governor of Stone Park Women's Prison who gradually liberalises the regime of the high security prison. The only people who could not watch the series were real prisoner as it went out at 9 pm and prisoners were shut up at 8.30 pm.

Max (19) was Max Bygraves new series: "Swingalong with me," that's the invitation as he kicks off a brand new show with his latest record. His previous series was called **Singalongamax**. The new show was slammed as being banal, but the viewers loved its old time melodies.

A YEAR IN THE SOAPS

Room In the Afternoon

Another afternoon soap appeared called very simply **Rooms**. It told the stories of tenants at 35 Mafeking Terrace. The large house had been converted into bed sitters. Only two characters were constant; Dorothy the landlady and Clive in the basement: 'They form the only thread linking the lives of the house's floating population.' Each week new characters would appear in one of the rooms and a two part drama on Tuesday and Wednesday afternoons would tell their story.

Some of the leading TV actors of the time passed through number 35: Jan Francis played a student and John Duttine played a secretive lodger. The series ran for a number of short seasons until 1977.

Took's TV Teasers

1. In Last of the Summer Wine who was the third original character with Clegg and Compo ?

2. Who was Michelle Dotrice – Betty – 'married' to ?

3. Who was the presenter of Stars on Sunday ?

1974

TOP TWENTY
Homes [millions]

1	This Is Your Life	ITV	9.9
2	Love Thy Neighbour	ITV	9.6
3	Miss World	BBC	9.1
4	Bless This House	ITV	9.0
5	Des O'Connor Show	ITV	9.0
6	Benny Hill Show	ITV	8.9
7	British Screen Awards	ITV	8.8
8	Tommy Cooper Hour	ITV	8.7
9	And Mother Makes Five	ITV	8.6
10	News At Ten	ITV	8.6
11	Opportunity Knocks	ITV	8.6
12	Val Doonican Show	ITV	8.6
13	Uri Geller	ITV	8.5
14	Generation Game	BBC	8.4
15	No, Honestly	ITV	8.4
16	Special Branch	ITV	8.4
17	Within These Walls	ITV	8.4
18	Coronation Street	ITV	8.3
19	Max	ITV	8.3
20	Eurovision Song Contest	BBC	8.2

• No 3 – Miss United Kingdom Helen Morgan won Miss World but it was only a five day reign. The revelation that she was an unmarried mum meant second-placed Miss South Africa was substituted.

• No 5 – Des O'Connor was voted the favourite male personality by viewers in the TV Times Awards.

• No 20 – Abba won with 'Waterloo'.

1974

FIRST NIGHTS
Comedy Tonight

1974

Porridge was an instant hit with viewers on the inside and outside. Unlike the women of Holloway who couldn't watch **Within These Walls**, Porridge, on at an earlier time, could be watched in the nick. One of the punishments used in some prisons was the withdrawal of the privilege to watch Norman Stanley Fletcher the star of Slade Prison, Ronnie Barker, and Richard Beckinsale as Godber his apprentice. Fulton Mackay was the chief warder with the regimental manner and squeaky boots and Brian Wilde as the softie warder Mr Barraclough.

Rising Damp was one of a series of six pilots from Yorkshire TV, run in

September. The others were: **You'll Never Walk Alone** starring Brian Glover and written by Simpson and Galton, **Brotherly Love** with Keith Barron, **Badger's Set** written by Barry Took, **Slater's Day** with John Junkin and **Oh No It's Selwyn Froggit** starring Bill Maynard. The latter, with Rising Damp, was the only show to make a successful series.

Get Some In was **The Army Game** in blue serge. This was a tale of National Service days when pimply youths were torn from their mothers and turned into trained killers by sadistic NCOs, or spent two years in Nether Wallop counting blankets. The series was set in the mid-fifties at RAF Skelton and later at RAF Midham. Tony Selby is best remembered as the nasty Corporal Marsh and Robert Lindsay as the ex-Teddy boy Jakey Smith.

Bootsie and Snudge was another military comedy. Originally it had been a hit for Alfie Bass and Bill Fraser as two characters from the Army Game who had been demobbed from the army and found jobs in a gentleman's club. Now 11 years later Granada TV reunited the characters. Bootsie has won £1 million on the pools and Snudge is the man with the big cheque...

It Ain't Half Hot Mum was the third big comedy hit to arrive in '74. **Dad's Army** writers Jimmy Perry and David Croft took more of their wartime memories and turned them into a hit camp comedy. A

platoon of army misfits posing as a concert party are marooned near the end of the War in India. Windsor Davies as the Sgt Major desperately tried to instil army discipline into Don Estelle. The two had a number one record, 'Whispering Grass'.

Just Like That

Tommy Cooper hadn't been doing his regular series on TV for some time. For three years he virtually disappeared from the TV screen, but in 1974 he came back and went straight to number one in the weekly charts. Like Benny Hill, he now confined himself to one-hour specials.

He was a born worrier: "Before a show I panic. I even worry about my artificial flowers dying." One of the running gags in his act at this time was the mystery man walking through the back of the shot. "He drives me mad, just when I'm in the middle of a miracle he's there."

He was an accomplished magician – a member of the Magic Circle and that's where he first realised that his nervous mistakes were getting more reaction than his magic act. "But the hard part is making sure the audience realise that the mistakes are deliberate, otherwise I'd get sympathy rather than laughter. And if a trick goes right – it's out... just like that!"

TEASER ANSWERS

1 Blamire, played by Michael Bates. He was the Indian bearer in It Ain't Half Hot Mum.
2 She played Betty and was married to Frank the walking disaster in Some Mothers Do 'Ave 'Em.
3 Jess Yates, who was also the producer, was sacked after revelations about his relationship with a young woman.

• The axe fell on Katie and her Oxo family. For 18 years Mary Holland as Katie had been seen serving up Oxo dishes to hubby Philip, Peter Moyniham, and an ever growing family.

• Russell Harty published a book of some of his more memorable interviews – 27 from the 180 stars that had been his guests on **Russell Harty Plus** including Barry Humphries and Frankie Howerd.

Hughie Green released a long player. It was a compilation of the winners from Opportunity Knocks, *including Freddie Starr, Peters and Lee and Mary Hopkin.*

NEAR MISSES

• **Candid Camera** returned to the screen after a break of seven years. The producer Peter Dulay now acted as the presenter of the Saturday night series. He replaced Jonathan Routh saying that the public were the stars and the show did not need a big personality. Though Dulay was no shrinking violet, he had spent many years touring the halls as a comedian before he became a producer.

• **Sounds Like Les Dawson** was a one-hour special in December for the comedian. 'He dreamed of singing, dancing, conducting and playing his way to musical disaster. And then he woke up and found it was all true...' Guests were the 'Madge Longbottom Trio' and the 'George and Thelma Grimsdyke Formation Team' (in reality Olivia Newton John and Roy Barraclough).

TV news

• ITV bought the TV rights to the first six James Bond films for £850,000. One cinema owner described the sale as: 'not only killing the golden goose, but auctioning off the eggs.' **Dr No**, **Goldfinger** and **From Russia With Love**, all starring Sean Connery, were to be massive TV hits over the years.

• In February the emergency power restriction was lifted and TV returned to its normal broadcasting hours, just in time for the General Election.

• In the new Labour Government, Anthony Wedgewood Benn's, period as the minister with responsibility for broadcasting only lasted a month. The job was handed to the Home Secretary Roy Jenkins, who announced the setting up of the Annan Committee to look into the future of broadcasting.

• Plans for a new Welsh language fourth TV channel for Wales were announced, with both BBC and ITV making its programmes. It didn't actually come on air for another eight years. No decision was made on a fourth channel for the rest of the United Kingdom.

• Bob Wilson, the Arsenal goalkeeper, announced his retirement, at 33. He joined the BBC as a sport's commentator to present **Football Focus** on **Grandstand**.

• The young man delivering Hovis began pushing his bike up a northern Victorian cobbled hill. Ridley Scott, the top movie director, created an image of long lost Yorkshire, with Dvorak's New World Symphony –

written by a Czech about America and the hill was actually in Dorset.

• William Franklyn finally ended his run of commercials for Indian Tonic Water with the catch phrase 'Sch, you know who.' He had been a hit as a secret agent in **Top Secret** in the early sixties and the commercial for Schweppes 'stole' the character for the nine-year campaign.

• Pop group New World appeared at the Old Bailey and admitted that they had tried to fix a win on **Opportunity Knocks** by getting their fans and friends to send in bogus votes.

• Arthur the TV cat was kidnapped. He became a star in 1967 in the commercials for Kattomeat, eating his food straight from the tin with his paw. He was found and returned to Spillers who now owned him. He died two years later aged 16. And Arthur was really a she cat called Samantha before stardom struck.

• Jeff Rawle brought to the TV screen Keith Waterhouse and Willis Hall's **Billy Liar**. George A Cooper played his blaspheming father, as he had done in the stage play. The original novel was set in 1959, but now Billy's fantasies are up-to-date. In the first episode he steals a model of Concorde and dreams he is a pilot.

• **The World of Hugh Hefner** documentary revealed 'an exclusive look into his private life surrounded by bunny girls with his permanent playmate Barbi Benton. If you've ever wondered what life is like for the Playboy Chief, tune in.' Over seven million homes did.

• **Up The Workers** turned the world of industrial relations, which was in turmoil in the early seventies, into a half hour comedy. Cockers Components Ltd. had Henry McGee as the boss, Lance Percival as the personnel manager and Norman Bird as the shop steward in a series that owed much to the Boulting brothers' movie **I'm Alright Jack**.

1975

TOP TWENTY
Homes [millions]

1	Royal Variety Performance	ITV	10.3
2	Benny Hill Show	ITV	9.5
3	European Football	BBC	9.4
4	Miss World 1975	BBC	9.4
5	Love Thy Neighbour	ITV	9.3
6	This Is Your Life	ITV	9.3
7	Dr No	ITV	9.2
8	Dad's Army	BBC	8.9
9	Generation Game	BBC	8.9
10	The Sweeney	ITV	8.8
11	Cilla's Comedy Six	ITV	8.8
12	Coronation Street	ITV	8.8
13	Edward the Seventh	ITV	8.8
14	Man About the House	ITV	8.8
15	Bless This House	ITV	8.7
16	Tommy Cooper Hour	ITV	8.4
17	The Two Ronnies	BBC	8.4
18	My Old Man	ITV	8.3
19	News At Ten	ITV	8.3
20	Upstairs Downstairs	ITV	8.3

• No 1 – Telly Savalas was in the royal show, as a song and dance man. Dad's Army, Count Basie, and Vera Lynn were among the usual strange mix of stars.

• No 3 – Leeds United lost 2-0 to Bayern Munich in the European Cup Final at Paris in May.

• No 7 – The first Bond film to run on TV and ITV sold every available second for the ad breaks, it was the highest ever earning programme for them.

Regan and Carter Fly In

The Sweeney (10) roared straight into the charts in January. John Thaw was Jack Regan, Dennis Waterman as Sergeant Carter and Garfield Morgan played the nasty Chief Inspector Haskins. The Sweeney Todd – cockney rhyming slang for the Flying Squad – again proved viewers can't get enough TV cops and robbers. It ran for three years and 52 episodes were made.

Cilla's Comedy Six (11) were plays specially written as a showcase for Cilla Black by ATV – her husband Bobbie Willis was 'Executive Producer'. There was lots of publicity trailing her first real acting job on television in which she played six different characters including: a brow-beaten house wife, spinster daughter, temp and a mum on holiday. Her leading men were the likes of Keith Barron, Norman Rossington, Henry McGee and Dinsdale Landen. The shows got mixed reviews. But critics were surprised by Cilla's acting talent. 'Cilla left her audience feeling that she could be a considerable TV comedienne' and she won the Writer's Guild award for the top comedy actress.

Edward the Seventh (13) on ITV was a £2 million costume blockbuster. Timothy West played Edward and Robert Hardy played his dad Albert with Annette Crosbie as Queen Victoria. Approval for the series was sought from Queen Elizabeth II, because the producers wished to film in Windsor Castle, Sandringham and Osborne House, and because it made a good line for publicity.

Man About the House (14) starred Richard O'Sullivan as the man sharing a flat with Paula Wilcox and Sally Thomsett. A successful series in its own right, it was also a spin-off factory. Brian Murphy and Yootha Joyce starred as their landlords, characters strong enough to support their own series: **George and Mildred**. Another spin-off was **Robin's Nest**, with O'Sullivan's character Robin Tripp running his own restaurant. The final accolade was an American series based on the format called **Three's Company**, which also ran over here.

Upstairs Downstairs (20), the other Edwardian drama, had now reached World War One. Hannah Gordon was the new Mrs Bellamy and Gareth Hunt was the new footman. These were the days before home video so *TV Times* had a reader's offer of audio tapes of the series read by Hannah Gordon, price £2.75.

Wedding of the Year

Confetti, bouquets – and 15 million to bless the bride

The marriage of Meg Richardson and Hugh Mortimer in Thursday's *Crossroads* is a long-awaited television event. But the ceremony turned out to be the biggest real-life hit since Princess Anne and Captain Mark Phillips walked up the aisle. ARLINE WHITTAKER talks to "bride" Noele Gordon about the work behind the happy day. The story starts overleaf.

At 5.25 pm on Thursday 3rd April tea times all over the country were severely disrupted. 'Today is the great day for Meg Richardson and Hugh Mortimer. After years of joys and grief, separations and reunions, they are at last to wed.'

The Crossroads Wedding Souvenir, price 35 pence, went on sale to cover the events in Birmingham. Noel Gordon and John Bently and the rest of the **Crossroads** cast and crew had to battle their way through huge crowds that had turned up to watch the wedding at the Registry Office.

The Rolls Royce taking the newlyweds on honeymoon was chauffeured by Larry Grayson. The marriage didn't last. Hugh was kidnapped by terrorists and died of a heart attack while in captivity.

FIRST NIGHTS

• Angela Baddeley who played Mrs Bridges the cook in **Upstairs Downstairs** received the CBE in the New Year's Honours List.
• Members of Parliament turned down the plan to put TV cameras in the Commons, but they did allow radio broadcasts for an initial four week experiment.
• ITN reporter Gerald Seymour published a best selling novel *Harry's Game*. The book was about the work of an undercover man in Northern Ireland, where Seymour was based for ITN. In 1982 it was made into a TV drama series with Ray Lonnen as Harry.
• Anna Ford got her first on-screen job with Granada TV's **Reports Action**, the first programme to use TV to try to place children for adoption. Anna had been a tutor with the **Open University**.
• The BBC sold over 7,000 hours of programmes abroad. The top three were: **The Ascent of Man** to 28 countries, **Onedin Line** – 26 and **Some Mothers Do 'Ave 'Em** – 16.
• **Why Don't You Just Switch Off the Television Set and Go and Do Something Less Boring Instead?** was the longest ever title to a TV programme. The Saturday morning summer show for children was designed to stimulate their play and activities. Judging by its viewing figures, most kids ignored the title.

Fawlty Towers was a 'slow burner'. It was not a big ratings hit when the six episodes were first shown on BBC2 in September 1975. Even the next year BBC1 repeats failed to make the weekly top 20s. But Basil Fawlty became one of the greatest TV comedy characters. John Cleese based him on an hotel owner that had clashed with the Python team in Torquay. Connie Booth, his wife who played Polly, co-wrote. The final seven episodes were made in 1979 before the jumbled up hotel sign to 'Watery Fowls', 'Farty Towels' or 'Fawty Flowers' came down for ever. Except that viewers demand will see the series repeated over and over.

The Good Life was the story of suburban man in revolt. Richard Briers and Felicity Kendal were the Goods of Surbiton who turned their des res into a self-sufficiency experiment. Penelope Keith and Paul Eddington were the bemused neighbours Margot and Jerry. Four series were made, the last in 1978.

Celebrity Squares: 'It's the most spectacular and certainly the most costly game of noughts and crosses in the world – the 18 foot high board cost £22,000.' Bob Monkhouse introduced a line up of nine 'stars' each Sunday afternoon. For the first show in July they were: Leslie Crowther, Diana Dors, Hermione Gingold, Aimi McDonald, Alfred Marks, Arthur Mullard, Vincent Price, William Rushton and Terry Wogan.

The Life of Riley began in January, a comeback series for comedian Bill Maynard. He had been one of the biggest names on TV in the mid-fifties but had virtually disappeared with the Inland Revenue in hot pursuit. Life of Riley was to be one of three successful series for him in 1975.

On the Move was a little ten minute adult education series that changed the lives of thousands of viewers and attitudes to illiteracy. Written by Barry Took, it featured Bob Hoskins and Donald Gee as Alf and Bert two removal men learning and teaching as they deliver their loads.

1975

Took's
TV TEASERS

1 What did the initials stand for in TISWAS, ITV's new Saturday morning children's programme ?

2 Who was Basil Brush's straight man ?

3 Where was Poldark set ?

1975

Regional Differences

Tastes in TV watching vary considerably across Britain. These are two top tens from the south and the north from December. In London no **Coronation Street**, but **Crossroads** makes No 9. In Lancashire, the Street is well up, but they're no fans of Crossroads.

LONDON

1 ITN News
2 The Generation Game
3 Upstairs, Downstairs
4 The Virgin Soldiers
5 Are You Being Served?
6 ITN News
7 The Saturday Special
8 This Is Your Life
9 Crossroads
10 The Doll

LANCASHIRE

1 The Generation Game
2 ITN News
3 Coronation Street
4 Opportunity Knocks
5 The Cuckoo Waltz
6 This Is Your Life
7 The Last Voyage
8 The Saturday Special
9 Upstairs, Downstairs
10 Our Man Flint

• American TV made their own version of two British TV hits; **Upstairs Downstairs** which was called **Beacon Hill** and was set in the smart quarter of Boston, and **Dad's Army** which became **Rear Guard**.

• The documentary **Johnny Go Home** revealed the secret world of London's homeless children and young runaways:

Drive-In, the Thames TV motoring programme celebrated its 100th edition. No doubt presenter Shaw Taylor road tested the new bargain priced Skoda S100.

'Behind the facade of Piccadilly Circus is a hidden world inhabited by hustlers, housebreakers, buskers and boy prostitutes.'

• **Coronation Street**'s Albert Tatlock celebrated his 80th birthday with a special old time street party and a giant cake. Actor Jack Howarth, was 79 at the time and had been in showbiz since 1908.

• **Time To Work** was for the 'growing number of married women returning to work. Perhaps they want to get away from the children for a while, or perhaps they need more money.'

A YEAR IN THE SOAPS

Couples

Couples was another new soap trying for afternoon success. It followed the work of a marriage guidance council. David Swift and Helen Shingler played the two experienced counsellors and Marjorie Yates was a trainee. Some well known TV faces played people with failing marriages, Maureen Lipman, Jean Boht, David Markham and in the first episode Judy Loe appeared as a young mum with problems. Her child was played by her real daughter Kathrin Beckinsale – daughter of Richard Beckinsale.

NEAR MISSES

• John Pilger continued his series of hard-hitting documentaries. In Bangladesh he found children starving following a year of disasters in that country. 'I get cynical about World Food Conferences costing £5 million. It costs 20 pence a day to keep a child alive in Bangladesh – you do your own figures...'

• **Don't Ask Me** made stars out of three doctors: Dr Magnus Pyke, Dr Miriam Stoppard and Dr David Bellamy. The Yorkshire TV programme set out to popularise science in peak time viewing. It was a grown-up version of **How**,

answering questions like: why do seed shoots always grow upwards? Why does hair stand on end when you get a shock? Why do golf balls have dimples? No one asked why did Magnus Pyke wave his arms about.

• **Carry On Laughing** brought the film team to television for a series of half hour comedies with titles like: Orgy and Bess, The Prisoner of Spenda, The Nine Old Cobblers and characters like Count Yerackers, Lady Houndsbotham and Lord Peter Flimsy. All the usual lovely load of smut and innuendo.

• **Are You Being Served?** served the BBC very well. The sitcom, set in a creaking department store, ran for 11 years. The scripts were well stocked with catch phrases and characters. John Inman, Mollie Sugden, Frank Thornton and Wendy Richard starred.

TEASER ANSWERS

1   This Is Saturday Wear a Smile. The show was presented by Chris Tarrant, Bob Carolgees, Sally James, Lenny Henry and Spit the dog.
2   Roy North was the fox's longest serving companion.
3   The romantic serial was set in 18th Century Cornwall.

The Ropers Move House

George and Mildred (5) saw the Ropers just edge out **Man About the House** in the year's ratings. The writers of both series Johnnie Mortimer and Brian Cooke decided the flat sharing sitcom was coming to an end, so the Ropers were off to the suburbs and 46 Peacock Crescent, Hampton Wick. There Brian Murphy and Yootha Joyce moved in next to Ann and Jeffrey Fairmile, 'the sort of snobby couple who would have musical toilet rolls,' said George.

Coronation Street (12) had slipped a bit from its regular top slot in the sixties. Now in the middle of the seventies, Fleet Street was starting to speculate on its future: 'Has Coronation Street Finally Had It?' they asked.

Starsky and Hutch (15) was the highest placed American cops and robbers show since **Dragnet** left the charts in 1956. David Starsky and Ken Hutchinson, played by Paul Michael Glaser and David Soul, were two cops out to keep crime off the streets and their car on the road. The series was full of car chases and was fairly violent until an anti-violence campaign frightened the producers and sponsors and the series settled down into an extended wisecracking buddie movie.

Kojak (16) had already been keeping the streets of Manhattan's 13th Precinct safe for two years. Lieutenant Theo Kojak, aka Telly Savalas, changed bald men's lives. Bald became beautiful and slap tops walked tall. Crocker and Stavros were his side-kicks, the latter played by Telly's brother George Savalas. 'Who loves ya, baby?' was the catch phrase that ran through 110 episodes in the run that ended in 1977.

The TV Times Awards (17). Richard O'Sullivan presented the prizes at the seventh annual awards where viewers voted for their favourite stars. Yootha Joyce was voted The Funniest Woman, Benny Hill The Funniest Man. Googie Withers won an award for **Within These Walls** and John Thaw for **The Sweeney**. It was seventh time lucky for Noele Gordon. She had won the award every year for Favourite Female Personality.

The **Money Wise** programme featured the problems of buying a house and looked at the price differences across the country for an 'average house'. In London it was £16,416 for a new house, the cheapest was in the North East of England at £10,563. The programme asked whether buying a home was an effective hedge against inflation!

The Old Grey Whistle Test broadcast Queen's Christmas Concert live from the Hammersmith Odeon, presented by 'Whispering' Bob Harris.

Took's TV Teasers

1 Who joined Steed in the New Avengers ?

2 Who played McMillan and Wife ?

3 Who were the two in Two's Company ?

1976

TOP TWENTY
Homes [millions]

1	Goldfinger	ITV	9.8
2	Generation Game	BBC	9.7
3	Miss World	BBC	9.6
4	The Sweeney	ITV	9.4
5	George and Mildred	ITV	9.4
6	Man About the House	ITV	9.2
7	From Russia With Love	ITV	9.2
8	Benny Hill Show	ITV	9.1
9	Royal Variety	BBC	9.1
10	This Is Your Life	ITV	9.1
11	Eurovision Song Contest	BBC	8.9
12	Coronation Street	ITV	8.8
13	The Italian Job	ITV	8.8
14	Sale of the Century	ITV	8.5
15	Starsky and Hutch	BBC	8.5
16	Kojak	BBC	8.4
17	TV Times Awards	ITV	8.4
18	The Two Ronnies	BBC	8.3
19	Morecambe and Wise	BBC	8.2
20	Opportunity Knocks	ITV	8.2

• No 1 – Goldfinger was 12 years old when it topped the year's ratings. It was the third Bond film made by Sean Connery.

• No 7 – From Russia With Love was even older at 13. Bond No 2 co-starred Robert Shaw and Daniela Bianchi.

• No 11 – Britain finally won with Brotherhood of Man and 'Save Your Kisses For Me'. It spent 16 weeks in the charts and reached No 1.

• No 13 – Michael Caine starred with a fleet of Minis in the 1969 movie.

1976

NEAR MISSES

• **When The Boat Comes In** starred husband and wife Susan Jameson and James Bolam in the Tyneside drama series set in the Depression. The Seatons were the Geordie family whose lives were followed in those politically charged days.

1976

• **Hadleigh**, played by Gerald Harper, was a spin-off from an earlier drama called **Gazette** in 1969. In 1976, with the fourth and final series, Harper, the local big-wig, was still having problems keeping his stately home, his life-style and his wife.

• **A Little Bit of Wisdom** starred Norman Wisdom as Norman a clerk in a builder's office – 'the little man who can never quite get things right'. Mix ups with the boss's daughter, various items of construction machinery and his flat mate and a smashing time with double glazing were all disasters carefully executed by the actor/clown/comedian.

• **Duchess of Duke Street** was the BBC's answer to **Upstairs Downstairs**. Gemma Jones starred as Louise Trotter, the proprietress of the Bentinck Hotel.

The story was based on the real-life story of Rosa Lewis who owned the Cavendish Hotel at the turn of the century. A lavish costume drama, it was a prize-winning hit and a big seller overseas.

• **Bouquet of Barbed Wire** 'A new seven part series concerning the Mansons who are happily married – until a young American intrudes into their family' arrived in January. Andrea Newman adapted her steamy sexy novel, a mix of lust, incest and infidelity that kept viewers glued. With Frank Finlay, Susan Penhaligon, Sheila Allen and Gavin Sorenson as the American who stirred the cocktail.

• **Husband of the Year** found foolhardy contestants from all over the UK who were willing to be scrutinised by celebrity husband and wife teams. Hosted by Pete Murray and Marjorie Proops.

• **Happy Ever After** was the archetypal domestic sitcom. Terry Scott and June Whitfield as the happy couple with a family of two daughters and a dotty aunt. The series evolved into the amazingly successful and long running **Terry and June**.

Marti Caine

Marti Caine starred in her own show **Nobody Does It Like Marti**. A year before she was 'a stringy, plain and lanky 30-year-old Sheffield housewife', working the beer and bingo club circuit. Then came **New Faces**. She won the all winners final at the London Palladium and as her prize got a two week booking at Las Vegas. ATV producer Colin Clews had seen her on New Faces and wanted to sign her up. 'I just knew she was a very talented singer and comedienne, but it has turned out better than I could have hoped.' Barbara Windsor was the guest on the first show.

A YEAR IN THE SOAPS

The Cedar Tree

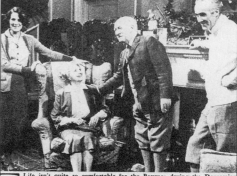

Life isn't quite so comfortable for the Bournes during the Depression but there's still some Christmas cheer: Susan Engel, Joyce Carey Cyril Luckham and Philip Latham show in *The Cedar Tree*

1.30 New Series
The Cedar Tree
Victoria
BY ALFRED SHAUGHNESSY
The depressed Thirties have begun—and the cold wind is felt in Larkfield Manor, elegant ancestral home of the Bourne family. As they assemble for another family Christmas, the youngest of their three daughters, 16-year-old Vicky, suffers the experience of growing up.
The graphics are by George Wallder, music arranged by Peter Knight.
The age of zip: see page 24
This week's cast:
Arthur Bourne .... Philip Latham
Helen Bourne .... Susan Engel
Elizabeth Bourne .... Sally Osborn
Anne Bourne .... Jennifer Lonsdale
Victoria Bourne .... Susan Skipper
Alice Bourne .... Joyce Carey
Charles Ashley .... Cyril Luckham
Phyllis Bourne .... Kate Coleridge
Nanny .... Jean Taylor Smith
Gates .... Peter Hill
Dr. Cropper .... Michael MacOwan
Dr. Brian Harrington .... James Fagan
Miss Pringle .... Pamela Mandell
THEME MUSIC STEPHEN FRANCIS: DEVISER/SCRIPT EDITOR ALFRED SHAUGHNESSY: DESIGNER HENRY GRAVENEY: DIRECTOR/PRODUCER IAN FORDYCE
ATV Network Production

The Cedar Tree was basically **Upstairs Downstairs** without the downstairs. The depressed thirties have begun – and the cold wind is felt in Larkfield Manor, the ancestral home of the Bourne family. They may have had money worries but, for daughters Elizabeths Anne and Victoria, played by Sally Osborn, Jennifer Lonsdale and Susan Skipper, their biggest headaches were new clothes and finding suitable male escorts. One such young cad was played by Nigel Havers. All was set for a long running saga of aristocratic decline but the family tree fell down after two years.

TEASER ANSWERS

1   Gareth Hunt played Mike Gambit and Joanna Lumley was Purdey. They joined Patrick McNee who appeared in every one of the 187 episodes in the old and new series.
2   Rock Hudson played Police Commissioner McMillan and his wife, Sally, was played by Susan Saint James.
3   Elaine Stritch and Donald Sinden starred in the story of an American woman and her terribly English butler.

FIRST NIGHTS

The Fosters was another family based sitcom, but this family were black. With Norman Beaton as dad and Isabelle Lucas as mum and a 17-year-old Lenny Henry as their son Sonny. It predated the **Cosby Show**'s Huxtables by many years, but was attacked over here for reinforcing negative stereotypes. The Fosters, based on an American show **Good Times**, did well initially in the charts, but slipped later in the run. Critics blamed poor scripts, not the 'black' theme. A second, and last, series was made the following year.

The Muppet Show had a very American feel with a transatlantic guest star most weeks and American voices, but it was made in Elstree by ATV. Jim Henson, of **Sesame Street** fame, created a music hall stuffed with over 200 strange creatures. The stars were Miss Piggy, Kermit, Ernie

---

Star of **The Sweeney**, Dennis Waterman set out on a recording career and recorded a single and an LP. "I'm too old to play for the England football team, so I thought I'd have a go at singing instead" said the soccer mad star. The records didn't make the charts, but four years later he had a hit with the **Minder** theme 'I Could Be So Good For You'.

Les Dawson also released an LP called 'An Evening With Les Dawson' which was a mixture of songs, chat and jokes.

Reporter Fyfe Robinson went **Around the World in 80 Hours** mimicking Phileas Fogg, who made the prediction: 'One day, when man has conquered the air, it will be possible to complete the journey in 80 hours'. Robertson made the journey in Concorde and the programme lasted 80 minutes.

- To celebrate the bicentennial of the USA, James Burke and Raymond Burr presented **The Inventing of America** an entertainment all about the household objects that the Yanks have given us.
- Show-jumper Harvey Smith made his TV debut as a wrestler in **World of Sport**. He wore a red robe as he climbed into the ring with a 'V' sign on the back.

and Bert (the old men watching the show from the box) and Fozzie Bear. It had awards showered on it, BAFTAs and Emmys, and Henson received the US's Congressional Medal for services to entertainment.

Multi-Coloured Swap Shop, hosted by Noel Edmonds, was the first children's show to give viewers the chance to really participate. Planned as a short winter fill-in for Saturday mornings, the three hour show proved such a success that the run was extended to 21 weeks. Children phoned-in with swaps, stories, questions for guests and comments on the show.

TV news

- Tom Baker took over as the fourth **Doctor Who** from Jon Pertwee and was on the front cover of the *Dr Who Annual*. And thanks to the fanatical following the series still has, the 75 pence book is worth about fifty times its original price. At six years in the role Baker was to become the longest lasting Doctor. He was followed by Peter Davison and later Sylvester McCoy, the last Doctor.
- Pan's People made their last appearance on **Top of the Pops**. For ten years their brand of erotic, scantily clad dancing to pop music had upset the clean-up TV lobby and raised male viewers' temperatures.
- Only one viewer called in to complain when some ITV regions showed the wrong episode of **Crossroads**. Viewers watching Granada, Southern, HTV and Scottish jumped an episode in that week's order. The missing one was dropped in the following week.
- Curry's put the first home video recorders on sale in their high street shops. Two systems were available from Philips and Sony and they cost about £500.
- Michael Douglas, star of the American cop series **The Streets of San Francisco**, asked the producers to have his character killed off as he was keen to take up movie offers.

Rock Follies was the story of three girl singers in 'The Little Ladies' rock band. With Rula Lenska, Charlotte Cornwell and Julie Covington it proved a critical success but never made any real impact in the ratings. Two series of six were made and they had a minor hit called 'OK?' in 1977 when Sue Jones-Davies had joined the group.

The Fall and Rise of Reginald Perrin starred Leonard Rossiter as the angst ridden suburban commuter. Pauline Yates played his wife, John Barron his boss CJ, Sue Nicholls his secretary. A hippopotamus played his mother-in-law.

THE DR WHO annual 1976

Starring TOM BAKER as DR WHO

Authorised edition as seen on BBC tv

1976

- A late night series **Sex In Our Time** was pulled from the autumn schedules by Thames TV. Television was under siege from Parliament and pressure groups at the time over 'too much sex on TV'. After consultation with the IBA about the six one-hour documentaries Thames said 'the programmes could not be transmitted without offending some viewers, even at that late hour.' They were then attacked for censorship by TV workers and the quality press.
- Two Harry Corbetts appeared in the New Year's Honours List. Harry H Corbett of **Steptoe and Son** and Harry Corbett the man behind, and inside, Sooty were both awarded OBEs.

1977

TOP TWENTY
Viewers [millions]

1	Mike Yarwood Xmas	BBC *	10.7
2	Morecambe and Wise Christmas Show	BBC *	10.7
3	Jubilee Royal Variety	ITV *	10.6
4	You Only Live Twice	ITV *	10.4
5	Sale of the Century	ITV *	10.3
6	Generation Game	ITV *	10.0
7	George and Mildred	ITV *	9.8
8	This Is Your Life	ITV	9.7
9	Benny Hill Show	ITV	9.6
10	Coronation Street	ITV	9.5
11	Oh No It's Selwyn Froggitt	ITV	9.5
12	Doctor On the Go	ITV	9.4
13	The Cuckoo Waltz	ITV	9.4
14	Miss Jones and Son	ITV	9.3
15	Robin's Nest	ITV	9.2
16	Eurovision	ITV	9.1
17	Miss World 1977	ITV	9.1
18	Wednesday At Eight	ITV *	9.0
19	Charlie's Angels	ITV	9.0
20	The Two Ronnies	BBC *	8.9

During 1977 AGB, who compiled the viewing figures, changed to measuring individuals. Entries marked with a * have been calculated on the equivalent of 2.2 people watching in each home.

• No 3 – The Royal Gala in that Jubilee year starred Julie Andrews, Bob Hope, Shirley MacLaine and the Muppets.

• No 16 – It was back to No 2 for Britain with 'Rock Bottom' sung by Lynsey De Paul and Mike Moran.

Christmas Ratings Battle

Mike Yarwood Christmas Show (1) was the winner in this year's Christmas competition. The BBC couldn't go wrong; at 7.15 pm **Bruce Forsyth and the Generation Game (6)**, with Anthea Redfern, 8.20 Mike Yarwood and his 'guests' Prince Charles, James Callaghan, President Carter and, in reality, Paul McCartney and Wings and then at 8.55 the Christmas institution **Morecambe and Wise (2)**. Shirley Bassey, Glenda Jackson, Andre Previn and many many more top stars willingly signed up to be sent up by Eric and Ernie in some of TV's golden moments, like the news readers singing 'There's Nothing Like A Dame'.

In reply ITV schedulers would seem to have waved a white flag. **Stars On Christmas Day** was their early evening response with Moira Anderson presenting a **Stars On Sunday** compilation. This was followed by the movie **Young Winston** starring Simon Ward and then **Stanley Baxter's Greatest Hits**.

Oh No It's Selwyn Froggitt (11) was one of the six sitcoms that made the year's list. Bill Maynard starred as a ham-fisted council workman, leading light in the Scarsdale Working Men's Club and walking disaster. It was a huge hit and in April managed to keep the **Coronation Street** wedding of Rita and Len off the No 1 spot.

Doctor On the Go (12) was more adventures of the young doctors from St Swithins. Only Robin Nedwell and Geoffrey Davies as Doctors Waring and Stuart-Clark survived from the original Doctor... series.

The Cuckoo Waltz (13) starred Diane Keene and David Roper as the couple, with the 'guest' Lewis Collins. This was the third series and the Hawthorns also have twins to cope with in the nest.

Miss Jones and Son (14) starred Paula Wilcox playing a single mum who planned to keep her baby and become an activist working for mother's rights. Roland Desmond Geoffrey Jones was played by tiny Luke Steensel.

Robin's Nest (15) was the final spin-off from **Man About the House**. Richard O'Sullivan was now the owner of a restaurant which he ran with the help of Tessa Wyatt and Tony Britton.

---

*TV writers Ray Galton and Alan Simpson creators of some of TV greatest comedy hits such as Hancock and Steptoe, launched a series of seven **Comedy Play-house** pilots. None repeated their earlier successes.*

FIRST NIGHTS

Gordon Burns introduced **The Krypton Factor** – wearing a massive kipper tie and long hair. It was the first British game show idea to be sold to American TV. In the States, according to Burns, they ruined it turning it into a kind of It's a Knockout and it didn't last long. The series was also sold to Australia, New Zealand and Germany.

Secret Army was another strong drama series about the Resistance in occupied Europe during World War II. Bernard Hepton ran the Belgian cafe and Clifford Rose was the Nazi baddie, Kessler. No doubt the writers of **'Allo 'Allo** were regular viewers of the three series that were made.

All Creatures Great and Small was the TV adaption of the James Herriott books of a vet's life in north Yorkshire. Christopher Timothy played the new young vet. Robert Hardy and Peter Davison were the other partners, Siegfried and Tristran Farnon in the 1930s country practice that re-christened the Dales to 'Herriott Country'.

Jesus of Nazareth 'marks a great development in world television history. The production took three years, and was constantly checked by a panel of religious authorities representing the great faith.' So ran the substantial claims for the greatest story ever told by Lord Grade's ATV. Robert Powell was Jesus and was supported by a quality cast from Anne Bancroft to Peter Ustinov.

6.15 *Jesus of Nazareth* marks a great development in world television history, a new and different look at the life and time of Jesus Christ.

The production took three years, and was constantly checked and supervised by a panel of religious authorities representing the great faiths.

Firmly based on the New Testament, the film highlights the divinity and humanity of Christ, His trials and His triumph. Research for the production revealed much that was new about the society and epoch in which Christ worked and lived.

The story is told in two parts, tonight and next Sunday. This first episode deals with His birth and the escape into Egypt when rumours of a Messiah's coming causes Herod to order the assassination of all boy babies. With Herod's death, Jesus returns and is baptised by John the Baptist, who tells his followers: "It is Him you must follow—not me." Jesus goes to preach in Galilee, and the miracles begin. Then John is beheaded and a leader of the Zealots—the Jewish Resistance of the day—calls for war on the Romans in revenge. However, Jesus has other ideas. And his following grows . . . **Jesus: the making of an epic—see page 18.**

ROBERT POWELL as JESUS
WITH GUEST STARS

ANNE BANCROFT *as* Mary Magdalene
JAMES FARENTINO *as* Simon Peter
IAN McSHANE *as* Judas
CHRISTOPHER PLUMMER *as* Herod Antipas
RALPH RICHARDSON *as* Simeon

VALENTINA CORTESE *as* Herodias
JAMES EARL JONES *as* Balthazar
DONALD PLEASENCE *as* Melchior
FERNANDO REY *as* Gaspar
PETER USTINOV *as* Herod the Great

MICHAEL YORK *as* John the Baptist
and OLIVIA HUSSEY *as* Mary

ALSO STARRING

CYRIL CUSACK *as* Yehuda   YORGO VOYAGIS *as* Joseph   IAN BANNEN *as* Amos
MARINA BERTI *as* Elizabeth   REGINA BIANCHI *as* Anna   OLIVER TOBIAS *as* Joel

ASSOCIATE PRODUCER DYSON LOVELL:
EXECUTIVE PRODUCER BERNARD J. KINGHAM
MUSIC COMPOSED AND CONDUCTED BY MAURICE JARRE
SCREENPLAY BY ANTHONY BURGESS, SUSO CECCHI D'AMICO, FRANCO ZEFFIRELLI
PRODUCED BY VINCENZO LABELLA: DIRECTED BY FRANCO ZEFFIRELLI

• Dennis Healey was the Chancellor of the Exchequer and both channels had Budget Specials. He made very few changes that year to the cost of: Petrol = 84p gallon, Beer = 27p a pint and 20 cigarettes = 46p.

• Burt Lancaster starred in a three million pound biblical epic series **Moses – the Lawgiver**. It went massively over budget when the Yom Kippur War drove the production *out* of Israel.

1977

Took's TV TEASERS

1   Who were the Blue Peter team this year?

2   Who was the west country poet discovered on Opportunity Knocks?

3   What was the name of the company in the Rag Trade?

NEAR MISSES

• **The Good Old Days** was still in the charts 24 years after the City Varieties Music Hall at Leeds went on air. It had a massive audience waiting list keen to dress up in Edwardian gear to sing old

music hall songs from a long lost era. Leonard Sachs was the master of ceremonies who with his mellifluous verbosity, sounded like a man who had swallowed a dictionary.

• **Dave Allen and Friends** was a change of direction for the comic. We were used to seeing Dave sitting on a stool, cigarette in hand and whisky within reach, telling stories. This series took him on a tour of the UK looking for the quirky, comic and unusual such as the world's women's shouting champion, a teacher devoted to the life cycle of the flea, and a man with a garden full of edible weeds.

• Jubilee Day was Tuesday 7th June and the BBC's coverage was No 1 in that week's chart. A **Nationwide Special** opened the day followed by the pomp and procession with Tom Fleming as the chief commentator. **Jubilee Jackanory** and a special Good Old Days followed later in the day.

• Dennis Norden said for the first time **It'll Be Alright On the Night**. A chance to see the TV and film clips that normally end up in a pile on the cutting room floor.

• **Citizen Smith** first shouted 'Power to the People.' Robert Lindsay as outrageous Wolfie Smith was leader of the Tooting Popular Front. Writer John Sullivan, who not long before had been cleaning carpets for a living, was hailed as a great new talent. The producer cast Cheryl Hall as Smith's girlfriend without realising she was married to Lindsay at the time.

• **Mr and Mrs** with Derek Batey asked 'How much do husbands and wives know about each other?' A procession of couples proved the answer was very little. It was Border TV's biggest hit.

A YEAR IN THE SOAPS

Aussie Soaps Arrive

Five years after it first arrived as an early afternoon soap opera, **Emmerdale Farm** had proved such a success it was given a peak time slot. This left a hole in the schedules and it was filled by **The Sullivans**, the first of Australia's soap operas to arrive on British TV.

The action took place as World War II loomed in late thirties' suburban Melbourne. One son is a pacifist and clashes with his father, there is love and conflict with another family of immigrants, the Kaufmanns. The saga carried on through the War and finally ended in 1982 after six years. The timelessness of the series made it readily repeatable and it has run again and again in numerous countries.

Lena Zavaroni

Lena Zavaroni was 13 in '77 and already a seasoned TV performer. That summer she was starring in the Sunday night variety show **Hi Summer**. She leapt to stardom as a winner on Hughie Green's **Opportunity Knocks** in 1973 aged nine and 4ft 1in in her stockinged feet. Appearances in the States followed, two top ten record hits, including 'Ma He's Making Eyes At Me' which won her a silver disc and she was on the bill of the **Royal Variety Show** in 1976. Now 4ft 10in she was earning £1,000 per week and wearing long dresses on stage. The little girl clothes had gone. But the success was a bit too much for the young star and problems with an eating disorder kept her out of the limelight until the middle of the eighties.

TEASER ANSWERS

1   John Noakes, Peter Purves and Lesley Judd.
2   Pam Ayres who had her own LWT series, The World of Pam Ayres.
3   Peter Jones as Mr Fenner, was the boss of Fenner Fashions Ltd.

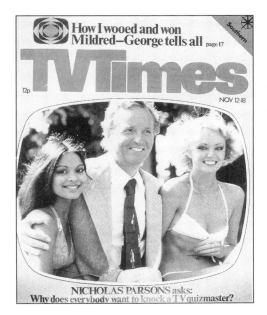

Prime time shows on Friday 22nd December 1978.

ITV
19.00	The Muppet Show
19.30	Survival Special
20.30	Sale of the Century

BBC1
19.10	Star Trek
20.00	Citizen Smith
20.30	The Liver Birds

BBC2
17.35	Christmas Matinee
20.00	Country Game
20.30	Leo Sayer

Took's TV Teasers

1   Ronnie Barker's Norman Stanley Fletcher came out of Slade Prison and into a new series in 1978. What was it called?

2   Who played Arthur Parker in Dennis Potter's controversial Pennies From Heaven?

3   What did the Heineken commercials start doing this year?

Strike Causes BBC Ratings Flop

An all-out strike at the BBC on 22nd December meant blank screens and victory for ITV in this year's top 20. Without an alternative main channel millions of viewers tuned in to that evening's programming on ITV.

The victory was particularly sweet for Anglia Television which made two of the shows transmitted in the all-important 'prime-time' slot between 7 pm and 9 pm.

'From Norwich...' as the opening sequence went, it was '...quiz of the week' **Sale of the Century (1)** at 7.30. By now in its seventh year, Nicholas Parsons was still smiling all the way to the bank as he offered contestants the chance to buy goods at bargain prices.

Because of the strike, it had the highest ever rating for a game show.

The bargains finally ran out in 1984 after about 500 contestants had won nearly half a million pounds' worth of prizes.

At 8.30 pm was a **Survival Special (2)** about a remarkable leopard, also high in the charts because of the strike.

At 7 pm was **The Muppet Show (5)**, featuring Kris Kristofferson and Rita Coolidge. Jim Henson's Miss Piggy and Kermit the Frog were by now household names having been given their own show in 1976 after being 'discovered' in **Sesame Street**.

Scheduled on BBC1 was **Star Trek** at 7.10 pm; **Citizen Smith** at 8 pm; and **The Liver Birds** at 8.30.

1978

TOP TWENTY
Viewers [millions]

1	Sale of the Century	ITV	21.2
2	Survival Special	ITV	21.1
3	George and Mildred	ITV	20.8
4	This Is Your Life	ITV	20.8
5	The Muppet Show	ITV	20.6
6	Coronation Street	ITV	20.5
7	Some Mothers Do 'Ave 'Em	BBC	20.0
8	Sharp Intake of Breath	ITV	19.8
9	The Eric Sykes Show	ITV	19.6
10	European Champion's Cup Final	ITV	19.2
11	The Sweeney	ITV	19.1
12	Edward & Mrs Simpson	ITV	18.9
13	Morecambe and Wise	ITV	18.7
14	Robin's Nest	ITV	18.7
15	Miss Jones and Son	ITV	18.6
16	Rising Damp	ITV	18.6
17	TV Eye	ITV	18.4
18	Mind Your Language	ITV	18.2
19	Lillie	ITV	18.2
20	All Creatures Great and Small	BBC	18.1

• No 6 – The Christmas edition saw Brian Tilsley gatecrash Elsie's Christmas party to arrange his first date with Gail Potter.

• No 13 – Eric and Ernie's first Christmas Special for ITV. Guests included Leonard Rossiter and Frank Finlay.

• No 10 – Liverpool won the final 1–0 against Bruges. Kenny Dalglish scored the winning goal.

1978

FIRST NIGHTS

Larry Grayson and Isla St Clair took over from Bruce Forsyth and Anthea Redfern on **The Generation Game**. Larry 'shut that door' on Brucie's 'good game, good game' and proved even more popular. Bruce meantime went to London Weekend Television, for **Bruce Forsyth's Big Night Out**, a series of two-hour unsuccessful Saturday night spectaculars. He progressed to **Play Your Cards Right** in 1980.

Butterflies began with Wendy Craig as Ria. The listing in the *Radio Times* said: 'Ria has enough to cope with: there is her husband Ben, who has his own hang-ups and her sons Adam and Russell who cause most of them. Then suddenly there's Leonard.' Geoffrey Palmer was Ben, Andrew Hall was Russell, Nicholas Lyndhurst was Adam and Bruce Montague was Leonard.

ITV's arts series **The South Bank Show** began with a profile of 'Paul McCartney - Songsmith'.

John Mortimer brought us Horace Rumpole in the shape of Leo McKern and **Rumpole of the Bailey**. The well-rounded barrister made his TV debut in a BBC play but the BBC took so long to make up its mind about a series that ITV jumped in.

Phil Redmond, later to create **Brookside**, brought us **Grange Hill**. Pupils in form 1A included Tucker Jenkins, later to be given his own series – **Tucker's Luck**. Tucker was actor Todd Carty, who

5.10 *New series*
Grange Hill
A series in nine parts by
PHIL REDMOND
1: It's the first day at a new school for the members of Form 1 Alpha. Benny is too early, Justin is lonely, Judy is scared, Trisha hates the uniform, but Tucker reckons he's got it all sewn up.
Grange Hill pupils:
Justin Bennett....ROBERT MORGAN
Winkle Graham
              CHRISTOPHER HALL
Benny Green......TERRY SUE PATT
Alan Hargreaves
              GEORGE ARMSTRONG
Jackie Heron....MIRIAM MANN
Tucker Jenkins.......TODD CARTY
David Lewis....GARY PETTERPLACE
Judy Preston....ABIGAIL BROWN
Thomas Watson...JAMES JEBBIA
Ann Wilson....LUCINDA DUCKETT
Carol Yates...........JULIA GALE
Trisha Yates....MICHELLE HERBERT
Caretaker...........GRAHAM ASHLEY
Mr Foster.........ROGER SLOMAN
Janet...............STELLA HAIME
Mrs Jenkins....HILARY CRANE

later became HIV carrier Mark Fowler in **EastEnders**.

Comedian Ted Rogers began making strange hand signals and contestants started winning Dusty Bins in the game show **3-2-1**.

Nicholas Ball, then the husband of comedian Pamela Stephenson, became ex-cop turned private eye James **Hazell**.

Ian Ogilvy became Simon Templar in the **Return of the Saint**. He replaced Roger Moore who had become James Bond.

America gave us former Miss USA Lynda Carter as **Wonder Woman**.

Kenny Everett introduced Sid Snott and Captain Kremmen in the **Kenny Everett Video Show**.

A YEAR IN THE SOAPS

A shot-gun hold-up at Mike Baldwin's denim factory meant the end for the **Street**'s Ernest Bishop. Bishop, played by Stephen Hancock, was blasted by a sawn off shot-gun and died later in hospital (rumour has it that Hancock had asked for a rise and the Street producers had answered by killing him off). But justice was seen to be done – his killers were jailed for life two months later.

The regulars at the Rovers rallied round a grieving Emily (Eileen Derbyshire), Ernest's wife of seven years. Emily never did have much luck with the men in her life – two years later she married Arnold Swain only to find out he was a bigamist. After that it was widowhood and Percy Sugden as a lodger.

No smoke...

After three episodes of **All Creatures Great and Small**, *I have yet to see any smoke coming from Robert Hardy's pipe. He doesn't seem to know what to do with it...*

F C Potter
Haywards Heath, Sussex

Radio Times
March 1978

TEASER ANSWERS

1   Going Straight. The sequel to Porridge which saw Fletch and Godber coping with life on the outside. (It won the 1978 BAFTA award for best comedy series.)
2   Bob Hoskins.
3   Heineken began 'Refreshing the parts other beers cannot reach'.

1978

Recognise the face behind the bar? Yes, before taking over the tenancy of the Rovers Alec Gilroy, aka Roy Barraclough, could be seen serving up drinks to the likes of leering landlord Rigsby in **Rising Damp (16)**.

Rigsby (Leonard Rossiter) had been insulting tenants Alan and Philip (Richard Beckinsale and Don Warrington) and lusting after the dotty Miss Jones (Frances de la Tour) since 1974.

LAST NIGHTS

The grandad of television talent shows **Opportunity Knocks** came to an end. It had been started by Hughie Green on radio in 1949 and moved to television in 1956. He auditioned 2,300 contestants for the first TV series, from the 20,000 that had applied. The number of stars he made famous is legendary: David Whitfield, The Bachelors, Mary Hopkin, Freddie Davis, Les Dawson, Little and Large, Bobby Crush, Peters and Lee, Lena Zavaroni, Frank Carson, Freddie Starr to name but a few.

Thirteen years after the demise of Opportunity Knocks, Barry Took, on **TV Weekly,** pondered on whatever happened to acts such as Mr and Mrs Hubert Bell, the hand balancing act from Leeds? Or Bruce Thompson, the one-man-band from Newbiggen-on-Sea? Bruce wrote in to tell Barry that he was still a warm-up man on **Every Second Counts**.

In 1987 the BBC tried the formula as **Bob Says Opportunity Knocks** with Bob Monkhouse stepping into Hughie's shoes and heavily on his toes. A complex court case ensued as Hughie tried to prove he held the copyright. It was never really resolved – Hughie's name was put on the credits as adviser.

1978

Dress Sense

Two big budget ITV period dramas made this year's top 20: **Edward and Mrs Simpson (12)**, winner of a BAFTA award for best drama series, and **Lillie (19)**.

Edward and Mrs Simpson starred Edward Fox as Edward VIII and American actress Cynthia Harris as Mrs Simpson. It was popular with the viewers but not so with the real Mrs Simpson, the Duchess of Windsor, by then in her eighties. The series took the cast to over 30 locations ranging from a Kenyan safari to a coal mine in Wales. Over 70 sets were designed from rooms in Buckingham Palace to a Glasgow slum.

It reportedly took nearly six months to buy the materials and trimmings for Cynthia. All the 1930s wigs and hair-pieces – including Mrs Simpson's – were individually made for the cast.

Lillie was a 13-part series about the life of Lillie Langtry, the Jersey girl who became the mistress to the Prince of Wales, later to be Edward VII. Francesca Annis played Lillie. Three years beforehand she had played her in a cameo role for **Edward the Seventh**. Anton Rodgers was her husband Edward, who finally ended up in a madhouse, Denis Lill played the Prince of Wales, and Peter Egan was the handsome young Oscar Wilde.

There were 3,000 costumes made for the series – 200 of them for Francesca's Lillie. As with Edward and Mrs Simpson, all the costumes were made the original way in natural fabrics – apparently man-made fabrics don't drape properly.

Eric and Ernie got caught up with the law in an episode of **The Sweeney (11)**. The two comedians, whose own show had switched to ITV only a few months before, starred as themselves in an episode called Hearts and Minds. They were entertainers in a night-club where the tough guys were investigating a murder. 'We *really* play ourselves – a cheap music hall act,' Eric joked. John Thaw and Denis Waterman had appeared on the **Morecambe and Wise Christmas Show** a couple of years beforehand – on the condition that Eric and Ernie appeared on theirs. Hearts and Minds also featured Jean Boht (Ma Boswell) as 'a woman neighbour'.

*Suzie Quatro returned home to the States and made a guest appearance on **Happy Days** playing in the Diner with the Fonz.*

*Bread's Boswell family weren't the first to be created by writer Carla Lane. Nerys Hughes character Sandra in **The Liver Birds** was a Boswell. The series regularly featured her mum and dad who were only ever referred to as Mr and Mrs Boswell.*

A feature on **Nationwide** prompted 16,000 letters in support of the mile against 500 for the kilometre.

1979

TOP TWENTY
Viewers [millions]

1	To the Manor Born	BBC	24.0
2	Larry Grayson's Generation Game	BBC	23.9
3	Blankety Blank	BBC	23.3
4	Are You Being Served	BBC	22.6
5	Mastermind	BBC	22.6
6	Mike Yarwood	BBC	22.4
7	Sykes	BBC	22.4
8	Secret Army	BBC	22.1
9	Last of the Summer Wine	BBC	21.9
10	Citizen Smith	BBC	21.8
11	Petrocelli	BBC	21.7
12	Rings On Their Fingers	BBC	21.1
13	Angels	BBC	20.9
14	The Benny Hill Show	ITV	20.9
15	Star Trek	BBC	20.8
16	Shoestring	BBC	20.7
17	Carry On Doctor	BBC	20.6
18	Shirley Bassey	BBC	20.4
19	Some Mothers Do 'Ave 'Em	BBC	20.4
20	Nine 0'Clock News	BBC	20.3

- No 7 – Eric Sykes and Hattie Jacques celebrated the 20th year of Sykes with a new series.

- No 14 – The only ITV programme to reach the charts. Transmitted week ending 18th March.

- No 17 – One of a season of Carry On films which ran this year and achieved high ratings.

1979

Eleven Week ITV Strike

It was a strike that helped ITV dominate the ratings in 1978 and a strike that helped the BBC dominate the ratings in 1979. The difference being that the BBC strike in 1978 lasted just one day and the ITV strike in 1979 lasted 11 weeks. From 10th August to 19th October ITV screens just broadcast a tasteful blue caption apologising for the lack of programmes. The strike ended with a victory for the unions and was estimated to have cost ITV £100 million in lost revenue. It was in the last weeks of the strike that the BBC achieved its highest ratings. All ten of the top programmes in the year's top 20 went out in the week ending 21st October.

To The Manor Born (1) was the only new show to make the list but it did spectacularly. Penelope Keith, at the time better known for her role as snob-next-door Margo Leadbetter in **The Good Life**, was snob-in-the-lodge Audrey Fforbes Hamilton, forced to move out of her stately home because of death duties. Peter Bowles was new monied Richard De Vere who moved into Grantley Manor under Audrey's disapproving eye.

Mastermind (5) that week came from Aberystwyth University in mid-Wales. Contenders were teacher Catherine Mason (specialist subject: Louis XIV of France), driver Ralph Handscomb (specialist subject: The James Bond novels of Ian Fleming), fitter Barry Jones (specialist subject: The Modern Summer

Vol 97 No. 44
October 25, 1979

IT'S MARVELLOUS to be back and we can't wait to tell you about the special issues we've been planning.

ITV is going to be brighter and better than ever and we've been making sure that your favourite magazine reflects the excellence of the programmes planned.

Olympics) and research assistant Philip Jenkins (specialist subject: The Development of Christianity AD 30-150) who went on to win the programme and the title that year. .

Angels (13) returned in 1979 as an early evening twice-weekly soap, produced by Julia Smith with Tony Holland as script editor (both went on to create **EastEnders**). Being a nurse at St Angela's hospital almost seemed to guarantee you a place later in Albert Square! Shirley Cheriton, Kathryn Apanowicz and Judith Jacob all went from nursing into EastEnders as Debbie Wilkins, Mags Czajkowski and Carmel Roberts. The first series of Angels back in 1976 had starred Fiona Fullerton as Patricia Rutherford, a new recruit with a private education and a rich daddy.

Coronation Street's Coming of Age party brought congratulations from all over Britain, including telegrams from some distinguished and surprising fans.

Poet Laureate John Betjeman wired: *'The Street grows richer and deeper and more lovable year by year. I thank God for it and live for Mondays and Wednesdays. May it last for centuries.'*

Another telegram read:
'Dateline: The Bull, Ambridge. Congratulations on being able to drink legally in the Rover's Return. Hope nobody gets too 'merry'. You'll be there in body as we will in spirit. Signed: The Archer family and all the regulars at the Bull.'

Travesty

*What insensitive idiot has turned **Last of the Summer Wine** into a half-hour 'comedy show', with audience participation - or canned laughter? What a travesty! Three wonderfully human characters transformed into three actors delivering punch-lines.*
Gone is the simplicity and the beauty of a once favourite half hour.

Pamela J Laidlaw
Princes Risborough, Bucks.

Radio Times
October 1979

Nearly four million extra viewers tuned in to Coronation Street to watch Brian Tilsley marry Gail Potter in November.

A YEAR IN THE SOAPS

Work Begins on Three New Soaps

Feverish work went on behind the scenes, after the Independent Television Authority announced it was looking for a new soap to put out during the day. Three new soaps were produced and tried out on the viewers in 1980 (delayed because of the ITV strike). Two ran for 13 weeks. The other was still running after 13 years.

Together, made by Southern Television, followed a group of characters living in a small block of Housing Association flats. One resident was presenter Sarah Greene as Tricia Webber. Other stars included Carol Hawkins of **Please Sir!** fame and Raymond Francis (Inspector Lockhart in **No Hiding Place**). Episodes in the first series were recorded three days before transmission – in the second and last series they went out live and Together entered television folk history. The studio canteen would empty at 1.30 as staff crowded around the TV sets waiting for the inevitable cock-ups. One story has it that the scene hands wallpapered a whole room during the commercial break.

Taff Acre, from HTV, was the Welsh Valley's answer to **Coronation Street**. The story centred around the Johnson family with Richard Davies (also of Please Sir! fame) as unemployed father Max and Rhoda Lewis as his employed wife Beth. The *Daily Mirror* called it 'breathlessly permissive and not to be missed'. Viewers thought differently.

And finally there was Scottish TV's **Take the High Road**, set in the fictional village of Glendarroch, in reality Luss. It centred around the comings and goings of the village. It was originally going to be called The Glendhu Factor (Glendhu is Gaelic for black valley and factor is the Scottish noun meaning estate manager). This was dropped because of the BBC's **Omega Factor** and Granada's **Krypton Factor** and concerns that the 'doo' might sound odd to English ears. It eventually became Take the High Road, easy to pronounce and without any 'doos' or factors.

FIRST NIGHTS

Anglia Television launched its first **Tales of the Unexpected**, based on the best-selling short stories of Roald Dahl. Tthe series was the most expensive project Anglia Television had ever taken on. Stars in that first series included Joan Collins, Sir John Gielgud, Elaine Stritch, Susan George and Timothy West.

American comedian Kelly Monteith was given his own BBC2 series written with Neil Shand.

On the game show front ITV launched **Give Us a Clue**, based on charades and hosted by Michael Aspel and the BBC gave us **Blankety Blank**.

Former Doctor Who John Pertwee hit upon the idea of adapting Barbara Euphan Todd's Worzel books for television and took the title role: **Worzel Gummage**.

Arthur Negus, the antiques expert who had found fame in the sixties with **Going For a Song**, did his first **Antiques Roadshow**.

1979

Took's
TV TEASERS

1   What were the names of the two families in the cult American comedy Soap ?

2   Geoffrey Burgon composed the theme music for Tinker, Taylor, Soldier, Spy, which reached number 56 in the music charts and stayed there for four weeks. What was it called ?

3   In a new sitcom Maureen Lipman played a problem page writer on a woman's magazine. Name her character and the series.

9.0 The Minder

DENNIS WATERMAN
GEORGE COLE

A thriller series starring Dennis Waterman as Terry, an ex-convict who must tackle a variety of difficult and dangerous bodyguard assignments arranged by his smooth boss.

Unglamorous Start For Minder

Second-hand car salesman Arthur Daley and ex-boxer Terry McCann had a quiet opening night. **Minder**, or **The Minder** as it was then called, began only a few weeks after ITV went back on air following the strike. It had no publicity. The *TV Times* gave it five lines (*see listing*) and very few people noticed it. In fact it took two years for the series to figure in the ratings. If it hadn't been for Thames Television's managing director Brian Cowgill it might not have lasted that long. ITV, unlike the BBC was not renowned for sticking with series which weren't instant hits.

1979

Blooming Good?

Richard Beckinsale played an out-of-work actor who gets a job in a florists in a new comedy series called **Bloomers**. Sadly Beckinsale never saw the series transmitted. The actor died suddenly before they recorded the final episode.

When his relations with Anna Calder-Marshall begin to wilt, Richard Beckinsale plants himself among the Bloomers to put things right: 9.30

![TV]news

• Ian Mackintosh, former Lieutenant-Commander in the Royal Navy and writer of the two TV blockbusters **Warship** and **The Sandbaggers** disappeared while crossing the Gulf of Alaska in a light aircraft. With him were his girlfriend Susan Insole and his friend British Airways pilot Graham Barber.

• Revlon lady Shelley Hack took over from Kate Jackson as one of the trio of TV crimefighters in **Charlie's Angels**. Hack, known to millions as the model in the Charlie Girl advertisements, played Tiffany Welles, daughter of a Connecticut police chief. She joined Jaclyn Smith and Cheryl Ladd.

• The Monica Sims working party on violence on television was published. New guidelines were laid down for programme makers.

• The tlevision licence fee increased to £12 for black and white sets, £34 for colour.

Fawlty TV

Fawlty Towers returned for a new series. The first series, made three years beforehand, had been shown three times in Britain and countless times all over the world. In America one channel had shown the whole lot in one evening. American television had wanted to cut some of it but John Cleese reportedly refused saying: "It's like saying to Beethoven, 'This symphony's a real treat, Ludwig, but it's 32 bars too long,'" Cleese and Connie Booth had started writing the second series in 1976 but there had been many interruptions - not least their split. Another reason why it had taken so long to come to screen, Cleese told the *Radio Times*, was because they took so long to write the scripts. 'Most 30 minute shows have about 65 pages of script. Ours are nearer 120 pages. We play it much faster than most people, so there's more to write.'

TEASER ANSWERS

1   The Tates and the Campbells.
2   'The Nunc Dimittis', it won a BAFTA award for best television theme (Geoffrey Burgon also composed the music for Brideshead Revisited in 1981).
3   Maureen Lipman played Jane Lucas in Agony. The series was devised by Anna Raeburn, then a real-life agony aunt, and Len Richmond. It ran for three years.

Only One New Hit

The only new series to make the chart this year was **Keep It In the Family (18)** an average sitcom about an average middle class family with average problems. Robert Gillespie played a cartoonist working from home. Pauline Yates was his wife and Stacy Dorning and Jenny Quayle were his daughters.

To say that the top 20 had a familiar look is an understatement. Two of the younger sitcoms were spin-offs from **Man About**

Who Shot JR?

It has to be the most successful cliff-hanger in the history of television. Who had crept up on soap's most hated man and blasted him in his own office at Ewing Towers? The question kept the world on tenterhooks, the bookies busy and T-shirt makers in business. In Britain viewers wondered, for eight months, was it half-mad Sue Ellen? Was it her sister and his mistress Kristin?

Was he dead? The truth was even the **Dallas** producers didn't know. They decided to shoot JR first and worry about it later.

In November over 20 million British viewers tuned in to find the culprit. It was Kristin, played by Bing Crosby's daughter Mary (JR recovered and had his revenge by drowning her in the South Fork swimming pool).

Took's TV Teasers

1 What in this year was claimed to be the most watched television show in the world?

2 Who told us 'You meet the nicest people on a Honda'?

3 Name Arthur's drinking haunt in Minder and where is it really located?

the House: George and Mildred (20), which had started in 1976 and **Robin's Nest (14)** which had begun in 1977. **My Wife Next Door (5)** had first appeared eight years earlier, and **The Benny Hill Show (16)** was first broadcast in 1955, which was the same year that **This Is Your Life (4)** arrived from America. **Coronation Street (8)**, was in its 20th year and as popular as ever.

Of the hit comedy acts in this year's charts, **The Two Ronnies (12)** and **Little and Large (19)** had been around for nearly a decade, **Morecambe and Wise (11)** for almost two.

Birthday Soap

In June **Coronation Street** celebrated its 2,000th edition and 20th year. Pat Phoenix adorned the front page of the *TV Times* saying inside: 'It feels like 200 years ago that Coronation Street started - and me with it.' Going on to talk about relationships and men - her estranged husband Alan Browning had died the previous year - she said: 'I feel like I am 90 per cent public property. I've got 30 million public friends but it means that most men look at me as Elsie. They expect me to turn it on strong, and I'm not like that at all.'

TV Times also published a bumper 96-page Extra which included an episode-by-episode rundown of the story to date and an 'actual' script of Coronation Street's first episode. It cost 60p.

1980

TOP TWENTY
Viewers [millions]

1	Live and Let Die	ITV	23.5
2	To the Manor Born	BBC	21.6
3	Dallas	BBC	20.3
4	This Is Your Life	ITV	19.8
5	My Wife Next Door	ITV	19.3
6	Jim'll Fix It	BBC	19.2
7	Blankety Blank	BBC	19.1
8	Coronation Street	ITV	19.0
9	The Dick Emery Show	BBC	18.9
10	All Creatures Great and Small	BBC	18.7
11	Morecambe and Wise	ITV	18.7
12	The Two Ronnies	BBC	18.6
13	Paint Your Wagon	ITV	18.5
14	Robin's Nest	ITV	18.4
15	Generation Game	BBC	18.3
16	The Benny Hill Show	ITV	18.1
17	Dick Emery Show	ITV	18.1
18	Keep It In the Family	ITV	18.1
19	Little and Large	ITV	18.1
20	George and Mildred	ITV	17.8

• No 4 – Among the guests being 'lifed' this year was Michael Aspel, later to host the show after Eamonn Andrews' death in 1987.

• No 5 – A repeat of the successful comedy starring John Alderton as George and Hannah Gordon as Suzy.

• No 13 – The New Year's afternoon film adaptation of the western musical with Clint Eastwood and Lee Marvin singing 'Wandrin' Star' and 'I Talk to the Trees'.

1980

FIRST NIGHTS

Best new comedy was **Yes Minister** starring Paul Eddington as Minister for Administrative Affairs Jim Hacker and Nigel Hawthorne as his permanent secretary Sir Humphrey Appleby. Hawthorne described the series as a 'parody of manipulation' and Hacker as 'an innocent beset by piratical civil servants'. Written by Jonathan Lynn and Antony Jay it soon became known as Prime Minister Margaret Thatcher's 'favourite programme' and picked up the BAFTA award for best comedy three years running, from 1980 to 1983. Hawthorne also won best actor in 1980 and 1981 and both he and Eddington were given CBE's in the 1986 New Year's Honours List.

The Other 'Alf saw cockney model Lorraine Chase made her acting debut as cockney model Lorraine Watts. John Standing, a real life baronet, was 'the other 'alf' upper class MP Charles Latimer.

Twenty-eight-year-old Lorraine had shot to fame as the 'Luton Airport' Campari girl, and was still taunted, unfairly, as being thick as two short planks merely because of her accent.

'People think that if you talk with a cockney accent you're a bit fick,' she pointed out in an interview. 'It's like the bird in the Luton Airport adverts. People think she's fick, but she's just the opposite. There's this mug trying to pick her up, giving this chat about "Were you truly wafted here from paradise?" You know, wot a load of rubbish. And instead of going "Ere leave it aht mate," "Knock it off," or something even stronger, she nicely says "No Luton Airport."'

ITV's **The Gentle Touch** was Britain's first TV series about a policewoman. Jill Gascoigne played London CID officer Maggie Forbes, widowed in the first episode and left to cope with the children and the career.

Juliet Bravo followed later in the year on the BBC with Stephanie Turner as Detective Inspector Jean Darbly, officer in charge of a provincial police station.

- A poll conducted by European Marketing Surveys showed that 60 per cent of television viewers thought police series were too far-fetched, 45 per cent thought they were inaccurate and 43 per cent thought they were too violent. But at least the majority of viewers preferred British to American series.
- BBC musicians went on strike in protest at the Corporations plans to axe five orchestras.
- The ITV drama documentary, **The Death of a Princess**, outraged Saudi Arabia. King Khaled cancelled his plans to visit Britain and millions of pounds were lost in exports.
- The Broadcasting Bill, which formerly gave the go-ahead for the establishment of two new channels – Channel 4 and its Welsh alternative S4C – was given the Royal Assent and became law on 13th November.
- Jeremy Isaacs, director of programmes at Thames Television, was chosen to head the new fourth channel. Other contenders for the job had been John Birt, controller of features and current affairs at London Weekend Television and Paul Bonner, former head of science and features at the BBC. Bonner was appointed channel controller, Isaacs deputy.
- Southern and Westward Television lost their IBA franchises and TV-am was awarded the contract for the new ITV breakfast service. ATV in the north was to be restructured to form Central Independent Television.

Ten thousand families applied to go on a new game show, **Family Fortunes**. But William G Stewart, the producer, still wasn't happy and wanted more to apply.

London taxi driver Fred Housego won the final of **Mastermind** and became a TV personality and presenter appearing on shows like **Blankety Blank**, **History On Your Doorstep** and **The Six O' Clock Show**.

TEASER ANSWERS

1   The Muppet Show. It had an estimated weekly audience of around 450 million.
2   Twiggy. According to the *Daily Mail* in 1980 she was among the top ten highest paid commercial earners, earning a reported £30,000 for the campaign.
3   The Winchester Club. The outside shot is of The Eton Club in Chalk Farm, North London.

NEAR MISSES

• Weekday evening ITV comedies included **Just Liz** on Mondays and **Hart of the Yard** on Wednesdays. They attracted about 15 million viewers but never made it to a second series.

• Just Liz starred Sandra Payne as Liz, a woman who's left alone to fend off suitors when her fiance takes a job abroad. Amongst those who came calling was Rodney Bewes as fussing Reg. It was written by John Esmonde and Bob Larbey the team behind **Please, Sir!**, **The Good Life** and **Get Some In**, but never really came up to scratch.

• Hart of the Yard was an American import, starring Ron Moody (remember him as Fagin in Oliver?) as Det. Roger Hart, an old-fashioned sleuth from Scotland Yard on temporary duty with the San Francisco Police Department. It was kind of Inspector Clouseau without the laughs. Hart's temporary duty in San Francisco turned out shorter than he might have hoped.

Commander Diana Dors confronting Betty and Janet (aka Ronnie Barker and Ronnie Corbett) in the final episode of the famous **Two Ronnies** sketch The Worm That Turned.

10.0 New Series
Tales of the Unexpected
JOAN COLLINS
PAULINE COLLINS
BREWSTER MASON in
A Girl Can't Always Have Everything
BY TONITA S. GARDNER, DRAMATISED BY JULIAN BOND
with JAMES FAULKNER

A further series of twist-in-the-tail dramas, based on short stories.

Witty, glamorous Suzy, siren of a touring theatre company, seeks a rich husband. When wealthy toy manufacturer Herbert appears, Suzy and her impish friend and flatmate Pat compete for the prize. But the situation develops into something frightening . . .

See Inside Television

Suzy	Joan Collins
Pat	Pauline Collins
Herbert	Brewster Mason
Patrick	James Faulkner
Grande Dame	Nancy Nevinson
Electrician	Marshall Ward
Man at airport	Ryan Michael
Stage manager	Richard Foxton
Messenger	Sylvester Williams

DESIGNER MARILYN TAYLOR : DIRECTOR GRAHAM EVANS : PRODUCER JOHN ROSENBERG : EXECUTIVE PRODUCER JOHN WOOLF
Anglia Television Production

The two Collins, Joan and Pauline, had their sights set on the same rich husband when they starred together in a **Tales of the Unexpected** as two touring rep. actresses. Both admitted to the *TV Times* that they had very little experience of the repertory circuit. 'I did nine months in Ireland in 1963 – seven nights a week, a different play every night, for £8 a week,' said Pauline. Joan's short stint was at Maidstone in 1952: 'I spent six weeks as an assistant stage manager. I remember rushing round acquiring props and playing very small roles.'

TV news

Franchise Changes

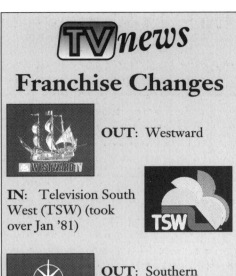

OUT: Westward

IN: Television South West (TSW) (took over Jan '81)

OUT: Southern Television

IN: Television South (TVS) (took over Jan '82)

OUT: Associated Television (ATV)

IN: Restructured form Central Independent Television (Jan '82)

IN: TV-am won breakfast franchise

1980

Two 'portable' home video systems went on sale – the Ferguson Videostar and National Panasonic 8400 costing about £1,500. Both had a large hand-held camera attached to a recorder that was larger than a briefcase.

• **The Kenny Everett Video Show** followed the **Benny Hill Show** to America. Thames TV hoped to build on Benny's success with a re-packaged series, but some of Kenny's 'naughty bits' had to be left on the cutting room floor.

• Viewers asked why David Jason was walking with a limp. He'd had a run-in with a lawn mower and his big tow had received a bit of a trim.

1981

TOP TWENTY
Viewers [millions]

1	Jaws	ITV	23.3
2	Diamonds Are Forever	ITV	22.2
3	Benny Hill Show	ITV	20.0
4	This Is Your Life	ITV	19.8
5	Coronation Street	ITV	18.8
6	To the Manor Born	BBC	17.8
7	Shelley	ITV	17.7
8	Magnum	ITV	17.6
9	Seven Dials of Mystery	ITV	17.6
10	Bergerac	BBC	17.4
11	Hart To Hart	ITV	17.4
12	ITN News	ITV	17.4
13	Last of the Summer Wine	BBC	17.0
14	London Night Out	ITV	17.0
15	Two Ronnies	BBC	17.0
16	Paul Daniels Magic Show	BBC	16.9
17	Sorry!	BBC	16.8
18	Crossroads	ITV	16.8
19	Morecambe and Wise Christmas Show	ITV	16.7
20	3 - 2 - 1	ITV	16.7

- No 1 – The 1979 Steven Speilberg epic about a man-eating shark.

- No 2 – Sean Connery's Bond in search of a diamond smuggler in Amsterdam.

- No 19 – Guests included Robert Hardy, Ralph Richardson, Alvin Stardust and Suzanne Danielle.

1981

Island Investigations

Two new detectives made the top 20 this year, both hunks, both from islands and both with women problems and smart cars.

From Hawaii was Tom Selleck as private investigator Thomas Sullivan (TS) **Magnum (8)**, a retired Naval intelligence officer who lives rent-free in a beach house in return for guarding it. The show was Selleck's eighth try at his own TV series and the one which made him big.

And from Jersey was John Nettles as Detective Sergeant Jim **Bergerac (10)**, working for the Channel Isles Bureau d' Etrangers and hindered by his frightfully rich ex-father-in-law Charlie Hungerford (Terence Alexander). Both series leapt into the charts with over 17 million viewers.

Not so hunky, but also new and popular was Ronnie Corbett's wimpy mummy's boy Timothy Lumsden in **Sorry! (17)**.

'Bankruptcy Revisited' Becomes Bankable BAFTA Winner

Brideshead Revisted may not have been the most watched programme of the year but it certainly was the most talked about. Filmed at Castle Howard in Yorkshire, it took more than two and a half years to make and cost four million pounds, more than twice what had been planned.

Filming was a catalogue of disasters. First the ITV strike in 1979 held up production. Committed to filming the **French Lieutenant's Woman** in 1980, Brideshead star Jeremy Irons ended up shuttling between productions. Everything finished late and editing was a nightmare. The newspapers predicted disaster calling it 'Bankruptcy Revisted' and 'The Curse That Visited Brideshead', among others.

An average of ten million viewers watched Brideshead – all 11 episodes and 13 hours of it. The series was nominated for 13 BAFTA awards and received seven of them, best actor for Anthony Andrews, best drama series, best design, best make-up, best film sound, best film editing and best costume design.

'I'm writing a very beautiful book, to bring tears, about the very rich, beautiful, high born people who live in palaces and have no troubles except what they make themselves and these are mainly the demons of sex and drink which after all are easy to bear as troubles go nowadays.' Evelyn Waugh, 1944.

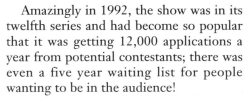

TVnews

- Angela Rippon and Anna Ford resigned from their respective jobs in the BBC and ITN newsrooms, both heading for TV-am. Selina Scott took over from Ford on **News At Ten**.
- The colour television licence went up from £34 to £46, black and white from £12 to £15.
- Scatterbrained scarecrow Worzel Gummidge was named TV personality of the year by the Variety Club.
- Small but perfectly formed ex-Tonight TV star Dudley Moore took America by storm. One Hollywood columnist cooed: 'He's so adorable, I could just tuck him under my arm and take him home.'
- The BBC and ITV companies agreed to pool resources for research into audience ratings. The Broadcasters Audience Research Board (BARB) was appointed to compile the figures for both channels.

BAFTA Awards

Judi Dench received the BAFTA best-actress award for not one but three different projects. The comedy **A Fine Romance** in which she starred with her real-life husband Michael Williams *and* the BBC play **Going Gently** *and* **The Cherry Orchard**.

Warren Mitchell began work on a new series of Alf Garnett stories but this time for ITV. The working title was 'Alf In Eastbourne' with Johnny Speight taking Garnett to a happy retirement by the sea. It went out in May called **Till Death...**

A Bullseye for Bowen

Jim Bowen is the first to admit that no-one thought **Bullseye** would last 12 minutes let alone 12 years. It all started in 1981 when Bowen, a stand-up comedian who had guested on **The Comedians**, was asked to present a British game show based around the game of darts. He claims he was the fifth choice for host. The first three turned it down and the fourth said he would check his diary.

The first two programmes were so awful they had to be scrapped, an expensive move considering a car had been won in one of the shows. "I thought I'd committed professional hari-kari," said Bowen later.

'My name is Bond, Brooke Bond' – the latest of the PG Tips chimps. The chimp campaign started in December 1956 and became the longest running in the history of television with over 100 different ads. The most famous chimp of all was Mr Shifter ('Do you know the piano's on my foot!') which entered the *Guinness Book of Records* as the most shown ad on telly – 2,000 appearances.

A modest start for the biggest TV success of the eighties, **Only Fools and Horses**, which concerned various generations of the Trotter family sharing a council flat in Peckham. Featuring Grandad (aka the late Lennard Pearce), Del Boy (David Jason) and younger brother 'Rodneeey' played by Nicholas Lyndhurst.

Jason's voice also launched another much-loved long running series this year, the children's cartoon **Dangermouse**.

Amazingly in 1992, the show was in its twelfth series and had become so popular that it was getting 12,000 applications a year from potential contestants; there was even a five year waiting list for people wanting to be in the audience!

During that time Bullseye had become cult viewing. The top ten Bullseye sayings ('super', 'smashing', 'great', 'lovely couple', 'look what you could have won') had been listed on the front cover of the trendy music magazine *New Musical Express*; Bowen played himself in a sketch on **The Laughter Show** called Chez Bullseye, set in the Bullseye household complete with a dart-board over the mantelpiece; in 1985 he was the subject of a **This Is Your Life** and finally, the ultimate accolade, **Spitting Image** made a Jim Bowen puppet.

A YEAR IN THE SOAPS

The unthinkable happened in **Crossroads**. On Monday 22nd June the nation awoke to the 'exclusive' revelation in the *Daily Mirror*: 'Noele Gordon sacked from star TV role as Meg Mortimer in Crossroads.' The tabloids went mad. The nation went into mourning. *The Star* asked its readers 'How would you get rid of Meg?' *The Sun* ran a Save Our Meg Campaign - viewers voted 25-1 in her support. But nothing could sway the men in high places at Central Television. Undercover filming went on aboard the QE2 in Southampton. The motel was burnt down and Meg was seen sailing off to a new life in New York.

1981

Took's TV TEASERS

1. What was the name of the holiday camp in Hi-de-Hi ?

2. Which role did Laurence Olivier play in Brideshead Revisited ?

3. Name the two presenters of the popular science show Where There's Life.

Royal Wedding

29th July was a big day for the Royal Family and a big day for British TV. Television coverage of the wedding of Prince Charles to Lady Diana Spencer was broadcast live to 74 countries and an estimated 750 million people tuned in across the world. In Britain the *Radio Times* and *TV Times* published special souvenir editions and 39 million people watched the event on both channels.

Commentators on the BBC were Angela Rippon and Michael Wood. On ITV it was Andrew Gardner, Selina Scott, Alastair Burnet and Ronald Allison – between them ITV and the BBC spent a million pounds on coverage.

Sales of videos doubled in the year leading up to the wedding from 700,000 to 1.5 million. In those days the viewing ratings didn't show the number of people who set their videos and watched the spectacle later.

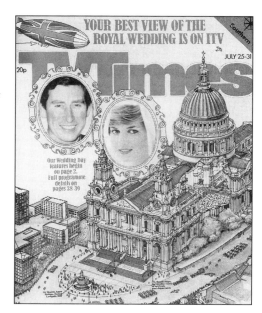

The Other Wedding of the Week

Ken Barlow married Deirdre Langton. The couple walked up the aisle on 27th of July, two days before the royals. A banner in **Coronation Street** read 'Good luck Charles and Di... and Ken and Deirdre.'

'It was a long and lovely velvet rut.' **Noele Gordon describing her time as Meg in Crossroads.**

LAST NIGHTS

Jack Hargreaves, the man who explained to 'townies' what went on in the country, finally bowed out of TV. His show, **Out of Town**, ended after 22 years. It began under the name **Gone Fishing** in 1956 and was due to run only for six weeks.

TEASER ANSWERS

1 Maplins.
2 Lord Marchmain, Sebastian's absent father.
3 Miriam Stoppard and Rob Buckman.

FIRST NIGHTS

Hill Street Blues
MICHAEL CONRAD
DANIEL J. TRAVANTI

Preview of a new series which takes a realistic look at an inner-city police precinct in America.

A teenage gang, robbery, kidnapping, drugs and explosives are all linked in this action-packed pilot episode.

See Inside Television

Sgt. Phil Esterhaus	Michael Conrad
Capt. Frank Furillo	Daniel J. Travanti
Mick Belker	Bruce Weitz
Johnny LaRue	Kiel Martin
Joyce Davenport	Veronica Hamel
Ray Calletano	Rene Enriquez
Neal Washington	Taurean Blacque
Sgt. Hunter	James Sikking
Henry Goldblume	Joe Spano
Hill	Michael Warren
Lucille Bates	Betty Thomas
Renko	Charles Haid
Hector	Ponchito Gomez
Jesus Martinez	Trinidad Silva
Woman	Veronica Redd
Girl	Eleanor McCoy

Cops, detectives and private eyes were the order of the year in 1981. Most long-lasting were the guys on the beat of the Hill Street Precinct. Creator and producer of **Hill Street Blues** was Steven Bochco whose credits included **Columbo** and **McMillan and Wife**. Television critics in the US who saw the pilot programme were so stunned by the violence and realism, that the original ending was changed before it got to the screen. The producers toned down the violence, turned up the comedy and billed it as a 'comedy drama'.

Soon viewers both sides of the Atlantic were hooked on its slick storylines and fast-cut action. Good news for the actors who were all relative newcomers and particularly good news for Veronica Hamel who played sexy lawyer Joyce Davenport. Until then she had only been famous for turning down a role in **Charlie's Angels** later offered to Jaclyn Smith.

As well as the top 20 newcommers the BBC brought us **The Chinese Detective** in the shape of Johnny Ho, played by David Yip.

Apart from the cop shows Wendy Craig created and starred in **Nanny**.

Susannah York and Ralph Bates played a divorcing couple in **Second Chance**.

Sarah Kennedy, Jeremy Beadle, Matthew Kelly and Henry Kelly were all **Game For a Laugh**, as were their contestants. The show was based on a forties American format **People Are Funny**.

ITV Dominant

Hart To Hart (3) was easy early-evening Sunday viewing. Robert Wagner was jet-setting millionaire Jonathan Hart and Stephanie Powers was his sophisticated and sexy wife Jennifer. Together with Max, the butler-cum-housekeeper, they found themselves embroiled in solving crimes and fighting evil.

Max was beautifully played by Lionel Stander – then 72 and on his sixth marriage. All his wives were 'around 20' when he married them. By now he claimed to be 'settled down'. 'I've always said no man should marry until he's over 60, and no woman until she's over 40,' he told the *TV Times*.

Robert Wagner's wife, film actress Natalie Wood, died tragically in a boating accident in November 1981. They had married for the first time in the fifties, divorced in the sixties and found each other again in the seventies.

Stephanie Powers was Wagner's first choice to play his screen wife. However, she was enjoying a colourful private life – travelling the world with actor William Holden looking for primitive and tribal art, practising her bullfighting and writing to her 22 adopted children living in an orphanage in Rome. Eventually, the scripts and Wagner's charm, convinced her to play the role of Jennifer.

Dead Ernest (14) concerned the life-after-death of one Ernest Springer played by Andrew Sachs. It was written by two **Coronation Street** writers Julian Roach and John Stevenson and was all set in heaven. This heaven had a pub – the Snake and Apple – bovver boys, nationality problems, trouble and strikes. Dead Ernest didn't survive long but Roach and Stevenson, went on to write **Brass**.

Shine On Harvey Moon (16) was Lawrence Marks and Maurice Gran's hit starring Kenneth Cranham as RAF Corporal Harvey Moon. Moon's battles began when he returned from World War Two duty in India. He couldn't find his family and everyone seemed to think he was dead. When he found the clan the series went from strength to strength and from half-hour episodes to one hour.

Perfect Plimsolls

A pair of old black canvas plimsolls helped Roy Marsden play Jack Ruskin, the lead character in **Airline**. Roy had problems visualising the part until he found the plimsolls in an old aircraft hangar at one of the locations for the series. They had obviously been worn by an early pilot. "I tried them on and immediately I got the walk and could see the character," he said. The plimsolls were stitched up and repaired and then worn throughout the filming. Roy treasured them.

Took's TV Teasers

1 Name the four main actors who appeared in The Young Ones ?

2 Which character went round chanting 'Gissa job' in Alan Bleasdale's drama series Boys From the Blackstuff ?

3 Who won a BAFTA award for her cameo role in Smiley's People ?

1982

TOP TWENTY
Viewers [millions]

1	Coronation Street	ITV	18.0
2	This Is Your Life	ITV	17.9
3	Hart To Hart	ITV	16.5
4	The Benny Hill Show	ITV	16.2
5	ITN News	ITV	16.1
6	Star Wars	ITV	16.1
7	Last of the Summer Wine	ITV	15.5
8	Moonraker	ITV	15.5
9	The Gaffer	ITV	15.5
10	Family Fortunes	ITV	15.0
11	Wish You Were Here	ITV	15.0
12	Minder	ITV	15.0
13	3 - 2 - 1	ITV	14.9
14	Dead Ernest	ITV	14.9
15	Starburst	ITV	14.7
16	Shine On Harvey Moon	ITV	14.7
17	The Fall Guy	ITV	14.5
18	The Gentle Touch	ITV	14.4
19	Nature Watch	ITV	14.2
20	Magnum Force	ITV	14.2

• No 6 – George Lucas's 1977 blockbuster starring Harrison Ford.

• No 8 – 1979 James Bond film starring Roger Moore.

• No 15 – ITV's popular Wednesday night variety show saw the likes of Bonnie Langford, Dennis Waterman, The Nolans, and Joe Longthorn topping the bill.

• No 19 – Julian Pettifer's new natural history and wildlife series.

Arthur Daley underwent a transformation in 1982. Still going strong as dodgy dealer Daley in **Minder (12)**, George Cole became Trevor Mountjoy, humourless estate agent and brother-in-law to Peter Bowles' charming ex-con Howard in **The Bounder**.

Cole described the difference between Arthur and Trevor as 'Arthur's like a windmill, arms and legs going all the time as he tries to talk his way in and out of things, while Trevor is like a lamp-post, solid and steady.'

The year also saw a new role for Daley's minder Terry McCann. Dennis Waterman turned up in June in **The Captain's Tale**, a true story about a Durham miners' football team winning the World Cup. Waterman himself had discovered the story while sitting on the loo. Buried deep in a Football Almanac was the fact that a West Auckland team

The Queen Treads the Coronation Street Cobbles

The Queen opened the real **Coronation Street** in May. For the first time in the soap's 21 year history it had a genuine, properly-built street of houses instead of a half-sized exterior set. The street cost £170,000 to build and was made from 4,000 concrete blocks and 49,000 bricks reclaimed from demolished houses in the area. The new street opened its doors to the viewing public on 7th June.

from the Northen Amateur League had beaten Juventus in Italy to win the first ever Cup back in 1910. Director Tom Clegg and writer Neville Smith took on the job of fleshing out the story and Waterman took the idea to Tyne Tees Television.

8.30
NEW SERIES
The Bounder
BY ERIC CHAPPELL

PETER BOWLES
GEORGE COLE

HE'S NOT HEAVY—HE'S MY BROTHER-IN-LAW

Comedy series about a sophisticated rogue, just released from prison after serving a sentence for embezzlement. His sister and brother-in-law hope he will turn over a new leaf. Unfortunately, he meets the widow next door — young, attractive and very rich. . . Music is by Peter Knight.

See page 8

Howard   Peter Bowles
Trevor   George Cole

10.0
The World Cup — A Captain's Tale
BY NEVILLE SMITH

DENNIS WATERMAN
RICHARD GRIFFITHS
ANDREW KEIR
NIGEL HAWTHORNE
DEREK FRANCIS

The amazing story, based on fact, of a unique sporting challenge. In 1910, Sir Thomas Lipton invited an amateur team to represent England in the first World Football Cup. These 'Men of Iron' from the West Auckland club, County Durham, were to face the might of Germany, Switzerland and Italy.

A YEAR IN THE SOAPS

Brookside was Britain's first soap to be set entirely on location. Its producers Mersey Television had bought 13 houses on a new housing estate outside Liverpool. Three houses made up the administrative offices, three were the technical block, one was used for catering and the rest were the homes of Brookside's fictional families. The first families on the Close were the Grants, headed by militant trade union official Robert Grant, who had moved up from a nearby council estate; the Collins, headed by recently redundant school headmaster Paul Collins, who had moved down from a posh house; and the newly married Huntingdons Roger and Heather who had moved out from his parents' place.

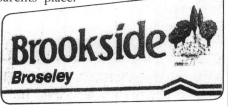

Brookside
Broseley

TV news

- Three new ITV stations - Central Television, Television South (TVS) and Television South West (TSW) – broadcast their first programmes.
- Film star Sophia Loren was sentenced to a month in prison for tax evasion.
- Sebastian Coe became the first British athlete to appear in a commercial as himself. He earned £30,000 for a series of Horlicks ads on the condition that he would not receive the money until he retired from athletics.
- Channel 4 was launched in November, a month later Home Secretary William Whitelaw voiced his concern about its 'bad language, political bias and many other undesirable qualities'.
- British Television's first three-dimensional programme, an edition of the science series **The Real World**, was broadcast – audiences watched through red and green spectacles.

TEASER ANSWERS

1   Rik Mayall, Ade Edmondson, Nigel Planer and Christopher Ryan (Alexei Sayle dropped in from time to time).
2   Bernard Hill's Yosser.
3   Beryl Reid.

FIRST NIGHTS

2 November

LATE TUESDAY

1982

4 CHANNEL FOUR

Britain's newest TV Channel

4.45
Join hostesses Beverley Isherwood (left) and Kathy Hytner on Channel Four's very first programme, *Countdown* — a quiz show that will be shown at 4.45pm every Monday to Thursday during the coming weeks.

9.0 The opening night film on Channel Four is *Walter*, starring Ian McKellen (left) and Barbara Jefford.

10.45 The Raving Beauties (above) star in tonight's late-night Channel Four revue, *In the Pink*, which traces women's attitudes from birth to middle-age through a witty potpourri of music, poetry and a little dance.

4.45 Countdown
RICHARD WHITELEY
TED MOULT
A great new quiz to launch Channel Four. *Countdown* combines entertainment and intellectual tease as it juggles letters, numbers, anagrams and sums. Contestants compete against the clock and against former *Brain of Britain* star, farmer Ted Moult and his team of statisticians and wordsmiths. It's lighthearted but educational as Ted tells us about the origins of certain words. And it's a game for the family at home — so have pens and paper ready. Presented by Richard Whiteley, *Countdown* will be on screen four nights a week from Monday to Thursday.
SCRIPT ASSOCIATES RICK VANES, JOHN JACKSON
DESIGNERS MIKE LONG, ROBERT SCOTT
DIRECTOR DEREK GOODALL
PRODUCER JOHN MEADE
EXECUTIVE PRODUCER FRANK SMITH
Yorkshire Television Production

5.15 Preview 4
Paul Coia, Olga Hubicka, David Stranks and Keith Harrison are the voices of Britain's new television channel. Tonight, they introduce themselves and some of the opening week's highlights on Channel Four.
Channel Four Presentation

5.30 The Body Show
YVONNE OCAMPO
A weekly series encouraging everyone to try some of the simpler exercises that dancers use to keep supple and healthy. Today, Yvonne introduces the basic exercise plan she will develop during the series which continues this Thursday. For a free leaflet on local opportunities to dance and keep fit, send a large SAE to: *The Body Show*, PO Box 7, London W3 6XJ. Scottish viewers only, send a large SAE to: *The Body Show*, Network, Glasgow G12.
See page 75
DIRECTOR SARAH BOSTON
PRODUCER VERONYKA BODNAREC
Fifty-One Percent Productions Ltd

6.0 People's Court
A series in which genuine legal cases, due to be tried in the Los Angeles Municipal Court, are settled out of court on a TV show. The actual plaintiffs and defendants (the real people, not actors) argue their cases before retired US Judge Joseph Wapner and agree to be bound by his decision. Today Judge Wapner rules on The Case of One Bald Tyre, and The Case of One Hot Roller Skate.

6.30 Book Four
Hermione Lee
First of a series looking at the best new books and interviewing top authors. Tonight, Len Deighton, Fay Weldon and William Boyd discuss writing about war. A booklist is available each week. Send SAE to: *Book Four*, Booklist 1, PO Box 400, Havelock Terrace, London SW8 4AU. Presented by Hermione Lee.
DIRECTOR PHILIP DRAYCOTT
PRODUCER JAMIE MUIR
EXECUTIVE PRODUCERS MELVYN BRAGG, NICK EVANS
London Weekend Television Production

7.0 Channel Four News
Peter Sissons introduces Britain's first hour-long news and news analysis programme. Godfrey Hodgson reports from Washington on key issues affecting America's mid-term elections. In London Trevor McDonald assesses other world news. Sarah Hogg presents regular expert reports on industry and finance including, tonight, Ian Ross on the final day of the CBI Conference at Eastbourne. Plus *Channel Four Comment*, an individual expression of opinion commissioned by Channel Four.
See page 24
DIRECTORS MICHAEL PIPER, ALAN RODMAN
PROGRAMME EDITORS PETER BLUFF, JOHN MAHONEY, JOHN MORRISON
EDITOR DERRIK MERCER
ITN Production

8.0 Brookside
BY PHIL REDMOND
Welcome to Brookside, a new housing estate on the outskirts of Liverpool. In the first episode of this twice-weekly serial, the Collins family are moving in — to a few unwelcome surprises and a confrontation with their new neighbours, the Grants. Another episode tomorrow.
See page 84
This week's cast:

Bobby Grant	Ricky Tomlinson
Sheila Grant	Sue Johnston
Barry Grant	Paul Usher
Damon Grant	Simon O'Brien
Karen Grant	Shelagh O'Hara
Heather Huntingdon	Amanda Burton
Roger Huntingdon	Rob Spendlove
Anabelle Collins	Doreen Sloane
Gordon Collins	Nigel Crowley
Paul Collins	Jim Wiggins
Lucy Collins	Katrin Cartlidge
Gizzmo Hawkins	Robert Smith
Ducksie Brown	Mark Birch
Matty Nolan	Tony Scoggo
Susi	Helen Murphy
Pauline	Jeanette Debs
Priest	Peter Holmes
Griff	Gary Roberts
Jacko	Paul Stanton
Fay	Michelle Edwards
Dawn	Mary Fay

DESIGNER LEIGH MALONE
DIRECTOR CHRIS CLOUGH
PRODUCER NICHOLAS PROSSER
EXECUTIVE PRODUCER PHIL REDMOND
Brookside Productions Ltd

8.30 The Paul Hogan Show
From Down Under, an irreverent mixture of humour, slapstick comedy, ugly characters and pretty girls — introduced by Australia's highest-rated television comic. Another episode on Friday.
See page 79

9.0 Film on Four
IAN McKELLEN
WALTER
BY DAVID COOK
FILM Some call Walter 'backward', some say he's 'handicapped', and others think of him as just a joke. Through the painstaking efforts of his mother, he has learned to read, write and talk a little, even to hold down a mundane job. But without the protection of his parents, the world is a harsh and terrifying place.
See page 45

Walter	Ian McKellen
Mother	Barbara Jefford
Father	Arthur Whybrow
Mr Hingley	Tony Melody
Mr Richards	David Ryall
Miss Rushden	Linda Polan
Mike	Keith Allen
Jean	Lesley Clare O'Neill
Mrs Ashby	Paul Tilbrook
Social worker	Marjorie Yates
Joseph	Jim Broadbent
Angus	Kenny Ireland
Mr Lipman	Donald McKillop
Ben Gunn	Nabil Shaban
Next bed man	Charles Lewsen
Staff nurse	Robert Walker
Male nurse	John Surman
Errol	Trevor Laird
Orderly	Robin Hooper
Dave	Stephen Petcher
Roger	Garry Cooper
Young Walter	Frankie Connolly

EDITOR MICK AUDSLEY
LIGHTING CAMERAMAN CHRIS MENGES
PRODUCER NIGEL EVANS
DIRECTOR STEPHEN FREARS
Central Production

10.15 The Comic Strip Presents...
ADRIAN EDMONDSON
DAWN FRENCH
PETER RICHARDSON
JENNIFER SAUNDERS
FIVE GO MAD IN DORSET
BY PETER RICHARDSON, PETER RICHENS
RAYMOND FRANCIS
SANDRA DORNE
First of six comedies. Four famous brats and a dog have a ripping time on their summer hols. Their self-righteous sleuthing leads them into perilous scrapes and wizard wheezes. And there's a surprise guest star.

Dick	Adrian Edmondson
George	Dawn French
Julian	Peter Richardson
Anne	Jennifer Saunders
Aunt Fanny	Sandra Dorne
Timmy	Bimbo
The inspector	Raymond Francis
The policeman	Barney Sharpe
The thugs	Ron Tarr, Nosher Powell
Shopkeeper and gipsy	Robbie Coltrane
Toby Thurlow	Daniel Peacock
Uncle Quentin	Surprise guest star

CAMERA PETER MIDDLETON
DIRECTOR BOB SPIERS
Filmworks/Comic Strip Production

10.45 In the Pink
ANNA CARTARET
SUE JONES-DAVIES
FANNY VINER
with
MILLI KOSOY GERVASI
DEE WELDING
A witty and provocative revue from the Raving Beauties celebrating women's lives through music, poetry and a little dancing. Compiled, performed and produced by women — with men in mind.
DESIGNER ANNA RIDLEY
DIRECTOR BARBARA DERKOW
PRODUCER JACKY STOLLER
Tempest Films Production

11.50 Closedown

Channel 4 Arrives

Channel 4 was launched on 2nd November, charged by an Act of Parliament to provide 'a distinctive service' and paid for by the 15 ITV companies.

The highlight of the first night was former **Crossroads** star Ronald Allen turning up as 'the surprise guest star' in The Comic Strip's Enid Blyton send up **Five Go Mad In Dorset**, shouting 'I'm a screaming homosexual, you little prigs.'

Channel 4 Top 10
w/e 7th November
Viewers [millions]

1	Brookside	4.10
2	Walter	3.75
3	Countdown	3.70
4	The Paul Hogan Show	3.50
5	Five Go Mad In Dorset	3.35
6	First Love	3.10
7	Preview 4	2.70
8	Family Special	2.15
9	The Body Show	2.10
10	The Paul Hogan Show	2.10

1983

TOP TWENTY
Viewers [millions]

1	Coronation Street	ITV	18.5
2	Superman	ITV	16.8
3	This Is Your Life	ITV	16.6
4	It'll Be Alright On the Night	ITV	16.0
5	Last of the Summer Wine	ITV	16.0
6	Jaws II	ITV	15.8
7	The Man With the Golden Gun	ITV	15.7
8	Family Fortunes	ITV	15.3
9	Miss World	ITV	15.0
10	Wish You Were Here	ITV	14.8
11	Name That tune	ITV	14.8
12	3-2-1	ITV	14.6
13	Tom, Dick and Harriet	ITV	14.6
14	The Winds of War	ITV	14.5
15	Carry On Laughing	ITV	14.4
16	London Night Out	ITV	14.4
17	Up the Elephant and Round the Castle	ITV	14.4
18	Cannon and Ball	ITV	14.4
19	The A-Team	ITV	14.3
20	On Her Majesty's Secret Service	ITV	14.3

• No 1 – Top rating episode transmitted on 23rd February, in the midst of the 'will Deirdre leave Ken for Mike?' saga.

• No 6 – Figure is just for one showing of the film. When it was repeated later in the year it gained another 13.75 million viewers.

• No 9 – Winner was Miss UK Sarah Hutt.

1983

Thin Year For the BBC

Last of the Summer Wine (5) was the only BBC top 20 hit of the year. Written by former policeman Roy Clarke it had by now been a hit for ten years. The setting was the same - the Yorkshire Dales, where three old friends, now retired, spent their days enjoying themselves and creating havoc. In 1983 Peter Sallis played former Co-op manager Clegg, Bill Owen was Compo the tramp and Brian Wilde was Foggy an ex-Army signwriter.

The Winds of War (14) was ITV's 16-hour epic mini-series, of Herman Wouk's novel shown on four successive Sunday and Monday evenings in September. It took 12 years to reach the screen, cost 65 million dollars to produce and involved 30,000 people in six countries, 267 locations, 50,000 costumes, 14 months of filming and 12 agonising months of editing the 185 hours shot into the 16 hours screened. The story focused on World War II and the exploits of Pug Henry, played by Robert Mitcham, an American naval attache based in Berlin.

Ali MacGraw played Natalie, his son's American-Jewish sweetheart. She was reportedly so upset at her American reviews that she refused to be interviewed at the time of the series' release in Britain. Victoria Tennant, in her first major TV role, played Pamela Tudsbury, a war correspondent's daughter with her eyes set on Pug.

Ace of Spies

Sam Neill, short, dark and handsome, hit the screens in September playing the title role in the Euston films drama **Reilly – Ace Of Spies**.

Monday, Wednesday: Reilly – Ace of Spies

A truly amazing life of Reilly

It's hard to believe the real-life exploits of any secret agent could match those of such fictional flights of fancy as Ian Fleming's James Bond. But earlier this century such a man, Sidney Reilly, did operate for Britain. In this edited extract from 'Reilly – Ace of Spies', Robin Bruce Lockhart, an expert on Reilly, recounts an extraordinary tale that is now dramatised in 12 parts for ITV in a story Fleming rejected as too outrageous for fiction.

The 12-part series told the true story of Sidney Reilly, born to a Jewish doctor in the late 19th century but brought up by a Russian aristocratic family. Fleeing Russia after discovering his true descendancy he joined the Secret Service to be entrusted with James Bond-style missions around the world. It had all the ingredients – love, intrigue, violence, sex, comedy but still failed to make the top.

Sam Neill was chosen for the part of Reilly after being spotted by producer Chris Burt, in Omen III. "We wanted someone with charm and sexiness yet someone whose eyes could kill," said Burt.

Wind In the Willows was the Christmas classic. Produced by animators Cosgrove Hall each model cost nearly £5,000 to make. The puppet skeletons were made of fibre glass – even the finger joints moved – and the skins were made from a specially developed rubber mixture which had to be replaced every couple of weeks. All the animals' clothes were individually designed and printed ordinary printed – fabric wouldn't have had the minute detail.

Two different sized models were needed for each character: a larger model for the interior scenes and scaled down replicas for the outside shots to give the impression that the scenes were larger than they actually were. Each model had its own animator and the whole production was shot frame by frame. The voices were provided by Richard Pearson as Mole, Ian Carmichael as Rat, David Jason as Toad and Michael Hordern as Ratty.

New Year's Honours

Broadcasting names were very much to the fore in the Queen's New Year's Honours List. Michael Hordern was given a knighthood, Max Bygraves an OBE and Jack Howarth – **Coronation Street**'s Albert Tatlock – an MBE. This made the third honour for Street stars: Violet Carson (Ena Sharples), received an OBE in 1965 and Doris Speed (Annie Walker) an MBE in 1977.

A YEAR IN THE SOAPS

Deirdre Barlow's affair with Mike Baldwin was the big soap sensation of the year. 'Will Deirdre leave Ken?' was the question on everyone's lips. 'Will Ken leave Deirdre?' 'Will Ken punch Mike?' Nearly every newspaper, even the serious ones, kept viewers up-to-date with the story-so-far.

She didn't. He didn't. Deirdre agreed to give the marriage a second chance and Ken booked a holiday in Malta.

A few months later Ken was asked to write a column for the *Weatherfield Recorder*. He agreed. A move which later led to his 'voluntary redundancy' from the Town Hall, his partnership in the newspaper and, ultimately, his affair the next year with assistant Sally Waterman.

A Year of Snap, Crackle and Pop

• 17th January – The BBC's **Breakfast Time** is launched with Frank Bough and Selina Scott taking pride of place on the red leather sofa. Diana 'Green Goddess' Moran is the exercise lady, Russell Grant tells the horoscopes and Francis Wilson tells the weather.

• 1st February – **TV-am** is launched from its hi-tech new studios in Camden Town. Peter Jay and his famous five (David Frost, Michael Parkinson, Robert Kee, Angela Rippon and Anna Ford) embark on their 'mission to explain'.
• March – Peter Jay, chairman and chief executive of TV-am resigns, Jonathan Aitken temporarily takes his place.
• April – Timothy Aitken takes over from his cousin. Anna Ford and Angela Rippon are kicked out of their jobs at TV-am by the company's financial boss Timothy Aitken.
• May – Greg Dyke is appointed from LWT as Editor-in-Chief. TV-am's viewing figures have fallen to 15 per cent of the BBC's Breakfast Time.
• June – Anna Ford throws a glass of wine over Timothy Aitken at a reception held by Lady Melchett.
• July – TV-am sees first signs of recovery. The station's share of the audience returns to 32 per cent.
• August – TV-am's share of audience

Woodentop

The Bill began as a one-off play called Woodentop, in a 1983 series called **Storyboard**. Woodentop, is the CID's nickname for anyone wearing the blue serge uniform, and the play concerned the first day on the beat for rookie PC Jimmy Carver played by Mark Wingett. It was an eventful day for Carver – first he discovered a decomposing body of an old lady in a bath, then he ran the risk of suspension when he clipped a young lad round the ear. The tearaway with a clipped ear was Gary Hailes later to find fame in **EastEnders** as Barry Clark.

Another now famous face from EastEnders in Woodentop was Peter Dean (Pete Beale) who played Sergeant Wilding. Woodentop was written by Geoff McQueen, the man behind the BBC series **Give Us a Break**, he still has his name on The Bill credits. It was directed by Peter Cregeen who had worked on nearly every other British cop series, and the producer was Michael Chapman.

goes up to 52 per cent, due to the success of Roland Rat in capturing a large children's audience during the school holidays and the popularity of new presenters Anne Diamond and Nick Owen.
• November – Fleet Holdings buys a 20 per cent stake and Kerry Packer a 10 per cent stake in TV-am.

1983

Took's TV Teasers

1 Before becoming an actor, The A-Team's Mr T was a body-guard for which former world heavy weight champion ?

2 Who took over from Paula Yates as co-presenter of Channel 4's The Tube ?

3 In which David Leyland play did Tim Roth star as a swastika-tattooed skinhead ?

1983

FIRST NIGHTS

Comedy was the order of the year – and good comedy at that.

Just Good Friends with working class Vince and middle class Penny went straight to the top of the BBC ratings when it was launched in the autumn. Paul Nicholas played the cockney hero and Jan Francis his prissy girlfriend Penny. The series was devised by John Sullivan after reading an agony column in one of his wife's magazines.

Then there was **Auf Wiedersehen Pet** about a gang of building workers who left the dole queues of Newcastle to find work in Germany. It was written by the team behind **Porridge** and **The Likely Lads**, Dick Clement and Ian La Frenais. At the time large numbers of building workers were flocking to Germany to find work and as part of their research Clement and La Frenais went to Dusseldorf with an ex-builder. On their return the man was arrested – it turned out on his last trip he had borrowed a vehicle without permission, driven it into a wall and left the country. All good source material for the series.

9.0 NEW SERIES
Auf Wiedersehen, Pet

BY DICK CLEMENT,
IAN LA FRENAIS,
FROM AN IDEA BY
FRANC RODDAM

IF I WERE A CARPENTER
The first in a drama series following the adventures of a gang of brickies in Germany. Unable to find jobs in Newcastle, three building workers make their way to Germany. Developed for television by Witzend Productions.

Channel 4 launched **Cheers**, a new US comedy from the producers of **Taxi**, set in a Boston bar. The first episode saw Diane (Shelley Long) being ditched by her fiance and Sam (Ted Danson), offering her a job as a waitress. She stayed five years.

And the BBC launched the off-beat comedy **Black Adder**, starring and co-written by Rowan Atkinson, with Brian Blessed co-starring in the first series.

Five Went Mad

'The famous five embark on an innocent holiday by the sea to stay with Mrs French at Hot Turkey Farm. On their travels – by cycle of course and laden with a picnic – they stop for ginger beers and directions. Only to be served by Janie, secret member of a cult dedicated to love, peace and drug abuse. They overhear on the radio that Uncle Quentin – scientist and homosexual – has escaped from prison – or was it **Crossroads**?

'They also learn of the strange happenings at Hot Turkey Farm and at Love Island across the water. Determined to get to the bottom of things they follow a series of clues which eventually lead to Love Island and the mysterious Dr Love and his disciples.' Yes, the Comic Strip was back a year after their debut on Channel 4's opening night. This time it was with **Five Go Mad On Mescalin** shown on Channel 4's first birthday. It didn't get within 10 million of the top 20 for the year but for the small audience who did watch it it was cult viewing.

The BBC's Spanish soap **Eldorado** was not even a glint in Auntie's eye in 1983. But over eight million viewers watched **El Dorado**, the film starring John Wayne as gunfighter Cole Thornton, when it was shown on BBC1 in August.

TV news

- The Equity dispute over actors' payments for appearing in commercials on Channel 4 continued, leading to blackouts between the programmes.
- Nearly 20 per cent of homes in the United Kingdom had video recorders, for the first time a higher percentage than other countries across the world, even Japan.
- The government ordered an inquiry into cancer around the nuclear power station Windscale, after a Yorkshire TV documentary reported the incidence of leukaemia among children in three villages close to the plant was three times the national average.
- London tube driver Christopher Hughes won **Mastermind**.
- Channel 4 launched its own teletext service called 4-Tel.
- Sir Ralph Richardson and David Niven died.

TEASER ANSWERS
1   Smokin' Joe Frazier (Mr T played B A Baracus – the B A stood for Bad Attitude).
2   Leslie Ash.
3   Made In Britain.

Women In Captivity

Tenko (12) was the story of a group of European women interned by the Japanese during the Second World War. It featured Stephanie Beacham, (later to star in **Connie** and **The Colbys**) as rape victim Rose. The idea for the series came when producer Lavinia Warner was a researcher on **This Is Your Life**. One of her subjects was Margo Turner, a brigadier general in the Queen Alexandra Royal Army Nursing Corps who was once a Japanese POW.

Her story haunted Warner who developed it into an **Omnibus** documentary **Women In Captivity** and ultimately dramatised it in Tenko. The first series shown in 1981 proved so successful that three years later the women returned for a new series covering the Allied victory and the liberation of the camps. The drama, **Tenko Reunion**, was made a year later.

• Eighty-five per cent of homes had colour television, 38 per cent had more than one set, 23 per cent had portable televisions, and six per cent were able to receive Oracle and Ceefax. Nearly one in four homes – 4,678,000 – had videos.
• Prince Andrew provided the voice over for a documentary, **Dawn To Dusk** – a day in the life of a naval officer. His commentary was written by Rosemary Anne Sissons, the writer of **Upstairs Downstairs**.

Took's TV Teasers

1 The Thorn Birds starred Richard Chamberlain and Rachel Ward. Who wrote the novel on which it was based ?

2 Which ITV comedy film saw Tim Curry play a star-struck cabbie on the run from the mafia ?

3 Who took over the role of Miss Ellie in Dallas ?

The A-Team (15) were America's group of Vietnam veterans turned vigilantes – out to do good even if in doing so they were very bad. Four years later the series was declared too violent for young viewers and taken off.

On a much softer note was **Fresh Fields (16)** with Julia McKenzie and Anton Rodgers as a scatty wife and a sensible husband, living a nice life in suburbia. They later moved to France and the series became **French Fields**.

This year a record six films featured in the top 20, seven if you include the telly movie **Lace (18)**. Four of the six went out in Christmas week: the 1964 Julie Andrews classic **Mary Poppins (10)** and Stephen Speilberg's **Raiders of the Lost Ark (4)** starring Harrison Ford both on Christmas Day; the Airport spoof **Airplane (6)** on Boxing Day and **Kramer v Kramer (7)** with Dustin Hoffman and Meryl Streep on the following Sunday.

Crash, Bang Wallop...

September... Billy Connolly, Peter Cook, Rik Mayall, Rowan Atkinson (to name but a few) descended upon the little known rural village of Nether Wallop in Hampshire for the most alternative of alternative arts festivals – **The First International Nether Wallop Festival**.

It had begun as a flippant suggestion by Stephen Pile of the *Sunday Times* ('What's wrong with holding a festival in Nether Wallop?') and two years later the fantastically bizarre idea turned into an even more fantastic fund raising reality.

The Royal Shakespeare Company's Trevor Nunn directed the village pageant in the Wallop Primary School, Wayne Sleep and the First Wallop Brownie Troupe danced a ballet about the life of the mayfly, and Bamber Gascoigne chaired the Nether Wallop versus The World's Greatest Philosophers quiz.

Charity Projects raised thousands of pounds for youth unemployment, Wallop got a new church roof, London Weekend Television got a two hour television special (shown on ITV in December) and the celebrities and Wallopians got a riotous weekend.

1984

TOP TWENTY
Viewers [millions]

1	Coronation Street	ITV	21.1
2	The Royal Variety	BBC	20.6
3	Porridge	BBC	19.4
4	Raiders of the Lost Ark	ITV	19.3
5	Miss World 1984	ITV	18.9
6	Airplane	ITV	18.1
7	Kramer vs Kramer	BBC	18.0
8	Bullseye	ITV	17.6
9	Minder	ITV	17.5
10	Mary Poppins	BBC	17.4
11	It'll Be Alright On the Night	ITV	16.9
12	Tenko	BBC	16.8
13	Duty Free	ITV	16.7
14	Thunderball	ITV	16.6
15	The A-Team	ITV	16.6
16	Fresh Fields	ITV	16.4
17	Any Which Way You Can	ITV	16.2
18	Lace	ITV	16.2
19	Give Us a Clue	ITV	16.1
20	This Is Your Life	ITV	16.1

• No 3 – A repeat of the classic comedy starring Ronnie Barker and Richard Beckinsale, which began on the BBC 10 years before.

• No 17 – The 1980 follow-up to Every Which Way You Can starring Clint Eastwood and Sondra Locke.

• No 18 – American television movie from the makers of Dallas adapted from the Shirley Conran novel.

1984

1984

FIRST NIGHTS

- The government announced its plans for a three channel Direct Broadcasting Satellite service to be set up by 1987. The BBC and ITV would be given one channel each, while a third would be awarded to a consortium consisting of Thorn EMI, Granada TV Rentals, S Pearson, Virgin Records and Consolidated Satellite Broadcasting – described as the 'Third Force'. The total cost was expected to amount to £560 million over seven years.
- A fatal heart attack ended the career of 58-year-old Eric Morecambe.
- Diana Dors died after a brave fight against cancer. And Gary Holton who played girl crazy Wayne in **Auf Wiedersehen Pet** died of a drug overdose.
- The Equity dispute over fees for actors who appeared in commercials on Channel Four and TV-am ended.
- The world saw for the first time the true horror of the Ethiopian famine. Pictures of Ethiopia's dying millions led news bulletins on 425 of the world's broadcasting organisations and reached almost a half a billion homes.
- David Hamilton-Grant, the distributor of the 'video nasty' Nightmares in a Damaged Brain was jailed for 18 months after being found guilty of possessing copies of an obscene video cassette for gain.
- In this Olympic year, ITV won the race for exclusive coverage of British athletics. They paid £15 million for an exclusive five year deal to televise all UK meetings.
- **Sportsnight** notched up its 500th edition after 16 years midweek coverage of sport. Harry Carpenter had been the presenter for nine years.

The **Spitting Image** puppet factory was born. The series that portrayed the Queen as a suburban housewife and wanted to know where President Reagan's brain had got to, offended, outraged and amused.

The show attracted 7.5 million viewers at 10 pm on a Sunday night, but at a price. The first series of 12 half hour shows cost around £2.6 million, almost twice as much per show as a prime time sitcom – so there had to be economies. No-longer-in-the-news bodies were fitted with new heads – or even melted down.

If having your own Spitting Image puppet was the ultimate accolade having it melted down was the ultimate insult.

The first Spitting Image went out at the same time Prince Philip was due to open Central Television's new Nottingham studios. The powers that be at Central were worried that the royal household would take offence at Spitting Image's portrayal and withdraw from the opening. As it happened, during the opening Philip quipped: "This is me, not one of those puppets."

The BBC phone lines were flooded with calls when viewers turned detective to help solve crimes in the first **Crimewatch UK** series. The series was based on the German programme **File XY Unsolved** which had been running for 17 years and claimed to have solved 40 per cent of its cases.

In addition to **Leaving**, Carla Lane had yet another new series this year – **As I Woke Up One Morning** – about four alcoholics in a drying out clinic.

Cilla Black returned to television with **Surprise, Surprise**.

Leslie Crowther asked members of an hysterical audience to 'Come on down' in **The Price Is Righ**t.

Lisa Goddard and Nigel Planer starred in **Roll Over Beethoven** as a piano teacher and an ex-heavy metal star.

THE LIMERICKMAN'S LIMERICK
Here's Terry in studio again
Forsaking his cheque book and pen
For laughter and chat.
If that's where you're at
Make sure to join Wogan at 10.0

Wogan

Wogan was on the box just one night a week – Saturdays at 10 pm. The Radio 2 DJ's chat show already laid claim to relaunching Cilla Black's career, putting the sparkle back into Omar Shariff's love life and putting Neil Kinnock on the path to Labour leadership.

The greatest problem facing a chat show, he told the *Radio Times* at the time, was coming up with a constant stream of new guests; 'The trouble is that there aren't that many personalities to go round. There is a small group of regulars who come on time and time again – and when you have Billy Connolly on for the fourth time, that's when you need to start worrying.' It was a problem he was to become all too familiar with when he moved to three nights a week in 1985. He took up the 7 pm slot on Mondays, Wednesdays and Fridays in February and stayed there for over seven years, 1,250 shows and some 3,000 guests.

The highest rating show featured an interview with badly burnt Falklands soldier Simon Weston. Gorden Kaye and Rory Bremner were the most frequent guests – they appeared six times each. Sue Lawley was his most frequent stand-in – others included Joanna Lumley, Anna Ford, Selina Scott, Derek Jameson, David Frost and Bruce Forsyth.

Keith Barron

Keith Barron, the man with the sexy voice who sold us Lux soap, was seen in two new sitcoms this year – on both channels, at the same time.

On ITV he was lusting after Linda in **Duty Free** and on the BBC he was equally unlucky in love in Carla Lane's **Leaving**.

How was he coping with the stardom? Stardom was not a word in the Barron vocabulary. "It's a word that should be reserved for someone of Sinatra's stature," he said at the time.

Barron delivered one line in an early episode of **The Avengers** going on to play Detective Sergeant Swift in **The Odd Man** and the angry young Nigel Barton in the two award-winning Dennis Potter plays **Vote, Vote, Vote for Nigel Barton** and **Stand Up For Nigel Barton**.

By the eighties he was the king of voice-overs – including eight years as the voice of the Andrex puppy ad. Later in the eighties he played a television station tyrant in **Room At the Bottom** (ITV 1986) and a lovelorn taxi-driver in **Take Me Home** (BBC 1989).

A YEAR IN THE SOAPS

1984

In **Emmerdale** Jack Sugden was being a naughty boy. After two and a half years of marriage to Pat, the hard-working farmer with a roving eye, was having a steamy affair with auctioneer Karen Moore. And all this while Pat was pregnant. How could he? The hate mail poured in.

Off-screen Clive Hornby who played Jack had just married his on-screen wife, Helen Weir. At the time of the on-screen affair Weir was really pregnant. The couple had planned that after the birth their off-screen baby would become their on-screen baby. That probably would have happened if they hadn't called the little boy Thomas. Weir was determined that the boy should have the same name on and off-screen. Unfortunately Thomas would not do for television – Pat would never have named her son after her hated ex-husband Tom Merrick. A row ensued, another little boy got the role of Robert and Pat was bumped off in a hit-and-run road accident.

• Elsie Tanner left **Coronation Street** to begin a new life in Portugal with old flame Bill Gregory. And Bert Tilsley and Stan Ogden died.

1985

TOP TWENTY
Viewers [millions]

1	EastEnders	BBC	23.6
2	Coronation Street	ITV	21.4
3	Wish You Were Here	ITV	19.0
4	Open All Hours	BBC	19.0
5	Last of the Summer Wine	ITV	18.8
6	Prince and Princess of Wales	ITV	18.6
7	It'll Be Alright/Night	ITV	18.6
8	That's Life	BBC	18.4
9	The Two Ronnies	BBC	18.5
10	Crossroads	ITV	18.1
11	Hollywood Wives	ITV	18.0
12	Boxing	ITV	18.0
13	Night of 100 Stars	ITV	17.7
14	Game For a Laugh	ITV	17.6
15	Superman II	ITV	17.6
16	Fresh Fields	ITV	17.5
17	Dr No	ITV	17.5
18	From Russia With Love	ITV	17.3
19	Goldfinger	ITV	17.0
20	Only Fools and Horses	BBC	16.9

• No 1 – This was the Boxing Day edition of the soap, repeated the following Sunday. The viewing figure is a total of both showings.

• No 6 – An interview with Alastair Burnet (before he became a Sir), the first full interview since the couple's wedding in 1981.

• No 12 – Barry Mcguigan beat Panamanian Eusebio Pedroza for the world featherweight title.

G..G..G..Granville

It took nine years for Ronnie Barker's Arkwright and David Jason's G..G..G.. Granville to make the top 20. **Open All Hours (4)** first opened the doors of Arkwright stores in 1976.

Written especially for Barker by Roy Clarke (**Last Of The Summer Wine**), it was taken off in 1984 to make way for another Clarke/Barker show, **The Magnificent Evans** about a small-town photographer in Wales. It failed and Open All Hours was brought back to great acclaim.

Barker was well established in the Top 20 as the rounder one of **The Two Ronnies (9)**, also writing for the series under the name Gerald Wiley. This year's chart topper was the first of a new series, shown on Christmas day. Phil Collins was the special guest.

Crossroads (10) by the end of the year was a new-look Crossroads. A new set, a new location, and a new managing director, Nicola Freeman (Gabriel Drake). The Hunters went off to run a hotel in Bermuda and never again was the soap to boast ratings of 18 million.

Hollywood Wives (11) was American television's three-part adaptation of the Jackie Collins novel starring Candice Bergen, Anthony Hopkins, Rod Steiger and Stefanie Powers. When it was shown in the UK a technician accidentally missed out one of the rolls of film – a crucial few minutes near the end of the five hours were never shown. Did anyone notice?

A YEAR IN THE SOAPS

On 19th of February at 7 pm Britain witnessed the birth of a new soap, the BBC's long awaited answer to **Coronation Street**. It was set in 'typical' Albert Square in the fictional London Borough of Walford. The model was Fassett Square in the London Borough of Hackney. A replica had been built at the old Elstree film studios, bought by the BBC the year before. They decided against East 8 and London Pride and called it **EastEnders**.

• In **Brookside** fireman George Jackson (Cliff Howells) was put away after being framed for a warehouse robbery. Brookside fans daubed 'Jackson is Innocent' and 'Free George Jackson' slogans throughout Liverpool.

• Among the stars at the National Theatre for **Night of 100 Stars (13)** were Les Dennis and Dustin Gee, Jimmy Tarbuck, Gary Wilmot, Bella Emberg, Bonny Langford and Lena Zavaroni. Guest of honour was Princess Anne and money was raised went to The Save the Children Fund.
ª Nine hundred years after the Domesday Book was started, the BBC began the **Domesday Project**. Using computer and laser disc technology, one million people were to help compile a 'picture' of twentieth century Britain for future generations to read.
• Sue Nicholls who joined **Coronation Street** as a regular in 1985 as Audrey Roberts is actually the Honourable Susan Frances Harmer Nicholls, daughter of Lord and Lady Harmer Nicholls of Staffordshire. She shares her life with Mark Eden who, as the Street's Alan Bradley, tried to kill Rita Fairclough in 1989.

FIRST NIGHTS

The 'Street of Shame' was the subject of two new dramas:
Hold the Back Page starring David Warner as Ken Wordsworth a sports writer who transfered from a quality Sunday to a daily tabloid; and **Lytton's Diary** with Peter Bowles as a Nigel Dempster-style gossip columnist (LWT at the time was also making **Hot Metal** a Fleet Street satire featuring Robert Hardy in his first comic role).

Stephanie Beacham played **Connie**, the bitch of the rag-trade, a role which led to American stardom as super rich bitch Sable Colby in **The Colbys**. Pam Ferris, later to become roly-poly Ma Larkin in **The Darling Buds of May**, played Connie's half-sister Nesta.

America brought us the **Miami Vice** squad in the shape of Crockett (Don Johnson) and Tubbs (Phillip Michael Thomas). They gave the world a new dress code: designer suits with T-shirts, Docksiders without socks, and constant facial stubble.

Britain hit back, halfway at least, with **Dempsey and Makepeace**, a mid-Atlantic mishmash. Michael Brandon was a thuggish New York Lieutenant Dempsey on reluctant attachment to Britain and Glynis Barber was Makepeace, the British half, an upper-class blonde with a degree and a titled daddy.

Alf Garnett (Warren Mitchell) returned **In Sickness and In Health** the long-delayed follow-up to **Til Death Us Do Part**. Dandy Nichols, forced into a wheelchair by arthritis, was also back as his down trodden wife Elsie, the 'silly old moo'. Was the humour old hat'? Apparently not – the series went straight into the charts.

Anna Karen (remember her as Olive in **On The Buses**?) starred in **Troubles and Strife** as Rosita, leader of a group of church wives all a flutter at the arrival of a handsome vicar (Stephen Pacey).

Tracey Ullman, Dawn French, Jennifer Saunders and Ruby Wax shared a flat in **Girls On Top**.

In **Happy Families** Jennifer Saunders played a 79-year-old grandmother and her four granddaughters, the youngest aged 26.

Bodymatters used audience participation, colourful models and flashing lights to help the layman understand everything from osteo-arthritis to why we blush.

Worth 16p Per Day

It may not have reached the millions but the few that did watch BBC2's trilogy Oscar in March loved it. The *Radio Times* letters pages were positively brimming with praise for Michael Gambon's 'most moving and personal' performance. It even made paying the licence fee OK:

Michael Gambon's acting was nothing less than inspired, particularly during the poignant scenes in Pentonville Prison, and for his personal anguish throughout. All concerned, from the supporting actors to Carl Davis with his haunting music, made it a production to rank with the BBC's finest.

Even with the licence fee at £58 per year, it was well worth the requisite 16p daily cost. To have seen such a masterpiece in the cinema would, of course, have cost at least £2 (a fortnight's viewing).

Alan Buttery, Rothwell, West Yorkshire.

Well said!

In the quiz world Noel Edmunds discovered **Telly Addicts** on the BBC and Julian Pettifer conducted **Busman's Holiday** on ITV.

Dirty Den

Only a few days after **EastEnders** was launched the newspapers found themselves an even bigger story – actor Leslie Grantham, who played the villainous 'Dirty' Den Watts, landlord of the Queen Vic, was a convicted murderer. He had served a life sentence – 11 years – for the murder of a taxi-driver while a soldier in Germany.

Grantham couldn't get outside his front door for reporters. He was paying yet again for his crime, and for soap stardom. He earned respect from the viewers, and from many members of the press for the way he handled it.

Grantham was 19 at the time of the sentence. Whilst in prison he became an actor and after his release in 1978 he trained at the Webber Douglas Academy, where he met his future wife Jane Laurie. After some television bit parts, he auditioned for EastEnders, initially for the role of Pete Beale. He was hired for six months for what was then seen as a minor role – Dirty Den. He stayed four years.

Grantham never did understand why Den was so loved. "I think Den is the most piggish man ever," he said later.

1985

Took's TV Teasers

1 Writer Carla Lane, the lady behind BBC comedies from Butterflies to Bread had two new series this year. What were they called ?

2 Who promoted Holsten Pils with a series of commercials using old black and white film clips ?

3 Where was the fictional setting for the BBC's Dynasty-style yachting saga Howard's Way ?

TVnews

- Thames Television tried to pinch **Dallas** from the BBC by offering £10,000 more per episode. Michael Grade, Controller of BBC1, called it an 'act of vandalism, breaking a gentlemen's agreement.' After a year-long squabble Thames gave it back.
- One and a half billion people in 160 countries watched the **Band Aid** concerts on television. The BBC's six hour extravaganza helped raise £40 million for Africa's famine-stricken poor. And Thames Television launched a 24-hour **Telethon** raising 2.5 million from homes in the London region.
- TV and radio journalists went on strike in protest against the banning of the BBC's **Real Lives** programme about Republican and Protestant extremists in Northern Ireland.
- The cost of a colour television licence increased from £46 to £58, a black and white licence from £15 to £18.
- BBC changed its logo for a revolving globe, revolutionised the weather with electronic graphics, and revamped the early evening schedule.

John Smiths Bitter won best commercial and best campaign

- John Smith's Bitter commercials scooped the prizes at the British Television Advertising Awards.
- Terry Wogan, the voice of early morning Radio 2 became the face of early evening BBC1. His reported salary for the thrice-weekly stint was £350,000 a year.
- EastEnders was launched.

1985

Nuclear Waste and Drugs Busts

The BBC's big BAFTA award-winner was **Edge Of Darkness** on BBC2, starring Bob Peck as Ronald Craven, a widowed Yorkshire detective who lost his beloved and beautiful daughter Emma (Joanne Whalley) to a loony gunman. Or so it seemed in the first episode. As he searched for his daughter's killers (with the help of Emma who kept turning up as a ghost) he realised just how little he knew her. In the beginning it was the vibrator and the automatic pistol in the knicker drawer, by the end it was raids on nuclear power plants.

Edge of Darkness was written by **Z-Cars** creator Troy Kennedy Martin and produced by Michael Wearing whose credits include **Boys From The Blackstuff**. Labour's shadow social services minister Michael Meacher appeared as himself speaking on the subject of nuclear energy.

On the other side (and to the detriment of both in the ratings) was ITV's **Operation Julie**, a drama reconstruction of one of the biggest drug busts to hit the headlines in the seventies.

Colin Blakely played Inspector Dick Lee, the policeman whose memoirs were the basis for the drama.

Edge Of Darkness was nominated for 11 BAFTAs and won six of them – best drama series, best actor for Peck, best original tv music, best film cameraman, best film sound and best film editing. Operation Julie was not even nominated for one.

TEASER ANSWERS

1   The Mistress starring Felicity Kendal and As I Woke Up One Morning about four alcoholics in a drying out clinic.
2   Griff Rhys Jones.
3   Tarrant (in reality Bursledon on the River Hamble, Hampshire).

Omnibus began its tenth series with a programme devoted to Tony Hancock. It celebrated his golden years in the late fifties with memories from his co-stars and clips from favourite shows.

1986

TOP TWENTY
Viewers [millions]

1	EastEnders	BBC	30.2
2	Just Good Friends	BBC	20.8
3	Only Fools and Horses	BBC	18.8
4	Coronation Street	ITV	18.7
5	Prince and Princess	ITV	18.4
6	Boxing	BBC	18.3
7	Blind Date	ITV	18.2
8	Last of the Summer Wine	BBC	18.1
9	People Do the Funniest Things	ITV	17.8
10	Duty Free	ITV	17.4
11	You Only Live Twice	ITV	17.3
12	Royal Variety	ITV	17.2
13	Late, Late Breakfast Show	BBC	16.8
14	Officer and a Gentleman	ITV	16.4
15	Russ Abbot's Xmas	BBC	16.1
16	Surprise, Surprise	ITV	15.9
17	Clash of the Titans	BBC	15.9
18	Dear John	ITV	15.6
19	Yanks	ITV	15.5
20	The Grand National	BBC	15.4

• No 1 – The Boxing Day edition of EastEnders, repeated the following Sunday – again the figure is a total of both showings.

• No 5 – A year in the life of the Prince and Princess of Wales presented by Alastair Burnet and transmitted over two nights.

• No 6 – American Steve Cruz took the world featherweight title from Irish champion Barry McGuigan.

Familiarity Breeds Ratings

Three out of the four BBC sitcoms to make this year's list were old favourites.

Vince and Penny, aka Paul Nicholas and Jan Francis, became more than **Just Good Friends (2)** in the ratings-winning Christmas Special which saw the couple get married.

Only Fools and Horses (3) was in its fifth year. Del Boy (David Jason) and Rodney (Nicholas Lyndhurst) had reached cult status. 'Right plonker' had entered the vocabulary. The 1985 Christmas Special made number 20 in the charts and every episode of the 1986 autumn run challenged the soaps **Coronation Street** and **EastEnders**.

Last of the Summer Wine (8) was no stranger to the top 20 but even that had taken eight years to really hit the big time.

Dear John (18) on the other hand had started that spring and jumped straight in. The story of wet teacher John (played by Ralph Bates) attending a weird singles group seemed to strike a comic nerve. Both Dear John and Just Good Friends were written by John Sullivan.

The Late, Late Breakfast Show (13) was Noel Edmonds early Saturday evening stunts and silliness show. It began in 1982 and ended tragically in 1986 after 25-year-old Michael Lush was killed when a Whirly Wheeler stunt went wrong.

Took's TV Teasers

1   Miami Vice heart-throb Don Johnson released a record which reached Number 46 in the British pop charts in November. What was it called ?

2   In which action series did Boy George make his American television debut in an episode called Cowboy George ?

3   Who starred as Maddie Hayes and David Addison in the American detective agency series Moonlighting ?

1986

FIRST NIGHTS

The BBC launched **Casualty**, a gritty new drama set around the night shift of a busy general hospital casualty department. It was set in the fictional city of Holby but much of the research was done at Bristol's Royal Infirmary. Writers Jeremy Brook and Paul Unwin got the idea after both being in hospital – Brook with colitis and Unwin after a car crash. 'We wanted it to be about a night shift because that's when a city chucks up its worst oddities,' Brook told the *Radio Times*.

The other BBC success story of the year was **Lovejoy** starring Ian McShane as the lovable East Anglian antiques dealer.

Hot Metal saw Robert Hardy as Terence 'Twiggy' Rathbone – ruthless tycoon buys failing quality newspaper – disaster soon follows.

Pat Phoenix became Phyllis Nugent a typical seaside landlady in **Constant Hot Water**.

John Thaw took on the role Henry Willows, a troubled father whose teenage son (Reece Dinsdale) had come **Home To Roost**.

Penelope Keith and Geoffrey Palmer played husband and wife publishers Caroline and Donald Fairchild in **Executive Stress**.

Brits abroad included Edward Woodward who became **The Equalizer** and Stephanie Beacham who joined the rich bitch set of **The Colbys**.

British television made stars out of former Labour MP Robert Kilroy-Silk; and would-be producer Jonathan Ross, who couldn't find a presenter for his new show **The Last Resort** so he did it himself.

NEW SERIES
7.50-8.40 Casualty

First of a 15-part series
1: *Gas*
by JEREMY BROCK
and PAUL UNWIN
Saturday evening in the Casualty Department of Holby City Hospital. It's a routine shift for the eight heroes – then there's an explosion at the docks.

Dannie	EMMA WATSON
Ralph	TREVOR COOPER
Charlie	DEREK THOMPSON
Susie	DEBBIE ROZA
Duffy	CATHERINE SHIPTON
Ewart	BERNARD GALLAGHER
Parker	ROGER OSTIME
Baz	JULIA WATSON
Robert Palmer	AL ASHTON
Kuba	CHRISTOPHER ROZYCKI
King	GEORGE HARRIS
Mrs Jones	JULIETTE GRASSBY
Sophie Jones	MADELEINE NASH
Mr Cartwright	BRIAN HAINES
Starchy Harris	PHIL MCCALL
Megan	BRENDA FRICKER
Ponting	ROBERT PUGH
Mute	LISA BOWERMAN
Brenner	COLIN FISHER
Mrs Price	NANCIE HERROD
Relative of Mrs Price	ROY EVANS
Television journalist	HELEN GWYN

9.30 Lovejoy
starring
Ian McShane as Lovejoy
in
Friends, Romans and Enemies
by IAN LA FRENAIS
with
Phyllis Logan as Lady Jane
Dudley Sutton as Tinker
Malcolm Tierney as Gimbert
Chris Jury as Eric
Junk or otherwise, death invariably yields up a fresh supply of objects to the antique trade. But old James Bexon saw everything in pairs, and Lovejoy's own life could be at stake.

Nicole	CATHERINE STRAUSS
Edward	BURNELL TUCKER
Amanda	CASSIE STUART
Helen	JO ROSS
Dandy Jack	GEOFFREY BATEMAN
Kate	CHARLOTTE EDWARDS
Bigelow	DENYS GRAHAM
Mrs Springer	FREDA DOWIE
Curator	SHEILA KEITH
Brian	ANTHONY JACKSON
Det Sgt Hill	PAUL ANTRIM

Created for television by
IAN LA FRENAIS
From the *Lovejoy* books by
JONATHAN GASH
Film editor RAY WINGROVE
Designer KEN LEDSHAM
Photographer COLIN MUNN
Producer ROBERT BANKS STEWART

Lady Jane (Phyllis Logan) joins antiques dealer Lovejoy (Ian McShane) who knows the value of the genuine article
BBC1 9.30 pm Lovejoy

• Conservative MP Matthew Parris resigned his seat in Parliament to take over as presenter of Weekend World. He replaced Brian Walden who had also been an MP before resigning to host the current affairs programme.

• Channel Four introduced on-screen triangles to warn viewers that 'special discretion was required' during movies of a violent or sexual nature. Rather than put people off, it actually boosted ratings for the films.

• John McCarthy, the television journalist, was kidnapped in Beirut and held captive for five years.

A YEAR IN THE SOAPS

Neighbours was introduced into Britain in October as part of the BBC's new daytime schedule. In Australia it had had a nervous start. Dropped from Channel 7, moved to Channel 10 with a major facelift, Neighbours only took off after much publicity hype.

The man behind Neighbours was former **Crossroads** creator and producer Reg Watson, an Australian who returned home in the seventies to shape **The Young Doctors**, **Sons and Daughters** and **Prisoner Cell Block H**. The theme tune was written by Tony Hatch who had also been responsible for the original Crossroads theme.

Giotto, the European spacecraft was heading towards an encounter with Halley's Comet. It was to send back live pictures as it passed through the Comet's tail.

TEASER ANSWERS

1   'Heartbeat' (It stayed in the pop charts for five weeks).
2   The A-Team (he appeared as himself as a kidnap victim).
3   Cybill Shepherd and Bruce Willis. According to newspaper reports they didn't get on off-screen as well as on. Willis had wanted his real wife Demi Moore to play Maddie.

Duty Free

Duty Free (10) was the wonderfully tacky sitcom about two couples on a package holiday in Spain. One critic described it as 'pathetic cardboard characters on a pathetic cardboard holiday'. It seems viewers had a penchant for cardboard. The holiday had already lasted three years and every episode featured high in the charts. All the shows to date had been recorded at Yorkshire Television's studios in Leeds but for this year's Christmas Special 'A Duty Free Christmas' four of the show's five stars, Joanna Van Gysegham (Linda), Keith Barron (David), Neil Stacy (Robert) and Carlos Douglas (Carlos the waiter), actually went to Spain. For the first time they were able to bring back some duty frees.

Compo, Clegg and... Seymour?

*I enjoyed the **Last of the Summer Wine** film Uncle of the Bride on New Year's Day very much, but I did miss Foggy, whose pedantic ways were such a wonderful foil to Clegg's quiet wit and Compo's exuberance.*

I can appreciate that Foggy is enjoying decorating eggs on the front at Bridlington, where he may even be able to exercise his signwriting talents. But please, what is the real reason for his leaving the series and will we see him back?

(Mrs) Mary E H Smith, London

Radio Times, 25-31 January 1986

TVnews

- The Independent Television Authority turned down a proposal that schools programmes should be transferred to Channel 4.
- The Peacock Report into alternative ways of financing the BBC was published.
- Conservative Party Chairman Norman Tebbit blasted the BBC for alleged political bias in its news coverage and in particular a Panorama programme on the US bombing of Libya.
- British Satellite Broadcasting (BSB) – a consortium including the Virgin Group, Granada TV, Anglia TV, Pearsons and Amstrad Consumer Electronics – was awarded the British DBS franchise. It undertook to spend at least £100 million on programmes in its first year.
- South Africa declared a state of emergency – TV coverage was limited.
- The BBC launched its new daytime schedule providing 1,000 extra hours a year at a cost of £8 million.
- *TV Times* readers voted the Oxo family the best ad on telly, for the second year running. The campaign had started with Kate and Philip (Mary Holland and Peter Moynihan) in the fifties and ran for 18 years until 1974. It was relaunched nine years

later with Linda Bellingham as Mum and Michael Redfern as Dad and

proved just as popular the second time round.

1986

1987

1987

TOP TWENTY
Viewers [millions]

1	EastEnders	BBC	27.1
2	Coronation Street	ITV	19.4
3	Question of Sport	BBC	19.0
4	Grand It's a Knockout	BBC	18.3
5	Children In Need	BBC	17.2
6	Don't Wait Up	BBC	16.7
7	Love Bug	ITV	16.6
8	Bruno v Bugner	ITV	16.3
9	Bread	BBC	16.0
10	Bergerac	BBC	15.8
11	Three Up, Two Down	BBC	15.6
12	Blind Date	ITV	15.4
13	Murder In Three Acts	ITV	15.3
14	The Palladium	ITV	15.2
15	Clive James On TV	ITV	15.1
16	Never Say Never Again	ITV	15.0
17	Aspel and Company	ITV	14.9
18	Wish You Were Here	ITV	14.8
19	Dr No	ITV	14.8
20	Inspector Morse	ITV	14.8

• No 7 – Disney's classic about the thinking Volkswagen was shown on New Year's Day.

• No 13 – Peter Ustinov played Hercule Poirot. From the book Three Act Tragedy, the film also starred Tony Curtis and Emma Samms.

• No 14 – Jimmy Tarbuck hosted this new series, the first night included Tom Jones, Bob Carolgees, Brian Conley and Five Star.

• No 16 – The 1983 Bond remake of Thunderball with Sean Connery and Kim Bassinger.

Royalty Bumps Up the Ratings

Princess Anne joined **A Question of Sport (3)** in February for its 2,000th edition resulting in it soaring to third place in the chart with over 19 million viewers. The appeal was short-lived however. A week later when **Treasure Hunt** began a new series opposite on Channel 4 the weekly sports quiz settled back to its average ratings of around 12 million viewers. The first A Question of Sport back in 1970 was introduced by David Vine with Henry Cooper and David Coleman as team captains. By 1987 Coleman was in the chair with team captains Emlyn Hughes and Bill Beaumont.

The Royals boosted the ratings again in June when over 18 million viewers tuned in for **The Grand Knockout Tournament (4)**. The team captains were Prince Edward, on behalf of the Duke Of Edinburgh's International Project '87; Princess Anne on behalf of the Save The Children Fund; Prince Andrew on behalf of the World Wildlife Fund and Fergie for the International Year of Shelter For the Homeless.

The Grand Knockout Tournament

Presenters Les Dawson, Su Pollard and Stuart Hall

HRH The Prince Edward captains his team on behalf of the Duke of Edinburgh's International Project 87.

HRH The Princess Anne captains her team on behalf of the Save The Children Fund.

HRH The Duke of York captains his team on behalf of the World Wildlife Fund.

HRH The Duchess of York captains her team on behalf of International Year of Shelter for the Homeless.

FIRST NIGHTS

The Two of Us saw ITV pluck Nicholas Lyndhurst from the BBC's **Only Fools and Horses**, change his name from Rodney to Ashley, and plonk him in a flat with a live-in girlfriend called Elaine, played by Janet Dibley. It proved unbelievably successful.

Rik Mayall became Alan B'Stard in **The New Statesman**, a rampant right-wing MP who gained his seat by arranging for his opponent to be maimed in a car crash.

The Roxy was ITV's first network chart show, and the first real challenger to **Top of the Pops**, which had been running for 23 years. It used independent local radio (ILR) charts and was set in a 1940s dance hall brought up to date with glaring neons.

New series from America included **LA Law** – a kind of **Hill Street Blues** in court – and **Highway To Heaven**, with Michael Landon.

A YEAR IN THE SOAPS

Brookside invented the Soap Bubble. Damon Grant (Simon O'Brien) met freckly schoolgirl Debbie McGrath (played by Gillian Kearney) and fell in love. By November the two lovers had done a runner – out of Brookside Close, out of Brookside itself and into their own three-part series **Damon and Debbie**. It was called a soap 'bubble' because it floated away from the main soap, though the two story-lines continued to run simultaneously. While the run-aways were seeking their fortune in York, Damon's parents Sheila and Bobby were seen worrying themselves sick in Brookside. The series ended in tragedy with Damon being stabbed to death.

Yarns

A wool shop in Tunbridge Wells was the setting for **Exclusive Yarns** starring Leslie Joseph, Maureen Lipman and Patricia Hodge. Joseph was Pippa, the self-made businesswoman who owned the shop, Hodge was elegant and inebriated Estelle, who ran the local nanny agency and Lipman was eccentric and neurotic Tamara, owner of Tapioca's restaurant. The play was one of the **First Sight** season on Channel 4, which introduced new writers to television.

EXCLUSIVE YARNS

On Channel 4
Sunday 12 July at 9.15pm

TVS

Project Yankee told the story of Richard Branson's trip across the Atlantic by hot-air balloon. The trip ended when the balloon ditched in the Irish Sea.

Soap War

Coronation Street (2) beat **EastEnders (1)** at its own game in Christmas week by broadcasting its first omnibus edition on the Sunday. Both soaps had an extra Friday episode and both soaps repeated the Friday episode on the Sunday. Adding both these figures together shows Coronation Street on top by over a million viewers.

Coronation Street's winning episode saw Hilda Ogden (Jean Alexander) leave hospital and leave the Street – she accepted an invitation from Dr Lowther to become his housekeeper in his new home.

However it didn't manage to topple EastEnders from the top spot in the yearly ratings. A record 27 million viewers tuned in to the EastEnders omnibus in the second week of the year.

Took's TV Teasers

1 Inspector Morse's side-kick Sgt Lewis is played by Kevin Whatley. In what cult comedy did he make his name and which character did he play?

2 Which advertiser claimed to 'take the grind out of ground coffee'?

3 Who played Skullion the porter in the TV adaptation of Tom Sharpe's Porterhouse Blue?

TV news

- Special Branch raided the BBC offices in Glasgow removing research material used for Duncan Campbell's banned **Secret Society** programme about the secret Sircon spy satellite.
- BBC Director General Alisdair Milne resigned.
- Clean Up TV campaigner Mary Whitehouse called **EastEnders** a 'peril' to viewers and their children after gay characters Barry and Colin were seen embracing on screen. BBC managing director Bill Cotton hit back saying Whitehouse was living in 'cloud cuckoo land'.
- Esther Rantzen won the Richard Dimbleby award for her campaigning work against child abuse.
- Comedian Jimmy Tarbuck left his long running game show **Winner Takes All** to host **Tarby's Frame Game** – a word game for married couples.
- Les Dennis took over as host of **Family Fortunes**. He followed in the footsteps of Bob Monkhouse and Max Bygraves.
- **Saint & Greavsie** hosts Ian St John and Jimmy Greaves published a book of soccer memories and stories called *Football Is a Funny Game*.

1987

Morse Code

Newcomer of the year and immediate chart entry was the television adaptation of Colin Dexter's classic **Inspector Morse (20)** books with John Thaw in the title role.

Part-time, Dexter compiled crosswords and for three years running was *The Observer's* crossword clue-writing champion – Morse was named after a fellow champion, Sir Jeremy Morse, chairman of Lloyds Bank. In fact all the surnames in Dexter's first novel were drawn from the list of *Observer* Crossword prizewinners. All except the murderers.

Morse was a poetic type, a lover of opera, real ale and classic cars. In the original books he drove a Lancia but the producers of the television series felt an old Jaguar was more suitable. The red Jag became so closely identified with the Oxford detective that in later editions of the novels Dexter replaced the Lancia with a red Jaguar *(see extracts)*.

Morse's passion for booze led to Beamish Stout sponsoring the series five years later. Viewers watched to see if Morse would change his drink from real ale to stout. He didn't.

1987

The case of the red Jaguar

A young, very wet traffic warden, the yellow band round her hat extremely new, was standing beside the Lancia, trying bravely to write down something on a bedrenched page of her notebook.

'All right, aren't I?' mumbled Morse defensively, as he walked down the shallow steps of the church towards her.

'You're over the white line and you'll have to back it up a bit. You've plenty of room.'

The Dead of Jericho, MacMillan 1981

A young, very wet traffic warden, the yellow band round her hat extremely new, was standing beside the Jaguar, trying bravely to write down something on a bedrenched page of her notebook.

'All right, aren't I?' mumbled Morse defensively, as he walked down the shallow steps of the church towards her.

'You're over the white line and you'll have to back it up a bit. You've plenty of room.'

The Dead of Jericho, MacMillan 1991

Colour Change

Blondes may have more fun but brunettes are taken much more seriously. Or so says Fiona Fullerton. When the former Bond girl and star of the BBC's **Angels** took on the role of Clarice Mannors in **The Charmer** she changed her hair colour from blonde to brunette and found that people were much more ready to listen to what she had to say.

The Charmer of the title was Nigel Havers, who at the time was also playing Tony Britton's son in the gentlemanly comedy **Don't Wait Up (6)**.

LWT hadn't banked on The Charmer being such a success (it got average audiences of about 13 million and hovered around No 10 in the charts) and regretted sticking to the plot and killing off the hero at the end of the series.

TEASER ANSWERS

1 Neville (the drippy one) in Auf Wiedersehen, Pet.
2 Brooke Bond Red Mountain.
3 David Jason.

When did Lynch of the Rovers marry Gilroy of the Graffiti Club? The answer: Wednesday 9th September 1987 – Elizabeth Theresa Lynch of the Rovers Return became Alec Gilroy.

'doing great, ta'

Bread (2) was in its second year, second in the charts and 'doing great, ta'. Carla Lane's story featured the Boswells, a large Liverpool family with no 'bread'.

It survived two major cast changes – Graham Bickley, replaced Peter Howitt as eldest son Joey and Melanie Hill replaced Gilly Coman as Aveline – and eventually finished in 1991.

The shows from Nos 10 to 13 in the charts featured as part of the BBC's **Comic Relief** night on Friday 5th February, which attracted an average of 10.6 million for the whole seven hours.

8.50 pm
Bread

Written by CARLA LANE
The story of the Boswells, a family of lovable rogues, their unity, loyalty and ability to survive in today's world of unemployment with the help of a little gentle skulduggery.
Mrs Boswell ....JEAN BOHT
Adrian Boswell
               JONATHON MORRIS
Joey Boswell .....PETER HOWITT
Aveline Boswell..GILLY COMAN
Jack Boswell ..VICTOR MCGUIRE
Julie ....CAROLINE MILMOE
Billy Boswell .....NICK CONWAY
Grandad.......KENNETH WALLER
Mr Kelly ....EDDIE ROSS
DHSS clerk ......PAMELA POWER
Boy.........................BEN DAVIS
DHSS claimants
       JOSIE KIDD, JAN DAVIES
Van driver ....TONY SCOGGO
Title song by DAVID MACKAY
Directed by SUSAN BELBIN
Produced by ROBIN NASH *(R)*

Wood, Walters and Wise (10) featured a selection of classic comedy sketches chosen by Radio 1 listeners and saw Victoria Wood, Julie Walters and Ernie Wise live in the Comic Relief studio.

COMIC RELIEF
BBC1 7.35pm-3.35am

Question of Sport/Spitting Image (11) saw the real Mike Gatting, Barry McGuigan, Daley Thomspon and David Coleman taking revenge on their Spitting Image puppets.

Dad's Army (12) was a vintage edition called The Royal Train introduced by Jimmy Perry.

Jasper Carrot Meets Blackadder (13) featured Jasper Carrot and a Blackadder Special, Blackadder – The Cavalier Years.

That's Life (14) with Esther Rantzen often features among the BBC's weekly top ten programmes. But after 15 years this is its first appearance in the annual top 20. This was the year the show launched a helpline for children suffering sexual and other kinds of abuse.

Took's TV Teasers

1 Name the actor and actress who played the new neighbours meeting over a cuppa in Gold Blend's advertising 'soap'.

2 Which award-winning series saw Ray McAnally play left wing Prime Minister Harry Perkins?

3 In Coronation Street what did Don Brennan accept in payment for a 30-mile taxi ride?

1988

TOP TWENTY
Viewers [millions]

1	EastEnders	BBC	24.5
2	Bread	BBC	21.0
3	Neighbours	BBC	18.7
4	Coronation Street	ITV	18.1
5	For Your Eyes Only	ITV	17.8
6	News	BBC	17.3
7	Last of the Summer Wine	BBC	17.1
8	'Allo, 'Allo	BBC	17.1
9	Only Fools and Horses	BBC	16.6
10	Wood, Walters and Wise	BBC	16.6
11	Question of Sport/ Spitting Image	BBC	16.4
12	Dad's Army	BBC	16.4
13	Blackadder Meets Jasper Carrot	BBC	15.9
14	That's Life	BBC	15.9
15	Octopussy	ITV	15.9
16	Santa Claus the Movie	BBC	15.6
17	The Man With the Golden Gun	ITV	15.4
18	Lift Off	BBC	15.2
19	This Is Your Life	ITV	15.1
20	Blind Date	ITV	14.9

• No 3 – Figure is lunch-time showing plus late-afternoon repeat. An average of Monday to Friday figures.

• No 5, 15 & 17 – All three Bond films starred Roger Moore.

• No 16 – 1984 film starring Dudley Moore.

1988

TV news

- In the US television evangelist Jimmy Swaggart fell from grace after admitting having had meetings with a prostitute.
- The BBC was criticised by the South African Government for televising a concert held to celebrate the 70th birthday of Nelson Mandela.
- The Defence Secretary George Younger attempted to persuade the BBC to make changes to **Tumbledown**, its drama about the Falklands War. The film was eventually transmitted minus two minutes.
- Health standards at BBC Broadcasting House were attacked after an outbreak of Legionnaires disease.
- Gay rights activists invaded the BBC **Six O'Clock News** studios. Sue Lawley read on as Nicholas Witchell battled off camera.
- Out went Saturday afternoon wrestling on ITV. In came Japanese sumo wrestling on Channel 4.
- George Cole played a character not unlike Arthur Daley in a commercial for the Leeds Permanent Building Society. Other building societies complained to the IBA.

1988

For the 1988 Seoul Olympics the Japanese TV company Panasonic, the main sponsor of the Games, introduced bar code video. With a special light-pen viewers could with one stroke programme their (Panasonic) video to automatically record the live coverage which was broadcast in the early hours of the morning in the UK.

The bar code shown above was for the opening ceremony transmitted at 0130 to 0500 on 17th September 1988.

TEASER ANSWERS
1. Anthony Head and Sharon Maughan.
2. A Very British Coup. It won a BAFTA for best drama.
3. A greyhound called Harry's Luck.

A YEAR IN THE SOAPS

On Easter Monday **Crossroads** came to an end after more than 23 years and 4,510 episodes.

Tommy 'Bomber' Lancaster, Terence Rigby, had decided to sell-up and Jill Chance, nee Richardson had to make a choice. Would she return to estranged husband Adam Chance, Tony Adams, who was trying to buy the place and wanted her back or would she go off with the landlord of the local pub, honest but poor John Maddington, Jeremy Nicholas? Nearly 13 million viewers tuned in to the bumper edition to find out. It turned out a bad day for Adam – Nicola Freeman's stepson Daniel, Philip Goodhew, took the hotel from under him and Jill went off with John in his sports car. The *TV Times* published a souvenir special of Jill's memories of the motel and Jane Rossington, the only member of the original cast to stay with the soap until the bitter end, published a book of her memories, *The Crossroads Years*.

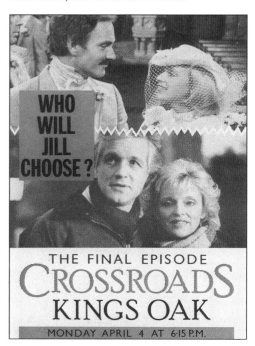

A Cat, a Dog and a Mouse...

A cat, a dog and a mouse, in harmony in front of a blazing Real Fire provided the theme for the best-loved commercial of the year. Viewers demanded to know if it was camera trickery. It wasn't. But it took hundreds of takes to get it just right. The cat and the dog were OK but life became downright dangerous for the mouse.

The Sexiest Man On TV

In the summer, the 'sexiest' man on TV left the small screen to become a star on the big one. Tom Selleck said goodbye to the beach house, Ferrari and Hawaii detective **Magnum**. The role had brought him success and fame in the 90 countries where the series was shown. He had been named Entertainer of the Year, favourite male star, sexiest man on TV... and so on. The film that brought him big screen fame was shown across Britain that summer as well – Three Men and a Baby, which also starred Steve Guttenburg and another TV favourite, Ted Danson from **Cheers**.

Maigret returned to the TV screen in the shape of Richard Harris playing the pipe-smoking French detective.

Goodbye To '88

The last programme of 1988 on ITV was **Cilla's Goodbye To '88**. And it was the first New Year's Eve extravaganza to be pre-recorded. At 30 seconds to midnight the recording was 'switched off' and the programme went live to Westminster for Big Ben's midnight chimes. Then it was back to the recording and a studio full of celebrating stars.

- Ringo Starr stoked up an old children's favourite by providing the voice for the series **Thomas the Tank Engine** which was written 40 years earlier by the Reverend Wilbert Vere Awdry.
- ITV staged the first network **Telethon**. Michael Aspel was the national host for the massive 27 hour programme which raised £22 million.

NEAR MISSES

Ruth Rendell's Chief Inspector Reg Wexford was based on two other writers' characters – George Simenon's Maigret and a detective called Fred Fellowes created by American mystery writer Hillary Waugh. He was called Reg after her favourite uncle and Wexford because she was on holiday in Ireland when she wrote the first book. George Baker took on the television role in 1987 and after that Rendell always thought of him as Wexford when she wrote a new book. Baker and Christopher Ravenscroft, who

played Detective Inspector Mike Burden, did 19 Wexford adaptations in five years – they ran out of novels in 1992.

Vision On

The comedy series **After Henry** was the first in a long line of BBC Radio Four hits that were snaffled by ITV and Channel Four from under the noses of BBC TV. Its two stars, Prunella Scales and Joan Sanderson, along with the scripts by Simon Brett, also made the switch. The long running **News Quiz** became the Channel Four award-winning hit **Have I Got News For You**. And the improvisation show **Whose Line Is It Anyway** went in the same direction. Two other successful sitcoms also made the transition with more or less the same stars and plots: **Second Thoughts** and **Up the Garden Path**.

Michael Caine returned to British television to lead the investigation into the **Jack the Ripper** murders as Inspector Frederick Abberline. The two hour drama was produced by the makers of **Minder**, Euston Films, and claimed to throw new light on who did it. They reckoned it was Sir William Gull, Queen Victoria's surgeon, played by Ray McAnally.

Kirstie Alley replaced Shelley Long in **Cheers** playing Rebecca, the Boston bar's new manager. Predictably she also replaced Diane in Sam's affections.

The two Rons, Gareth Hale and Norman Pace, two former PE teachers turned comedians were given their own series **The Management** on Channel 4.

ITV launched its own sports quiz called **Sporting Triangles** which was hosted by Nick Owen with Jimmy Greaves and Tessa Sanderson as team captains.

Colin's Sandwich was billed as a 'Hancock for the eighties'. Mel Smith starred in the six-part comedy series written by two of the writers on **Not the Nine O'Clock News** and **Alias Smith and Jones**, Paul Smith and Terry Kyan. It told the story of an under-achieving British Rail clerk who dreams of being a writer.

Wyatt's Watchdogs starred Brian Wilde, the softie warder in **Porridge** and Trevor Bannister from **Are You Being Served?** as residents forming a cross between a neighbourhood watch scheme and a local vigilante group.

Are you sitting comfortably? Lots of viewers were for a new series from Muppet creator Jim Henson which began in May. **The Storyteller** featured a combination of actors and fantasy creatures re-telling famous folk tales.

The storyteller himself was played by John Hurt. He had to be in the studio at five in the morning for a two hour make-up session, then it was on set for filming until eight at night – all spent in a wig with a rubber nose, ears and cheeks glued to his face.

1988

1989

TOP TWENTY
Viewers [millions]

1	Coronation Street	ITV	24.4
2	EastEnders	BBC	24.1
3	Crocodile Dundee	BBC	21.8
4	Neighbours	BBC	20.1
5	Only Fools and Horses	BBC	20.1
6	Tyson v Bruno	BBC	17.9
7	Bread	BBC	16.5
8	Blind Date	ITV	16.2
9	Forever Green	ITV	15.7
10	Royal Variety Performance	ITV	15.5
11	The Man With the Golden Gun	ITV	15.5
12	Inspector Morse	ITV	15.5
13	Beadle's About	ITV	15.2
14	The Heroes	ITV	15.1
15	This Is Your Life	ITV	15.1
16	Russ Abbot Christmas Show	BBC	15.0
17	A Bit of a Do	ITV	14.8
18	'Allo, 'Allo	BBC	14.7
19	The Good Life	BBC	14.7
20	Tanamera	ITV	14.5

• No 1 – Back at the top of the charts, but only just, after introducing a weekly Sunday omnibus repeat in February.

• No 3 – First showing of the Paul Hogan Aussie blockbuster.

• No 6 – Frank Bruno failed in his bid for the World Heavyweight Championship, after losing to America's Mike Tyson in the fifth round.

1989

My Husband and I

ITV had an immediate hit on its hands with **Forever Green (9)** on Sunday nights starring husband and wife team Pauline Collins and John Alderton. They played Jack and Harriet Boult a married couple who gave up the pressures of London life for a run-down cottage in the country. It was their fifth television series together, the others being **Upstairs, Downstairs**; **No, Honestly**; **Yes Honestly**; and **Thomas and Sarah**. The series jumped straight into the top 20 charts with over 15 and a half million avid viewers.

Another immediate hit was Yorkshire Television's comedy drama **A Bit of a Do (17)**, which centred around a series of social gatherings of two incompatible Northern families only brought together because of the first 'Do' – the marriage of Jenny, only daughter of snobbish dentist Laurence Rodenhurst and his wife Liz, to Paul, unkempt younger son of socially inferior iron foundry boss Ted Simcock and his wife. David Jason and Nicola Pagett led the all-star cast. Pagett who, like Collins and Alderton, shot to fame in Upstairs, Downstairs, claimed she owed the role to Diana Rigg, who was offered it first and turned it down. Other 'Dos' included the Dentists' Dance, the Angling Club Christmas do, a charity do and the Miss Cock-a-Doodle Chicken do.

Both **The Heroes (14)** and **Tanamera – Lion of Singapore (20)** were ITV co-productions with Australian companies.

The Heroes, was a true World War II adventure starring **Neighbours** heart-throb Jason Donovan as the youngest of 14 men who sailed 5,000 miles from Cairns across the Indian Ocean to Singapore harbour in a leaky Japanese fishing boat to blow up the Japanese navy. The fishing boat used was an exact replica of the real boat used for 'Operation Jaywick' – the problem was it had to

accommodate not only the 14 actors but a 30-strong film crew. So the wooden clad boat was mounted on a steel pontoon that became a floating set.

In Tanamera, Singapore's colonial past was recreated on the hills overlooking Sydney harbour. It was based on the book by former *Daily Mail* foreign correspondent Noel Barber and centred on the forbidden love affair between an Asian woman and an English man, both the offspring of rich and powerful families.

Coronation Street was looking for a new moggie for its opening titles and 5,000 applied. After exhaustive auditions they chose Frisky a pretty tortoiseshell who is seen basking on the roof three times a week.

• Prime Minister Margaret Thatcher rejected an independent inquiry clearing Thames Television of criticisms against its **Death On The Rock** documentary.

• Rupert Murdoch launched Sky Television's first four satellite channels.

• Newspapers claimed Jimmy Savile had had his legs insured for one million pounds against injury in the London Marathon.

• Lightning strikes blacked out BBC programmes as the unions campaigned for an improved pay offer. The three month dispute was resolved after staff were offered an 8.8 per cent increase.

• Comedian Ken Dodd was cleared of eight charges of tax fraud after a trial lasting 23 days.

• A court ruled that a television viewer who claimed he only watched Sky television did not need a television licence.

• Madonna was paid £3 million to appear in a Pepsi commercial. The ad was dropped after its theme 'Like a Prayer' was attacked for being blasphemous.

• Newsreader Gordon Honeycombe retired from newsreading when he left TV-am. He had first joined ITN in 1965.

• After experiments televising the House of Lords, the Commons finally allowed TV cameras into Parliament with the debate following the State Opening.

A Day In the Life

A two-hour experimental documentary on ITV in November was hailed as a unique TV event. The TV companies turned the cameras in on themselves for the biggest ever look behind the scenes.

One Day In the Life of Television used over 50 film and tape crews to see programmes of all kinds in the making, and then watched the public's reaction to them in private houses, pubs, army barracks – even Dartmoor prison! A book about the experiment was also published.

Among the millions who tuned in to watch **A Bit of a Do** was Mr Arthur White. He described himself as David Jason's biggest fan – because he is David's older brother. Although their paths never cross professionally, Arthur is also a busy actor – and the man who encouraged David into acting – 'We're a very close family," said Arthur, "and great mates."

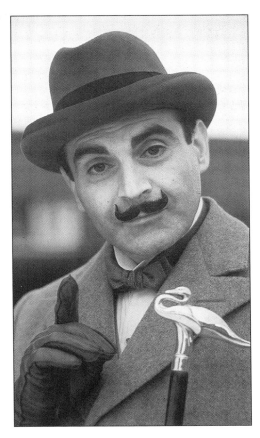

• David Suchet, donned a waxed moustache and took on the role of Agatha Christie's Belgian sleuth Hercule **Poirot**. The series jumped straight into the charts with over 14 million viewers, and the classical actor who had found popular fame in **Blott On the Landscape**, was on his way to becoming the Poirot of all Poirots. The secret of becoming Poirot, he said, was in the moustache which was freshly waxed and curled every time it was put on.

• Meanwhile over at ITN brother John Suchet moved from **SuperChannel News** to **News At 12.30** in May.

Ben Kingsley played Nazi hunter Simon Wiesenthal in a four-hour mini-series based on Wiesenthal's memoirs called **Murderers Among Us**. Wiesenthal – who lost 89 members of his and his wife's family through Nazi Germany's persecution of the Jews had himself survived a dozen labour camps and two execution squads – was 80 at the time the film was made and had dedicated his life to tracking down and bringing to justice the people who perpetrated the Holocaust. Kingsley spent two days with him in Vienna before filming began. "Within ten minutes we were crying together." Kingsley said. As well as looking similar the two men also shared the same birthday – 31st December – although Kingsley was born in 1943, and Wiesenthal in 1908. "I felt he was a man who could jump into my skin" said Wiesenthal. "He asked me such detailed questions, I knew he understood me and could make a good Wiesenthal." He was right.

1989

Took's TV Teasers

1 Who sang the theme tune for ITV's A Bit of a Do ?

2 From what did impressionist Bobby Davro take his surname ?

3 What was the name of Britain's first teletext soap ?

Aussies Push Out Neighbours

Move over Kylie, **Home and Away** is here to get its own back. In Australia Home and Away had been developed by Channel 7, who had originally dumped **Neighbours** in 1985. It was bought by ITV, to counter Neighbours' spectacular success on the BBC.

The idea for the series came after producer Alan Bateman stopped in a small Australian country town and found the community divided by the building of a foster home to house city kids. In the series the foster home is a run-down caravan park in the fictional Summer Bay somewhere up the coast from Sydney. Foster parents Tom and Pippa Fletcher couldn't have kids of their own and moved there after Tom lost his job in the city. After a couple of years Pippa miraculously had a baby, Tom died in a car accident, and Vanessa Downing, who played Pippa, left the show. Pippa remained, but she looked very different.

Stars to be wooed from Neighbours included Guy Pearce (Mike in Neighbours, David in Home and Away) and Craig McLachlan (Henry in Neighbours, Grant in Home and Away).

1989

Dirty Den Watts, former landlord of the Queen Vic leaves Dickens Hill prison for his trial, in which he faces arson charges for burning down the Dagmar pub. For actor Leslie Grantham Den's time inside meant he could work elsewhere. He turned up later as boxing promoter Eddie Burt in ITV's **Winners and Losers** and club owner Danny Kane in BBC's **Paradise Club**. Den was eventually killed off at the hands of local gangsters.

Judi Dench began **Behaving Badly** as Bridget in a four-part Channel 4 drama. Bridget's husband Mark, Ronald Pickup, had left her for a younger woman and she had moved out of their London home and behaved beautifully – until she decided behaving badly was much more fun.

The man with whom she behaved badly was her daughter's gay flat-mate, played by Douglas Hodge, who later in the year turned up as smoothie heart-throb Declan in **Capital City**, the senior trader at Shane Longman merchant bank. The critics didn't really like Capital City and viewers didn't really understand it.

Other newcomers included Barber and Duffy, two agents for **Saracen** systems, a security company dealing in protection and counter terrorism. Christian Burgess was Barber, a former SAS major and Jimmy Clarke was Duffy, formerly of the US army's Delta Force.

Dennis Waterman and Jan Francis teamed up for **Stay Lucky**, which centred on the personality clash between cockney 'wide-boy' Thomas Gynn and northerner Sally Hardcastle.

Keith Barron went serious in **Take Me Home** as a taxi-driver who fell in love with one of his lifts; Simon Dutton had a short spell as the newest **Saint**; and fast-talking quick-witted barrister Clive Anderson was given his own show **Clive Anderson Talks Back**.

Last, but hopefully not least, **TV Weekly** began.

TEASER ANSWERS

1   George Melly.
2   From his father's hardware store, which in turn had been named after Bobby and brother David (David = Dav / Robert = ro).
3   Park Avenue.

Power to Change MPs' Loos

Sitcoms usually take at least a year to get really good ratings. That is unless they star Penelope Keith. At a time when repeats of **To the Manor Born** were still pulling in 10 million viewers, nearly 14 and a half million viewers tuned in to the first episode of **No Job For a Lady (20)** in February as Keith made her first appearance as Labour MP Jean Price.

In the event the show became only memorable for changing the toilet arrangements in the House of Commons – by making fun of the lack of a ladies' loo for female MPs. The Mother of Parliaments was rapidly equipped with one.

Watching (18) starred Emma Wray and Paul Brown as Brenda and Malcolm, two bird-watching ex-lovers ('Let me spell it out. Malcolm Stoneway is my "ex", with a capital "X"') who can't stop watching each other.

Michael Barrymore's game show **Strike It Lucky (19)** was into its fifth series. The format meant that the quiz could be won in two minutes or 25 minutes. To accommodate this Michael Barrymore's introductory interviews, a feature of the show, were recorded at length and cut to fit. And 'at length' meant just that. One Scottish farmer talked and read poetry for 90 minutes. Barrymore and the studio audience loved it, though the viewers at home only saw two minutes of it. It was Barrymore's success with his Strike It Lucky guests that led to him being snapped up for his own series **Barrymore**, in 1991.

NEAR MISSES

• If **Spycatcher** was the beginning, **The Piglet Files** was the absolute end. Nicholas Lyndhurst was Peter Chapman (codename: Piglet), a senior lecturer in electronics who found himself unwittingly recruited by MI5 to instruct their field agents in the use of high technology equipment.
• In **El CID**, Alfred Molina and John Bird played Blake and Bromley, two Scotland Yard detectives who handed in their handcuffs for some private investigating on the Costa Del Sol. By the third series in 1992 Molina was committed to other projects and Amanda Redman joined the cast as Bromley's estranged daughter Ross.
• Other programmes just outside the charts included Rowan Atkinson's **Mr Bean**; John Nettles' **Bergerac**; the sitcom **The Upper Hand** with Joe McGann as an ex-footballer turned housekeeper; and the drama series **Stolen** which gripped the nation early in the year on Friday nights as we waited to see if Cheryl Prime would get her children back from Art Malik.

Took's TV TEASERS

1 Michael Parker is the real name of which game show host?

2 Who played Dr Henry Jekyll in ITV's £4 million film adaptation of Robert Louis Stevenson's classic horror?

3 Which soap stars celebrated their 25th wedding anniversary in an episode in September?

ITV and the BBC shared the 1990 World Cup football – covering alternate matches.

Germany beat Argentina 1-0 in the final on the Sunday night, watched by over 13 million viewers.

Top Five World Cup 1990 Matches			Viewers [millions]
1 England v Germany	4 July	BBC	16.7
2 England v Eire	11 June	ITV	16.0
3 England v Cameroon	1 July	BBC	15.7
4 England v Egypt	21 June	BBC	15.3
5 England v Belgium	26 June	BBC	13.3

1990

TOP TWENTY
Viewers [millions]

1	Coronation Street	ITV	22.8
2	EastEnders	BBC	20.8
3	Neighbours	BBC	20.6
4	Only Fools and Horses	BBC	18.0
5	It'll Be Alright On the Night	ITV	17.9
6	E.T.	BBC	17.5
7	A View To a Kill	ITV	16.9
8	Generation Game	BBC	16.7
9	World Cup W Germany v England	BBC	16.7
10	News and Weather	BBC	16.6
11	Inspector Morse	ITV	16.2
12	Octopussy	ITV	15.9
13	Blind Date	ITV	15.8
14	Wish You Were Here	ITV	15.8
15	This Is Your Life	ITV	15.7
16	The Bill	ITV	15.3
17	For Your Eyes Only	ITV	15.2
18	Watching	ITV	14.8
19	Strike It Lucky	ITV	14.6
20	Bergerac	BBC	14.2

• No 5 – The sixth in Dennis Norden's series of ITV television blunders – shown 2nd December.

• No 6 – Steven Spielberg's modern fairytale about a young boy's friendship with an extra-terrestrial.

• No 7 – Roger Moore's last Bond, made in 1985 and featuring Grace Jones.

• No 9 – The World Cup features four times in the Top 20. This list shows only the highest rated match.

1990

FIRST NIGHTS

One Foot In the Grave was best new sitcom of the year. Richard Wilson was

Top to bottom Keith Barron, Reece Dinsdale and Sam Kelly in **Haggard**.

Victor Meldrew, 60 years old, temperamental and faced with early retirement: 'I feel officially a lower form of life than a Duracell battery.' Annette Crosbie played his poor wife Margaret. The series was written by David Renwick and went from strength to strength.

From the pen of Roy Clarke, the man behind **Last of the Summer Wine**, came **Keeping Up Appearances** with Patricia Routledge as Hyacinth Bucket (pronounced 'Bouquet').

Rising Damp writer Eric Chappell turned from contemporary people and problems to costume capers with **Haggard**, inspired by the *Daily Telegraph* column Squire Haggard's Diary. Keith Barron played the 18th century squire given to drink, wenching and the accumulation of debt. And Haggard junior was Reece Dinsdale last seen as the husband of the girl Barron was having an affair with in **Take Me Home**.

Dennis Waterman turned up in a comedy as a self-made man **On the Up** but not sure how to cope with it all.

A Sense of Guilt, starred Trevor Eve as obsessive writer Felix Cramer, who seemed, by the end, to have had an affair with almost everyone in the cast. The most scandalous being with his best friend's daughter Sally, played by Beryl Bainbridge's daughter Rudi Davies. Like a good book you couldn't put it down.

Peter Bowles and Bryan Murray were **Perfect Scoundrels**: a suave, sophisticated but down-on-his-luck Englishman and a smooth-talking quick-thinking Irish conman. The two actors came up with the idea while standing in muddy fields waiting for filming to start on The Irish RM.

Hugh Laurie and Stephen Fry were bumbling Bertie Wooster and unflappable Percy Jeeves in **Jeeves and Wooster**. Fry particularly was a great fan

of PG Wodehouse. He wrote to the author when he was a young lad of eight, and Wodehouse, then in his eighties, replied with a short note and a signed photograph. Fry kept the photograph with him during filming as a good luck token.

Waterfront Beat was the BBC's answer to **The Bill**, except that it was set in Liverpool, not London.

And **The $64,000 Question** was: why on earth did they bring back this fifties game show? Bob Monkhouse replaced original host Jerry Desmond and the set was hi-tech, even space age.

Twenty four years after it boldly appeared, a new series of **Star Trek** arrived. **Star Trek: the Next Generation** starring Patrick Stewart went into orbit with a brand new crew and a mark two Enterprise.

A YEAR IN THE SOAPS

Families

Hitting back at the success of the Aussie soaps Granada Television had the bright idea of launching a new daytime soap – **Families** – set half in Australia and half in England. Mike Thompson, played by Malcolm Stoddard, was the link. He was running a garage in Cheshire when a mid-life crisis led him to walk out on his wife and three children in pursuit of his first love, Diana Stevens, recently widowed in Sydney. Diana was played by British-born Australian actress Briony Behets, a veteran of Aussie soap having featured in everything from **Prisoner Cell Block H** to **Neighbours**.

Families was a complicated project. All the exterior Australian scenes were shot in Sydney and the corresponding interior scenes recreated in Manchester many months later. For make-up it meant reproducing the exact shade of tan when they were back in England. For props, everything, down to the Australian crisp packets, had to be shipped to Britain.

By 1992 most of the original cast of Families had moved on, exhausted no doubt!

TEASER ANSWERS

1   Michael Barrymore. He changed his name because the actors' union Equity had another Mike Parker on its lists.
2   Michael Caine.
3   Pauline and Arthur Fowler in EastEnders.

Chancer

Heart-throb of the year was 25-year-old newcomer Clive Owen who played city business analyst Steven Crane in **Chancer**, a 13-part series brimming with fast cars, money, romance and boardroom battles. Owen's character was a city whizz kid called up to Manchester to sort out an ailing family car business. According to one critic he made Dirty Den and JR look like mummy's boys.

But the real star of the show was Leslie Phillips, Crane's old boss, city financier Jimmy Blake, 'a smooth-talking manipulator being a total villain'.

Phillips was also the star of three other shows this year: two **Comic Strip** films playing Horace Cutler and the Dean of Oxford and a **World In Action** drama **Who Bombed Birmingham** about the Birmingham Six court case in which he played Lord Lane. In his seventies Leslie Phillips saw his career take on a new dimension with powerful screen roles which even overtook his immense talent for comedy.

> • The comedian who had given the nation a new catch phrase – loadsa-money – won his own series. **The Harry Enfield Television Programme** saw Enfield saying goodbye to Stavros and the flash plasterer with the bulging wad. But in came the Double Take Brothers, Mr 'You Didn't Want To Do That', Little Brother and The Old Gits.
> • Who killed Laura Palmer? After weeks of watching **Twin Peaks** become increasingly more bizarre, viewers that stayed with it discovered that it was Bob the alien spirit who did the deed.

Two of the many faces of Maureen Lipman in **About Face**, a series of half-hour plays written by her husband Jack Rosenthal. Other faces included a loo attendant in a posh London nightclub, an American stage manager at a provincial theatre, the long-suffering wife of a politician and a dowdy telephonist who blossomed into a passionate flamenco dancer.

1990

TVnews

- The BBC announced that it would make savings of £75 million by 1993 as part of a radical re-organisation plan.
- Two firsts for ITN Newscaster Trevor McDonald: He was the first British broadcaster to interview Nelson Mandela on his release from prison and the first to interview Saddam Hussein after his invasion of Kuwait. The BBC hit out at ITN for agreeing to transmit Hussein's interview unedited.
- Rowan Atkinson as **Mr Bean** won the Golden Rose of Montreux award. Britain picked up all the light entertainment awards except the bronze which went to Finland. Atkinson was also given the 1989 BAFTA best comedy award for **Blackadder Goes Forth**. John Thaw won best actor for **Morse** and the Channel 4 drugs drama **Traffik** received best drama series.
- Sir Alastair Burnet resigned as director of ITN following a clash with the company over future ownership. He continued as anchorman of **News At Ten** for a further 18 months.
- The battle of the satellite dishes ended when BSB merged with Sky TV. BSB had been beset by delays and problems with its squarial and just had not attracted enough viewers.

1991

TOP TWENTY
Viewers [millions]

1	Coronation Street	ITV	21.5
2	EastEnders	BBC	21.0
3	Neighbours	BBC	19.4
4	Only Fools and Horses	BBC	18.9
5	London's Burning	ITV	18.7
6	Darling Buds of May	ITV	18.4
7	Auntie's Bloomers	BBC	18.2
8	You've Been Framed	ITV	17.8
9	Dennis Norden's Laughter File	ITV	17.4
10	Blind Date Wedding of the Year	ITV	16.9
11	Big	ITV	16.5
12	Watching	ITV	16.4
13	Best of Blind Date	ITV	16.4
14	Ruth Rendell Mysteries	ITV	16.3
15	Casualty	BBC	16.1
16	It'll Be Alright On the Night	ITV	15.8
17	Inspector Morse	ITV	15.6
18	Holiday '91	BBC	15.4
19	Antiques Roadshow	BBC	15.3
20	News and Weather	BBC	15.3

• No 11 – Starring Tom Hanks as a young boy who becomes a man overnight with the help of a wishing machine at a carnival fairground.

• No 14 – A two-part mystery called Means of Evil.

• No 20 – The Gulf War in January and February meant high ratings for the news shows.

YORKSHIRE TELEVISION

The DARLING BUDS OF MAY

Darling Buds and Blind Dates

Darling Buds of May (6) was the television phenomenon of the year. It starred David Jason and made overnight stars out of relative unknowns Pam Ferris, Catherine Zeta Jones and Philip Franks. "I like to be able to wander around Tescos without anyone recognising me," Ferris said before the series began. She never had that pleasure again. She opened supermarkets instead. The series was based on the H.E. Bates novels about the Larkins, a large and loving, brash, boozy and beautiful English rural family who lived in a world where everything was 'Perfick... just perfick.' It was brought to the screen by Bates's son Richard. An American television company had bought the rights to the books but had spent so long making up their minds about turning them into a series that Bates jnr bought the rights back again and took the project to Yorkshire Television. H.E. Bates widow visited the location during filming and ended up appearing as an extra in one of the scenes.

Blind Date (10 and 13), Cilla Black's boy-meets-girl game show, reached its seventh series and 100th show in 1991 and was getting a lorra lorra viewers. In that time the show had matched up 200 couples but managed few on-going relationships and only one wedding. In 1988 Alex Tatham an accountant from London picked out Sue Middleton, a recruitment consultant from the West Midlands and they went on a blind date to a mediaeval banquet in Ireland. After much reported coaxing from the Blind Date team they eventually tied the knot. Nearly 17 million viewers tuned in to watch.

When we weren't watching Darling Buds and Blind Date we were tuning in to video bloopers: the bloopers of the famous on **Dennis Norden's Laughter File (9)** and his **It'll Be Alright On the Night (16)** or Terry Wogan's Christmas alternative **Auntie's Bloomers (7)**.

But the real stars were the ones in **You've Been Framed (8)**, the stars at home cocking it up with their camcorders. For the first series Jeremy Beadle's researchers worked their way through 20,000 home videos at a rate of 70 a day.

FIRST NIGHTS

Funny man Harry Enfield made his acting debut in **Gone To the Dogs** a series all about money, relationships and greyhound racing. Alison Steadman was Lauren Patterson, a lady with no career, no children and an oaf of a husband – self-made millionaire and mad dog racer Larry (Warren Clarke) and a besotted old flame, jailbird Jim Morley, (Jim Broadbent). Enfield played Morley's son Little Ji.m He went on to star in the comedy **Men Behaving Badly** the following year with Leslie Ash and Martin Clunes. Both shows went to a second series but Enfield, being a man who never likes to do two of anything, gracefully bowed out of both.

Warren Clarke also starred in the BBC2 four-part comedy thriller **Sleepers**. He and Nigel Havers played two Soviet spies packed off to Britain in the 60s. They were enjoying their new lives in the 90s until the KGB decided it was time to catch up with them.

John Thaw temporarily abandoned his role in **Inspector Morse** to play middle-aged advertising executive Stanley Duke in a black comedy based on Kingsley Amis's **Stanley and the Women**. Sheila Gish and Penny Downie were his past and present wives and Geraldine James played the positively awful publicity-concious psychiatrist, who blamed Stanley for his son's problems.

Jean Alexander was a posher Hilda Ogden as Patricia Hodge's mum in **Rich Tea and Sympathy** a six-part series about a Labour divorcee and a Conservative widower socially and politically opposed.

The BBC radio series **Second Thoughts** came to television, on ITV, with the same stars James Bolam and Lynda Bellingham as Bill and Faith, two divorcees facing marriage second time around.

And seeking a sporting soap to replace **Howard's Way**, the BBC went for the racing game with **Trainer** a Sunday night serial with newcomer Mark Greenstreet.

Jimmy Nail, the beefy brickie Oz in **Auf Weidersehen Pet**, turned up on the Tyne as an off-beat copper called **Spender**. And Tim Healy, the foreman, tuned up in Australia in **The Boys From The Bush**, playing an expatriate cockney running a detective agency.

- Complaints poured in after a scene in **Morse** involving a crying baby being held over a stairwell by actress Jan Harvey. The producers of the series assured viewers that the baby's mother had been within touching distance with instructions to stop filming if she felt concerned. And Junior Health Minister Baroness Hooper told the Lords there had been no infringement of the law governing child actors.
- Channel 4 refused permission for Merseyside Police's fraud squad to see episodes of its drama **GBH** in advance of transmission. The police claimed the series might have implications for their investigation, involving former deputy leader of Liverpool City Council Derek Hatton, into land deals on Merseyside. Hatton believed the central character Michael Murray was modelled on himself. Alan Bleasdale, who wrote the series, said it wasn't.
- US television evangelist Morris Cerullo announced he was planning to launch a 24-hour channel in Europe.
- Television journalist John McCarthy was released after five years and three months in captivity in Beirut.
- Thames Television, Television South, Television South West, and TV-am lost their franchises, after an unprecedented ITV auction. Winning companies Carlton, Meridian, Westcountry and Sunrise geared up to take over in January 1993.

A YEAR IN THE SOAPS

Brookside Murder Saves Ratings

Brookside celebrated its 1,000th episode in October. The event was marked with a murder and the opening of a new parade of shops behind the Close – in reality many miles away on the site of a converted school which housed the new production offices. Ratings had been on the slide, even the Brookside faithfuls were saying it was boring. A boost was needed and what better way to up the ratings than a gory murder? Sue Sullivan and baby Daniel were the victims – found dead on the day of the grand opening of the shops. Whodunnit? The saga went on for weeks. Was it hubby Terry? Former lover Barry Grant? Or Graeme, an obsessed admirer from work? Several different endings were shot. The ratings soared. Barry eventually turned out to be the culprit.

1991

Took's TV Teasers

1 What was the name of Channel 4's new improvisation show featuring Tony Slattery and Ian McShane?

2 Who wrote ITV's thriller Red Fox, starring John Hurt?

3 What was the name of John Mortimer's sequel to Paradise Postponed?

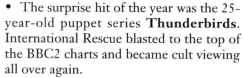

• The surprise hit of the year was the 25-year-old puppet series **Thunderbirds**. International Rescue blasted to the top of the BBC2 charts and became cult viewing all over again.

• After spending four years in prison, **Lovejoy** was back into the antiques trade. Ian McShane hadn't really been inside – he'd been appearing in **Dallas**.

NEAR MISSES

Noel's Houseparty, featured Noel Edmonds, no longer on the road but ensconced in a 'country house' set – featuring the Gotcha Oscar which saw various teams of celebrities competing, The Gung Tank and Grab-a-Grand.

1990

The *Radio Times* and *TV Times* monopoly on publishing weekly programme listings ended in March. Both magazines began publishing details of the other side's programmes. Newspapers were given the go-ahead to print the weekly listings – at a price – and many new mags were launched – some lasted, some didn't.

Grange Hill, the school saga of teenage life, which was loved by the kids and loathed by the mums and dads, was now a teenager itself. Since 1978 the BBC had been under siege with charges of bad language, bad behaviour and violence, but they stuck it out.

Second-hand car dealer Arthur Daley caught red-handed in possession of the same Daimler Sovereign as PD James' tv detective Adam Dalgleish. Check the registration number – exactly the same car was used in both productions.

Bruce Forsyth took back the reins of the **Generation Game** in 1991 after an absence of 13 years. His new assistant was Rosemarie Ford.

But whatever happened to 'give us a twirl' Anthea Redfern? Or Larry Grayson's assistant Isla St Clair?

Anthea married property developer Freddie Hoffman and settled down ten minutes away from Bruce in Berkshire.

Isla left Britain to run a bar and restaurant in Portugal with her husband Tony Sawford and their two children Elliot and Calum.

TEASER ANSWERS
1   S & M.
2   Gerald Seymour.
3   Titmuss Regained.

Top Shows

As well as the old favourites such as **Only Fools and Horses, Blind Date, Wish You Were Here, The Antiques Roadshow, Morse, The Bill, Lovejoy** and **Watching**, 1992 saw some high ratings for new series and one-offs.

Murder Squad (14 million) followed the Metropolitan Police Force on real life murder investigations. Two 'fly-on-the-wall' documentary crews spent four months with the force shadowing them 24 hours a day as they went about their grim business. Each programme followed a different murder from the moment the investigating officers arrived on the scene, through the post-mortems, forensic analysis and the interviewing of witnesses, to the arrest, interrogation and charging of the suspect.

1992

At the time of publication no ratings had been published for the latter half of the year. The listed programmes are just a sample of the top-rating shows for the first six months. The figure in brackets is an average viewing figure.

In Suspicious Circumstances (13 million) also looked at real crimes – but past crimes where doubt remains over the original verdict. Each investigation was re-enacted with the voice of Edward Woodward questioning the evidence. In one, Michael Melia, (last seen being bumped off as Eddie, the landlord of the Queen Vic in **EastEnders**) met another violent end as Freddie Mills *(see re-touched photo)*, the former boxing champion who was found dead outside his Soho night-club in 1965. The verdict at the time was suicide but the programme uncovered new evidence which suggested that it may have been a gangland killing.

As Time Goes By (13 million) starred Dame Judi Dench and Geoffrey Palmer as old flames attempting to relight the fire. Dench was Jean, a widowed managing director of a secretarial firm and Palmer was Lionel, a client of her agency who was writing his autobiography.

1992

A YEAR IN THE SOAPS

The BBC launched **Eldorado** in July, a sun, sea, sex and sangria soap, set amid a community of ex-pats living on the Costa Del Sol.

It was created by the team behind **EastEnders** and **Angels**, Julia Smith and Tony Holland, and had its own Den and Angie in the shape of smoothie Mark Tandy (seen tossing his pregnant girl-friend out onto the streets in the first episode) and ageing night-club singer Trish Valentine, with a troublesome toyboy and a sharp tongue. Eldorado is Spanish for 'the golden place'. The *Daily Mirror* suggested it might have been better to have called it El Brasso, but went on to predict it would be a 'huge and lasting success'. *The Guardian* described it as 'going straight for the young drunk vote with a directness which leaves you winded'. Mary White-house, typically, called it a "shambles". "The BBC should be ashamed of itself. How could such a great British institution with a reputation for quality sink to this appalling level I do not know."

Took's TV Teasers

1   Who were the three angels in ITV's after-life comedy drama?

2   In which series did Spandau Ballet singer Martin Kemp play the devil in disguise.

3   Who was the only original member of the Brookside cast still there when the soap celebrated its tenth birthday?

FIRST NIGHTS

A naked Ronald Pickup shocked viewers when he was seen as 54-year-old bank manager Andrew Powell, cavorting with an 18-year-old on a Lakeland fell in Melvyn Bragg's three-part adaptation of his novel **A Time To Dance**.

Adam Faith returned to television in the BBC drama series **Love Hurts** playing plumber turned self-made millionaire Frank Carver. Zoe Wanamaker was Tessa Piggott – the woman he fell in love with.

Karl Howman, better known as Jacko in **Brush Strokes**, played another lovable odd-job man in **Mulberry**, a new comedy from the Brush Strokes team, John Esmonde and Bob Larbey.

Nigel Havers and Keith Barron were **The Good Guys**, southerner Guy McFadyean and northerner Guy Binks, an unlikely pairing who found themselves unwittingly involved in solving crimes.

Tom Conti and John Standing were another unlikely alliance in **The Old Boy Network** but instead of solving crimes they were committing them. Conti was Lucas Fry, a disgraced former MI5 agent and Standing was his old adversary and new partner in espionage Peter Duckham.

Rides focused on the affairs of a London cabbie service run by, and for, women. It was produced by the woman behind **Tenko**, Lavinia Warner, under her independent production company – Warner Sisters.

Ordinary people were the stars of Michael Barrymore's **Barrymore**, which saw the host of **Strike It Lucky** doing what he does best – chatting and performing with members of the public. Star of the series was five-year-old Roxanne from Portsmouth who belted out "I'm 'enry the eighth I am" to a delighted audience.

1992

Spitting Image provided a strong dose of satire and comedy to relieve viewers' fatigue on the eve of polling day.

Elizabeth R

Nearly 19 million viewers tuned in to **Elizabeth R**, a fascinating film documentary following a year in the life of the Queen, made to celebrate the 40th anniversary of her accession to the throne.

Documentary producer and director Edward Mirzoeff was given unprecedented access to film the Queen's day-to-day working life and viewers were able to witness Royal family occasions such as a party at Sandringham following the christening of Princess Eugenie, a day out at Epsom Derby, the Queen on holiday with her grandchildren and at a ball at Balmoral. The *Radio Times* published a special souvenir edition featuring a photograph taken by Dorothy Wilding 40 years previously to mark her accession to the throne.

TEASER ANSWERS

1   Alfred Molina, Tom Bell and Cathy Tyson.
2   Growing Rich. A six-part drama written by Fay Weldon.
3   Paul Usher who played Barry Grant.

Former **EastEnders** heart-throb Nick Berry moved to the Yorkshire Moors to play village bobby Nick Rowan in **Heartbeat**, based on the 'Constable' books by former Yorkshire policeman Peter Walker (pen-name Nicholas Rhea).

Irish actress Niamh Cusack played Rowan's recently-qualified doctor wife Kate. The hit Friday night series was set in the swinging sixties and the Buddy Holly hit 'Heartbeat', re-recorded by Berry, provided the theme.

1992

Bobby Davro kicked off his new series of impressions with Gazza. "Gazza's a gift," he said. "He's got a big mouth and he's always sticking his tongue out."

Remakes

Remakes were the order of the year in 1992. First it was the BBC's 60's drama series **Maigret** remade on ITV with Michael Gambon playing the pipe-smoking chief inspector. The original Maigret was the late Rupert Davies, a smoker himself possessing a rumoured 40 pipes. His Maigret was accused of drinking too much on screen. In the new series booze and tobacco were limited and non-smoker Gambon was seen more often sucking his pipe than smoking it.

On Channel 4 **The Magic Roundabout** returned with a new series using the original puppets but with Nigel Planer's voice replacing the dulcet tones of Eric Thompson. Planer's version was ecologically sound – Dougal's worries were about such things as global warming.

On the BBC five of the original members of **Are You Being Served** reunited for **Grace and Favour**, which saw the staff of Grace Brothers leave the department store and move out of town to the Millstone Manor country hotel.

And finally Des O'Connor took on the role of the quiz inquisitor in a remake of Michael Miles' 60s hit **Take Your Pick**. The yes/no interlude returned and everything else was more or less the same – except in colour.

1955 to 1992
MONTH BY MONTH LISTINGS

The following charts are a representative list of top programmes from one week in each month of the years from 1955 to 1992. As some of the original records and data have been lost there are omissions and amendments, however every effort has been made to keep the tables accurate.

From October 1955 to August 1961 only top ten lists are available, from then on most listings are for the top twenty.

Sources:
Television Audience Measurement (TAM) 1955-1968
Audits Of Great Britain (AGB) 1968-1981
AGB for British Audience Research Board (BARB) 1981-

1955
[London% share]

OCTOBER

1	Sunday Night At the London Palladium	ITV	78
2	Take Your Pick	ITV	73
3	Double Your Money	ITV	70
4	Saturday Showtime	ITV	69
5	Roy Rogers	ITV	69
6	Highland Fling	BBC	69
7	I Love Lucy	ITV	68
8	Boxing	BBC	66
9	Adventures of Robin Hood	ITV	66
10	Movie Magazine	ITV	66

NOVEMBER

1	Take Your Pick	ITV	78
2	Sunday Night At the London Palladium	ITV	75
3	I Love Lucy	ITV	74
4	Adventures of Robin Hood	ITV	73
5	Theatre Royal	ITV	71
6	People Are Funny	ITV	71
7	Dragnet	ITV	71
8	Saturday Showtime	ITV	71
9	Roy Rogers	ITV	69
10	Gun Law	ITV	69

DECEMBER

1	Sunday Night At the London Palladium	ITV	84
2	Theatre Royal	ITV	79
3	I Love Lucy	ITV	79
4	Dragnet	ITV	78
5	Roy Rogers	ITV	77
6	Figure Skating	ITV	72
7	Adventures of Robin Hood	ITV	71
8	Take Your Pick	ITV	71
9	Stage One	ITV	71
10	Gun Law	ITV	69

1956
[London % Share]

JANUARY

1	Adventures of Robin Hood	ITV	78
2	Roy Rogers	ITV	76
3	Take Your Pick	ITV	70
4	Escaper's Club	ITV	68
5	Colonel March of Scotland Yard	ITV	68
6	Dragnet	ITV	66
7	Saturday Showtime	ITV	66
8	Sunday Night At the London Palladium	ITV	65
9	Inner Sanctum	ITV	65
10	TV Playhouse	ITV	65

FEBRUARY

1	Sunday Night At the London Palladium	ITV	78
2	Theatre Royal	ITV	75
3	I Love Lucy	ITV	73
4	Dragnet	ITV	70
5	Escaper's Club	ITV	69
6	Professional Boxing	ITV	69
7	Inner Sanctum	ITV	68
8	Douglas Fairbanks Presents	ITV	67
9	Jack Hylton Presents	ITV	66
10	Chance of a Lifetime	ITV	65

MARCH

1	Take Your Pick	ITV	76
2	Adventures of Robin Hood	ITV	68
3	Noddy Stories	ITV	67
4	Sunday Night At the London Palladium	ITV	67
5	I Love Lucy	ITV	67
6	Jack Jackson Show	ITV	67
7	Dragnet	ITV	65
8	Theatre Royal	ITV	64
9	Roy Rogers	ITV	63
10	Before Your Very Eyes	ITV	62

APRIL

1	Dragnet	ITV	70
2	Douglas Fairbanks Presents	ITV	66
3	Adventures of Robin Hood	ITV	64
4	Escaper's Club	ITV	58
5	Inner Sanctum	ITV	58
6	Adventures of Noddy	ITV	58
7	Take Your Pick	ITV	58
8	Jack Jackson Show	ITV	57
9	What's My Line?	BBC	55
10	Tony Hancock Show	ITV	55

MAY

1	Douglas Fairbanks Presents	ITV	69
2	Dragnet	ITV	61
3	Gun Law	ITV	61
4	I Love Lucy	ITV	61
5	Sunday Night At the London Palladium	ITV	58
6	Double Your Money	ITV	57
7	Theatre Royal	ITV	57
8	Take Your Pick	ITV	55
9	Variety Star Time	ITV	54
10	The Cup Final	BBC	54

JUNE

1	Dragnet	ITV	61
2	Adventures of Robin Hood	ITV	60
3	Roy Rogers	ITV	58
4	Jack Jackson Show	ITV	55
5	Celebrity Playhouse	ITV	54
6	Summer Theatre	ITV	53
7	Dixon of Dock Green	BBC	52
8	We Are Your Servants	BBC	50
9	My Wildest Dream	ITV	50
10	I've Got a Secret	ITV	50

JULY

1	Close Up	ITV	58
2	Gun Law	ITV	58
3	My Wildest Dream	ITV	57
4	Holiday Night	ITV	57
5	Look In On London	ITV	54
6	The 64,000 Question	ITV	50
7	Opportunity Knocks	ITV	50
8	I Love Lucy	ITV	50
9	Summer Theatre	ITV	50
10	Big City	ITV	48

AUGUST

1	Dragnet	ITV	54
2	Gun Law	ITV	54
3	The 64,000 Question	ITV	54
4	My Wildest Dream	ITV	50
5	Friday Night With Terry Thomas	ITV	50
6	Close Up	ITV	47
7	They're Off	ITV	46
8	The Garrison Ramblers	ITV	46
9	The Gambler	ITV	46
10	This Week	ITV	45

SEPTEMBER

1	The Crazy Gang	ITV	82
2	Dragnet	ITV	75
3	Sunday Night At the London Palladium	ITV	70
4	Gun Law	ITV	70
5	Play Gems	ITV	69
6	Sailor of Fortune	ITV	66
7	Assignment Foreign Legion	ITV	66
8	Man Trap	ITV	64
9	The Bob Cummings Show	ITV	63
10	Take Your Pick	ITV	63

OCTOBER

1	Armchair Theatre	ITV	74
2	Sunday Night At the London Palladium	ITV	70
3	Frontier Doctor	ITV	66
4	Dragnet	ITV	66
5	The 64,000 Question	ITV	66
6	Take Your Pick	ITV	66
7	Joan and Leslie	ITV	63
8	Man Trap	ITV	62
9	Double Your Money	ITV	62
10	Make Up Your Mind	ITV	60

NOVEMBER

1	Sunday Night At the London Palladium	ITV	75
2	Armchair Theatre	ITV	73
3	The 64,000 Question	ITV	70
4	Assignment Foreign Legion	ITV	69
5	Take Your Pick	ITV	69
6	Douglas Fairbanks Presents	ITV	67
7	Roy Rogers	ITV	67
8	Adventures of Robin Hood	ITV	65
9	This Week	ITV	65
10	Wyatt Earp	ITV	65

DECEMBER

1	Before Your Very Eyes	ITV	70
2	Dragnet	ITV	69
3	Film Festival	ITV	64
4	Secret Mission	ITV	63
5	Take Your Pick	ITV	63
6	Roy Rogers	ITV	62
7	Assignment Foreign Legion	ITV	62
8	Frontier Doctor	ITV	62
9	Sunday Night At the London Palladium	ITV	61
10	Adventures of Robin Hood	ITV	61

1957

[Homes in Millions]

MONTH BY MONTH 1957

JANUARY

1	Caroll Levis Discoveries	ITV	1.9
2	Double your Money	ITV	1.9
3	Take your Pick	ITV	1.8
4	Sunday Night At the		
	London Palladium	ITV	1.8
5	Boyd Q.C.	ITV	1.7
6	My Wife's Sister	ITV	1.7
7	The 64,000 Question	ITV	1.6
8	Variety Star Time	ITV	1.6
9	Professional Boxing	ITV	1.6
10	The Trollenberg Terror	ITV	1.6

FEBRUARY

1	Sunday Night At the		
	London Palladium	ITV	2.0
2	Armchair Theatre	ITV	2.0
3	Take Your Pick	ITV	2.0
4	Double Your Money	ITV	1.9
5	Carroll Levis Discoveries	ITV	1.8
6	Spot the Tune	ITV	1.8
7	Jack Jackson Show	ITV	1.8
8	Chelsea Review	ITV	1.8
9	Jack Hylton Presents	ITV	1.7
10	Do You Trust Your Wife	ITV	1.7

MARCH

1	Armchair Theatre	ITV	2.2
2	Take Your Pick	ITV	2.1
3	Play of the Week	ITV	2.1
4	Sunday Night At the		
	London Palladium	ITV	2.0
5	Double your Money	ITV	2.0
6	Spot the Tune	ITV	2.0
7	Professional Boxing	ITV	1.9
8	Robert Dherry Show	ITV	1.9
9	Saturday Spectacular	ITV	1.9
10	The Gentle Killers	ITV	1.9

APRIL

1	Jack Hylton Presents	ITV	2.2
2	Sunday Night At the		
	London Palladium	ITV	2.2
3	Armchair Theatre	ITV	2.2
4	Double Your Money	ITV	2.1
5	Spot the Tune	ITV	2.0
6	Take Your Pick	ITV	2.0
7	Emergency Ward Ten	ITV	2.0
8	Emergency Ward Ten	ITV	1.9
9	The Gentle Killers	ITV	1.9
10	Jack Jackson Show	ITV	1.8

MAY

1	Take Your Pick	ITV	2.2
2	Flannagan & Allen	ITV	2.0
3	Play of the Week	ITV	2.0
4	Sunday Night At the		
	London Palladium	ITV	2.0
5	Double Your Money	ITV	2.0
6	Emergency Ward Ten	ITV	2.0
7	Jack Jackson Show	ITV	2.0
8	Spot the Tune	ITV	2.0
9	The Gentle Killers	ITV	1.9
10	Emergency Ward Ten	ITV	1.9

JUNE

1	Take Your Piclk	ITV	2.1
2	Carroll Levis Discoveries	ITV	2.0
3	Emergenecy Ward Ten	ITV	1.9
4	Sunday Night At the		
	London Palladium	ITV	1.9
5	The Maltese Falcon	ITV	1.7
6	TV Playhouse	ITV	1.7
7	Saturday Spectacular	ITV	1.7
8	Startime	ITV	1.6
9	Jack Hylton Presents	ITV	1.6
10	Motive for Murder	ITV	1.6

JULY

1	Criss Cross Quiz	ITV	2.0
2	Jump for Joy	ITV	2.0
3	Blackpool Night	ITV	1.9
4	Emergency Ward Ten	ITV	1.9
5	Criss Cross Quiz	ITV	1.9
6	Personal Appearance	ITV	1.9
7	Emergency Ward Ten	ITV	1.9
8	Army Game	ITV	1.9
9	Criss Cross Quiz	ITV	1.9
10	The Prime Minister	BBC/ITV	1.8

AUGUST

1	Criss Cross Quiz	ITV	2.2
2	Not Wanted	ITV	2.1
3	Emergency Ward Ten	ITV	2.0
4	Blackpool Night	ITV	1.9
5	Caroll Levis Discoveries	ITV	1.8
6	Saturday Spectacular	ITV	1.8
7	TV Playhouse	ITV	1.8
8	Beside the Seaside	ITV	1.8
9	Criss Cross Quiz	ITV	1.8
10	Emergency Ward Ten	ITV	1.7

SEPTEMBER

1	Criss Cross Quiz	ITV	2.6
2	Emergency Ward Ten	ITV	2.6
3	TV Playhouse	ITV	2.6
4	Blackpool Night	ITV	2.5
5	Play of the Week	ITV	2.4
6	Emergency Ward Ten	ITV	2.4
7	Alexander Korda	ITV	2.3
8	Criss Cross Quiz	ITV	2.3
9	Saturday Spectacular	ITV	2.2
10	Shadow Squad	ITV	2.2

OCTOBER

1	Life With the Lyons	ITV	2.9
2	Criss Cross Quiz	ITV	2.8
3	Emergency Ward Ten	ITV	2.8
4	Tell the Truth	ITV	2.7
5	TV Playhouse	ITV	2.7
6	Murder Bag	ITV	2.6
7	Armchair Theatre	ITV	2.6
8	Criss Cross Quiz	ITV	2.6
9	Emergency Ward Ten	ITV	2.6
10	Sunday Night At the		
	London Palladium	ITV	2.5

NOVEMBER

1	Take Your Pick	ITV	3.2
2	The Prince of Wales Show	ITV	3.1
3	Emergency Ward Ten	ITV	2.9
4	O.S.S.	ITV	2.9
5	Caroll Levis Discoveries	ITV	2.9
6	Startime	ITV	2.7
7	Double Your Money	ITV	2.6
8	TV Playhouse	ITV	2.6
9	Emergency Ward Ten	ITV	2.6
10	Saturday Spectacular	ITV	2.5

DECEMBER

1	TV Playhouse	ITV	3.2
2	Take Your Pick	ITV	3.2
3	Sunday Night At the		
	London Palladium	ITV	3.1
4	O.S.S	ITV	3.1
5	Spot the Tune	ITV	3.0
6	Bid For Fame	ITV	3.0
7	Double Your Money	ITV	2.9
8	Alfred Marks Time	ITV	2.8
9	Emergency Ward Ten	ITV	2.8
10	The Film Show	ITV	2.8

1958

[Homes in millions]

JANUARY

1	Take Your Pick	ITV	3.8
2	Army game	ITV	3.7
3	Play of the Week	ITV	3.7
4	TV Playhouse	ITV	3.6
5	Emergency Ward Ten	ITV	3.6
6	Emergency Ward Ten	ITV	3.5
7	Armchair Theatre	ITV	3.5
8	Sunday Night At the Palladium	ITV	3.4
9	Double Your Money	ITV	3.3
10	Shadow Squad	ITV	3.0

FEBRUARY

1	Take Your Pick	ITV	3.8
2	Army Game	ITV	3.8
3	TV Playhouse	ITV	3.6
4	Emergency Ward Ten	ITV	3.6
5	Sunday Night At the Palladium	ITV	3.6
6	Double Your Money	ITV	3.5
7	Emergency Ward Ten	ITV	3.5
8	Shadow Squad	ITV	3.4
9	USSR Now	ITV	3.0
10	Armchair Theatre	ITV	2.8

MARCH

1	Take Your Pick	ITV	4.1
2	Army game	ITV	4.1
3	Armchair Theatre	ITV	3.8
4	Emergency Ward Ten	ITV	3.8
5	Sunday Night At the Palladium	ITV	3.7
6	Double Your Money	ITV	3.6
7	TV Playhouse	ITV	3.6
8	Emergency Ward Ten	ITV	3.5
9	Shadow Squad	ITV	3.1
10	Play of the Week	ITV	3.1

APRIL

1	Army Game	ITV	3.9
2	TV Playhouse	ITV	3.8
3	Professional Boxing	ITV	3.7
4	Emergency Ward Ten	ITV	3.6
5	Val Parnell's Star Time	ITV	3.5
6	Criss Cross Quiz	ITV	3.5
7	Caroll Levis Show	ITV	3.5
8	Emergency Ward Ten	ITV	3.5
9	Double Your Money	ITV	3.4
10	Sunday Night At the Palladium	ITV	3.3

MAY

1	Take Your Pick	ITV	3.6
2	Emergency Ward Ten	ITV	3.5
3	Wagon Train	ITV	3.5
4	TV Playhouse	ITV	3.4
5	Criss Cross Quiz	ITV	3.4
6	Emergency Ward Ten	ITV	3.3
7	Army Game	ITV	3.3
8	Double Your Money	ITV	3.2
9	Armchair Theatre	ITV	2.9
10	Shadow Squad	ITV	2.9

JUNE

1	Army Game	ITV	4.2
2	Wagon Train	ITV	4.0
3	Take Your Pick	ITV	3.9
4	TV Playhouse	ITV	3.8
5	Emergency Ward Ten	ITV	3.4
6	Emergency Ward Ten	ITV	3.4
7	Shadow Squad	ITV	3.3
8	Double Your Money	ITV	3.1
9	Criss Cross Quiz	ITV	3.0
10	Sunday Night At the Palladium	ITV	2.9

JULY

1	Wagon Train	ITV	3.9
2	Murder Bag	ITV	3.3
3	Emergency Ward Ten	ITV	3.2
4	Jack Hylton Presents	ITV	3.2
5	TV Playhouse	ITV	3.1
6	Emergency Ward Ten	ITV	3.1
7	My Wife and I	ITV	3.0
8	Val Parnell's Spectacular	ITV	2.9
9	Make Up Your Mind	ITV	2.8
10	The Verdict Is Yours	ITV	2.7

AUGUST

1	Wagon Train	ITV	3.9
2	Murder Bag	ITV	3.3
3	Emergency Ward Ten	ITV	3.1
4	Jubilee Show	ITV	3.1
5	Emergency Ward Ten	ITV	3.0
6	Bernard Delfont Presents	ITV	2.9
7	TV Playhouse	ITV	2.9
8	Make Up Your Mind	ITV	2.8
9	Jack Hylton Presents	ITV	2.7
10	Jack Hylton's Thursday Show	ITV	2.6

MONTH BY MONTH 1958

SEPTEMBER

1	Wagon Train	ITV	4.1
2	Blackpool Tower Circus	ITV	3.9
3	Murder Bag	ITV	3.3
4	Val Parnell's Startime	ITV	3.3
5	Emergency Ward Ten	ITV	3.3
6	Jubilee Show	ITV	3.2
7	Twenty One	ITV	3.2
8	Play of the Week	ITV	3.0
9	Emergency Ward Ten	ITV	2.8
10	Jack Hylton Presents	ITV	2.7

OCTOBER

1	Wagon Train	ITV	4.6
2	Army Game	ITV	4.5
3	Double Your Money	ITV	4.5
4	Sunday Night At the Palladium	ITV	4.4
5	Dotto	ITV	4.4
6	Val Parnell's Startime	ITV	4.3
7	TV Playhouse	ITV	4.3
8	Twenty One	ITV	4.3
9	Take Your Pick	ITV	4.2
10	Spot the Tune	ITV	4.2

NOVEMBER

1	Dotto	ITV	4.9
2	Sunday Night At the Palladium	ITV	4.8
3	Wagon Train	ITV	4.7
4	Army Game	ITV	4.6
5	Take Your Pick	ITV	4.3
6	TV Playhouse	ITV	3.9
7	Twenty One	ITV	3.9
8	Val Parnell's Spectacular	ITV	3.9
9	Spot the Tune	ITV	3.7
10	Emergency Ward Ten	ITV	3.7

DECEMBER

1	Sunday Night At the Palladium	ITV	4.7
2	Wagon Train	ITV	4.6
3	Dotto	ITV	4.6
4	Spot the Tune	ITV	4.5
5	Twenty One	ITV	4.5
6	Army Game	ITV	4.5
7	Take Your Pick	ITV	4.3
8	TV Playhouse	ITV	4.2
9	Double Your Money	ITV	4.1
10	Val Parnell's Spectacular	ITV	3.8

1959

[Homes in Millions]

MONTH BY MONTH 1959

JANUARY

1	Wagon Train	ITV	5.3
2	Army Game	ITV	5.2
3	TV Playhouse	ITV	5.0
4	Spot the Tune	ITV	4.9
5	Sunday Night At the Palladium	ITV	4.8
6	Take Your Pick	ITV	4.8
7	Dotto	ITV	4.8
8	Professional Boxing	ITV	4.4
9	Armchair Theatre	ITV	4.3
10	Emergency Ward Ten	ITV	4.2

FEBRUARY

1	Army Game	ITV	5.1
2	Wagon Train	ITV	5.1
3	Dotto	ITV	5.0
4	Spot the Tune	ITV	4.9
5	The Larkins	ITV	4.8
6	Take Your Pick	ITV	4.8
7	Saturday Spectacular	ITV	4.8
8	Sunday Night At the Palladium	ITV	4.7
9	Double Your Money	ITV	4.7
10	Emergency Ward Ten	ITV	4.5

MARCH

1	Army Game	ITV	5.1
2	Wagon Train	ITV	5.1
3	Double Your Money	ITV	4.9
4	Spot the Tune	ITV	4.9
5	Take Your Pick	ITV	4.6
6	TV Playhouse	ITV	4.6
7	Sunday Night At the Palladium	ITV	4.5
8	Emergency Ward Ten	ITV	4.4
9	The Larkins	ITV	4.4
10	Hippodrome	ITV	4.1

APRIL

1	Army Game	ITV	5.7
2	Wagon Train	ITV	5.3
3	Take Your Pick	ITV	5.0
4	Spot the Tune	ITV	4.9
5	Double Your Money	ITV	4.7
6	Sunday Night At the Palladium	ITV	4.5
7	Emergency Ward Ten	ITV	4.5
8	Emergency Ward Ten	ITV	4.3
9	Criss Cross Quiz	ITV	4.2
10	Saturday Spectacular	ITV	4.1

MAY

1	Wagon Train	ITV	5.4
2	Army Game	ITV	4.8
3	Sunday Night At the Palladium	ITV	4.4
4	Hippodrome	ITV	4.3
5	Take Your Pick	ITV	4.2
6	Spot the Tune	ITV	4.2
7	Double Your money	ITV	4.1
8	Play of the Week	ITV	4.0
9	Emergency Ward Ten	ITV	3.8
10	Jack Hylton Monday Show	ITV	3.7

JUNE

1	Wagon Train	ITV	5.0
2	Play of the Week	ITV	4.7
3	Army Game	ITV	4.5
4	Spot the Tune	ITV	4.3
5	Sunday Night At the Palladium	ITV	4.2
6	Emergency Ward Ten	ITV	4.1
7	Take Your Pick	ITV	4.1
8	Emergency Ward Ten	ITV	3.9
9	Double Your Money	ITV	3.9
10	Take Your Pick	ITV	3.9

JULY

1	Moscow State Circus	ITV	4.9
2	Wagon Train	ITV	4.9
3	Emergency Ward Ten	ITV	3.9
4	TV Playhouse	ITV	3.9
5	Armchair Theatre	ITV	3.9
6	Crime Street	ITV	3.9
7	Concentration	ITV	3.9
8	Play of the Week	ITV	3.7
9	Emergency Ward Ten	ITV	3.4
10	Concentration	ITV	3.4

AUGUST

1	Wagon Train	ITV	5.1
2	Concentration	ITV	4.2
3	Sunday Variety	ITV	4.1
4	Emergency Ward Ten	ITV	4.1
5	Concentration	ITV	3.8
6	Emergency Ward Ten	ITV	3.6
7	The Big Steal	BBC	3.6
8	Play of the Week	ITV	3.5
9	Skyport	ITV	3.5
10	Armchair Theatre	ITV	3.4

SEPTEMBER

1	Wagon Train	ITV	5.4
2	Play of the Week	ITV	4.6
3	Circus Comes To Town	ITV	4.5
4	Emergency Ward Ten	ITV	4.4
5	Eisenhower At Number Ten	ITV	4.4
6	Crime Street	ITV	4.3
7	Concentration	ITV	4.3
8	Emergency Ward Ten	ITV	4.2
9	Bernard Delfont's Sunday Variety	ITV	4.2
10	Concentration	ITV	4.1

OCTOBER

1	Double Your Money	ITV	5.5
2	Dotto	ITV	5.5
3	Take Your Pick	ITV	5.3
4	Concentration	ITV	5.1
5	Probation Officer	ITV	4.9
6	Liberal Party	ITV	4.9
7	Wagon Train	ITV	4.8
8	Emergency Ward Ten	ITV	4.8
9	Emergency Ward Ten	ITV	4.8
10	Sunday Night At the London Palladium	ITV	4.8

NOVEMBER

1	Wagon Train	ITV	5.9
2	Take Your Pick	ITV	5.6
3	Sunday Night At the London Palladium	ITV	5.4
4	Play of the Week	ITV	5.2
5	Saturday Spectacular	ITV	5.0
6	Emergency Ward Ten	ITV	5.0
7	Concentration	ITV	4.9
8	Armchair Theatre	ITV	4.9
9	Emergency Ward Ten	ITV	4.8
10	Probation Officer	ITV	4.7

DECEMBER

1	Wagon Train	ITV	6.1
2	Sunday Night At the London Palladium	ITV	5.9
3	Armchair Theatre	ITV	5.3
4	Emergency Ward Ten	ITV	5.2
5	Concentration	ITV	5.2
6	Take Your Pick	ITV	5.1
7	Army Game	ITV	5.1
8	Knight Errant	ITV	5.0
9	Hippodrome	ITV	4.8
10	Emergency Ward Ten	ITV	4.6

1960

[Homes in millions]

JANUARY

1	Wagon Train	ITV	5.9
2	Sunday Night At the Palladium	ITV	5.7
3	Take Your Pick	ITV	5.6
4	Army Game	ITV	5.6
5	Concentration	ITV	5.5
6	Emergency Ward Ten	ITV	5.5
7	Lord Saville's Crime	ITV	5.2
8	Emergency Ward Ten	ITV	5.2
9	The Signal	ITV	5.1
10	No Hiding Place	ITV	5.1

FEBRUARY

1	Sunday Night At the Palladium	ITV	7.1
2	Wagon Train	ITV	7.0
3	Night Panic	ITV	6.5
4	Take Your Pick	ITV	6.2
5	Emergency Ward Ten	ITV	6.1
6	Army Game	ITV	5.8
7	Knight Errant	ITV	5.4
8	Rawhide	ITV	5.3
9	Concentration	ITV	5.3
10	Probation Officer	ITV	5.2

MARCH

1	Wagon Train	ITV	6.9
2	Sunday Night At the Palladium	ITV	6.9
3	The Larkins	ITV	6.8
4	Take Your Pick	ITV	6.6
5	China Doll	ITV	6.5
6	Football	ITV	5.9
7	Living For Kicks	ITV	5.9
8	Breakaway	ITV	5.8
9	Rawhide	ITV	5.6
10	Emergency Ward Ten	ITV	5.5

APRIL

1	The Budget	BBC/ITV	7.6
2	Wagon Train	ITV	7.1
3	Sunday Night At the Palladium	ITV	7.0
4	The Budget Reply	BBC/ITV	7.0
5	The Leather Jungle	ITV	6.6
6	Arthur Haynes Show	ITV	6.3
7	Take Your Pick	ITV	6.2
8	Rawhide	ITV	6.0
9	Emergency Ward Ten	ITV	5.7
10	Emergency Ward Ten	ITV	5.7

MAY

1	Wagon Train	ITV	6.9
2	The Innocent	ITV	6.4
3	Probation Officer	ITV	6.3
4	Liberal Party	BBC/ITV	6.1
5	The Green Pack	ITV	5.9
6	Arthur's Treasured Volumes	ITV	5.8
7	Sunday Night At the Palladium	ITV	5.8
8	Take Your Pick	ITV	5.6
9	Double Your Money	ITV	5.4
10	Rawhide	ITV	5.3

JUNE

1	Sunday Night At the Palladium	ITV	6.7
2	No Hiding Place	ITV	6.5
3	Take Your Pick	ITV	5.8
4	Army Game	ITV	5.7
5	An Arabian Night	ITV	5.5
6	Emergency Ward Ten	ITV	5.5
7	Wagon Train	ITV	5.4
8	Spot the Tune	ITV	5.4
9	Rawhide	ITV	5.1
10	Emergency Ward Ten	ITV	5.0

JULY

1	Rawhide	ITV	6.1
2	After the Party	ITV	5.7
3	No Hiding Place	ITV	5.4
4	Emergency Ward Ten	ITV	5.3
5	Bernard Delfont's Sunday Show	ITV	5.1
6	Emergency Ward Ten	ITV	5.0
7	Tess	ITV	4.9
8	Tribute To Mr Bevan	ITV	4.9
9	Deadline Midnight	ITV	4.6
10	Maverick	ITV	4.5

AUGUST

1	Rawhide	ITV	5.2
2	No Hiding Place	ITV	5.0
3	Bernard Delfont's Sunday Show	ITV	5.0
4	The Mirror Maze	ITV	4.7
5	False Witness	ITV	4.7
6	Emergency Ward Ten	ITV	4.4
7	Mess Mates	ITV	4.3
8	The Variety Show	ITV	4.3
9	Emergency Ward Ten	ITV	4.2
10	Ladies of the Corridor	ITV	4.0

SEPTEMBER

1	Rawhide	ITV	6.5
2	No Hiding Place	ITV	6.1
3	The Harsh World	ITV	5.8
4	The Larkins	ITV	5.5
5	Emergency Ward Ten	ITV	5.4
6	Mess Mates	ITV	5.4
7	Emergency Ward Ten	ITV	5.3
8	Sparrow, Sparrow	ITV	5.0
9	Sunday Night At the Palladium	ITV	5.0
10	77 Sunset Strip	ITV	4.6

OCTOBER

1	No Hiding Place	ITV	6.8
2	Emergency Ward Ten	ITV	6.6
3	Sunday Night At the Palladium	ITV	6.6
4	Bootsie and Snudge	ITV	6.3
5	Arthur Haynes Show	ITV	6.2
6	Thunder On the Snowy	ITV	6.2
7	Double Your Money	ITV	6.1
8	The Larkins	ITV	6.1
9	The Circus Comes To Town	ITV	6.0
10	Emergency Ward Ten	ITV	5.9

NOVEMBER

1	Bootsie and Snudge	ITV	7.1
2	The Cake Baker	ITV	6.8
3	Sunday Night At the Palladium	ITV	6.8
4	Take Your Pick	ITV	6.6
5	Double Your Money	ITV	6.6
6	Independent Man	ITV	6.4
7	Emergency Ward Ten	ITV	6.4
8	The Four Dutchmen	ITV	6.2
9	Emergency Ward Ten	ITV	6.1
10	Knight Errant	ITV	6.1

DECEMBER

1	The Cupboard	ITV	7.7
2	Sunday Night At the Palladium	ITV	7.4
3	Take Your Pick	ITV	7.2
4	The Accomplices	ITV	7.2
5	Bootsie and Snudge	ITV	6.3
6	Army Game	ITV	6.3
7	Emergency Ward Ten	ITV	6.2
8	Arthur Haynes Show	ITV	6.1
9	Emergency Ward Ten	ITV	5.9
10	Dickie Henderson Show	ITV	5.8

MONTH BY MONTH 1960

1961

[Homes in millions]

JANUARY

1	Russ Conway Show	ITV	6.8
2	Sunday Night At the Palladium	ITV	6.6
3	Emergency Ward Ten	ITV	6.5
4	Bootsie and Snudge	ITV	6.5
5	Romantic Young Lady	ITV	6.5
6	Take Your Pick	ITV	6.4
7	Emergency Ward Ten	ITV	6.3
8	Army Game	ITV	6.3
9	Armchair Theatre	ITV	6.3
10	Dickie Henderson Show	ITV	6.0

FEBRUARY

1	No Hiding Place	ITV	7.3
2	Bootsie and Snudge	ITV	6.9
3	Take Your Pick	ITV	6.8
4	Emergency Ward Ten	ITV	6.7
5	Army Game	ITV	6.5
6	Emergency Ward Ten	ITV	6.5
7	Sunday Night At the Palladium	ITV	6.4
8	Dickie Henderson Show	ITV	6.2
9	Double Your Money	ITV	6.2
10	Armchair Theatre	ITV	6.1

MARCH

1	No Hiding Place	ITV	7.4
2	Bootsie and Snudge	ITV	6.7
3	Dickie Henderson Show	ITV	6.6
4	Sunday Night At the Palladium	ITV	6.6
5	Emergency Ward Ten	ITV	6.4
6	Emergency Ward Ten	ITV	6.4
7	Take Your Pick	ITV	6.0
8	Armchair Theatre	ITV	6.0
9	Coronation Street	ITV	5.8
10	Hell Hath No Fury	ITV	5.8

APRIL

1	No Hiding Place	ITV	7.2
2	Conservative Party	BBC/ITV	6.7
3	Emergency Ward Ten	ITV	6.4
4	Take Your Pick	ITV	6.2
5	Army Game	ITV	6.2
6	Bootsie and Snudge	ITV	6.1
7	Coronation Street	ITV	6.1
8	Play of the Week	ITV	6.0
9	Armchair Theatre	ITV	5.9
10	Drama '61	ITV	5.8

MAY

1	No Hiding Place	ITV	7.1
2	Bootsie and Snudge	ITV	7.0
3	Dickie Henderson Show	ITV	6.9
4	Conservative Party	BBC/ITV	6.5
5	Emergency Ward Ten	ITV	6.3
6	Coronation Street	ITV	6.3
7	Tales of Mystery	ITV	6.2
8	Emergency Ward Ten	ITV	6.1
9	Arthur Haynes Show	ITV	6.1
10	Army Game	ITV	6.0

JUNE

1	No Hiding Place	ITV	6.4
2	Boyd Q.C.	ITV	6.2
3	President Kennedy	ITV	6.2
4	Bootsie and Snudge	ITV	6.2
5	Emergency Ward Ten	ITV	6.1
6	Probation Officer	ITV	5.9
7	Coronation Street	ITV	5.8
8	Startime	ITV	5.8
9	Army Game	ITV	5.7
10	Three Live Wires	ITV	5.7

JULY

1	Harpers West One	ITV	5.9
2	No Hiding Place	ITV	5.7
3	Emergency Ward Ten	ITV	5.6
4	Coronation Street	ITV	5.4
5	Coronation Street	ITV	5.4
6	Emergency Ward Ten	ITV	5.4
7	Bernard Delfont's Show	ITV	5.3
8	Play of the Week	ITV	5.1
9	Three Live Wires	ITV	5.0
10	Television Playhouse	ITV	5.0

AUGUST

1	Harpers West One	ITV	5.7
2	No Hiding Place	ITV	5.7
3	Coronation Street	ITV	5.4
4	Boyd Q.C.	ITV	5.4
5	Abracadabra	ITV	5.0
6	Coronation Street	ITV	4.9
7	Emergency Ward Ten	ITV	4.8
8	Emergency Ward Ten	ITV	4.7
9	Three Live Wires	ITV	4.6
10	Bernard Delfont's Show	ITV	4.6

SEPTEMBER

1	Sunday Palladium	ITV	6.7
2	Coronation Street	ITV	6.5
3	Coronation Street	ITV	6.0
4	Emergency Ward Ten	ITV	5.9
5	Harpers West One	ITV	5.9
6	Three Live Wires	ITV	5.6
7	Top Secret	ITV	5.6
8	Emergency Ward Ten	ITV	5.5
9	Echo Four Two	ITV	5.5
10	Armchair Theatre	ITV	5.5
11	Gilt and Gingerbread	ITV	5.3
12	Sophie Tucker Show	ITV	5.2
13	Play of the Week	ITV	5.0
14	Abradabra	ITV	5.0
15	Rawhide	ITV	4.9
16	Winning Widows	ITV	4.8
17	Twenty Questions	ITV	4.8
18	Tell the Truth	ITV	4.6
19	Family Solicitor	ITV	4.4
20	This Week	ITV	4.3

OCTOBER

1	Coronation Street	ITV	7.1
2	Sunday Palladium	ITV	7.1
3	Coronation Street	ITV	6.7
4	Echo Four Two	ITV	6.7
5	Emergency Ward Ten	ITV	6.5
6	Emergency Ward Ten	ITV	6.4
7	Probation Officer	ITV	6.2
8	Double Your Money	ITV	6.2
9	Take Your Pick	ITV	5.7
10	Top Secret	ITV	5.6
11	The Rose Affair	ITV	5.5
12	Play of the Week	ITV	5.4
13	Three Live Wires	ITV	5.1
14	Mess Mates	ITV	5.1
15	The General Strike	ITV	5.1
16	Family Solicitor	ITV	5.0
17	All Kinds of Music	ITV	5.0
18	Rawhide	ITV	4.9
19	Winning Widows	ITV	4.8
20	TV Playhouse	ITV	4.6

NOVEMBER

1	Royal Variety Show	ITV	8.4
2	Coronation Street	ITV	7.2
3	Coronation Street	ITV	7.0
4	Top Secret	ITV	6.9
5	Emergency Ward Ten	ITV	6.8
6	Crime Sheet	ITV	6.6
7	Emergency Ward Ten	ITV	6.4
8	Double Your Money	ITV	6.4
9	Miss World	BBC	5.9
10	Charlie Drake	ITV	5.8
11	Three Live Wires	ITV	5.7
12	International Football	ITV	5.5
13	Family Solicitor	ITV	5.4
14	Ghost Squad	ITV	5.3
15	Dr Kildare	BBC	5.2
16	Morecambe and Wise Show	ITV	5.1
17	Bootsie and Snudge	ITV	5.1
18	Our House	ITV	5.1
19	Overland Trail	BBC	5.1
20	Criss Cross Quiz	ITV	4.8

DECEMBER

1	Coronation Street	ITV	7.3
2	Sunday Palladium	ITV	7.3
3	Coronation Street	ITV	6.2
4	Double Your Money	ITV	5.9
5	Dickie Henderson Show	ITV	5.8
6	Dr Kildare	BBC	5.4
7	Morecambe and Wise Show	ITV	5.4
8	One Step Beyond	ITV	5.3
9	Here's Harry	BBC	5.2
10	Drama '61	ITV	5.2
11	The Escape of RD 7	ITV	5.1
12	Perry Mason	BBC	5.0
13	Rag Trade	BBC	4.9
14	Bootsie and Snudge	ITV	4.9
15	Playdate	ITV	4.8
16	Probation Officer	ITV	4.7
17	Devil's Canyon	ITV	4.7
18	Take Your Pick	ITV	4.5
19	Ken Dodd Show	ITV	4.3
20	Impact	ITV	4.3

1962
[Homes in Millions]

JANUARY

1	Coronation Street	ITV	7.6
2	Sunday Palladium	ITV	7.4
3	Coronation Street	ITV	6.9
4	Double Your Money	ITV	6.1
5	Bootsie and Snudge	ITV	5.9
6	One Step Beyond	ITV	5.7
7	Take Your Pick	ITV	5.7
8	Drama '62	ITV	5.7
9	Dr. Kildare	BBC	5.4
10	Love In Another Land	ITV	5.3
11	Parade	ITV	5.2
12	Mess Mates	ITV	4.9
13	Bronco	BBC	4.9
14	All Our Yesterdays	ITV	4.7
15	Candid Camera	ITV	4.7
16	The Singing Years	ITV	4.5
17	Juke Box Jury	BBC	4.4
18	Dixon of Dock Green	BBC	4.3
19	Wrestling	ITV	4.2
20	This Is Your Life	BBC	4.1

FEBRUARY

1	Coronation Street	ITV	8.1
2	Coronation Street	ITV	7.6
3	One Step Beyond	ITV	6.7
4	Take Your Pick	ITV	6.4
5	Double Your Money	ITV	6.1
6	Bootsie and Snudge	ITV	5.9
7	Rawhide	ITV	5.8
8	Eric Sykes	BBC	5.7
9	Sunday Palladium	ITV	5.7
10	Bronco	BBC	5.5
11	Playdate	ITV	5.4
12	South America	ITV	5.2
13	Laramie	BBC	5.2
14	All That Jazz	ITV	5.2
15	Perry Mason	BBC	5.1
16	Black and White Minstrels	BBC	5.0
17	All Our Yesterdays	ITV	4.8
18	Come Dancing	BBC	4.7
19	Parade	ITV	4.6
20	Take a Letter	ITV	4.5

MARCH

1	Coronation Street	ITV	8.1
2	Coronation Street	ITV	7.9
3	Take Your Pick	ITV	6.3
4	Sunday Palladium	ITV	6.0
5	Rawhide	ITV	5.7
6	Take a Letter	ITV	5.7
7	Double Your Money	ITV	5.7
8	Some Talk of Alexander	ITV	5.6
9	Laramie	BBC	5.6
10	Eric Sykes	BBC	5.3
11	Bootsie And Snudge	ITV	5.3
12	Over the Moon	ITV	5.1
13	Tenderfoot	BBC	5.1
14	Perry Mason	BBC	5.1
15	Thirty Minute Theatre	ITV	4.9
16	Compact	BBC	4.8
17	Black and White Minstrels	BBC	4.8
18	Candid Camera	ITV	4.7
19	All Our Yesterdays	ITV	4.7
20	Z Cars	BBC	4.7

APRIL

1	Coronation Street	ITV	8.1
2	Coronation Street	ITV	8.0
3	Sunday Palladium	ITV	7.7
4	European Cup	ITV	7.3
5	Playdate	ITV	6.3
6	Take Your Pick	ITV	6.0
7	Rawhide	ITV	5.8
8	Double Your Money	ITV	5.7
9	Laramie	BBC	5.6
10	Take a Letter	ITV	5.5
11	Rag Trade	BBC	5.1
12	Perry Mason	BBC	5.1
13	Find the Singer	ITV	5.0
14	Bootsie and Snudge	ITV	4.8
15	All Our Yesterday	ITV	4.7
16	Compact	BBC	4.7
17	Z Cars	BBC	4.5
18	Candid Camera	ITV	4.4
19	Black and White Minstrels	BBC	4.3
20	Sportsview	BBC	4.3

MAY

1	Coronation Street	ITV	7.7
2	Coronation Street	ITV	7.7
3	Labour Broadcast	BBC/ITV	7.3
4	Conservative Broadcast	BBC/ITV	7.2
5	No Hiding Place	ITV	6.3
6	Top Secret	ITV	6.2
7	Sunday Palladium	ITV	6.1
8	Take Your Pick	ITV	5.9
9	Armchair Theatre	ITV	5.9
10	Dickie Henderson Show	ITV	5.6
11	Emergency Ward Ten	ITV	5.5
12	Emergency Ward Ten	ITV	5.2
13	Double Your Money	ITV	5.0
14	Bootsie and Snudge	ITV	5.0
15	Take a Letter	ITV	4.9
16	Hippodrome	ITV	4.9
17	This Week	ITV	4.8
18	The Odd Man	ITV	4.7
19	London v Paris Twist	ITV	4.7
20	Hard, Fast., Beautiful	BBC	4.6

JUNE

1	Coronation Street	ITV	7.4
2	Coronation Street	ITV	6.9
3	Labour Broadcast	BBC/ITV	5.9
4	Dickie Henderson Show	ITV	5.4
5	Play of the Week	ITV	5.3
6	No Hiding Place	ITV	5.1
7	Top Secret	ITV	5.1
8	Probation Officer	ITV	4.4
9	Sunday Palladium	ITV	4.4
10	Emergency Ward Ten	ITV	4.3
11	Armchair Theatre	ITV	4.3
12	The Odd Man	ITV	4.2
13	Take Your Pick	ITV	4.0
14	Take a Letter	ITV	4.0
15	Double Your Money	ITV	3.9
16	This Week	ITV	3.7
17	Emergency Ward Ten	ITV	3.6
18	Farson Meets Williams	ITV	3.6
19	All Our Yesterdays	ITV	3.4
20	World Cup '62	BBC	3.4

JULY

1	Coronation Street	ITV	7.4
2	Coronation Street	ITV	7.0
3	Tales of Mystery	ITV	6.0
4	My Three Angels	ITV	5.7
5	Top Secret	ITV	5.3
6	No Hiding Place	ITV	4.9
7	Probation Officer	ITV	4.7
8	This Week	ITV	4.7
9	Bernard Delfont's Show	ITV	4.7
10	The Hard Knock	ITV	4.7
11	Emergency Ward Ten	ITV	4.5
12	Emergency Ward Ten	ITV	4.4
13	The State of the Union	ITV	4.3
14	Steptoe and Son	BBC	4.3
15	Morecambe and Wise Show	ITV	4.3
16	Take a Letter	ITV	4.2
17	Saki	ITV	3.9
18	Holiday Town Parade	ITV	3.7
19	Abracadabra	ITV	3.6
20	Compact	BBC	3.4

AUGUST

1	Coronation Street	ITV	6.4
2	Bernard Delfont's Show	ITV	5.6
3	No Hiding Place	ITV	5.3
4	Drama '62	ITV	5.3
5	Coronation Street	ITV	5.1
6	This Week	ITV	5.1
7	Play of the Week	ITV	5.0
8	Tales of Mystery	ITV	4.9
9	Probation Officer	ITV	4.7
10	Emergency Ward Ten	ITV	4.6
11	Emergency Ward Ten	ITV	4.6
12	Abracadabra	ITV	4.3
13	Morecambe and Wise Show	ITV	4.2
14	Take a Letter	ITV	4.0
15	Holiday Town Parade	ITV	3.8
16	Wells Fargoe	BBC	3.6
17	Circus From Paris	BBC	3.5
18	The Double Blind	BBC	3.5
19	Watch Over the Mekong	ITV	3.5
20	All Our Yesterdays	ITV	3.4

MONTH BY MONTH 1962

SEPTEMBER

1	Coronation Street	ITV	7.6
2	Coronation Street	ITV	7.2
3	No Hiding Place	ITV	7.1
4	Bernard Delfont's Show	ITV	7.1
5	Play of the Week	ITV	6.4
6	Drama '62	ITV	6.4
7	The Verdict Is Yours	ITV	5.1
8	Emergency Ward Ten	ITV	5.1
9	Emergency Ward Ten	ITV	4.9
10	Take a Letter	ITV	4.7
11	Tales of Mystery	ITV	4.6
12	Morecambe and Wise Show	ITV	4.6
13	Abracadabra	ITV	4.5
14	Probation Officer	ITV	4.4
15	Billy Cotton Band Show	BBC	4.4
16	Silent Evidence	BBC	4.2
17	Bronco	BBC	4.2
18	The Chubby Checker Show	ITV	4.2
19	Steptoe and Son	BBC	4.2
20	This Week	ITV	4.1

OCTOBER

1	Coronation Street	ITV	8.4
2	Coronation Street	ITV	8.1
3	Armchair Theatre	ITV	6.3
4	No Hiding Place	ITV	6.1
5	Maigret	BBC	6.0
6	Double Your Money	ITV	6.0
7	Emergency Ward Ten	ITV	6.0
8	Val Parnell's Sunday Show	ITV	6.0
9	Take Your Pick	ITV	5.6
10	Emergency Ward Ten	ITV	5.5
11	Zero One	BBC	5.5
12	Drama '62	ITV	5.2
13	Z Cars	BBC	5.1
14	Television Playhouse	ITV	5.1
15	Winning Widows	ITV	5.1
16	Harpers West.One	ITV	5.1
17	Take a Letter	ITV	5.1
18	Sportsview	BBC	5.0
19	Bruce Forsyth Show	ITV	5.0
20	Man of the World	ITV	4.8

NOVEMBER

1	Coronation Street	ITV	8.4
2	Labour Broadcast	BBC/ITV	8.2
3	Miss World	BBC	7.5
4	Coronation Street	ITV	7.4
5	Take Your Pick	ITV	6.7
6	No Hiding Place	ITV	6.4
7	Double Your Money	ITV	6.4
8	Thank You and Good Night	ITV	6.4
9	The Bob Hope Show	ITV	6.3
10	Bootsie and Snudge	ITV	6.2
11	Emergency Ward Ten	ITV	6.2
12	Take a Letter	ITV	6.1
13	Professional Boxing	BBC	6.0
14	Bronco	BBC	5.9
15	Val Parnell's Sunday Show	ITV	5.8
16	Man of the World	ITV	5.8
17	Bruce Forsyth Show	ITV	5.6
18	Emergency Ward Ten	ITV	5.4
19	Z Cars	BBC	5.4
20	Notorious	BBC	5.4

DECEMBER

1	Coronation Street	ITV	8.4
2	Coronation Street	ITV	8.1
3	Double Your Money	ITV	6.8
4	Take Your Pick	ITV	6.8
5	No Hiding Place	ITV	6.7
6	Val Parnell's Sunday Show	ITV	6.7
7	A Letter From the General	ITV	6.6
8	Emergency Ward Ten	ITV	6.4
9	Joker	ITV	6.4
10	Bootsie and Snudge	ITV	6.2
11	Bronco	BBC	6.2
12	Dickie Henderson Show	ITV	6.0
13	Emergency Ward Ten	ITV	5.9
14	Take a Letter	ITV	5.7
15	Here's Harry	BBC	5.7
16	Z Cars	BBC	5.7
17	Time Gentlemen Please	ITV	5.7
18	Harpers West One	ITV	5.5
19	Arthur Hayne's Show	ITV	5.5
20	The Pinkness of It All	ITV	5.3

1963
[Homes in Millions]

JANUARY

1	Coronation Street	ITV	9.1
2	Coronation Street	ITV	8.8
3	No Hiding Place	ITV	7.5
4	Take Your Pick	ITV	7.0
5	Val Parnell's Sunday Show	ITV	6.8
6	Steptoe and Son	BBC	6.7
7	Double Your Money	ITV	6.7
8	Emergency Ward Ten	ITV	6.5
9	Bronco	BBC	6.5
10	Emergency Ward Ten	ITV	6.1
11	Harpers West One	ITV	5.9
12	Dickie Henderson Show	ITV	5.9
13	All Good Children	ITV	5.9
14	Take a Letter	ITV	5.8
15	The Lucy Show	BBC	5.7
16	Bootsie and Snudge	ITV	5.7
17	Drama '63	ITV	5.7
18	Hancock	ITV	5.5
19	Arthur Haynes Show	ITV	5.5
20	Z Cars	BBC	5.4

FEBRUARY

1	Coronation Street	ITV	8.8
2	Coronation Street	ITV	8.7
3	Steptoe and Son	BBC	8.5
4	Val Parnell's Sunday Show	ITV	7.6
5	Laughter USA	BBC	7.5
6	No Hiding Place	ITV	7.4
7	Play of the Week	ITV	7.1
8	Take Your Pick	ITV	7.1
9	Emergency Ward Ten	ITV	6.9
10	Wagon Train	ITV	6.6
11	Double Your Money	ITV	6.5
12	Sportsview	BBC	6.4
13	Z Cars	BBC	6.1
14	Take a Letter	ITV	6.0
15	Emergency Ward Ten	ITV	6.0
16	This Week	ITV	6.0
17	Tales of Mystery	ITV	5.9
18	Television Playhouse	ITV	5.7
19	Arthur Haynes Show	ITV	5.7
20	Plane Makers	ITV	5.6

MARCH

1	Coronation Street	ITV	8.4
2	Coronation Street	ITV	8.4
3	Liberal Broadcast	BBC/ITV	8.3
4	Take Your Pick	ITV	7.3
5	Val Parnell's Sunday Show	ITV	7.1
6	Emergency Ward Ten	ITV	6.8
7	Lords, Ladies & Gentlemen	ITV	6.5
8	Double Your Money	ITV	6.4
9	Eric Sykes	BBC	6.4
10	Professional Boxing	ITV	6.3
11	Wagon Train	ITV	6.3
12	The Lucy Show	BBC	5.9
13	The Rag Trade	BBC	5.9
14	Take a Letter	ITV	5.8
15	Here Come the Girls	ITV	5.8
16	Emergency Ward Ten	ITV	5.7
17	Eden End	ITV	5.5
18	Bootsie and Snudge	ITV	5.5
19	Thank Your Lucky Stars	ITV	5.5
20	Z Cars	BBC	5.4

APRIL

1	The Budget	BBC/ITV	9.5
2	The Budget Reply	BBC/ITV	8.9
3	Coronation Street	ITV	8.4
4	Coronation Street	ITV	8.3
5	The Odd Man	ITV	7.0
6	Eric Sykes	BBC	6.9
7	Take Your Pick	ITV	6.9
8	Play of the Week	ITV	6.8
9	The Harry Secombe Show	ITV	6.8
10	Drama '63	ITV	6.7
11	Double Your Money	ITV	6.5
12	Emergency Ward Ten	ITV	6.3
13	Crane	ITV	6.2
14	Moon Strike	BBC	6.0
15	Bootsie and Snudge	ITV	5.9
16	Emergency Ward Ten	ITV	5.7
17	Z Cars	BBC	5.4
18	Take a Letter	ITV	5.3
19	The Lucy Show	BBC	5.3
20	Jane Eyre	BBC	5.3

MAY

1	Labour Broadcast	BBC/ITV	8.7
2	Coronation Street	ITV	8.3
3	Coronation Street	ITV	7.7
4	The Odd Man	ITV	7.6
5	Jungle Juice	ITV	6.7
6	Take Your Pick	ITV	6.6
7	Emergency Ward Ten	ITV	6.3
8	Jane Eyre	BBC	6.3
9	The Harry Secombe Show	ITV	6.2
10	Double Stakes	ITV	6.1
11	Double Your Money	ITV	5.7
12	Take a Letter	ITV	5.6
13	Emergency Ward Ten	ITV	5.6
14	Bootsie and Snudge	ITV	5.2
15	The Lucy Show	BBC	5.2
16	Crane	ITV	5.2
17	Sportsview	BBC	5.2
18	The Plane Makers	ITV	5.1
19	The Human Jungle	ITV	5.1
20	Here Come the Girls	ITV	5.1

JUNE

1	Coronation Street	ITV	7.3
2	Playhouse	ITV	5.7
3	Coronation Street	ITV	5.3
4	Emergency Ward Ten	ITV	5.2
5	Pope John XXIII	ITV	5.1
6	Monkey and the Mohawk	ITV	5.1
7	This Week	ITV	5.0
8	Double Your Money	ITV	5.0
9	Val Parnell's Sunday Show	ITV	5.0
10	Crane	ITV	4.8
11	Take Your Pick	ITV	4.8
12	Zero One	BBC	4.7
13	The Victorians	ITV	4.7
14	Alfred Hitchcock Hour	ITV	4.6
15	Emergency Ward Ten	ITV	4.6
16	Comedy Four	ITV	4.6
17	The Hard Case	ITV	4.6
18	Take a Letter	ITV	4.5
19	Thank Your Lucky Stars	ITV	4.2
20	Love Story	ITV	4.1

JULY

1	Coronation Street	ITV	7.7
2	Coronation Street	ITV	7.4
3	Morecambe and Wise Show	ITV	6.9
4	Summer Spectacular	ITV	5.9
5	No Hiding Place	ITV	5.8
6	Armchair Theatre	ITV	5.8
7	Lucky Stars	ITV	5.7
8	Sergeant Cork	ITV	5.6
9	Steptoe and Son	BBC	5.3
10	University Challenge	ITV	5.2
11	Emergency Ward Ten	ITV	5.0
12	Love Story	ITV	4.9
13	Emergency Ward Ten	ITV	4.9
14	Alfred Hitchcock Hour	ITV	4.7
15	Maupassant	ITV	4.5
16	The Lucy Show	BBC	4.4
17	This Week	ITV	4.4
18	Play of the Week	ITV	4.3
19	Z Cars	BBC	4.3
20	Take a Letter	ITV	4.2

AUGUST

1	Coronation Street	ITV	7.1
2	This Week	ITV	5.8
3	The Odd Man	ITV	5.7
4	No Hiding Place	ITV	5.5
5	Television Playhouse	ITV	5.2
6	Emergency Ward Ten	ITV	5.0
7	Lucky Stars	ITV	5.0
8	Take a Letter	ITV	5.0
9	Coronation Street	ITV	4.9
10	Don't Say a Word	ITV	4.7
11	Emergency Ward Ten	ITV	4.7
12	Steptoe and Son	BBC	4.7
13	Alfred Hitchcock Hour	ITV	4.6
14	Little Big Business	ITV	4.5
15	Morecambe and Wise Show	ITV	4.5
16	Love Story	ITV	4.4
17	Stars and Garters	ITV	4.4
18	This Is Your Life	BBC	4.4
19	Zero One	BBC	4.4
20	Drama '63	ITV	4.1

SEPTEMBER

1	Coronation Street	ITV	8.2
2	Coronation Street	ITV	7.6
3	Morecambe and Wise Show	ITV	6.8
4	Love Story	ITV	6.7
5	The Odd Man	ITV	6.3
6	Stars and Garters	ITV	6.2
7	No Hiding Place	ITV	6.1
8	Emergency Ward Ten	ITV	5.9
9	Emergency Ward Ten	ITV	5.7
10	University Challenge	ITV	5.3
11	Chipperfield's Circus	ITV	5.3
12	Drama '63	ITV	5.3
13	Sergeant Cork	ITV	5.2
14	Lucky Stars	ITV	5.2
15	Television Playhouse	ITV	5.1
16	Don't Say a Word	ITV	5.0
17	Take a Letter	ITV	5.0
18	Alfred Hitchcock Hour	ITV	4.9
19	Z Cars	BBC	4.8
20	This Week	ITV	4.8

OCTOBER

1	Coronation Street	ITV	8.4
2	Coronation Street	ITV	8.3
3	Sunday Palladium	ITV	7.9
4	Take Your Pick	ITV	7.2
5	Dickie Henderson Show	ITV	7.0
6	No Hiding Place	ITV	7.0
7	Emergency Ward Ten	ITV	7.0
8	Armchair Theatre	ITV	7.0
9	Double Your Money	ITV	6.8
10	Emergency Ward Ten	ITV	6.5
11	The Avengers	ITV	6.0
12	Thank Your Lucky Stars	ITV	6.0
13	The Charlie Drake Show	ITV	5.6
14	Espionage	ITV	5.6
15	The Dick Powell Theatre	BBC	5.5
16	Our Man At Saint Marks	ITV	5.4
17	Maupassant	ITV	5.4
18	This Week	ITV	5.2
19	Maigret	BBC	5.1
20	The Dick Van Dyke Show	BBC	5.1

NOVEMBER

1	Royal Variety	ITV	10.4
2	Coronation Street	ITV	9.1
3	Coronation Street	ITV	9.0
4	Miss World '63	BBC	8.2
5	Max Bygraves Show	ITV	8.2
6	Take Your Pick	ITV	7.8
7	The Larkins	ITV	7.4
8	No Hiding Place	ITV	7.3
9	London Wall	ITV	7.2
10	Double Your Money	ITV	6.9
11	Emergency Ward Ten	ITV	6.9
12	Thank Your Lucky Stars	ITV	6.9
13	Sentimental Agent	ITV	6.9
14	Dickie Henderson Show	ITV	6.5
15	Our Man At Saint Marks	ITV	6.4
16	The Avengers	ITV	6.3
17	Z Cars	BBC	6.1
18	Espionage	ITV	6.1
19	Take a Letter	ITV	5.9
20	Pie In the Sky	ITV	5.9

DECEMBER

1	Coronation Street	ITV	8.9
2	Coronation Street	ITV	8.7
3	Drama '63	ITV	8.2
4	Sunday Palladium	ITV	8.0
5	Take Your Pick	ITV	7.8
6	No Hiding Place	ITV	7.5
7	Juke Box Jury	BBC	7.5
8	Double Your Money	ITV	7.3
9	Stars and Garters	ITV	7.2
10	It's the Beatles	BBC	6.9
11	Dickie Henderson Show	ITV	6.9
12	Emergency Ward Ten	ITV	6.8
13	Vicky and the Sultan	ITV	6.7
14	Emergency Ward Ten	ITV	6.3
15	The Good Old Days	BBC	5.9
16	Fourteen-Eighteen	ITV	5.8
17	Friday Night	ITV	5.8
18	University Challenge	ITV	5.6
19	Take a Letter	ITV	5.4
20	Dixon of Dock Green	BBC	5.4

1964
[Homes in Millions]

JANUARY

1	Steptoe and Son	BBC	9.4
2	Coronation Street	ITV	9.0
3	Coronation Street	ITV	8.8
4	No Hiding Place	ITV	8.1
5	Take Your Pick	ITV	8.0
6	Sunday Palladium	ITV	8.0
7	Armchair Theatre	ITV	7.9
8	Dick Powell Theatre	BBC	7.6
9	Double Your Money	ITV	7.4
10	It's Dark Outside	ITV	7.0
11	The Avengers	ITV	6.8
12	Emergency Ward Ten	ITV	6.7
13	Thank Your Lucky Stars	ITV	6.7
14	Foreign Affairs	ITV	6.7
15	Stars and Garters	ITV	6.4
16	Touch of Norman Vaughan	ITV	6.2
17	Espionage	ITV	6.1
18	Emergency Ward Ten	ITV	5.9
19	World In Action	ITV	5.9
20	This Week	ITV	5.8

FEBRUARY

1	Steptoe and Son	BBC	9.7
2	Liberal Broadcast	BBC/ITV	9.3
3	Coronation Street	ITV	8.8
4	Coronation Street	ITV	8.7
5	Dick Powell Theatre	BBC	8.3
6	Take Your Pick	ITV	7.9
7	Crane	ITV	7.8
8	Emergency Ward Ten	ITV	7.8
9	Double Your Money	ITV	7.5
10	The Avengers	ITV	7.5
11	Sunday Palladium	ITV	7.1
12	It's Dark Outside	ITV	6.3
13	Arthur Haynes Show	ITV	6.3
14	Thank Your Lucky Stars	ITV	6.1
15	They've Sold a Million	ITV	5.9
16	Espionage	ITV	5.8
17	Foreign Affairs	ITV	5.8
18	Maigret	BBC	5.7
19	Emergency Ward Ten	ITV	5.7
20	Touch of NormanVaughan	ITV	5.5

MARCH

1	Coronation Street	ITV	9.0
2	Coronation Street	ITV	8.7
3	Take Your Pick	ITV	8.1
4	Crane	ITV	7.3
5	Sunday Palladium	ITV	7.3
6	Double Your Money	ITV	7.1
7	Sportsview	BBC	7.0
8	Emergency Ward Ten	ITV	6.5
9	The Villians	ITV	6.5
10	Thank Your Lucky Stars	ITV	6.5
11	Z Cars	BBC	6.4
12	A Wicked World	ITV	6.2
13	Play of the Week	ITV	6.1
14	Sykes and a Plank	BBC	6.1
15	The Dick Powell Theatre	BBC	6.1
16	Touch of NormanVaughan	ITV	6.1
17	The Avengers	ITV	6.0
18	Top of the Pops	BBC	5.8
19	Arthur Haynes Show	ITV	5.7
20	Second City Reports	ITV	5.7

APRIL

1	Labour Broadcast	BBC/ITV	9.6
2	Conservative Broadcast	BBC/ITV	9.0
3	Coronation Street	ITV	8.3
4	Coronation Street	ITV	8.3
5	Ready Steady Go – Mod Ball	ITV	7.9
6	No Hiding Place	ITV	7.8
7	Take Your Pick	ITV	7.2
8	Double Your Money	ITV	6.6
9	Morecambe and Wise Show	ITV	6.5
10	Sunday Palladium	ITV	6.5
11	Cradle Song	ITV	6.5
12	They've Sold a Million	ITV	6.4
13	Emergency Ward Ten	ITV	6.1
14	G.S. Five	ITV	6.1
15	The Villains	ITV	6.0
16	The Protectors	ITV	6.0
17	Big Night Out	ITV	5.8
18	Sykes in a Band	BBC	5.7
19	The Dick Powell Theatre	BBC	5.7
20	Love Story	ITV	5.7

MAY

1	Conservative Broadcast	BBC/ITV	9.1
2	Labour Broadcast	BBC/ITV	9.0
3	Coronation Street	ITV	8.6
4	No Hiding Place	ITV	8.1
5	Coronation Street	ITV	8.0
6	Around The Beatles	ITV	7.6
7	Take Your Pick	ITV	7.3
8	Double Your Money	ITV	6.9
9	Love Story	ITV	6.6
10	A Fear of Strangers	ITV	6.4
11	Emergency Ward Ten	ITV	6.2
12	Morecambe and Wise Show	ITV	6.2
13	Sunday Palladium	ITV	6.1
14	Top of the Pops	BBC	5.9
15	Thank Your Lucky Stars	ITV	5.9
16	Jazz Girl	ITV	5.6
17	The Protectors	ITV	5.6
18	Emergency Ward Ten	ITV	5.5
19	This Week	ITV	5.5
20	Our Man At Saint Marks	ITV	5.4

JUNE

1	Coronation Street	ITV	8.6
2	Coronation Street	ITV	8.1
3	No Hiding Place	ITV	8.0
4	Double Your Money	ITV	6.8
5	Take Your Pick	ITV	6.8
6	Sunday Palladium	ITV	6.5
7	Thank Your Lucky Stars	ITV	6.3
8	Play of the Week	ITV	6.1
9	Love Story	ITV	6.1
10	This Week	ITV	6.0
11	Emergency Ward Ten	ITV	6.0
12	The Protectors	ITV	6.0
13	Morecambe and Wise Show	ITV	5.9
14	Meet the Wife	ITV	5.7
15	Emergency Ward Ten	ITV	5.6
16	Our Man At Saint Marks	ITV	5.4
17	The Dickie Henderson Show	ITV	5.2
18	Armchair Theatre	ITV	5.2
19	The Odd Man	ITV	5.2
20	University Challenge	ITV	5.1

JULY

1	Room At the Top	ITV	8.3
2	Coronation Steet	ITV	6.5
3	Sunday Mystery Theatre	ITV	6.5
4	No Hiding Place	ITV	5.9
5	The Villains	ITV	5.9
6	Opportunity Knocks	ITV	5.6
7	Emergency Ward Ten	ITV	5.5
8	Blackpool Night Out	ITV	5.5
9	Don't Say a Word	ITV	5.3
10	Emergency Ward Ten	ITV	5.2
11	Lucky Stars	ITV	5.2
12	The Dickie Henderson Show	ITV	5.2
13	The Celebrity Game	ITV	5.1
14	Voyage To England	ITV	5.0
15	Mainly Millicent	ITV	4.8
16	The Larkins	ITV	4.8
17	Our Man At Saint Marks	ITV	4.7
18	Cricket	ITV	4.7
19	Play of the Week	ITV	4.7
20	Love Story	ITV	4.7

AUGUST

1	Coronation Street	ITV	6.5
2	Emergency Ward Ten	ITV	6.1
3	Armchair Mystery Theatre	ITV	5.9
4	The Dickie Henderson Show	ITV	5.8
5	Love Story	ITV	5.5
6	The Celebrity Game	ITV	5.5
7	Blackpool Night Out	ITV	5.5
8	Opportunity Knocks	ITV	5.4
9	The Larkins	ITV	5.4
10	Room Down Under	ITV	5.1
11	Don't Say a Word	ITV	5.1
12	Lucky Stars	ITV	5.0
13	Play of the Week	ITV	4.9
14	Emergency Ward Ten	ITV	4.7
15	The Hidden Truth	ITV	4.7
16	Coronation Street	ITV	4.6
17	This Week	ITV	4.3
18	H.M.S. Paradise	ITV	4.3
19	Triangle	ITV	4.3
20	No Hiding Place	ITV	4.2

SEPTEMBER

1	Coronation Street	ITV	8.1
2	Coronation Street	ITV	7.8
3	No Hiding Place	ITV	7.8
4	Sunday Palladium	ITV	7.4
5	Emergency Ward Ten	ITV	7.2
6	Emergency Ward Ten	ITV	7.0
7	Take Your Pick	ITV	6.9
8	Love Story	ITV	6.8
9	Drama'64	ITV	6.8
10	Double Your Money	ITV	6.7
11	Opportunity Knocks	ITV	6.2
12	This Week	ITV	6.0
13	The Hidden Truth	ITV	5.8
14	Boyd Q.C.	ITV	5.7
15	Ready Steady Go – Winners	ITV	5.7
16	Fire Crackers	ITV	5.6
17	This Week' Special	ITV	5.6
18	Z Cars	BBC	5.4
19	World In Action	ITV	5.2
20	It's a Woman's World	ITV	5.2

OCTOBER

1	Coronation Street	ITV	9.4
2	Coronation Street	ITV	8.6
3	No Hiding Place	ITV	8.2
4	Take Your Pick	ITV	7.5
5	Double Your Money	ITV	7.2
6	They've Sold a Million	ITV	6.8
7	Sunday Palladium	ITV	6.6
8	Emergency Ward Ten	ITV	6.4
9	Emergency Ward Ten	ITV	6.4
10	Cinema	ITV	6.4
11	All Our Yesterdays	ITV	6.2
12	Steptoe and Son	BBC	6.2
13	The Rogues	ITV	6.2
14	Arthur Haynes Show	ITV	6.0
15	The Pop Spot	ITV	6.0
16	Thank Your Lucky Stars	ITV	5.7
17	Tokyo '64	ITV	5.6
18	Top of the Pops	BBC	5.5
19	Drama'64	ITV	5.4
20	Call In On Wynter	ITV	5.3

NOVEMBER

1	Coronation Street	ITV	9.4
2	Coronation Street	ITV	9.3
3	Royal Variety Show	BBC	8.3
4	Take Your Pick	ITV	7.9
5	Crane	ITV	7.6
6	All Our Yesterdays	ITV	6.7
7	Play of the Week	ITV	6.7
8	Emergency Ward Ten	ITV	6.7
9	Emergency Ward Ten	ITV	6.7
10	Dave's Kingdom	ITV	6.4
11	The Plane Makers	ITV	6.3
12	The Billy Fury Show	ITV	6.3
13	Double Your Money	ITV	6.3
14	Arthur Haynes Show	ITV	6.3
15	Cinema	ITV	6.3
16	Thank Your Lucky Stars	ITV	5.9
17	It's a Square World	BBC	5.9
18	This Week	ITV	5.4
19	The Benny Hill Show	ITV	5.4
20	World In Action	ITV	5.2

DECEMBER

1	Coronation Street	ITV	9.2
2	Coronation Street	ITV	9.2
3	Armchair Theatre	ITV	8.2
4	Take Your Pick	ITV	8.1
5	Sunday Palladium	ITV	7.5
6	Crane	ITV	7.4
7	Double Your Money	ITV	7.3
8	The Villains	ITV	7.1
9	The Plane Makers	ITV	6.9
10	Emergency Ward Ten	ITV	6.9
11	Emergency Ward Ten	ITV	6.7
12	All Our Yesterdays	ITV	6.6
13	Arthur Haynes Show	ITV	6.3
14	Cinema	ITV	6.2
15	Perry Mason	BBC	6.1
16	Dave's Kingdom	ITV	6.1
17	The Sullivan Brothers	ITV	5.9
18	World In Action	ITV	5.8
19	Thank Your Lucky Stars	ITV	5.6
20	Dr. Kildare	BBC	5.4

MONTH BY MONTH 1964

1965

[Homes in Millions]

MONTH BY MONTH 1965

JANUARY

1	Coronation Street	ITV	9.2
2	Coronation Street	ITV	9.1
3	Take Your Pick	ITV	8.1
4	Crane	ITV	7.8
5	Double Your Money	ITV	7.8
6	It's Tarbuck	ITV	7.2
7	Emergency Ward Ten	ITV	7.0
8	Emergency Ward Ten	ITV	6.9
9	All Our Yesterdays	ITV	6.6
10	Perry Mason	BBC	6.6
11	The Plane Makers	ITV	6.6
12	Millie In Jamaica	ITV	6.6
13	The Villains	ITV	6.5
14	Sunday Palladium	ITV	6.3
15	Ironside	BBC	5.9
16	This Week	ITV	5.9
17	University Challenge	ITV	5.8
18	Professional Wrestling	ITV	5.8
19	Armchair Theatre	ITV	5.8
20	Thank Your Lucky Stars	ITV	5.6

FEBRUARY

1	Coronation Street	ITV	9.2
2	Coronation Street	ITV	9.2
3	No Hiding Place	ITV	8.4
4	Take Your Pick	ITV	8.3
5	Double Your Money	ITV	8.0
6	The Villains	ITV	7.2
7	This Week	ITV	7.2
8	Emergency Ward Ten	ITV	7.2
9	All Our Yesterdays	ITV	7.0
10	Stars and Garters	ITV	6.9
11	Emergency Ward Ten	ITV	6.9
12	Front Page Story	ITV	6.8
13	Sunday Palladium	ITV	6.2
14	Henderson Hospital	ITV	6.1
15	University Challenge	ITV	6.1
16	America	ITV	5.7
17	Thank Your Lucky Stars	ITV	5.5
18	Sunday Playhouse	ITV	5.5
19	Call In On Valentine	ITV	5.4
20	Wrestling	ITV	5.3

MARCH

1	Coronation Street	ITV	9.4
2	Coronation Street	ITV	9.4
3	No Hiding Place	ITV	8.4
4	Take Your Pick	ITV	8.4
5	Double Your Money	ITV	8.2
6	Emergency Ward Ten	ITV	7.2
7	Emergency Ward Ten	ITV	7.0
8	All Our Yesterdays	ITV	6.9
9	Stars and Garters	ITV	6.8
10	The Worker	ITV	6.6
11	Front Page Story	ITV	6.5
12	University Challenge	ITV	6.2
13	Sunday Palladium	ITV	6.2
14	It's Dark Outside	ITV	6.1
15	Cinema	ITV	5.9
16	Top of the Pops	BBC	5.9
17	This Week	ITV	5.8
18	Wrestling	ITV	5.8
19	Armchair Theatre	ITV	5.8
20	World In Action	ITV	5.5

APRIL

1	Coronation Street	ITV	8.6
2	Coronation Street	ITV	8.5
3	Take Your Pick	ITV	8.2
4	No Hiding Place	ITV	7.8
5	This Week	ITV	7.6
6	Emergency Ward Ten	ITV	7.2
7	Stars and Garters	ITV	6.5
8	Emergency Ward Ten	ITV	6.5
9	It's Dark Outside	ITV	6.5
10	Sunday Palladium	ITV	6.5
11	All Our Yesterdays	ITV	6.2
12	Call In On Valentine	ITV	6.1
13	University Challenge	ITV	6.1
14	New Christie Minstrels	ITV	6.0
15	Cinema	ITV	5.8
16	Thank Your Lucky Stars	ITV	5.3
17	The Human Jungle	ITV	5.2
18	World In Action	ITV	5.0
19	Wrestling	ITV	4.8
20	Eamonn Andrews Show	ITV	4.8

MAY

1	Coronation Street	ITV	8.8
2	Coronation Street	ITV	8.6
3	No Hiding Place	ITV	7.8
4	Take Your Pick	ITV	7.5
5	Emergency Ward Ten	ITV	6.7
6	Dickie Henderson Show	ITV	6.6
7	Emergency Ward Ten	ITV	6.4
8	Six Shades of Black	ITV	6.3
9	Our Man At Saint Marks	ITV	6.3
10	This Week	ITV	6.2
11	All Our Yesterdays	ITV	6.1
12	Sunday Palladium	ITV	6.1
13	University Challenge	ITV	6.0
14	You're On Your Own	ITV	5.7
15	Cinema	ITV	5.6
16	Front Page Story	ITV	5.5
17	Thank Your Lucky Stars	ITV	5.4
18	Slight White Paper On Love	ITV	5.1
19	Perry Mason	BBC	5.0
20	The Bedsit Girl	BBC	5.0

JUNE

1	Coronation Street	ITV	7.8
2	Take Your Pick	ITV	6.5
3	Double Your Money	ITV	6.4
4	Sunday Palladium	ITV	6.4
5	Coronation Street	ITV	6.3
6	The Man In Room 17	ITV	6.3
7	Cinema	ITV	6.2
8	Emergency Ward Ten	ITV	6.0
9	This Week	ITV	5.8
10	No Hiding Place	ITV	5.7
11	Front Page Story	ITV	5.7
12	Emergency Ward Ten	ITV	5.7
13	Our Man At Saint Marks	ITV	5.4
14	World In Action	ITV	5.4
15	Pardon the Expression	ITV	5.4
16	The Western	BBC	5.1
17	Armchair Theatre	ITV	5.1
18	Wrestling	ITV	5.0
19	The Joe Baker Show	ITV	4.9
20	Carroll Calling	ITV	4.8

JULY

1	Coronation Street	ITV	8.1
2	Coronation Street	ITV	8.1
3	No Hiding Place	ITV	7.4
4	Blackpool Night Out	ITV	6.5
5	Our Man At Saint Marks	ITV	6.4
6	Pardon the Expression	ITV	6.1
7	Front Page Story	ITV	5.9
8	Emergency Ward Ten	ITV	5.6
9	This Week	ITV	5.6
10	All Our Yesterdays	ITV	5.5
11	World In Action	ITV	5.5
12	Cinema	ITV	5.5
13	The Des O'Connor Show	ITV	5.5
14	Emergency Ward Ten	ITV	5.4
15	The Man In Room 17	ITV	5.4
16	Suspense Hour	ITV	5.4
17	Opportunity Knocks	ITV	5.1
18	Sing a Song of Sixpence	ITV	5.0
19	Morecambe and Wise Show	ITV	4.9
20	Groucho	ITV	4.5

AUGUST

1	Riviera Police	ITV	8.1
2	Coronation Street	ITV	7.8
3	Coronation Street	ITV	6.9
4	Our Man At Saint Marks	ITV	6.4
5	Blackpool Night Out	ITV	5.9
6	Cinema	ITV	5.7
7	Play of the Week	ITV	5.5
8	Love Story	ITV	5.5
9	All Our Yesterdays	ITV	5.4
10	Sing a Song of Sixpence	ITV	5.3
11	Emergency Ward Ten	ITV	5.2
12	Pardon The Expression	ITV	5.1
13	The Man In Room 17	ITV	5.1
14	The Des O'Connor Show	ITV	5.1
15	Armchair Mystery Theatre	ITV	4.9
16	Morecambe and Wise Show	ITV	4.8
17	Emergency Ward Ten	ITV	4.7
18	World In Action	ITV	4.7
19	Comedy Playhouse	BBC	4.7
20	This Week	ITV	4.7

SEPTEMBER

1	Coronation Street	ITV	9.1
2	Coronation Street	ITV	8.4
3	Riviera Police	ITV	8.4
4	This Week	ITV	7.7
5	Emergency Ward Ten	ITV	7.2
6	Emergency Ward Ten	ITV	7.2
7	The Dickie Henderson Show	ITV	6.8
8	Blackmail	ITV	6.7
9	Sing a Song of Sixpence	ITV	6.6
10	Cinema	ITV	6.5
11	All Our Yesterdays	ITV	6.3
12	Blackpool Night Out	ITV	6.2
13	University Challenge	ITV	6.1
14	Love Story	ITV	5.7
15	Six of the Best	ITV	5.4
16	Opportunity Knocks	ITV	5.4
17	Play of the Week	ITV	5.1
18	Professional Boxing	ITV	5.1
19	Top of the Pops	BBC	5.1
20	Suspense Hour	ITV	5.1

OCTOBER

1	Coronation Street	ITV	8.4
2	Riviera Police	ITV	8.0
3	Take Your Pick	ITV	7.8
4	Love Story	ITV	7.7
5	Double Your Money	ITV	7.0
6	Cliff Richard/The Shadows	ITV	6.8
7	Emergency Ward Ten	ITV	6.5
8	Blackmail	ITV	6.5
9	The Big Valley	ITV	6.5
10	Cinema	ITV	6.3
11	The Return of Steptoe	BBC	6.3
12	University Challenge	ITV	6.1
13	The Worker	ITV	6.1
14	Coronation Street	ITV	5.8
15	The New Palladium Show	ITV	5.8
16	All Our Yesterdays	ITV	5.7
17	Emergency Ward Ten	ITV	5.7
18	The Man From Uncle	BBC	5.7
19	The Four of Hearts	ITV	5.5
20	The World Tonight	ITV	5.5

NOVEMBER

1	Coronation Street	ITV	8.4
2	Double Your Money	ITV	8.0
3	Steptoe and Son	BBC	7.8
4	Love Story	ITV	7.7
5	Take Your Pick	ITV	7.3
6	University Challenge	ITV	6.4
7	Emergency Ward Ten	ITV	6.3
8	All Our Yesterdays	ITV	6.2
9	The Man Who Never Was	ITV	6.1
10	The Avengers	ITV	6.1
11	The Big Valley	ITV	6.1
12	Blackmail	ITV	6.0
13	No Hiding Place	ITV	6.0
14	This Week	ITV	6.0
15	Perry Mason	BBC	5.9
16	Top of the Pops	BBC	5.9
17	The Man From Uncle	BBC	5.9
18	The Van Doonican Show	BBC	5.9
19	The Prince of Wales Show	ITV	5.9
20	Fenella Fielding	ITV	5.9

DECEMBER

1	Coronation Street	ITV	8.5
2	Take Your Pick	ITV	8.4
3	No Hiding Place	ITV	8.3
4	Love Story	ITV	8.1
5	Double Your Money	ITV	8.1
6	Hello Dolly	ITV	8.1
7	The Avengers	ITV	7.3
8	Coronation Street	ITV	6.9
9	All Our Yesterdays	ITV	6.8
10	University Challenge	ITV	6.7
11	Emergency Ward Ten	ITV	6.4
12	Emergency Ward Ten	ITV	6.3
13	Armchair Theatre	ITV	6.3
14	Cinema	ITV	6.2
15	Blackmail	ITV	6.2
16	The Western	BBC	6.2
17	Play of the Week	ITV	6.2
18	The Gang Show	ITV	6.2
19	The Val Doonican Show	BBC	6.2
20	The World Tomorrow	ITV	6.1

1966

[Homes in Millions]

JANUARY

1	Take Your Pick	ITV	8.6
2	Double Your Money	ITV	8.5
3	Coronation Street	ITV	8.4
4	No Hiding Place	ITV	8.0
5	Coronation Street	ITV	7.8
6	The Liars	ITV	7.3
7	Cinema	ITV	7.3
8	Emergency Ward Ten	ITV	7.1
9	The Power Game	ITV	7.0
10	Emergency Ward Ten	ITV	7.0
11	University Challenge	ITV	7.0
12	The World Tomorrow	ITV	6.8
13	The Avengers	ITV	6.8
14	All Our Yesterdays	ITV	6.7
15	Sunday Palladiumn	ITV	6.6
16	This Week	ITV	6.4
17	International Football	ITV	6.4
18	The Benny Hill Show	BBC	6.2
19	Stories of D.H. Lawrence	ITV	6.0
20	The Western	BBC	6.0

FEBRUARY

1	Coronation Street	ITV	8.7
2	Double Your Money	ITV	8.6
3	Coronation Street	ITV	8.5
4	Take Your Pick	ITV	8.5
5	The Avengers	ITV	8.4
6	Emergency Ward Ten	ITV	7.8
7	Morecambe and Wise Show	ITV	7.8
8	The Power Game	ITV	7.6
9	The Rat Catchers	ITV	7.5
10	Emergency Ward Ten	ITV	7.4
11	Cinema	ITV	7.4
12	The Liars	ITV	7.3
13	Sunday Palladium	ITV	7.1
14	This Week	ITV	7.0
15	University Challenge	ITV	6.8
16	All Our Yesterdays	ITV	6.5
17	Mystery and Imagination	ITV	6.2
18	The Man From Uncle	BBC	6.1
19	The World Tomorrow	ITV	6.1
20	Dixon of Dock Green	BBC	5.8

MARCH

1	Coronation Street	ITV	8.7
2	Take Your Pick	ITV	8.6
3	Double Your Money	ITV	8.4
4	Coronation Street	ITV	8.2
5	The Avengers	ITV	7.6
6	Emergency Ward Ten	ITV	7.5
7	Morecambe and Wise Show	ITV	7.2
8	Emergency Ward Ten	ITV	7.1
9	The Liars	ITV	6.9
10	Sunday Palladium	ITV	6.8
11	Pardon the Expression	ITV	6.8
12	University Challenge	ITV	6.8
13	Cinema	ITV	6.6
14	All Our Yesterdays	ITV	6.5
15	The Man From Uncle	BBC	6.5
16	Hope and Keen	ITV	6.2
17	This Week	ITV	6.2
18	Mystery and Imagination	ITV	5.6
19	Perry Mason	BBC	5.4
20	Softly, Softly	BBC	5.4

APRIL

1	Mrs. Thursday	ITV	8.9
2	Coronation Street	ITV	8.3
3	Double Your Money	ITV	8.2
4	Coronation Street	ITV	7.7
5	Cinema	ITV	7.7
6	The Man In Room 17	ITV	7.3
7	Weavers Green	ITV	6.9
8	The Des O'Connor Show	ITV	6.8
9	Pardon the Expression	ITV	6.7
10	Emergency Ward Ten	ITV	6.5
11	University Challenge	ITV	6.3
12	The Love Affair	BBC	6.2
13	This Week	ITV	6.1
14	Sportsview	BBC	6.0
15	All Our Yesterdays	ITV	5.9
16	Play of the Week	ITV	5.9
17	The Rat Catchers	ITV	5.9
18	The Man From Uncle	BBC	5.9
19	Black and White Minstrels	BBC	5.7
20	Emergency Ward Ten	ITV	5.6

MAY

1	Coronation Street	ITV	8.5
2	No Hiding Place	ITV	8.2
3	Mrs Thursday	ITV	8.0
4	Coronation Street	ITV	7.4
5	Double Your Money	ITV	6.8
6	Football	BBC	6.8
7	It's Tarbuck	ITV	6.6
8	Play of the Week	ITV	6.6
9	Checkmate	ITV	6.5
10	The Man In Room 17	ITV	6.4
11	Cinema	ITV	6.2
12	University Challenge	ITV	6.2
13	Pardon the Expression	ITV	6.1
14	Emergency Ward Ten	ITV	5.8
15	Emergency Ward Ten	ITV	5.7
16	Black and White Minstrels	BBC	5.6
17	The Wednesday Play	BBC	5.5
18	The Western	BBC	5.3
19	International Football	ITV	5.2
20	All Our Yesterdays	ITV	5.1

JUNE

1	Mrs Thursday	ITV	7.7
2	Coronation Street	ITV	7.3
3	Coronation Street	ITV	7.0
4	Sunday Palladium	ITV	7.0
5	Pardon the Expression	ITV	6.7
6	No Hiding Place	ITV	6.7
7	Cinema	ITV	6.6
8	The Man In Room 17	ITV	6.4
9	Seven Deadly Sins	ITV	6.2
10	Double Your Money	ITV	6.2
11	Emergency Ward Ten	ITV	5.4
12	The World Tomorrow	ITV	5.4
13	The Frost Report	BBC	5.3
14	Redcap	ITV	5.2
15	All Our Yesterdays	ITV	5.1
16	University Challenge	ITV	5.0
17	This Week	ITV	4.9
18	Emergency Ward Ten	ITV	4.9
19	Love Affair	BBC	4.7
20	Millicent	ITV	4.7

JULY

1	The Blackpool Show	ITV	7.7
2	Coronation Street	ITV	6.9
3	Cilla At the Savoy	ITV	6.9
4	No Hiding Place	ITV	6.8
5	Our Man At Saint Marks	ITV	6.6
6	Cinema	ITV	6.2
7	Love Story	ITV	6.1
8	The Dickie Valentine Show	ITV	6.1
9	Coronation Street	ITV	6.0
10	You Can't Win	ITV	5.7
11	Sixth Form Challenge	ITV	5.4
12	This Is Petula Clark	BBC	5.4
13	Emergency Ward Ten	ITV	5.3
14	This England	ITV	5.1
15	All About You	ITV	5.1
16	Weavers Green	ITV	5.1
17	All Our Yesterdays	ITV	4.8
18	Emergency Ward Ten	ITV	4.8
19	Public Eye	ITV	4.8
20	Know Your Rights	BBC	4.8

AUGUST

1	The Informer	ITV	7.0
2	Coronation Street	ITV	6.9
3	Play of the Week	ITV	5.9
4	The Blackpool Show	ITV	5.8
5	Professional Boxing	ITV	5.8
6	This Week	ITV	5.7
7	Love Story	ITV	5.6
8	You Can't Win	ITV	5.5
9	Dickie Valentine Show	ITV	5.5
10	Cinema	ITV	5.5
11	Our Man At Saint Marks	ITV	5.4
12	This England	ITV	5.2
13	Sixth Form Challenge	ITV	5.1
14	Emergency Ward Ten	ITV	5.1
15	All Our Yesterdays	ITV	4.8
16	Public Eye	ITV	4.7
17	The Love Affair	BBC	4.6
18	Emergency Ward Ten	ITV	4.6
19	All About You	ITV	4.5
20	Weavers Green	ITV	4.5

SEPTEMBER

1	Heavyweight Boxing	BBC	8.1
2	Coronation Street	ITV	7.6
3	Coronation Street	ITV	7.4
4	The Bruce Forsyth Show	ITV	7.3
5	The Informer	ITV	7.1
6	Cinema	ITV	6.9
7	Our Man At Saint Marks	ITV	6.7
8	Till Death Us Do Part	BBC	6.6
9	This Week	ITV	6.0
10	University Challenge	ITV	5.9
11	Plays of Married Life	ITV	5.8
12	Steptoe and Son	BBC	5.8
13	Tom Jones	ITV	5.6
14	The Love Affair	BBC	5.5
15	Emergency Ward Ten	ITV	5.5
16	Public Eye	ITV	5.4
17	All Our Yesterdays	ITV	5.4
18	Swimming	BBC	5.1
19	Love Story	ITV	4.7
20	The Corridor People	ITV	4.7

OCTOBER

1	Coronation Street	ITV	8.6
2	Sunday Palladium	ITV	8.5
3	Double Your Money	ITV	8.2
4	Take Your Pick	ITV	7.7
5	Coronation Street	ITV	7.4
6	Hippodrome	ITV	7.1
7	The Love Affair	BBC	6.6
8	University Challenge	ITV	6.6
9	Blackmail	ITV	6.6
10	This Week	ITV	6.3
11	The Power Game	ITV	6.2
12	All Our Yesterdays	ITV	6.1
13	Cinema	ITV	6.1
14	All Square	ITV	6.1
15	The Likely Lads	BBC	6.0
16	Emergency Ward Ten	ITV	6.0
17	Intrigue	ITV	5.9
18	Millicent and Roy	ITV	5.5
19	Home and Beauty	ITV	5.3
20	The Eamonn Andrews Show	ITV	5.2

NOVEMBER

1	Secombe and Friends	ITV	9.4
2	Coronation Street	ITV	8.9
3	Double Your Money	ITV	8.8
4	Take Your Pick	ITV	8.6
5	Cinema	ITV	7.7
6	Blackmail	ITV	7.3
7	Coronation Street	ITV	7.1
8	University Challenge	ITV	7.1
9	Hippodrome	ITV	6.9
10	The Des O'Connor Show	ITV	6.8
11	Emergency Ward Ten	ITV	6.4
12	All Our Yesterdays	ITV	6.2
13	Mystery and Imagination	ITV	6.1
14	The Likely Lads	BBC	6.0
15	All Square	ITV	6.0
16	The Love Affair	BBC	5.9
17	The Norman Vaughan Show	ITV	5.7
18	The Val Doonican Show	BBC	5.7
19	Sportsview	BBC	5.6
20	The Power Game	ITV	5.5

DECEMBER

1	Coronation Street	ITV	8.7
2	Sunday Palladium	ITV	8.7
3	Take Your Pick	ITV	8.6
4	Double Your Money	ITV	7.6
5	Morecambe and Wise Show	ITV	7.2
6	Blackmail	ITV	7.2
7	Coronation Street	ITV	7.1
8	University Challenge	ITV	7.0
9	The Val Doonican Show	BBC	6.3
10	Cinema	ITV	6.1
11	The Love Affair	BBC	6.0
12	Emergency Ward Ten	ITV	6.0
13	The Rat Catchers	ITV	6.0
14	All Our Yesterdays	ITV	5.9
15	Illustrated Weekly Hudd	BBC	5.9
16	High Adventure	BBC	5.9
17	Daktari	BBC	5.6
18	Meet the Wife	BBC	5.6
19	Hugh and I	BBC	5.6
20	George and the Dragon	ITV	5.5

MONTH BY MONTH 1966

1967

[Homes in Millions]

JANUARY

1	Take Your Pick	ITV	8.5
2	London Palladium Show	ITV	7.9
3	Mr Aitch	ITV	7.7
4	Morecambe and Wise Show	ITV	7.6
5	Double Your Money	ITV	7.6
6	Doddy's Music Box	ITV	7.6
7	Life With Cooper	ITV	7.3
8	Turn Out the Lights	ITV	7.2
9	Till Death Us Do Part	BBC	6.5
10	Mrs Thursday	ITV	6.5
11	On the Island	ITV	6.4
12	The Rat Patrol	BBC	6.2
13	The Rat Catchers	ITV	6.1
14	Emergency Ward Ten	ITV	6.0
15	Coronation Street	ITV	6.0
16	Softly, Softly	BBC	6.0
17	The Wednesday Play	BBC	6.0
18	Nixon At Nine-Five	BBC	6.0
19	You Can't Sleep Here	BBC	6.0
20	The Monroes	BBC	5.9

FEBRUARY

1	London Palladium Show	ITV	9.1
2	Mrs. Thursday	ITV	8.5
3	Take Your Pick	ITV	8.5
4	Coronation Street	ITV	8.0
5	The Avengers	ITV	8.0
6	Double Your Money	ITV	7.8
7	Who Is Sylvia?	ITV	7.8
8	Sportsview Special	BBC	7.4
9	Till Death Us Do Part	BBC	7.0
10	Doddy's Music Box	ITV	6.9
11	University Challenge	ITV	6.8
12	Turn Out the Lights	ITV	6.3
13	Nixon At Nine-Five	BBC	6.2
14	Cinema	ITV	6.1
15	World Tomorrow Special	ITV	6.1
16	Daktari	BBC	6.0
17	Softly, Softly	BBC	6.0
18	Eamonn Andrews Show	ITV	6.0
19	Coronation Street	ITV	6.0
20	The Crossfire	ITV	5.9

MARCH

1	Mrs Thursday	ITV	8.4
2	Z Cars	BBC	8.2
3	Take Your Pick	ITV	8.0
4	Coronation Street	ITV	7.3
5	The Avengers	ITV	7.3
6	Mr Rose	ITV	7.3
7	London Palladium Show	ITV	7.2
8	Coronation Street	ITV	6.9
9	Double Your Money	ITV	6.7
10	Daktari	BBC	6.5
11	The Rolf Harris Show	BBC	6.4
12	Doddy's Music Box	ITV	6.4
13	Mr Aitch	ITV	6.3
14	University Challenge	ITV	6.3
15	Softly, Softly	BBC	6.2
16	Nixon At Nine-Five	ITV	6.2
17	The League of Gentlemen	ITV	6.2
18	Z Cars	BBC	6.2
19	Emergency Ward Ten	ITV	5.7
20	This Week	ITV	5.7

APRIL

1	Market In Honey Lane	ITV	8.8
2	Eurovision Song Contest	BBC	8.8
3	London Palladium Show	ITV	8.1
4	Mr Rose	ITV	7.5
5	Coronation Street	ITV	7.4
6	No Hiding Place	ITV	7.4
7	Cinema	ITV	7.3
8	Take Your Pick	ITV	7.3
9	Coronation Street	ITV	7.1
10	Z Cars	BBC	6.7
11	Double Your Money	ITV	6.4
12	High Street Mayfair	ITV	6.4
13	Mr Aitch	ITV	6.4
14	This Week	ITV	6.1
15	Mike & Bernie's Music Hall	ITV	6.1
16	Best of Benny Hill	BBC	6.1
17	Seven Deadly Virtues	ITV	5.9
18	University Challenge	ITV	5.9
19	The Avengers	ITV	5.9
20	Daktari	BBC	5.6

MAY

1	London Palladium Show	ITV	8.2
2	Cinema	ITV	7.8
3	No Hiding Place	ITV	7.3
4	Coronation Street	ITV	7.2
5	Take Your Pick	ITV	7.2
6	Market In Honey Lane	ITV	7.1
7	Mr Rose	ITV	7.1
8	Seven Deadly Virtues	ITV	6.9
9	Coronation Street	ITV	6.8
10	The Frost Report	BBC	6.7
11	The Delivery Man	ITV	6.3
12	The Benny Hill Show	BBC	6.2
13	Double Your Money	ITV	5.9
14	Tom Jones	ITV	5.6
15	Opportunity Knocks	ITV	5.5
16	Eamonn Andrews Show	ITV	5.5
17	Z Cars	BBC	5.3
18	Tomorrow's World	BBC	5.3
19	The Avengers	ITV	5.2
20	University Challenge	ITV	5.2

JUNE

1	Coronation Street	ITV	7.4
2	No Hiding Place	ITV	7.4
3	London Palladium Show	ITV	7.3
4	Coronation Street	ITV	6.8
5	World In Action Special	ITV	6.7
6	The Des O'Connor Show	ITV	6.1
7	Market In Honey Lane	ITV	6.0
8	The Price of a Record	ITV	5.9
9	The Frost Report	BBC	5.8
10	University Challenge	ITV	5.8
11	George and the Dragon	ITV	5.4
12	Trapped	ITV	5.4
13	The Fellows	ITV	5.2
14	Stories Of D.H. Lawrence	ITV	5.2
15	War – Both Sides	ITV	5.0
16	This Week	ITV	5.0
17	Opportunity Knocks	ITV	4.9
18	Eamonn Andrews Show	ITV	4.8
19	Z Cars	BBC	4.4
20	All Our Yesterdays	ITV	4.4

JULY

1	Coronation Street	ITV	7.7
2	Summer Playhouse	ITV	7.6
3	World In Action	ITV	7.1
4	Coronation Street	ITV	6.9
5	News At Ten	ITV	6.9
6	The Blackpool Show	ITV	6.5
7	Perry Mason	BBC	6.1
8	News At Ten	ITV	5.8
9	Cinema	ITV	5.8
10	Love Story	ITV	5.8
11	Golden Shot	ITV	5.8
12	News At Ten	ITV	5.4
13	News At Ten	ITV	5.4
14	Half Hour Story	ITV	5.4
15	Steptoe and Son	BBC	5.3
16	The Love Affair	BBC	5.2
17	Till Death Us Do Part	BBC	4.7
18	This Week	ITV	4.6
19	Opportunity Knocks	ITV	4.5
20	News At Ten	ITV	4.4

AUGUST

1	Summer Playhouse	ITV	6.6
2	Coronation Street	ITV	6.6
3	Coronation Street	ITV	6.3
4	News At Ten	ITV	5.8
5	The Blackpool Show	ITV	5.7
6	News At Ten	ITV	5.5
7	Boy Meets Girl	BBC	5.4
8	Love Story	ITV	5.4
9	Steptoe and Son	BBC	5.3
10	Till Death Us Do Part	BBC	5.3
11	News At Ten	ITV	5.2
12	World In Action	ITV	5.1
13	Half Hour Story	ITV	5.0
14	Opportunity Knocks	ITV	5.0
15	Billy Cotton's Music Hall	BBC	4.8
16	Take It From Us	ITV	4.7
17	This Week	ITV	4.5
18	Cinema	ITV	4.5
19	The Fugitive	ITV	4.4
20	The Love Affair	BBC	4.3

SEPTEMBER

1	Coronation Street	ITV	9.4
2	Coronation Street	ITV	9.2
3	The Bruce Forsyth Show	ITV	7.0
4	World In Action	ITV	6.4
5	News At Ten	ITV	6.4
6	It's a Knockout	BBC	6.2
7	The Wrestlers	ITV	6.1
8	Summer Playhouse	ITV	5.7
9	News At Ten	ITV	5.5
10	All Our Yesterdays	ITV	5.4
11	Not In Front of the Children	BBC	5.4
12	News At Ten	ITV	5.4
13	Opportunity Knocks	ITV	5.4
14	The Golden Shot	ITV	5.2
15	The Man From Uncle	BBC	5.1
16	A Bit of an Experience	BBC	5.1
17	Love Story	ITV	5.1
18	Tonight With Dave Allen	ITV	5.1
19	Sir Arthur Conan Doyle	BBC	4.7
20	Escape	ITV	4.7

OCTOBER

1	Coronation Street	ITV	8.3
2	Coronation Street	ITV	8.2
3	World In Action	ITV	7.8
4	Playhouse	ITV	6.9
5	Take Your Pick	ITV	6.9
6	Spotlight	ITV	6.7
7	Mrs Thursday	ITV	6.4
8	The Avengers	ITV	6.3
9	The Val Doonican Show	BBC	6.2
10	University Challenge	ITV	6.2
11	The Informer	ITV	5.9
12	Cinema	ITV	5.9
13	News At Ten	ITV	5.9
14	Saturday Thriller	BBC	5.8
15	News At Ten	ITV	5.7
16	Opportunity Knocks	ITV	5.7
17	News At Ten	ITV	5.7
18	This Week	ITV	5.4
19	The Golden Shot	BBC	5.4
20	Steptoe and Son	BBC	5.4

NOVEMBER

1	Morecambe and Wise Show	ITV	8.7
2	Coronation Street	ITV	8.3
3	Take Your Pick	ITV	7.8
4	Max Bygraves	ITV	7.5
5	World In Action	ITV	7.4
6	Dr Finlay's Casebook	BBC	7.2
7	News At Ten	ITV	7.2
8	News At Ten	ITV	7.0
9	Englebert	ITV	6.9
10	Coronation Street	ITV	6.7
11	The Avengers	ITV	6.5
12	The Golden Shot	ITV	6.5
13	Tarzan	ITV	6.4
14	Inheritance	ITV	6.4
15	University Challenge	ITV	6.2
16	Cinema	ITV	6.2
17	Cimarron Strip	ITV	6.2
18	Steptoe and Son	BBC	6.2
19	Opportunity Knocks	ITV	6.2
20	The Des O'Connor Show	ITV	6.2

DECEMBER

1	Coronation Street	ITV	8.7
2	Coronation Street	ITV	8.6
3	World In Action	ITV	8.0
4	Playhouse	ITV	7.9
5	Take Your Pick	ITV	7.6
6	The Saturday Thriller	BBC	7.4
7	Morecambe and Wise Show	ITV	7.3
8	The Val Doonican Show	BBC	7.0
9	Opportunity Knocks	ITV	7.0
10	The Informer	ITV	6.8
11	University Challenge	ITV	6.7
12	Dixon of Dock Green	BBC	6.7
13	Englebert	ITV	6.6
14	Mrs Thursday	ITV	6.5
15	News At Ten	ITV	6.3
16	News At Ten	ITV	6.3
17	British Film Comedy	BBC	6.3
18	The Enchanted Isles	ITV	6.2
19	This Is Petula Clark	BBC	6.1
20	All Gas and Gaiters	BBC	6.1

1968

[Homes in Millions]

JANUARY

1	Till Death Us Do Part	BBC	8.3
2	Coronation Street	ITV	8.2
3	World In Action	ITV	8.0
4	Playhouse	ITV	7.7
5	Double Your Money	ITV	7.6
6	Take Your Pick	ITV	7.1
7	Coronation Street	ITV	7.1
8	The Saturday Thriller	BBC	7.1
9	This Is Petula Clark	BBC	6.9
10	News At Ten	ITV	6.8
11	Softly, Softly	BBC	6.7
12	George and the Dragon	ITV	6.5
13	Mike and Bernie's Show	ITV	6.4
14	News At Ten	ITV	6.4
15	The Virginian	BBC	6.1
16	News At Ten	ITV	5.9
17	Cinema	ITV	5.8
18	News At Ten	ITV	5.7
19	British Film Comedy	BBC	5.6
20	Top of the Pops	BBC	5.6

FEBRUARY

1	Coronation Street	ITV	8.3
2	World In Action	ITV	8.2
3	Piccadilly Palace	ITV	7.9
4	Coronation Steet	ITV	7.9
5	Till Death Us Do Part	ITV	7.7
6	Playhouse	ITV	7.2
7	Double Your Money	ITV	7.2
8	News At Ten	ITV	7.2
9	Take Your Pick	ITV	7.1
10	Francis Durbridge Presents	BBC	7.1
11	George and the Dragon	ITV	7.0
12	Doddy's Music Box	ITV	6.9
13	News At Ten	ITV	6.8
14	Cinema	ITV	6.8
15	News at Ten	ITV	6.5
16	Beggar My Neighbour	BBC	6.4
17	Cilla	BBC	6.4
18	Man In a Suitcase	ITV	6.4
19	Professional Boxing	ITV	6.4
20	A Man of Our Times	ITV	6.2

MARCH

1	Coronation Street	ITV	8.2
2	Life With Cooper	ITV	8.1
3	Coronation Street	ITV	7.8
4	The Dark Number	BBC	7.6
5	World In Action	ITV	7.5
6	Doddy's Music Box	ITV	7.5
7	Double Your Money	ITV	7.2
8	Sportsview	BBC	7.2
9	News At Ten	ITV	7.1
10	Cilla	BBC	7.0
11	Softly, Softly	BBC	6.8
12	The Saint	ITV	6.8
13	Man In a Suitcase	ITV	6.6
14	Not In Front of the Children	BBC	6.5
15	Take Your Pick	ITV	6.5
16	Playhouse	ITV	6.4
17	News At Ten	ITV	6.3
18	News at Ten	ITV	6.1
19	The London Palladium	ITV	6.1
20	The Saturday Thriller	BBC	6.0

APRIL

1	Eurovision Song Contest	BBC	9.4
2	Life With Cooper	ITV	8.5
3	Coronation Street	ITV	8.4
4	Coronation Street	ITV	7.4
5	Playhouse	ITV	7.2
6	Opportunity Knocks	ITV	7.1
7	LBJ – What Next?	ITV	7.0
8	British Film Comedy	BBC	7.0
9	Double Your Money	ITV	7.0
10	The Big Show	ITV	6.8
11	Take Your Pick	iTV	6.8
12	The Saint	ITV	6.7
13	News At Ten	ITV	6.4
14	Softly, Softly	BBC	6.4
15	News At Ten	ITV	6.4
16	Man In a Suitcase	ITV	6.3
17	Moira Anderson Sings	BBC	6.2
18	Z Cars	BBC	6.0
19	News At Ten	ITV	5.9
20	Sportsview	BBC	5.9

MAY

1	Howerd's Hour	ITV	9.1
2	Coronation Steet	ITV	8.0
3	The Des O'Connor Show	ITV	7.7
4	A Man Called Ironside	BBC	7.4
5	World in Action	ITV	7.2
6	Coronation Street	ITV	7.0
7	Opportunity Knocks	ITV	6.9
8	Double Your Money	ITV	6.7
9	Take Your Pick	ITV	6.6
10	Comedy Playhouse	BBC	6.5
11	The Saint	ITV	6.2
12	This Week	ITV	6.2
13	Spindoe	ITV	6.1
14	News At Ten	ITV	6.1
15	News At Ten	ITV	6.0
16	Margins of the Mind	ITV	5.9
17	News At Ten	ITV	5.8
18	British Film Comedy	BBC	5.6
19	Sportsview	BBC	5.6
20	Cinema	ITV	5.6

JUNE

1	International Football	BBC	8.8
2	The Big Show	ITV	7.0
3	Take Your Pick	ITV	6.9
4	News At Ten	ITV	6.8
5	News At Ten	ITV	6.4
6	Coronation Street	ITV	6.4
7	Lulu's Back In Town	BBC	6.1
8	Sportsview	BBC	5.9
9	The Kennedy Shooting	ITV	5.8
10	The Saint	ITV	5.8
11	Opportunity Knocks	ITV	5.7
12	The Des O'Connor Show	ITV	5.7
13	Coronation Street	ITV	5.6
14	This Week	ITV	5.6
15	Sink the Bismark	BBC	5.6
16	Mr Rose	ITV	5.6
17	The Avengers	ITV	4.9
18	News At Ten	ITV	4.8
19	Armchair Theatre	ITV	4.8
20	British Film Comedy	BBC	4.6

JULY

1	News At Ten	ITV	6.5
2	News At Ten	ITV	6.4
3	Coronation Street	ITV	6.3
4	News At Ten	ITV	6.1
5	Coronation Street	iTV	6.0
6	Cinema	ITV	5.8
7	The Big Show	ITV	5.8
8	News At Ten	ITV	5.5
9	News At Ten	ITV	5.5
10	Playhouse	ITV	5.3
11	Take Your Pick	ITV	5.3
12	Opportunity Knocks!	ITV	5.2
13	Love Story	ITV	5.1
14	Double Your Money	ITV	5.1
15	Life With Cooper	ITV	5.1
16	University Challenge	ITV	5.0
17	Sportsview	BBC	4.8
18	Detective	BBC	4.8
19	All We Want Is Everything	ITV	4.7
20	Lulu's Back in Town	BBC	4.6

AUGUST

1	Coronation Street	ITV	6.0
2	Miss United Kingdom	BBC	5.8
3	The Goon Show	ITV	5.5
4	Football – European Finals	BBC	5.4
5	Coronation Street	ITV	5.3
6	According To Dora	BBC	5.3
7	Crooks Anonymous	ITV	5.2
8	Thursday Film	ITV	4.9
9	Black and White Minstrels	BBC	4.8
10	Ride the High Iron	ITV	4.8
11	Crime Buster	ITV	4.8
12	World In Action	ITV	4.7
13	Saturday Thriller	BBC	4.6
14	Sportsview	BBC	4.6
15	Film – Mr Music	BBC	4.6
16	News	ITV	4.6
17	Best of Enemies	ITV	4.5
18	Vendetta	BBC	4.5
19	So You Think You Know	BBC	4.5
20	Morecambe and Wise	ITV	4.5

MONTH BY MONTH 1968

SEPTEMBER

1	Coronation Street	ITV	6.0
2	Nearest and Dearest	ITV	5.8
3	Cry Terror	BBC	5.4
4	Crime Buster	ITV	5.4
5	Never Mind the Quality	ITV	5.4
6	Black and White Minstrels	BBC	5.3
7	Coronation Street	ITV	5.1
8	Marty	BBC	5.1
9	Opportunity Knocks	ITV	5.1
10	News At Ten	ITV	4.9
11	This Week	ITV	4.8
12	News At Ten	ITV	4.8
13	Motorway	ITV	4.7
14	The Forsyte Saga	BBC	4.6
15	According To Dora	BBC	4.6
16	Frontier	ITV	4.6
17	Frost on Sunday	ITV	4.5
18	News At Ten	ITV	4.5
19	News At Ten	ITV	4.5
20	Top of the Pops	BBC	4.5

OCTOBER

1	Coronation Street	ITV	7.3
2	Coronation Street	ITV	7.1
3	Sherlock Holmes	BBC	6.4
4	Up In the World	BBC	6.4
5	Val Doonican Show	BBC	6.3
6	Opportunity Knocks	ITV	6.2
7	Dixon of Dock Green	BBC	6.1
8	Oh! Brother	BBC	6.0
9	Olympics Opening Ceremony	BBC	6.0
10	World In Action	ITV	5.8
11	Softly, Softly	BBC	5.8
12	Marty	BBC	5.6
13	Forsyte Saga	BBC	5.6
14	George and the Dragon	ITV	5.5
15	The Avengers	ITV	5.4
16	Z Cars	BBC	5.3
17	Top of the Pops	BBC	5.1
18	A Man Called Harry Brent	BBC	5.1
19	News At Ten	ITV	5.0
20	Sportsnight With Coleman	BBC	5.0

NOVEMBER

1	Coronation Street	ITV	7.5
2	Coronation Street	ITV	7.2
3	Opportunity Knocks	ITV	6.9
4	The Jimmy Tarbuck Show	ITV	6.9
5	The Forsyte Saga	BBC	6.8
6	Cooper At Large	ITV	6.7
7	Not In Front of the Children	BBC	6.5
8	San Francisco	BBC	6.5
9	The Val Doonican Show	BBC	6.1
10	The Saturday Stars	ITV	6.0
11	Sherlock Holmes	BBC	6.0
12	World In Action	ITV	5.9
13	News At Ten	ITV	5.8
14	Dixon of Dock Green	BBC	5.8
15	News at Ten	ITV	5.8
16	News At Ten	ITV	5.7
17	Frost on Sunday	ITV	5.7
18	Uncle Silas	ITV	5.6
19	Top of the Pops	BBC	5.6
20	Softly, Softly	BBC	5.6

DECEMBER

1	Coronation Street	ITV	7.6
2	Coronation Street	ITV	7.1
3	Father, Dear Father	ITV	7.0
4	Sherlock Holmes	BBC	6.9
5	The Val Doonican Show	BBC	6.9
6	Till Death Us Do Part	BBC	6.7
7	The Jimmy Tarbuck Show	ITV	6.7
8	The Forsyte Saga	BBC	6.6
9	Mike and Bernie's Show	ITV	6.6
10	Frost On Sunday	ITV	6.6
11	News At Ten	ITV	6.5
12	Dixon of Dock Green	BBC	6.4
13	Please Sir!	ITV	6.4
14	Day the Earth Caught Fire	BBC	6.4
15	Man of the Month	ITV	6.3
16	News At Ten	ITV	6.0
17	Pride and Prejudice	BBC	6.0
18	News At Ten	ITV	6.0
19	Horne A'Plenty	ITV	5.9
20	Softly, Softly	BBC	5.9

1969

[Homes in Millions]

MONTH BY MONTH 1969

JANUARY

1	Coronation Street	ITV	7.5
2	Till Death Us Do Part	BBC	7.5
3	Max	ITV	7.5
4	Coronation Street	ITV	7.2
5	The Frobisher Game	ITV	6.9
6	Mr Digby, Darling	ITV	6.9
7	The Forsyte Saga	BBC	6.9
8	The Avengers	ITV	6.8
9	Two-Way Stretch	BBC	6.7
10	Opportunity Knocks	ITV	6.7
11	The Power Game	ITV	6.6
12	World In Action	ITV	6.6
13	The Rolf Harris Show	BBC	6.5
14	The Reporters	ITV	6.5
15	Morecambe and Wise Show	BBC	6.3
16	News At Ten	ITV	6.2
17	News At Ten	ITV	6.2
18	So Evil My Love	BBC	6.2
19	The Dick Emery Show	BBC	6.0
20	The Fossett Saga	ITV	6.0

FEBRUARY

1	Max	ITV	8.2
2	Coronation Steet	ITV	7.9
3	The Power Game	ITV	7.9
4	Opportunity Knocks	ITV	7.5
5	Coronation Street	ITV	7.5
6	The Rolf Harris Show	BBC	7.1
7	The Dick Emery Show	BBC	7.1
8	The Forsyte Saga	BBC	7.1
9	Morecambe and Wise Show	BBC	7.0
10	News At Ten	ITV	6.8
11	Mike Yarwood Stand Up	ITV	6.8
12	European Skating	BBC	6.8
13	Dad's Army	BBC	6.7
14	House of Strangers	BBC	6.7
15	This Is Tom Jones	ITV	6.5
16	Mr. Digby, Darling	ITV	6.4
17	The Saturday Crowd	ITV	6.3
18	Maigret At Bay	BBC	6.3
19	The Avengers	ITV	6.2
20	Go On – It'll Do You Good	ITV	6.2

MARCH

1	The Power Game	ITV	7.8
2	Coronation Street	ITV	7.8
3	Coronation Steet	ITV	7.6
4	Opportunity Knocks	ITV	7.2
5	Two In Clover	ITV	7.2
6	News At Ten	ITV	6.9
7	World In Action	ITV	6.6
8	Her Majesty's Pleasure	ITV	6.6
9	The Unguarded Moment	BBC	6.5
10	The Rolf Harris Show	BBC	6.5
11	The Dick Emery Show	BBC	6.4
12	Dr Finlay's Casebook	BBC	6.4
13	Armchair Theatre	ITV	6.4
14	The Roy Hudd Show	ITV	6.3
15	The Avengers	ITV	6.2
16	News At Ten	ITV	6.2
17	Softly, Softly	BBC	6.2
18	On the Buses	ITV	6.1
19	This Is Tom Jones	ITV	6.0
20	News At Ten	ITV	6.0

APRIL

1	Max	ITV	6.9
2	Coronation Steet	ITV	6.4
3	Callan	ITV	6.3
4	John Browne's Body	ITV	6.1
5	Black Widow	BBC	6.0
6	Life With Cooper	ITV	5.7
7	News At Ten	ITV	5.4
8	Oh! Brother	BBC	5.4
9	Coronation Street	ITV	5.4
10	The Saturday Crowd	ITV	5.4
11	This Week	ITV	5.3
12	Judge Dee	ITV	5.3
13	News At Ten	ITV	5.2
14	News At Ten	ITV	5.2
15	This Is Tom Jones	ITV	5.2
16	The Stanley Baxter Show	BBC	5.1
17	News At Ten	ITV	5.1
18	On the Buses	ITV	5.1
19	The Virginian	BBC	5.0
20	HMS Defiant	ITV	5.0

MAY

1	Football: England v Wales	BBC	7.0
2	Coronation Street	ITV	6.9
3	Football: England v Scotland	BBC	6.9
4	Football: Scotland v N Ireland	BBC	6.7
5	The Dark Past	BBC	6.6
6	Spate of Speight	ITV	6.3
7	Opportunity Knocks	ITV	6.3
8	News At Ten	ITV	6.2
9	World In Action	ITV	6.0
10	News At Ten	ITV	6.2
11	Life With Cooper	ITV	5.9
12	News At Ten	ITV	5.9
13	Coronation Street	ITV	5.8
14	Des O'Connor Show	ITV	5.8
15	Old Bill	BBC	5.6
16	The Prior Commitment	BBC	5.6
17	John Browne's Body	ITV	5.5
18	Oh! Brother	BBC	5.5
19	Francis Albert Sinatra	BBC	5.4
20	Race You To the Top	BBC	5.4

JUNE

1	News at Ten	ITV	7.6
2	Fraud Squad	ITV	7.5
3	The Mind of Mr J G Reeder	ITV	7.0
4	News At Ten	ITV	6.9
5	Coronation Street	ITV	6.5
6	Father, Dear Father	ITV	6.5
7	It's The Bachelors	ITV	6.4
8	Whicker's New World	ITV	6.3
9	Coronation Street	ITV	6.3
10	News At Ten	ITV	6.2
11	Opportunity Knocks	ITV	6.0
12	Playhouse – Uncle Jonathan	ITV	5.8
13	This Week	ITV	5.7
14	News At Ten	ITV	5.6
15	The Liberace Show	ITV	5.1
16	News At Ten	ITV	5.0
17	The Gold Robbers	ITV	5.0
18	On the Buses	ITV	4.9
19	D-Day 25 Years On	ITV	4.8
20	Match of the Decade	BBC	4.6

JULY

1	Fraud Squad	ITV	6.6
2	News At Ten	ITV	6.4
3	Coronation Street	ITV	6.3
4	Coronation Street	ITV	6.1
5	Nearest and Dearest	ITV	6.1
6	Whicker's World	ITV	6.0
7	The Main Chance	ITV	5.9
8	News At Ten	ITV	5.9
9	News	ITV	5.8
10	Playhouse	ITV	5.4
11	Mike and Bernie's Show	ITV	5.2
12	News At Ten	ITV	5.1
13	The Gold Robbers	ITV	5.1
14	News At Ten	ITV	5.0
15	Doctor In the House	ITV	4.9
16	Join Jim Dale	ITV	4.9
17	The Liberace Show	ITV	4.9
18	Z Cars	BBC	4.4
19	The Troubleshooters	BBC	4.5
20	Laugh With Hope	BBC	4.5

AUGUST

1	News At Ten	ITV	5.8
2	Fraud Squad	ITV	5.7
3	Coronation Street	ITV	5.7
4	Public Eye	ITV	5.5
5	Coronation Street	ITV	5.4
6	Nearest and Dearest	ITV	5.4
7	News At Ten	ITV	5.0
8	News At Ten	ITV	5.0
9	The Gold Robbers	ITV	4.9
10	News At Ten	ITV	4.8
11	Doctor In the House	ITV	4.6
12	Mike and Bernie's Show	ITV	4.4
13	News At Ten	ITV	4.4
14	Tarbuck's Back	ITV	4.3
15	Wojeck	BBC	4.2
16	Boy Meets Girl	BBC	4.2
17	World In Action	ITV	4.1
18	The Frankie Howerd Show	ITV	4.1
19	Join Jim Dale	ITV	4.0
20	Applause! Applause!	ITV	4.0

SEPTEMBER

1	Who Dun It	ITV	6.6
2	News At Ten	ITV	6.4
3	The Best Things In Life	ITV	6.3
4	Coronation Street	ITV	6.3
5	Justice Is a Woman	ITV	5.7
6	Public Eye	ITV	5.4
7	News At Ten	ITV	5.2
8	Doctor In the House	ITV	5.2
9	Coronation Street	ITV	5.1
10	Jeux Sans Frontieres	BBC	5.0
11	News At Ten	ITV	5.0
12	Never Mind the Quality	ITV	5.0
13	News At Ten	ITV	4.9
14	News At Ten	ITV	4.9
15	The Mark of Zorro	BBC	4.7
16	The Frankie Howerd Show	ITV	4.6
17	Black and White Minstrels	BBC	4.6
18	This Week	ITV	4.5
19	The L-Shaped Room	BBC	4.5
20	Disney Time	BBC	4.5

OCTOBER

1	The Dustbinmen	ITV	7.4
2	Coronation Street	ITV	7.1
3	Coronation Street	ITV	6.9
4	Please Sir!	ITV	6.8
5	Special Branch	ITV	6.8
6	Dear Mother, Love Albert	ITV	6.7
7	Nearest and Dearest	ITV	6.6
8	Playhouse – Mixed Foursome	ITV	6.5
9	News At Ten	ITV	6.2
10	Opportunity Knocks	ITV	6.2
11	Softly, Softly	BBC	6.2
12	Not In Front of the Children	BBC	6.1
13	World In Action	ITV	6.1
14	Dad's Army	BBC	6.1
15	Music Hall	ITV	6.1
16	News At Ten	ITV	6.0
17	Ours Is a Nice House	ITV	6.0
18	Who Dun It	ITV	5.9
19	The Saturday Crowd	ITV	5.8
20	Top of the Pops	BBC	5.4

NOVEMBER

1	In Loving Memory	ITV	8.6
2	Coronation Street	ITV	8.2
3	Please Sir!	ITV	8.0
4	Coronation Street	ITV	7.4
5	Nearest and Dearest	ITV	7.3
6	Special Branch	ITV	7.1
7	The Password Is Courage	BBC	7.1
8	World In Actioin	ITV	7.0
9	Opportunity Knocks	ITV	6.9
10	Who Dun It	ITV	6.9
11	News At Ten	ITV	6.9
12	Mr Digby, Darling	ITV	6.7
13	Playhouse	ITV	6.6
14	The Saturday Crowd	ITV	6.5
15	Ours Is a Nice House	ITV	6.5
16	News At Ten	ITV	6.4
17	Softly, Softly	BBC	6.3
18	Not In Front of the Children	BBC	6.3
19	News At Ten	ITV	6.2
20	Dad's Army	BBC	6.2

DECEMBER

1	Coronation Street	ITV	8.2
2	This Is Your Life	ITV	8.0
3	Special Branch	ITV	7.7
4	Coronation Street	ITV	7.6
5	News At Ten	ITV	7.6
6	News At Ten	ITV	7.2
7	Curry and Chips	ITV	7.2
8	Opportunity Knocks	ITV	7.0
9	World In Action	ITV	7.0
10	Please Sir!	ITV	6.8
11	Softly, Softly	BBC	6.6
12	Dad's Army	BBC	6.5
13	Twilight For the Gods	BBC	6.4
14	Cribbins	ITV	6.4
15	News At Ten	ITV	6.4
16	Morecambe and Wise	BBC	6.3
17	News At Ten	ITV	6.2
18	Not In Front of the Children	BBC	6.2
19	The Saturday Crowd	ITV	6.2
20	The Root of All Evil	ITV	6.1

1970

[Homes in Millions]

JANUARY

1	Coronation Street	ITV	8.2
2	This Is Your Life	ITV	8.0
3	Coronation Street	ITV	8.0
4	The Max Bygraves Hour	ITV	7.8
5	Opportunity Knocks	ITV	7.4
6	A Present For Dickie	ITV	7.3
7	Kate	ITV	7.3
8	The Worker	ITV	7.2
9	On the Buses	ITV	7.2
10	The Last Voyage	BBC	7.2
11	World In Action	ITV	7.1
12	News At Ten	ITV	7.0
13	The Val Doonican Show	BBC	6.7
14	News At Ten	ITV	6.7
15	Playhouse	ITV	6.6
16	Happy Ever After	ITV	6.5
17	The Dave King Show	ITV	6.5
18	Manhunt	ITV	6.5
19	Whicker In Europe	ITV	6.4
20	Not In Front of the Children	BBC	6.3

FEBRUARY

1	Coronation Street	ITV	8.6
2	The Benny Hill Show	ITV	8.5
3	This Is Your Life	ITV	8.4
4	Kate	ITV	8.2
5	Coronation Street	ITV	8.1
6	Max	ITV	8.0
7	Opportunity Knocks	ITV	7.7
8	News At Ten	ITV	7.7
9	On the Buses	ITV	7.7
10	Gun Fighter	BBC	7.4
11	Whicker In Europe	ITV	7.2
12	The Val Doonican Show	BBC	7.0
13	A Present For Dickie	ITV	6.9
14	It's Cliff Richard	BBC	6.9
15	Take Three Girls	BBC	6.8
16	Manhunt	ITV	6.8
17	News At Ten	ITV	6.7
18	Frost On Sunday	ITV	6.7
19	This is...Tom Jones	ITV	6.5
20	Oh Brother!	BBC	6.4

MARCH

1	This Is Your Life	ITV	8.7
2	News At Ten	ITV	8.7
3	Steptoe and Son	BBC	8.7
4	Coronation Street	ITV	8.6
5	Coronation Street	ITV	8.1
6	Kate	ITV	8.0
7	Opportunity Knocks	ITV	7.8
8	Max	ITV	7.8
9	On the Buses	ITV	7.4
10	Frost At the Palladium	ITV	7.1
11	The Val Doonican Show	BBC	7.0
12	It's Cliff Richard	BBC	7.0
13	Two In Clover	ITV	6.9
14	World In Action	ITV	6.8
15	Manhunt	ITV	6.8
16	Playhouse	ITV	6.7
17	This Week	ITV	6.7
18	News At Ten	ITV	6.7
19	A Man Called Ironside	BBC	6.7
20	Battle At Apache Pass	BBC	6.6

APRIL

1	This Is Your Life	ITV	8.3
2	Coronation Street	ITV	7.8
3	Callan	ITV	7.7
4	Steptoe and Son	BBC	7.6
5	The Dustbinmen	ITV	7.2
6	News At Ten	ITV	7.2
7	Coronation Street	ITV	6.9
8	Miss England	BBC	6.5
9	Norman	ITV	6.3
10	The Dick Emery Show	BBC	6.3
11	Girls About Town	ITV	6.2
12	The Misfit	ITV	6.2
13	Doctor In the House	ITV	6.2
14	World In Action	ITV	6.2
15	The Golden Shot	ITV	6.2
16	David Nixon's Magic Box	ITV	6.1
17	Black and White Minstrels	BBC	5.9
18	Crime of Passion	ITV	5.9
19	News At Ten	ITV	5.9
20	Manhunt	ITV	5.8

MAY

1	This Is Your Life	ITV	7.4
2	Coronation Street	ITV	7.2
3	Coronation Street	ITV	6.6
4	For the Love of Ada	ITV	6.4
5	A Family At War	ITV	6.3
6	European Cup Final	BBC	6.3
7	Norman	ITV	6.2
8	Manhunt	ITV	6.2
9	Doctor In the House	ITV	6.1
10	The Dustbinmen	ITV	5.9
11	News At Ten	ITV	5.9
12	Black and White Minstrels	BBC	5.9
13	News At Ten	ITV	5.8
14	Yellow Sky	BBC	5.7
15	Up Pompeii	BBC	5.6
16	Away all Boats	BBC	5.6
17	News At Ten	ITV	5.4
18	The Expert	BBC	5.4
19	The Des O'Connor Show	ITV	5.3
20	Mike and Bernie's Scene	ITV	5.3

JUNE

1	Manhunt	ITV	5.7
2	Callan	ITV	5.6
3	Genevieve	BBC	5.5
4	News At Ten	ITV	5.5
5	World Cup Grandstand	BBC	5.4
6	Doctor In the House	ITV	5.2
7	The Best Things In Life	ITV	5.1
8	Father Dear Father	ITV	5.1
9	News At Ten	ITV	5.1
10	News At Ten	ITV	4.8
11	News At Ten	ITV	4.8
12	Playhouse	ITV	4.6
13	Eddie In August	ITV	4.5
14	Saturday Night Theatre	ITV	4.5
15	This Week	ITV	4.4
16	Mike and Bernie's Scene	ITV	4.4
17	It's a Knockout	BBC	4.4
18	Wheel of Fortune	ITV	4.3
19	Max	ITV	4.2
20	News At Ten	ITV	4.2

JULY

1	Coronation Street	ITV	7.4
2	A Family At War	ITV	7.1
3	Coronation Street	ITV	6.5
4	News At Ten	ITV	6.5
5	Never Mind the Quality	ITV	6.4
6	Doctor In the House	ITV	6.4
7	His and Hers	iTV	6.3
8	News At Ten	ITV	6.1
9	Opportunity Knocks	ITV	6.1
10	Confession (Python Method)	ITV	6.0
11	News At Ten	ITV	5.9
12	News At Ten	ITV	5.9
13	News At Ten	ITV	5.8
14	World in Action	ITV	5.5
15	The Best Things In Life	ITV	5.4
16	Armchair Theatre	ITV	5.1
17	Dick Emery's Grand Prix	BBC	5.0
18	Music Hall	ITV	4.8
19	This Week	ITV	4.8
20	Ten Tall Men	BBC	4.7

AUGUST

1	Coronation Street	ITV	6.6
2	Whicker's Walkabout	ITV	6.3
3	Opportunity Knocks	ITV	6.1
4	Coronation Street	ITV	6.1
5	A Family At War	ITV	5.8
6	Never Mind the Quality	ITV	5.4
7	News At Ten	ITV	5.4
8	Playhouse	ITV	5.3
9	It's a Knockout	BBC	5.3
10	The Dustbinmen	ITV	5.1
11	This Week	ITV	5.0
12	News At Ten	ITV	4.9
13	Husbands and Lovers	ITV	4.9
14	The Des O'Connor Show	ITV	4.9
15	His and Hers	ITV	4.8
16	News At Ten	ITV	4.8
17	News At Ten	ITV	4.7
18	The Troubleshooters	BBC	4.5
19	Hark At Barker	ITV	4.4
20	Cinema	ITV	4.4

SEPTEMBER

1	Coronation Street	ITV	6.9
2	News At Ten	ITV	6.5
3	Special Branch	ITV	6.4
4	The Sinners	ITV	6.4
5	Coronation Street	ITV	6.2
6	It's a Knockout	BBC	6.2
7	News At Ten	ITV	5.9
8	The Worker	ITV	5.9
9	News At Ten	ITV	5.7
10	A Man Called Ironside	BBC	5.4
11	This Week	ITV	5.4
12	Nearest and Dearest	ITV	5.3
13	The Dustbinmen	ITV	5.3
14	Never Say Die	ITV	5.2
15	Me Mammy	BBC	5.2
16	War of the Worlds	ITV	5.1
17	The Golden Shot	ITV	5.1
18	News At Ten	ITV	5.0
19	Opportunity Knocks	ITV	4.9
20	Cinema	ITV	4.7

OCTOBER

1	Prizewinners	BBC	8.0
2	Please Sir!	ITV	7.3
3	Coronation Street	ITV	7.2
4	News At Ten	ITV	7.2
5	Morecambe and Wise	BBC	7.0
6	Nine O'Clock News	BBC	6.9
7	Coronation Street	ITV	6.8
8	The Main Chance	ITV	6.7
9	Cribbins	ITV	6.7
10	Special Branch	ITV	6.7
11	Diamond Crack Diamond	ITV	6.6
12	Opportunity Knocks	ITV	6.5
13	News At Ten	ITV	6.4
14	Mike and Bernie's Special	ITV	6.4
15	Armchair Theatre	ITV	6.3
16	Fraud Squad	ITV	6.3
17	World In Action	ITV	6.3
18	Crowther's In Town	ITV	6.3
19	The Golden Shot	ITV	6.2
20	For the Love of Ada	ITV	6.2

NOVEMBER

1	Please Sir!	ITV	7.7
2	Steptoe and Son	BBC	7.6
3	Coronation Street	ITV	7.5
4	Coronation Street	ITV	7.3
5	Opportunity Knocks!	ITV	7.0
6	Armchair Theatre	ITV	6.8
7	Dad's Army	BBC	6.8
8	The Main Chance	ITV	6.7
9	Queenie's Castle	ITV	6.6
10	Fraud Squad	ITV	6.6
11	News At Ten	ITV	6.6
12	Special Branch	ITV	6.3
13	Softly, Softly	BBC	6.3
14	World In Action	ITV	6.2
15	The Lovers	ITV	6.2
16	Blue Murder At St. Trinians	BBC	6.2
17	News At Ten	ITV	6.1
18	Mary Hopkins Land of Films	BBC	6.1
19	Boy On a Dolphin	BBC	6.1
20	Z Cars	BBC	6.0

DECEMBER

1	On the Buses	ITV	7.8
2	Please Sir!	ITV	7.8
3	News At Ten	ITV	7.2
4	International Boxing	ITV	7.0
5	Steptoe and Son	BBC	6.9
6	Coronation Street	BBC	6.9
7	Dixon of Dock Green	BBC	6.8
8	Coronation Street	ITV	6.7
9	Opportunity Knocks	ITV	6.7
10	Morecambe and Wise Show	BBC	6.7
11	This Is Your Life	ITV	6.5
12	Dad's Army	BBC	6.4
13	The Rolf Harris Show	BBC	6.3
14	The Sound of Anger	BBC	6.2
15	Happy Ever After	ITV	6.1
16	Bachelor Father	BBC	6.0
17	The Golden Shot	ITV	5.8
18	Softly, Softly	BBC	5.7
19	The Main Chance	ITV	5.6
20	Saturday With Nimmo	BBC	5.6

MONTH BY MONTH 1970

1971

[Homes in Millions]

MONTH BY MONTH 1971

JANUARY

1	This Is Your Life	ITV	8.1
2	Nearest and Dearest	ITV	7.9
3	Coronation Street	ITV	7.8
4	A Family At War	ITV	7.7
5	Hadleigh	ITV	7.6
6	Coronation Street	ITV	7.6
7	News At Ten	ITV	7.4
8	Dixon of Dock Green	BBC	7.3
9	The World of Whicker	ITV	7.3
10	On the Buses	ITV	7.2
11	Softly, Softly	BBC	6.9
12	News At Ten	ITV	6.9
13	Laughter In Paradise	BBC	6.8
14	Six Dates With Barker	ITV	6.7
15	Z Cars	BBC	6.6
16	The Rolf Harris Show	BBC	6.6
17	The Cliff Richard Show	BBC	6.5
18	Man At the Top	ITV	6.4
19	Shadow Over Elveron	BBC	6.3
20	The Val Doonican Show	BBC	6.1

FEBRUARY

1	Coronation Street	ITV	8.6
2	Coronation Street	ITV	8.6
3	A Family At War	ITV	8.5
4	This Is Your Life	ITV	8.2
5	Nearest and Dearest	ITV	8.1
6	News At Ten	ITV	8.0
7	Bless This House	ITV	7.9
8	On the Buses	ITV	7.9
9	Shadows Of Fear	ITV	7.6
10	Man At the Top	ITV	7.5
11	Dixon of Dock Green	BBC	7.5
12	Hadleigh	ITV	7.2
13	Cilla	BBC	7.2
14	News At Ten	ITV	6.9
15	Dear Mother, Love Albert	ITV	6.7
16	The Cliff Richard Show	BBC	6.7
17	A Man Called Ironside	BBC	6.6
18	David Nixon's Magic Box	ITV	6.6
19	News At Ten	ITV	6.5
20	Softly, Softly	BBC	6.5

MARCH

1	This Is Your Life	ITV	8.3
2	Coronation Street	ITV	8.3
3	Coronation Street	ITV	8.1
4	A Family At War	ITV	7.8
5	Dixon of Dock Green	BBC	7.8
6	Bless This House	ITV	7.2
7	Doctor At Large	ITV	7.2
8	The British Screen Awards	BBC	7.1
9	Cilla	BBC	7.1
10	News At Ten	ITV	6.8
11	Hadleigh	ITV	6.8
12	World In Action	ITV	6.7
13	Dear Mother, Love Albert	ITV	6.7
14	State Secret	BBC	6.7
15	David Nixon's Magic Box	ITV	6.7
16	Joey Boy	BBC	6.6
17	News At Ten	ITV	6.6
18	Shadows of Fear	ITV	6.5
19	Sykes and a Big, Big Show	BBC	6.5
20	The Dick Emery	BBC	6.5

APRIL

1	This Is Your Life	ITV	8.2
2	Coronation Street	ITV	7.8
3	Coronation Street	ITV	7.8
4	Bless This House	ITV	7.8
5	For the Love of Ada	ITV	7.4
6	Hine	ITV	7.1
7	News At Ten	ITV	6.9
8	Budgie	ITV	6.9
9	The Ten Commandments	ITV	6.8
10	Opportunity Knocks	ITV	6.6
11	World In Action	ITV	6.4
12	News At Ten	ITV	6.1
13	Ironside	BBC	5.8
14	The Misfit	ITV	5.7
15	Slapstick and Old Lace	ITV	5.6
16	News At Ten	ITV	5.5
17	News At Ten	ITV	5.5
18	The Two Ronnies	BBC	5.5
19	Doctor At Large	ITV	5.3
20	Easy Street	BBC	5.3

MAY

1	Coronation Street	ITV	7.4
2	This Is Your Life	iTV	7.2
3	For the Love of Ada	ITV	7.1
4	Coronation Street	ITV	6.8
5	Doctor At Large	ITV	6.8
6	And Mother Makes Three	ITV	6.7
7	Opportunity Knocks	ITV	6.7
8	News At Ten	ITV	6.5
9	The Mind of J.G.Reader	ITV	6.4
10	World In Action	ITV	6.0
11	News At Ten	ITV	6.0
12	Budgie	ITV	5.8
13	The Great Train Race	ITV	5.8
14	A Man Called Ironside	BBC	5.8
15	The Dick Emery Show	BBC	5.7
16	The Two Ronnies	BBC	5.7
17	News At Ten	ITV	5.6
18	Z Cars	BBC	5.4
19	The Sky's the Limit	ITV	5.3
20	Comanche	BBC	5.3

JUNE

1	Opportunity Knocks	ITV	6.6
2	Coronation Street	ITV	6.6
3	Mike and Bernie's Show	ITV	6.2
4	News At Ten	ITV	6.1
5	The Sky's the Limit	ITV	6.1
6	The Mind of J.G.Reader	ITV	6.0
7	Coronation Street	ITV	6.0
8	Queenie's Castle	ITV	5.9
9	Budgie	ITV	5.9
10	Black and White Minstrels	BBC	5.9
11	The Last of the Baskets	ITV	5.8
12	News At Ten	ITV	5.8
13	News At Ten	ITV	5.8
14	News At Ten	ITV	5.8
15	A Man Called Ironside	BBC	5.7
16	World In Action	ITV	5.7
17	And Mother Makes Three	ITV	5.5
18	Kindly Leave the Kerb	ITV	5.5
19	Wreck of the Mary Deare	BBC	5.4
20	Hine	ITV	5.4

JULY

1	Coronation Street	ITV	6.4
2	Opportunity Knocks	ITV	6.0
3	News At Ten	ITV	6.0
4	Public Eye	ITV	5.9
5	Kate	ITV	5.9
6	Father, Dear Father	ITV	5.6
7	News At Ten	ITV	5.5
8	Coronation Street	ITV	5.5
9	Queenie's Castle	ITV	5.4
10	Crime of Passion	ITV	5.4
11	The Sky's the Limit	ITV	5.3
12	World In Action	ITV	5.2
13	You're Only Young Twice	ITV	5.2
14	Seasons of the Year	ITV	5.0
15	Sykes- With the Lid Off	ITV	5.0
16	The Comedians	ITV	5.0
17	News At Ten	ITV	4.9
18	News At Ten	ITV	4.9
19	News At Ten	ITV	4.8
20	A Man Called Ironside	BBC	4.8

AUGUST

1	Coronation Street	ITV	6.3
2	Coronation Street	ITV	6.1
3	Public Eye	ITV	5.9
4	Never Mind the Quality	ITV	5.8
5	Opportunity Knocks	ITV	5.7
6	Edward Woodward Hour	ITV	5.7
7	News At Ten	ITV	5.6
8	Alexander the Greatest	ITV	5.5
9	The Sky's the Limit	ITV	5.5
10	News At Ten	ITV	5.4
11	Apollo 15	BBC	5.4
12	The World of Whicker	ITV	5.2
13	You're Only Young Twice	ITV	5.2
14	The Sinners	ITV	5.2
15	Up Pompeii	BBC	5.0
16	Kate	ITV	4.9
17	Nine O'Clock News	BBC	4.9
18	It's a Knockout	BBC	4.8
19	The Des O'Connor Show	ITV	4.8
20	News At Ten	ITV	4.7

SEPTEMBER

1	Public Eye	ITV	7.3
2	Frankie Howerd's Hour	ITV	7.3
3	For the Love of Ada	ITV	7.1
4	News At Ten	ITV	6.4
5	Coronation Street	ITV	6.2
6	News At Ten	ITV	5.9
7	The Heroes of Telemark	BBC	5.7
8	Armchair Theatre	ITV	5.7
9	It's a Knockout!	BBC	5.6
10	A Man Called Ironside	BBC	5.5
11	News At Ten	ITV	5.3
12	This Week	ITV	5.3
13	Never Mind the Quality	ITV	5.2
14	Journey To Centre of Earth	BBC	5.2
15	Coronation Street	ITV	5.1
16	Disney Time	BBC	5.1
17	Kate	ITV	5.1
18	Billy Smart's Circus	BBC	5.0
19	Getaway With Cliff	BBC	5.0
20	Sunday Night Theatre	ITV	5.0

OCTOBER

1	The Persuaders	ITV	7.5
2	The Fenn Street Gang	ITV	7.5
3	A Family At War	ITV	7.4
4	Coronation Street	ITV	7.3
5	Coronation Street	ITV	7.0
6	Father, Dear Father	ITV	6.9
7	Justice	ITV	6.6
8	The Lovers	ITV	6.4
9	World In Action	ITV	6.4
10	The Sky's the Limit	ITV	6.4
11	Steptoe and Son	BBC	6.2
12	On the Buses	ITV	6.2
13	News At Ten	ITV	6.1
14	Softly, Softly	BBC	5.9
15	The Comedians	ITV	5.9
16	David Nixon's Magic Box	ITV	5.8
17	News At Ten	ITV	5.7
18	Z Cars	BBC	5.6
19	Lilies of the Field	BBC	5.6
20	Armchair Theatre	ITV	5.6

NOVEMBER

1	Coronation Street	ITV	7.6
2	A Family At War	ITV	7.5
3	Coronation Street	ITV	7.4
4	Carry On Cabby	BBC	7.4
5	The Lovers	ITV	7.4
6	On the Buses	ITV	7.2
7	Cilla	BBC	7.1
8	The Persuaders	ITV	7.1
9	The Val Doonican Show	ITV	7.0
10	The Passenger	BBC	7.0
11	The Fenn Street Gang	ITV	6.7
12	The Man Who Never Was	BBC	6.7
13	Justice	ITV	6.6
14	The Sky's the Limit	ITV	6.6
15	Z Cars	BBC	6.5
16	Lollipop Loves Mr Mole	ITV	6.5
17	News At Ten	ITV	6.5
18	Up Pompeii	BBC	6.4
19	The Flaxton Boys	ITV	6.4
20	Golden Shot	ITV	6.3

DECEMBER

1	This Is Your Life	ITV	8.4
2	Coronation Steet	ITV	7.8
3	Coronation Street	iTV	7.7
4	The Persuaders	ITV	7.7
5	A Family At War	ITV	7.5
6	On the Buses	ITV	7.4
7	Opportunity Knocks	ITV	7.3
8	And Mother Makes Three	ITV	7.3
9	The Fenn Street Gang	ITV	6.8
10	The Sky's the Limit	ITV	6.7
11	Justice	ITV	6.7
12	Generation Game	BBC	6.7
13	Cilla	BBC	6.6
14	Dixon of Dock Green	BBC	6.6
15	Z Cars	BBC	6.5
16	News At Ten	ITV	6.5
17	Softly, Softly	BBC	6.4
18	Lollipop Loves Mr. Mole	ITV	6.3
19	News At Ten	ITV	6.3
20	Rivals of Sherlock Holmes	ITV	6.2

1972

[Homes in Millions]

JANUARY

1	This Is Your Life	ITV	8.5
2	A Family At War	ITV	8.2
3	Suspicion	ITV	8.1
4	Coronation Street	ITV	7.7
5	The Dick Emery Show	BBC	7.4
6	News At Ten	ITV	7.2
7	Opportunity Knocks!	ITV	7.2
8	Dixon of Dock Green	BBC	7.2
9	News At Ten	ITV	7.1
10	And Mother Makes Three	ITV	7.0
11	Coronation Street	ITV	6.9
12	Witches - New Fashion	ITV	6.7
13	Hollywood Premiere	BBC	6.6
14	News At Ten	ITV	6.5
15	It's Cliff Richard	BBC	6.4
16	The Persuaders	ITV	6.3
17	The Alamo	BBC	6.2
18	Justice	ITV	6.2
19	Mike and Bernie	ITV	6.1
20	Softly, Softly	BBC	5.9

FEBRUARY

1	This Is Your Life	ITV	8.5
2	Opportunity Knocks!	ITV	8.0
3	Coronation Street	ITV	7.7
4	A Family At War	ITV	7.7
5	Coronation Street	ITV	7.6
6	Love Story	ITV	7.0
7	News At Ten	ITV	6.8
8	The Persuaders	ITV	6.7
9	Whicker's Orient	ITV	6.6
10	News At Ten	ITV	6.6
11	Sez Les	ITV	6.4
12	The Sky's the Limit	ITV	6.4
13	Softly, Softly	BBC	6.3
14	The Dick Emery Show	BBC	6.2
15	Upstairs, Downstairs	ITV	6.1
16	Dixon of Dock Green	BBC	6.0
17	The Fenn Street Gang	ITV	5.9
18	A European Journey	ITV	5.8
19	Nine O'Clock News	BBC	5.7
20	News At Ten	ITV	5.6

MARCH

1	This Is Your Life	ITV	8.6
2	Opportunity Knocks!	ITV	8.0
3	Steptoe and Son	BBC	8.0
4	On the Buses	ITV	8.0
5	Coronation Street	ITV	7.6
6	Coronation Street	ITV	7.5
7	My Good Woman	ITV	7.5
8	The Comedians	ITV	7.2
9	Bless This House	ITV	7.1
10	Love Story	ITV	7.1
11	Des	ITV	7.0
12	Softly, Softly	BBC	6.9
13	The Dick Emery Show	BBC	6.9
14	The Sky's the Limit	ITV	6.7
15	News At Ten	ITV	6.3
16	A European Journey	ITV	6.3
17	The Liver Birds	BBC	6.3
18	Both Ends Meet	ITV	6.2
19	Spyder's Web	ITV	6.2
20	Callan	ITV	6.1

APRIL

1	This Is Your Life	ITV	8.7
2	Coronation Street	ITV	8.3
3	A Place In the Sun	ITV	7.0
4	Max	ITV	6.9
5	Callan	ITV	6.9
6	Doctor In Charge	ITV	6.9
7	The Sky's the Limit	ITV	6.8
8	Cade's County	ITV	6.8
9	Girls Galore	BBC	6.7
10	Steptoe and Son	BBC	6.7
11	News At Ten	ITV	6.6
12	The Liver Birds	BBC	6.5
13	Des	ITV	6.1
14	Carry On Spying	BBC	6.0
15	The Brothers	BBC	5.9
16	Coronation Street	ITV	5.8
17	Ken Dodd	ITV	5.8
18	Sportsnight With Coleman	BBC	5.7
19	Tarbuck's Luck	BBC	5.7
20	News At Ten	ITV	5.5

MAY

1	This Is Your Life	ITV	8.5
2	Love Thy Neighbour	ITV	8.1
3	Bless This House	ITV	8.0
4	Crimes of Passion	ITV	7.5
5	Six Days of Justice	ITV	7.5
6	Cade's County	ITV	7.3
7	Coronation Street	ITV	7.2
8	Coronation Street	ITV	7.1
9	Opportunity Knocks!	ITV	6.9
10	World In Action	ITV	6.8
11	Callan	ITV	6.8
12	Doctor In Charge	ITV	6.8
13	The Sky's the Limit	ITV	6.6
14	News At Ten	ITV	6.6
15	Albert!	ITV	6.5
16	The Liver Birds	BBC	6.2
17	Budgie	ITV	5.9
18	News At Ten	ITV	5.9
19	The Brothers	BBC	5.8
20	News At Ten	ITV	5.8

JUNE

1	Crime of Passion	ITV	7.4
2	News At Ten	ITV	7.0
3	Nearest and Dearest	ITV	6.9
4	Man At the Top	ITV	6.8
5	The Main Chance	ITV	6.8
6	Alcock and Gander	ITV	6.8
7	News At Ten	ITV	6.7
8	News At Ten	ITV	6.6
9	Coronation Street	ITV	6.5
10	Look - Mike Yarwood	BBC	6.1
11	The Sky's the Limit	ITV	6.0
12	Coronation Street	ITV	6.0
13	World In Action	ITV	5.8
14	News At Ten	ITV	5.8
15	Doctor In Charge	ITV	5.7
16	It's a Knockout	BBC	5.7
17	Operation Amsterdam	BBC	5.7
18	Football: Anglo Italian	ITV	5.6
19	The David Nixon Show	ITV	5.5
20	Albert!	ITV	5.4

JULY

1	Man At the Top	ITV	7.2
2	Coronation Street	ITV	6.9
3	News At Ten	ITV	6.6
4	Father, Dear Father	ITV	6.5
5	Playhouse	ITV	6.3
6	The David Nixon Show	ITV	6.2
7	Alcock And Gander	ITV	6.2
8	The Main Chance	ITV	6.2
9	News At Ten	ITV	6.2
10	News At Ten	ITV	6.1
11	Nearest and Dearest	ITV	6.0
12	World In Action	ITV	5.8
13	The Sky's the Limit	ITV	5.8
14	Coronation Street	ITV	5.6
15	In For a Penny	ITV	5.6
16	Budgie	ITV	5.5
17	S.O.S. Pacific	BBC	5.3
18	Doctor In Charge	ITV	5.1
19	Black and White Minstrels	BBC	5.1
20	News At Ten	ITV	5.0

AUGUST

1	Crime of Passion	ITV	6.9
2	Max Bygraves At the Royalty	ITV	6.8
3	Man At The Top	ITV	6.5
4	News At Ten	ITV	6.5
5	Coronation Street	ITV	6.3
6	Mike and Bernie's Show	ITV	6.0
7	Whicker: A Woman's World	ITV	6.0
8	The Main Chance	ITV	5.9
9	News At Ten	ITV	5.8
10	Coronation Street	ITV	5.8
11	News At Ten	ITV	5.7
12	Nine O'Clock News	BBC	5.7
13	Opportunity Knocks	ITV	5.6
14	The Dead End Lads	ITV	5.6
15	Queenie's Castle	ITV	5.6
16	Who Do You Do?	ITV	5.5
17	It's a Knockout	BBC	5.5
18	Lollipop	ITV	5.3
19	It's All In a Life	ITV	5.2
20	News At Ten	ITV	5.2

MONTH BY MONTH 1972

SEPTEMBER

1	Shut That Door	ITV	6.5
2	Man At the Top	ITV	6.4
3	Nine O'Clock News	BBC	6.4
4	Nine O'Clock News	BBC	6.3
5	Max Bygraves At the Royalty	ITV	6.3
6	Coronation Street	ITV	6.1
7	Doctor In Charge	ITV	6.1
8	Are You Being Served?	BBC	5.9
9	Coronation Street	ITV	5.8
10	A Man Called Ironside	BBC	5.8
11	Queenie's Castle	ITV	5.7
12	The Dick Emery Show	BBC	5.7
13	Opportunity Knocks	ITV	5.6
14	Lollipop	ITV	5.6
15	Nine O'Clock News	BBC	5.6
16	Generation Game	BBC	5.4
17	Comedy Playhouse	BBC	5.4
18	No Highway	BBC	5.3
19	Whicker: A Woman's World	ITV	5.2
20	Hurricane Higgins	ITV	5.1

OCTOBER

1	Love Thy Neighbour	ITV	8.2
2	Dad's Army	BBC	7.4
3	And Mother Makes Three	ITV	7.2
4	Coronation Street	ITV	7.2
5	World In Action	ITV	7.2
6	Opportunity Knocks	ITV	7.1
7	Softly, Softly	BBC	6.8
8	Kate	ITV	6.6
9	Armchair Theatre	ITV	6.6
10	Doctor In Charge	ITV	6.6
11	Coronation Street	ITV	6.3
12	Dixon of Dock Green	BBC	6.2
13	Nine O'Clock News	BBC	6.2
14	Nine O'Clock News	BBC	6.1
15	The Two Ronnies	BBC	6.1
16	My Good Woman	ITV	6.1
17	Crossroads	ITV	6.1
18	My Wife Next Door	BBC	6.0
19	News At Ten	ITV	5.8
20	Crossroads	ITV	5.8

NOVEMBER

1	Opportunity Knocks	ITV	7.5
2	Dixon of Dock Green	BBC	7.2
3	Colditz	BBC	7.2
4	Dad's Army	BBC	7.2
5	Coronation Street	ITV	7.1
6	Upstairs, Downstairs	ITV	7.1
7	Public Eye	ITV	6.9
8	News At Ten	ITV	6.9
9	Generation Game	BBC	6.8
10	The Strauss Family	ITV	6.8
11	The Fenn Street Gang	ITV	6.8
12	Des	ITV	6.7
13	Softly, Softly	BBC	6.7
14	News At Ten	ITV	6.6
15	Coronation Street	ITV	6.6
16	The Sheepman	BBC	6.5
17	News At Ten	ITV	6.4
18	Thirty Minutes Worth	ITV	6.4
19	Crossroads	ITV	6.2
20	Crossroads	ITV	6.1

DECEMBER

1	This Is Your Life	ITV	8.5
2	The Strauss Family	ITV	7.6
3	Opportunity Knocks	ITV	7.4
4	Dad's Army	BBC	7.2
5	Upstairs, Downstairs	ITV	7.1
6	Coronation Street	ITV	7.1
7	Colditz	BBC	7.1
8	Public Eye	ITV	7.0
9	Coronation Street	ITV	6.9
10	Generation Game	BBC	6.8
11	Dixon of Dock Green	BBC	6.8
12	News At Ten	ITV	6.8
13	Thirty Minutes Worth	ITV	6.6
14	Crossroads	ITV	6.6
15	Softly, Softly	BBC	6.6
16	News At Ten	ITV	6.6
17	Adventures of Black Beauty	ITV	6.4
18	The Harry Secombe Show	ITV	6.4
19	My Wife Next Door	BBC	6.2
20	Opportunity Knocks	ITV	6.0

1973

[Homes in Millions]

JANUARY

1	This Is Your Life	ITV	8.2
2	Public Eye	ITV	7.8
3	Miss TV Europe	ITV	7.7
4	Upstairs Downstairs	ITV	7.5
5	Father Dear Father	ITV	7.2
6	Coronation Street	ITV	7.1
7	Love Story	ITV	7.0
8	Fenn Street Gang	ITV	7.0
9	Colditz	BBC	6.9
10	Morecambe and Wise Show	BBC	6.8
11	News At Ten	ITV	6.8
12	News At Ten	ITV	6.7
13	Death of Adolf Hitler	ITV	6.6
14	Crossroads	ITV	6.6
15	Generation Game	ITV	6.5
16	Softly, Softly	BBC	6.2
17	News At Ten	ITV	6.1
18	Cilla	BBC	6.1
19	News At Ten	ITV	6.0
20	A Man Called Ironside	BBC	6.0

FEBRUARY

1	This Is Your Life	ITV	8.9
2	Love Story	ITV	7.8
3	Cilla	BBC	7.7
4	Opportunity Knocks	ITV	7.6
5	A Man Called Ironside	BBC	7.5
6	Father Dear Father	ITV	7.4
7	Coronation Street	ITV	7.3
8	Coronation Street	ITV	7.1
9	Morecambe and Wise Show	BBC	7.0
10	Rivals of Sherlock Holmes	ITV	6.9
11	Crossroads	ITV	6.7
12	Nearest and Dearest	ITV	6.7
13	Bless This House	ITV	6.7
14	Public Eye	ITV	6.7
15	Torpedo Boy	BBC	6.6
16	Nine O'Clock News	ITV	6.5
17	Crossroads	ITV	6.4
18	Country Matters	ITV	6.4
19	Adventures of Black Beauty	ITV	6.3
20	Crossroads	ITV	6.3

MARCH

1	This Is Your Life	ITV	8.8
2	Whicker's South Seas	ITV	7.7
3	Opportunity Knocks	ITV	7.6
4	Dick Emery Show	BBC	7.5
5	Coronation Street	ITV	7.4
6	Bless This House	ITV	7.3
7	Morecambe and Wise Show	BBC	7.3
8	Coronation Street	ITV	7.1
9	Love Story	ITV	7.1
10	A Man Called Ironside	BBC	7.0
11	Crossroads	ITV	6.8
12	Playhouse	ITV	6.7
13	News At Ten	ITV	6.6
14	On the Buses	ITV	6.5
15	Rivals of Sherlock Holmes	ITV	6.5
16	News At Ten	ITV	6.5
17	Some Mothers Do 'Ave 'Em	BBC	6.5
18	The Burke Special	BBC	6.5
19	Justice	ITV	6.4
20	All Our Saturdays	ITV	6.3

APRIL

1	Eurovision Song Contest	BBC	9.8
2	This Is Your Life	ITV	8.7
3	Love Thy Neighbour	ITV	8.2
4	Opportunity Knocks	ITV	7.5
5	Coronation Street	ITV	7.5
6	Coronation Street	ITV	7.1
7	Special Branch	ITV	7.1
8	Justice	ITV	6.8
9	Crossroads	ITV	6.7
10	Shut That Door	ITV	6.7
11	Playhouse	ITV	6.4
12	News At Ten	ITV	6.4
13	A Man Called Ironside	BBC	6.4
14	World In Action	ITV	6.3
15	Crossroads	ITV	6.3
16	News At Ten	ITV	6.3
17	Crossroads	ITV	6.3
18	Rivals of Sherlock Holmes	ITV	6.2
19	It's Tarbuck	ITV	6.1
20	The Sky's the Limit	ITV	6.0

MAY

1	This Is Your Life	ITV	8.7
2	Bless This House	ITV	7.9
3	Coronation Street	ITV	7.8
4	The Dick Emery Show	BBC	7.1
5	Shut That Door	ITV	7.1
6	Coronation Street	ITV	6.9
7	Crossroads	ITV	6.9
8	The David Nixon Show	ITV	6.8
9	Special Branch	ITV	6.7
10	Crossroads	ITV	6.6
11	It's Tarbuck	ITV	6.5
12	Crossroads	ITV	6.5
13	World In Action	ITV	6.4
14	News At Ten	ITV	6.0
15	Crossroads	ITV	5.9
16	The Sky's the Limit	ITV	5.9
17	Rivals of Sherlock Holmes	ITV	5.8
18	James Paul McCartney	ITV	5.7
19	Six Days of Justice	ITV	5.7
20	The Sun TV Awards	ITV	5.7

JUNE

1	Special Branch	ITV	6.9
2	My Good Woman	ITV	6.8
3	Hunter's Walk	ITV	6.7
4	News At Ten	ITV	6.6
5	And Mother Makes Three	BBC	6.6
6	Coronation Street	ITV	6.4
7	Six Days of Justice	ITV	6.3
8	World In Action	ITV	6.1
9	The Dick Emery Show	BBC	6.1
10	It's a Knockout	BBC	6.0
11	Coronation Street	ITV	5.8
12	David Nixon Show	ITV	5.7
13	Crossroads	ITV	5.7
14	World Cup Grandstand	BBC	5.7
15	The Fenn Street Gang	ITV	5.7
16	News At Ten	ITV	5.6
17	News At Ten	ITV	5.6
18	Crossroads	ITV	5.5
19	The Sky's the Limit	ITV	5.4
20	Football: Russia v England	ITV	5.4

JULY

1	Thirty Mintues Worth	ITV	6.4
2	Special Branch	ITV	6.3
3	Hadleigh	ITV	6.3
4	Sam	ITV	6.2
5	Coronation Street	ITV	6.2
6	News At Ten	ITV	6.1
7	Coronation Street	ITV	6.0
8	My Good Woman	ITV	6.0
9	News At Ten	ITV	5.9
10	News At Ten	ITV	5.9
11	Hunter's Walk	ITV	5.8
12	News At Ten	ITV	5.7
13	News At Ten	ITV	5.6
14	Crossroads	ITV	5.4
15	Crossroads	ITV	5.4
16	Who Dunnit	ITV	5.4
17	World In Action	ITV	5.4
18	Crossroads	ITV	5.2
19	Nobody Is Norman Wisdom	ITV	5.2
20	Crossroads	ITV	5.0

AUGUST

1	Coronation Street	ITV	6.8
2	Coronation Street	ITV	6.5
3	Thirty Minutes Worth	ITV	6.5
4	Sam	ITV	6.4
5	Opportunity Knocks	ITV	6.2
6	Hunter's Walk	ITV	5.9
7	News At Ten	ITV	5.9
8	Spring and Autumn	IYV	5.7
9	News At Ten	ITV	5.7
10	Crossroads	ITV	5.6
11	Crossroads	ITV	5.5
12	Shabby Tiger	ITV	5.5
13	Crossroads	ITV	5.5
14	Hadleigh	ITV	5.4
15	Nobody Is Norman Widsom	ITV	5.4
16	News At Ten	ITV	5.3
17	Look - Mike Yarwood	BBC	5.3
18	It's Mike Reid	ITV	5.3
19	It's a Knockout	BBC	5.3
20	A Man Called Ironside	BBC	5.0

SEPTEMBER

1	Van der Valk	ITV	7.8
2	Man About the House	ITV	7.5
3	Coronation Street	ITV	7.3
4	Sam	ITV	7.0
5	Reg Varney	ITV	6.9
6	Coronation Street	ITV	6.8
7	Opportunity Knocks	ITV	6.7
8	News At Ten	ITV	6.5
9	News At Ten	ITV	6.3
10	Hadleigh	ITV	6.2
11	Singalonga Max	ITV	6.1
12	Crossroads	ITV	6.0
13	Crossroads	ITV	5.9
14	News At Ten	ITV	5.8
15	It's a Knockout	BBC	5.8
16	Crossroads	ITV	5.7
17	The Generation Game	BBC	5.3
18	Chester: Portrait of a City	ITV	5.2
19	Hunter's Walk	ITV	5.1
20	News At Ten	ITV	5.1

OCTOBER

1	Coronation Street	ITV	7.3
2	Whicker Way Out West	ITV	7.2
3	Crossroads	ITV	6.8
4	Coronation Street	ITV	6.8
5	The Generation Game	BBC	6.8
6	Van der Valk	ITV	6.6
7	Crossroads	ITV	6.5
8	Opportunity Knocks	ITV	6.4
9	Crossroads	ITV	6.4
10	Crossroads	ITV	6.2
11	What a Carry On	ITV	6.2
12	Thirty Minutes Worth	ITV	6.1
13	Top of the Pops	BBC	6.0
14	Men of Affairs	ITV	5.9
15	Armchair Theatre	ITV	5.9
16	Singalonga Max	ITV	5.7
17	It's Lulu	BBC	5.7
18	Dave Allen At Large	BBC	5.7
19	Helen, a Woman of Today	ITV	5.6
20	Crime of Passion	ITV	5.6

NOVEMBER

1	The Generation Game	BBC	7.4
2	Coronation Street	ITV	7.3
3	Crossroads	ITV	7.1
4	Crossroads	ITV	7.1
5	Crossroads	ITV	7.1
6	Opportunity Knocks	ITV	6.9
7	Coronation Street	ITV	6.9
8	Beryl's Lot	ITV	6.7
9	Upstairs Downstaris	ITV	6.6
10	Steptoe and Son	BBC	6.5
11	Sunday Night Palladium	ITV	6.4
12	Dad's Army	BBC	6.4
13	Armchair Theatre	ITV	6.4
14	News At Ten	ITV	6.4
15	Helen, a Woman of Today	ITV	6.3
16	Softly, Softly	BBC	6.3
17	Crossroads	ITV	6.3
18	Whicker Way Out West	ITV	6.3
19	Thirty Minutes Worth	BBC	6.2
20	Wonderful World of Disney	BBC	6.0

DECEMBER

1	The Benny Hill Show	ITV	8.2
2	Some Mother Do 'Ave 'Em	BBC	7.8
3	Coronation Street	ITV	7.7
4	This Is Your Life	ITV	7.5
5	The Generation Game	BBC	7.5
6	Opportunity Knocks	ITV	7.3
7	Helen, a Woman of Today	ITV	7.3
8	My Good Woman	ITV	7.2
9	Coronation Street	ITV	7.0
10	Crossroads	ITV	7.0
11	Crossroads	ITV	6.9
12	Crossroads	ITV	6.8
13	Nine O'Clock News	BBC	6.7
14	Sunday Night Palladium	ITV	6.5
15	Crossroads	ITV	6.4
16	News At Ten	ITV	6.3
17	Upstairs Downstairs	ITV	6.2
18	Harry Secombe Show	BBC	6.2
19	Heaven Knows Mr Allison	BBC	6.1
20	Billy Liar	ITV	6.0

1974

[Homes in Millions]

JANUARY

1	This Is Your Life	ITV	8.8
2	Opportunity Knocks	ITV	8.3
3	Val Doonican Show	ITV	8.0
4	Till Death Us Do Part	BBC	7.8
5	Coronation Street	ITV	7.6
6	Love Thy Neighbour	ITV	7.5
7	Beryl's Lot	ITV	7.4
8	Man About the House	ITV	7.3
9	Upstairs Downstairs	ITV	7.3
10	Crossroads	ITV	7.2
11	Crossroads	ITV	7.2
12	Coronation Street	ITV	7.2
13	Generation Game	BBC	7.1
14	Nine O'Clock News	BBC	7.0
15	Crossroads	ITV	7.0
16	Love Story	ITV	6.9
17	Crossroads	ITV	6.8
18	Billy Liar	ITV	6.7
19	Within These Walls	ITV	6.6
20	Candid Camera	ITV	6.4

FEBRUARY

1	This Is Your Life	ITV	9.4
2	Benny Hill Show	ITV	9.3
3	Opportunity Knocks	ITV	8.5
4	Love Thy Neighbour	ITV	8.3
5	Man About the House	ITV	8.0
6	Coronation Street	ITV	7.8
7	Within These Walls	ITV	7.6
8	Coronation Street	ITV	7.5
9	Crossroads	ITV	7.4
10	Election Special	ITV	7.4
11	Val Doonican Special	ITV	7.3
12	Crossroads	ITV	7.2
13	Candid Camera	ITV	7.2
14	Crossroads	ITV	7.1
15	Nine O'Clock News	BBC	7.1
16	News At Ten	ITV	7.0
17	Bless This House	ITV	6.7
18	Till Death Us Do Part	BBC	6.7
19	Adventures of Black Beauty	ITV	6.5
20	The Likely Lads	BBC	6.5

MARCH

1	This Is Your Life	ITV	8.8
2	British Screen Awards	ITV	8.8
3	Love Thy Neighbour	ITV	8.6
4	Within These Walls	ITV	8.4
5	Des O'Connor	ITV	8.2
6	Opportunity Knocks	ITV	8.1
7	News At Ten	ITV	8.0
8	Coronation Street	ITV	7.9
9	Coronation Street	ITV	7.7
10	Napoleon and Love	ITV	7.4
11	Crossroads	ITV	7.2
12	News At Ten	ITV	7.2
13	Crossroads	ITV	6.9
14	World In Action	ITV	6.8
15	Crossroads	ITV	6.8
16	Special Branch	ITV	6.7
17	Crossroads	ITV	6.7
18	Adventures of Black Beauty	ITV	6.7
19	Sez Les	ITV	6.6
20	Candid Camera	ITV	6.6

APRIL

1	Love Thy Neighbour	ITV	9.5
2	Bless This House	ITV	8.5
3	This Is Your Life	ITV	8.3
4	Max	ITV	8.3
5	Eurovision Song Contest	BBC	8.2
6	Coronation Street	ITV	7.8
7	Special Branch	ITV	7.6
8	Opportunity Knocks	ITV	7.5
9	Des O'Connor Show	ITV	7.4
10	World In Action	ITV	7.3
11	Coronation Street	ITV	7.0
12	Colditz	BBC	7.0
13	The Zoo Gang	ITV	6.9
14	Crossroads	ITV	6.9
15	World At War	ITV	6.7
16	News At Ten	ITV	6.5
17	Crossroads	ITV	6.5
18	Not On Your Nellie	ITV	6.4
19	Crossroads	ITV	6.4
20	The Awful Mr Goodhall	ITV	6.2

MAY

1	This Is Your Life	ITV	8.4
2	And Mother Makes Five	ITV	8.2
3	Special Branch	ITV	8.0
4	Coronation Street	ITV	7.7
5	My Name Is Harry Worth	ITV	7.2
6	Hunter's Walk	ITV	7.2
7	Coronation Street	ITV	7.1
8	Up the Workers	ITV	6.9
9	A Little Bit of Wisdom	ITV	6.9
10	Crossroads	ITV	6.8
11	Crossroads	ITV	6.7
12	News At Ten	ITV	6.6
13	The David Nixon Show	ITV	6.5
14	World At War	ITV	6.5
15	Crossroads	ITV	6.5
16	The Awful Mr Goodhall	ITV	6.5
17	World In Action	ITV	6.4
18	It's a Knockout	BBC	6.4
19	News At Ten	ITV	6.3
20	Crossroads	ITV	6.1

JUNE

1	Justice	ITV	7.1
2	Sam	ITV	7.0
3	And Mother Makes Five	ITV	7.0
4	News At Ten	ITV	7.0
5	Coronation Street	ITV	6.9
6	News At Ten	ITV	6.8
7	Up the Workers	ITV	6.5
8	Crossroads	ITV	6.4
9	Coronation Street	ITV	6.4
10	Crossroads	ITV	6.3
11	Playhouse	ITV	6.3
12	Crossroads	ITV	6.2
13	This Is Your Life	ITV	6.1
14	Doctor At Sea	ITV	6.1
15	Hunter's Walk	ITV	6.0
16	My Name Is Harry Worth	ITV	5.9
17	Crossroads	ITV	5.8
18	News At Ten	ITV	5.8
19	The David Nixon Show	ITV	5.7
20	News At Ten	ITV	5.7

JULY

1	Coronation Street	ITV	7.3
2	Sam	ITV	6.7
3	Coronation Street	ITV	6.4
4	Jimmy Tarbuck Show	ITV	6.3
5	Justice	ITV	6.3
6	Sprout	ITV	6.2
7	Whodunnit?	ITV	6.1
8	News At Ten	ITV	6.1
9	Sez Les	ITV	6.0
10	Crossroads	ITV	5.9
11	Crossroads	ITV	5.9
12	Crossroads	ITV	5.7
13	Doctor At Sea	ITV	5.7
14	Hunter's Walk	ITV	5.7
15	News At Ten	ITV	5.6
16	Love Affair	ITV	5.6
17	The Piano Smashers	ITV	5.5
18	Thriller	ITV	5.5
19	World Cup Football	ITV	5.5
20	The 1000 Plane Raid	BBC	5.4

AUGUST

1	Spring and Autumn	ITV	6.3
2	Sam	ITV	6.0
3	Coronation Street	ITV	5.9
4	Cannon	BBC	5.9
5	Love Thy Neighbour	ITV	5.8
6	Justice	ITV	5.8
7	Crossroads	ITV	5.6
8	Crossroads	ITV	5.6
9	Coronation Street	ITV	5.5
10	Opportunity Knocks	ITV	5.4
11	Village Hall	ITV	5.4
12	It's a Knockout	BBC	5.3
13	My Good Woman	ITV	5.2
14	Moody and Pegg	ITV	5.1
15	How's Your Father	ITV	5.1
16	Don't Drink the Water	ITV	5.1
17	Crossroads	ITV	5.1
18	Don't Ask Me	ITV	5.0
19	News At Ten	ITV	4.9
20	News At Ten	ITV	4.9

MONTH BY MONTH 1974

SEPTEMBER

1	Steptoe and Son	BBC	7.8
2	Nine O'Clock News	BBC	7.8
3	Coronation Street	ITV	6.8
4	Opportunity Knocks	ITV	6.7
5	Nine O'Clock News	BBC	6.7
6	Sutherland's Law	BBC	6.4
7	Crossroads	ITV	6.3
8	Moody and Pegg	ITV	6.2
9	Coronation Street	ITV	6.2
10	Porridge	BBC	6.2
11	Rising Damp	ITV	6.1
12	Softly, Softly	BBC	6.1
13	Crossroads	ITV	6.1
14	Some Mothers Do 'Ave 'Em	BBC	6.1
15	Crossroads	ITV	6.0
16	World In Action	ITV	6.0
17	Don't Ask Me	ITV	5.9
18	Don't Drink the Water	ITV	5.9
19	Crossroads	ITV	5.9
20	Nine O'Clock News	BBC	5.8

OCTOBER

1	Man About the House	ITV	7.2
2	Dave Allen In Search	ITV	7.2
3	Coronation Street	ITV	7.0
4	Crossroads	ITV	6.9
5	My Good Woman	ITV	6.8
6	Steptoe and Son	BBC	6.8
7	Morecambe and Wise	ITV	6.8
8	Crossroads	ITV	6.7
9	Coronation Street	ITV	6.7
10	Crossroads	ITV	6.6
11	Porridge	BBC	6.6
12	Generation Game	BBC	6.4
13	The Dick Emery Show	BBC	6.4
14	Nine O'Clock News	BBC	6.4
15	Survival	ITV	6.3
16	Opporunity Knocks	ITV	6.3
17	Sale of the Century	ITV	6.3
18	Nine O'Clock News	BBC	6.2
19	Upstairs Downstairs	ITV	6.2
20	This Is Your Life	ITV	6.1

NOVEMBER

1	Bless this House	ITV	8.6
2	Coronation Street	ITV	7.8
3	Man About the House	ITV	7.8
4	Generation Game	BBC	7.5
5	Coronation Street	ITV	7.4
6	Crossroads	ITV	7.4
7	Crossroads	ITV	7.4
8	Upstairs Downstairs	ITV	7.3
9	Jennie	ITV	7.2
10	Opportunity Knocks	ITV	7.1
11	Bootsie and Snudge	ITV	7.0
12	Heidi	BBC	7.0
13	Crossroads	ITV	6.9
14	Survival	ITV	6.9
15	Mastermind	BBC	6.9
16	No, Honestly	ITV	6.9
17	And Mother Makes Five	ITV	6.8
18	World In Action	ITV	6.7
19	Crossroads	ITV	6.6
20	Sale of the Century	ITV	6.6

DECEMBER

1	Bless This House	ITV	8.3
2	This Is Your Life	ITV	8.3
3	Mastermind	BBC	8.2
4	Generation Game	BBC	8.0
5	Opportunity Knocks	ITV	7.8
6	Coronation Street	ITV	7.6
7	Coronation Street	ITV	7.5
8	Jennie	ITV	7.4
9	Crossroads	ITV	7.4
10	Crossroads	ITV	7.4
11	Upstairs Downstairs	ITV	7.1
12	Sounds Like Les Dawson	ITV	7.1
13	Crossroads	ITV	7.0
14	News At Ten	ITV	6.9
15	World In Action	ITV	6.7
16	No, Honestly	ITV	6.5
17	Crossroads	ITV	6.5
18	Dad's Army	BBC	6.5
19	Ken Dodd	BBC	6.4
20	The Dick Emery Show	BBC	6.4

1975

[Homes in Millions]

MONTH BY MONTH 1975

JANUARY

1	Love Thy Neighbour	ITV	8.8
2	Generation Game	BBC	8.1
3	Coronation Street	ITV	8.0
4	This Is Your Life	ITV	7.9
5	Opportunity Knocks	ITV	7.8
6	Coronation Street	ITV	7.4
7	The Sweeney	ITV	7.2
8	Crossroads	ITV	7.1
9	Haunted	ITV	7.1
10	Topaz	ITV	7.0
11	The Val Doonican Show	ITV	6.8
12	The Canterville Ghost	ITV	6.8
13	News At Ten	ITV	6.6
14	Crossroads	ITV	6.6
15	Rising Damp	ITV	6.5
16	No, Honestly	ITV	6.4
17	Pilger	ITV	6.3
18	Monte Carlo Or Bust	ITV	6.2
19	Sale of the Century	ITV	6.2
20	Columbo	ITV	6.1

FEBRUARY

1	Love Thy Neighbour	ITV	9.2
2	This Is Your Life	ITV	8.9
3	Cilla's Comedy Six	ITV	8.5
4	Coronation Street	ITV	8.3
5	The Life of Riley	ITV	8.2
6	Public Eye	ITV	8.2
7	Opportunity Knocks	ITV	8.0
8	Coronation Street	ITV	8.0
9	Crossroads	ITV	7.6
10	The Sweeney	ITV	7.6
11	News At Ten	ITV	7.5
12	Crossroads	ITV	7.5
13	Crossroads	ITV	7.5
14	Sale of the Century	ITV	7.4
15	Six Million Dollar Man	ITV	7.4
16	This Week	ITV	6.9
17	Within These Walls	ITV	6.9
18	A Little Bit of Wisdom	ITV	6.9
19	World In Action	ITV	6.8
20	Crossroads	ITV	6.6

MARCH

1	Man About the House	ITV	8.6
2	This Is Your Life	ITV	8.0
3	Opportunity Knocks	ITV	7.9
4	The Sweeney	ITV	7.8
5	Whicker's World	ITV	7.7
6	Sale of the Century	ITV	7.7
7	Coronation Street	ITV	7.6
8	This Week	ITV	7.5
9	Coronation Street	ITV	7.5
10	Last of the Summer Wine	BBC	7.5
11	How's Your Father	ITV	7.4
12	You're On Your Own	BBC	7.4
13	The Main News	BBC	7.4
14	Crossroads	ITV	7.3
15	Crossroads	ITV	7.3
16	Crossroads	ITV	7.1
17	News At Ten	ITV	7.0
18	Des O'Connor Entertains	ITV	6.9
19	New Faces	ITV	6.9
20	Within These Walls	ITV	6.6

APRIL

1	This Is Your Life	ITV	8.3
2	Man About the House	ITV	8.1
3	My Old Man	ITV	7.9
4	Special Branch	ITV	7.8
5	Opportunity Knocks	ITV	7.7
6	Crossroads	ITV	7.7
7	Crossroads	ITV	7.7
8	Within These Walls	ITV	7.7
9	Coronation Street	ITV	7.6
10	Crossroads	ITV	7.6
11	Are You Being Served?	BBC	7.5
12	How's Your Father	ITV	7.5
13	Des O'Connor Entertains	ITV	7.3
14	Crossroads	ITV	7.3
15	News At Ten	ITV	7.0
16	Edward the Seventh	ITV	6.9
17	The Wackers	ITV	6.9
18	News At Ten	ITV	6.7
19	Mike Yarwood	BBC	6.6
20	High Society	ITV	6.5

MAY

1	Edward the Seventh	ITV	8.7
2	This Is Your Life	ITV	8.7
3	Bless This House	ITV	8.7
4	Coronation Street	ITV	8.3
5	Are You Being Served?	BBC	7.7
6	Crossroads	ITV	7.7
7	Love Thy Neighbour	ITV	7.7
8	News At Ten	ITV	7.4
9	Crossroads	ITV	7.4
10	Crossroads	ITV	7.1
11	Crossroads	ITV	7.1
12	The Main Chance	ITV	7.0
13	Coronation Street	ITV	6.9
14	The Loner	ITV	6.6
15	Sale of the Century	ITV	6.6
16	Sadie, It's Cold Outside	ITV	6.5
17	Shut That Door	ITV	6.5
18	Kojak	BBC	6.4
19	Special Branch	ITV	6.4
20	The David Nixon Show	ITV	6.3

JUNE

1	Kojak	BBC	7.8
2	And Mother Makes Five	ITV	6.7
3	Edward the Seventh	ITV	6.6
4	Coronation Street	ITV	6.5
5	Sam	ITV	6.5
6	Main News & Weather	BBC	6.5
7	Crossroads	ITV	6.5
8	Crossroads	ITV	6.4
9	Sutherland's Law	BBC	6.3
10	Coronation Street	ITV	6.3
11	Dad's Army	BBC	6.2
12	Crossroads	ITV	6.1
13	The David Nixon Show	ITV	6.0
14	Don't Ask Me	ITV	6.0
15	News At Ten	ITV	6.0
16	Jacques Cousteau	BBC	5.8
17	The Main Chance	ITV	5.7
18	The World of Television	ITV	5.6
19	Top of the Pops	BBC	5.5
20	Are You Being Served?	BBC	5.4

JULY

1	Coronation Street	ITV	6.8
2	And Mother Makes Five	ITV	6.8
3	Coronation Street	ITV	6.6
4	Crossroads	ITV	6.5
5	Crossroads	ITV	6.4
6	It's a Celebrity Knockout	BBC	6.4
7	Three Comedies of Marriage	ITV	6.3
8	Crossroads	ITV	6.3
9	Sale of the Century	ITV	6.1
10	The Passing of Leviathan	ITV	5.9
11	Crossroads	ITV	5.9
12	Jacques Cousteau	BBC	5.8
13	News At Ten	ITV	5.7
14	Rising Damp	ITV	5.6
15	Don't Ask Me	ITV	5.6
16	Cannon	BBC	5.6
17	The David Nixon Show	ITV	5.5
18	Sam	ITV	5.5
19	That's Life	BBC	5.4
20	News At Ten	ITV	5.3

AUGUST

1	Man About the House	ITV	6.3
2	Cannon	BBC	6.3
3	Down the Gate	ITV	6.2
4	Seaside Special	BBC	6.1
5	Coronation Street	ITV	6.1
6	Crossroads	ITV	5.9
7	Crossroads	ITV	5.8
8	Crossroads	ITV	5.7
9	Coronation Street	ITV	5.6
10	Moody and Pegg	ITV	5.6
11	News At Ten	ITV	5.5
12	The Squirrels	ITV	5.5
13	Crossroads	ITV	5.4
14	Don't Ask Me	ITV	5.3
15	News At Ten	ITV	5.3
16	Sam	ITV	5.2
17	Gosling's Travels	ITV	5.0
18	News At Ten	ITV	4.9
19	Comedy Premiere	ITV	4.9
20	Whodunnit?	ITV	4.8

SEPTEMBER

1	Man About the House	ITV	7.9
2	The Sweeney	ITV	7.2
3	Miss Great Britain	ITV	7.1
4	The Stars Look Down	ITV	7.1
5	Upstairs, Downstairs	ITV	6.9
6	Crossroads	ITV	6.8
7	Crossroads	ITV	6.6
8	Crossroads	ITV	6.5
9	Sale of the Century	ITV	6.4
10	Crossroads	ITV	6.3
11	General Hospital	ITV	6.3
12	Liver Birds	BBC	6.3
13	Great Zaire River Expedition	ITV	6.2
14	Frankie and Bruce	ITV	6.1
15	News At Ten	ITV	6.0
16	The Two Ronnies	BBC	5.9
17	Coronation Street	ITV	5.9
18	Nine O'Clock News	BBC	5.9
19	The Dick Emery Show	BBC	5.9
20	Coronation Street	ITV	5.7

OCTOBER

1	The Sweeney	ITV	8.3
2	The Two Ronnies	BBC	8.1
3	Man About the House	ITV	8.1
4	The Generation Game	ITV	7.8
5	Crossroads	ITV	7.5
6	The Liver Birds	BBC	7.3
7	Upstairs, Downstairs	ITV	7.3
8	Crossroads	ITV	7.2
9	Crossroads	ITV	7.1
10	Crossroads	ITV	7.0
11	Dad's Army	BBC	7.0
12	Opportunity Knocks	ITV	7.0
13	Coronation Street	ITV	7.0
14	My Son Reuben	ITV	7.0
15	World In Action	ITV	6.6
16	The Dick Emery Show	BBC	6.5
17	The Invisible Man	BBC	6.4
18	Beryl's Lot	ITV	6.4
19	Coronation Street	ITV	6.3
20	Softly, Softly	BBC	6.3

NOVEMBER

1	The Generation Game	BBC	8.4
2	The Sweeney	ITV	8.2
3	Crossroads	ITV	8.0
4	Crossroads	ITV	7.7
5	Opportunity Knocks	ITV	7.7
6	Crossroads	ITV	7.6
7	Coronation Street	ITV	7.5
8	Upstairs, Downstairs	ITV	7.5
9	Ken Dodd'	BBC	7.3
10	Crossroads	ITV	7.3
11	Get Some In!	ITV	7.3
12	The Cuckoo Waltz	ITV	7.1
13	Coronation Street	ITV	6.8
14	Carry On Laughing	ITV	6.7
15	Porridge	BBC	6.7
16	Beryl's Lot	ITV	6.7
17	Sale of the Century	ITV	6.5
18	Dr Who	BBC	6.4
19	The Dick Emery Show	BBC	6.3
20	News At Ten	ITV	6.3

DECEMBER

1	The Generation Game	BBC	8.7
2	This Is Your Life	ITV	8.6
3	News	ITV	8.5
4	Upstairs, Downstairs	ITV	8.1
5	Opportunity Knocks	ITV	7.9
6	Crossroads	ITV	7.9
7	Crossroads	ITV	7.9
8	Coronation Street	ITV	7.6
9	Our Man Flint	ITV	7.6
10	Crossroads	ITV	7.6
11	Coronation Street	ITV	7.5
12	Crossroads	ITV	7.5
13	Ken Dodd	BBC	7.5
14	The Saturday Special	BBC	7.4
15	Rising Damp	ITV	7.0
16	The Cuckoo Waltz	ITV	7.0
17	Are You Being Served?	BBC	6.9
18	The Last Voyager	BBC	6.8
19	Kojak	BBC	6.8
20	Dr Who	BBC	6.6

1976

[Homes in Millions]

JANUARY

1	This Is Your Life	ITV	8.3
2	Morecambe and Wise Show	BBC	8.2
3	Sale of the Century	ITV	8.0
4	Crossroads	ITV	7.8
5	Crossroads	ITV	7.6
6	Opportunity Knocks	ITV	7.6
7	Crossroads	ITV	7.5
8	Coronation Street	ITV	7.4
9	Coronation Street	ITV	7.4
10	Crossroads	ITV	7.4
11	Happy Ever After	BBC	7.3
12	Celebrity Squares	ITV	7.3
13	Yes My Dear	ITV	7.3
14	Love Thy Neighbour	ITV	7.2
15	New Faces	ITV	7.0
16	Life and Death of Penelope	BBC	6.7
17	Top of the Pops	BBC	6.4
18	When the Boat Comes In	BBC	6.4
19	It Ain't Half Hot Mum	BBC	6.4
20	Bouquet of Barbed Wire	ITV	6.4

FEBRUARY

1	This Is Your Life	ITV	8.5
2	Crossroads	ITV	7.9
3	Crossroads	ITV	7.8
4	Crossroads	ITV	7.7
5	Sale of the Century	ITV	7.7
6	Crossroads	ITV	7.7
7	Coronation Street	ITV	7.6
8	Coronation Street	ITV	7.6
9	Opportunity Knocks	ITV	7.5
10	Happy Ever After	BBC	7.4
11	Bouquet of Barbed Wire	ITV	7.3
12	And Mother Makes Five	ITV	7.2
13	New Faces	ITV	7.2
14	Life and Death of Penelope	BBC	7.0
15	That's Life	BBC	6.8
16	Oh No It's Selwyn Froggitt	ITV	6.7
17	Celebrity Squares	ITV	6.7
18	Bless This House	ITV	6.6
19	News At Ten	ITV	6.5
20	Yes My Dear	ITV	6.5

MARCH

1	This Is Your Life	ITV	9.0
2	Man About the House	ITV	8.6
3	Coronation Street	ITV	8.1
4	Crossroads	ITV	7.7
5	Crossroads	ITV	7.6
6	Crossroads	ITV	7.6
7	Opportunity Knocks	ITV	7.5
8	Coronation Street	ITV	7.5
9	Sale of the Century	ITV	7.5
10	Crossroads	ITV	7.1
11	Celebrity Squares	ITV	7.0
12	The Good Old Days	BBC	7.0
13	Bless This House	ITV	6.9
14	Sez Les	ITV	6.8
15	When the Boat Comes In	BBC	6.8
16	Up the Workers	ITV	6.9
17	Happy Ever After	BBC	6.7
18	Steptoe and Son	BBC	6.7
19	The Liver Birds	BBC	6.5
20	New Faces	ITV	6.5

APRIL

1	Man About the House	ITV	9.2
2	This Is Your Life	ITV	8.9
3	Coronation Street	ITV	8.8
4	Up the Workers	ITV	7.9
5	Coronation Street	ITV	7.6
6	Crossroads	ITV	7.6
7	Sale of the Century	ITV	7.5
8	A Little Bit of Wisdom	ITV	7.4
9	Crossroads	ITV	7.4
10	Crossroads	ITV	7.3
11	The Fosters	ITV	7.3
12	Police Woman	ITV	7.1
13	Crossroads	ITV	7.1
14	New Faces	ITV	6.9
15	Rising Damp	ITV	6.8
16	The Two Ronnies	BBC	6.6
17	Are You Being Served?	BBC	6.6
18	The David Nixon Show	ITV	6.6
19	Luke's Kingdom	ITV	6.6
20	Bless This House	ITV	6.6

MAY

1	This Is Your Life	ITV	7.9
2	Coronation Street	ITV	7.6
3	Coronation Street	ITV	7.6
4	Crossroads	ITV	7.4
5	Crossroads	ITV	7.4
6	Rising Damp	ITV	7.2
7	A Little Bit of Wisdom	ITV	6.9
8	European Cup	ITV	6.9
9	Crossroads	ITV	6.9
10	The Fosters	ITV	6.9
11	The David Nixon Show	ITV	6.8
12	Sale of the Century	ITV	6.8
13	Crossroads	ITV	6.7
14	That's Life	BBC	6.6
15	Are You Being Served?	BBC	6.4
16	New Faces	ITV	6.2
17	Hadleigh	ITV	6.1
18	World In Action	ITV	6.0
19	Nurse of the Year	ITV	6.0
20	Kill Two Birds	ITV	5.9

JUNE

1	Crossroads	ITV	6.9
2	Crossroads	ITV	6.9
3	Crossroads	ITV	6.7
4	Coronation Street	ITV	6.7
5	Luke's Kingdom	ITV	6.5
6	Sale of the Century	ITV	6.3
7	News At Ten	ITV	6.2
8	Crossroads	ITV	6.2
9	My Brother's Keeper	ITV	6.1
10	World Cup Football	ITV	6.1
11	Winner Takes All	ITV	6.0
12	Don't Ask Me	ITV	5.9
13	Whicker's World	ITV	5.9
14	Coronation Street	ITV	5.8
15	Starsky and Hutch	BBC	5.8
16	New Faces	ITV	5.8
17	Morecambe and Wise Show	ITV	5.8
18	General Hospital	ITV	5.8
19	Porridge	BBC	5.6
20	Husband of the Year	ITV	5.4

JULY

1	News At Ten	ITV	6.9
2	The Bionic Woman	ITV	6.5
3	Crossroads	ITV	6.4
4	Crossroads	ITV	6.3
5	Bonnie and Clyde	BBC	6.2
6	Crossroads	ITV	6.1
7	Crossroads	ITV	6.0
8	The Great Race	ITV	5.8
9	Coronation Street	ITV	5.6
10	It's a Celebrity Knockout	BBC	5.6
11	Coronation Street	ITV	5.6
12	Man About the House	ITV	5.6
13	The Good Life	BBC	5.5
14	General Hospital	ITV	5.5
15	Get Some In	ITV	5.4
16	News At Ten	ITV	5.4
17	Starsky and Hutch	BBC	5.4
18	Nine O'Clock News	BBC	5.4
19	Nine O'Clock News	BBC	5.4
20	The Cuckoo Waltz	ITV	5.4

AUGUST

1	News At Ten	ITV	6.5
2	The Benny Hill Show	ITV	6.5
3	Get Some In	ITV	6.2
4	The Bionic Woman	ITV	6.1
5	Coronation Street	ITV	6.1
6	Hunter's Walk	ITV	6.1
7	Crossroads	ITV	6.0
8	The Cuckoo Waltz	ITV	6.0
9	The Pride and the Passion	ITV	5.9
10	Nine O'Clock News	BBC	5.9
11	The Squirrels	ITV	5.8
12	Crossroads	ITV	5.8
13	Crossroads	ITV	5.8
14	Coronation Street	ITV	5.7
15	Crossroads	ITV	5.7
16	General Hospital	ITV	5.7
17	The Sweepstake Game	ITV	5.7
18	Spartacus	ITV	5.6
19	Killers	ITV	5.6
20	Whodunnit?	ITV	5.5

MONTH BY MONTH 1976

SEPTEMBER

1	George and Mildred	ITV	8.8
2	The Sweeney	ITV	8.2
3	Generation Game	BBC	7.9
4	Crossroads	ITV	7.6
5	Pilger	ITV	7.4
6	The Two Ronnies	BBC	7.2
7	The Good Life	BBC	7.1
8	The Benny Hill Show	BBC	7.1
9	The Duchess of Duke Street	BBC	7.1
10	Crossroads	ITV	7.0
11	Crossroads	ITV	6.8
12	The Bionic Woman	ITV	6.8
13	Coronation Street	ITV	6.7
14	Crossroads	ITV	6.3
15	Spring and Autumn	ITV	6.3
16	Coronation Street	ITV	6.2
17	Nine O'Clock News	BBC	6.2
18	News At Ten	ITV	6.1
19	The Dick Emery Show	BBC	6.0
20	Dr Who	BBC	6.0

OCTOBER

1	George and Mildred	ITV	9.0
2	The Sweeney	ITV	8.8
3	Generation Game	BBC	8.4
4	Kojak	BBC	8.2
5	The Two Ronnies	BBC	8.0
6	Crossroads	ITV	7.5
7	The Duchess of Duke Street	BBC	7.5
8	Coronation Street	ITV	7.4
9	Crossroads	ITV	7.4
10	Happy Ever After	BBC	7.4
11	The Good Life	BBC	7.4
12	The Benny Hill Show	ITV	7.3
13	Crossroads	ITV	7.3
14	Coronation Street	ITV	7.2
15	Crossroads	ITV	7.1
16	Nine O'Clock News	ITV	7.1
17	Sale of the Century	ITV	7.1
18	Opportunity Knocks	ITV	7.0
19	Nine O'Clock News	BBC	6.8
20	General Hospital	ITV	6.7

NOVEMBER

1	Goldfinger	ITV	9.8
2	Generation Game	BBC	9.4
3	George and Mildred	ITV	9.2
4	The Sweeney	ITV	9.0
5	This Is Your Life	ITV	8.4
6	Starsky and Hutch	BBC	8.2
7	Coronation Street	ITV	7.9
8	Crossroads	ITV	7.7
9	Crossroads	ITV	7.7
10	Coronation Street	ITV	7.6
11	Crossroads	ITV	7.6
12	Sale of the Century	ITV	7.4
13	Opportunity Knocks	ITV	7.4
14	Crossroads	ITV	7.3
15	The Duchess of Duke Street	BBC	7.2
16	Dr Who	BBC	7.1
17	World In Action	ITV	6.9
18	The New Avengers	ITV	6.8
19	Shirley Bassey	BBC	6.8
20	News At Ten	ITV	6.8

DECEMBER

1	Generation Game	BBC	9.7
2	The Sweeney	ITV	8.9
3	Starsky and Hutch	BBC	8.5
4	Sale of the Century	ITV	8.3
5	This Is Your Life	ITV	8.2
6	Wednesday At Eight	ITV	8.0
7	Crossroads	ITV	7.9
8	Crossroads	ITV	7.8
9	The Best of Dick Emery	BBC	7.7
10	Crossroads	ITV	7.7
11	Crossroads	ITV	7.6
12	Opportunity Knocks	ITV	7.6
13	Coronation Street	ITV	7.6
14	The New Avengers	ITV	7.5
15	The Duchess of Duke Street	BBC	7.5
16	Coronation Street	ITV	7.3
17	The Six Million Dollar Man	ITV	7.1
18	Into Infinity	BBC	7.1
19	News At Ten	ITV	6.9
20	It Ain't Half Hot Mum	BBC	6.8

1977

[Homes and then Viewers in Millions]

From August of this year TV audience ratings were switched from millions of homes viewing to the total of individuals viewing.

JANUARY

1	This Is Your Life	ITV	9.2
2	Coronation Street	ITV	8.5
3	Beyond Bermuda Triangle	ITV	8.2
4	Sale of the Century	ITV	8.2
5	The Good Old Days	BBC	8.1
6	Crossroads	ITV	8.1
7	Dave Allen and Friends	ITV	8.0
8	Mike Yarwood In Persons	BBC	8.0
9	Crossroads	ITV	7.9
10	Get Some In	ITV	7.9
11	Crossroads	ITV	7.9
12	Opportunity Knocks	ITV	7.7
13	Coronation Street	ITV	7.6
14	Crossroads	ITV	7.6
15	Starsky and Hutch	BBC	7.5
16	Charlie's Angels	ITV	7.4
17	Another Bouquet	ITV	7.3
18	Twin Detectives	ITV	7.0
19	The Squirrels	ITV	6.9
20	Yanks Go Home	ITV	6.7

FEBRUARY

1	This Is Your Life	ITV	9.5
2	Coronation Street	ITV	8.9
3	The Cuckoo Waltz	ITV	8.8
4	Robin's Nest	ITV	8.8
5	Coronation Street	ITV	8.6
6	Conspiracy of Terror	ITV	8.6
7	Sale of the Century	ITV	8.5
8	Get Some In	ITV	8.3
9	Opportunity Knocks	ITV	8.1
10	Doctor On the Go	ITV	8.0
11	Crossroads	ITV	8.0
12	Crossroads	ITV	7.9
13	Ronnie Corbett's Sat Special	BBC	7.7
14	Charlie's Angels	ITV	7.6
15	Crossroads	ITV	7.6
16	This Year, Next Year	ITV	7.5
17	Another Bouquet	ITV	7.5
18	Crossroads	ITV	7.4
19	News At Ten	ITV	7.2
20	Dave Allen and Friends	ITV	7.2

MARCH

1	Oh No, It's Selwyn Frogitt	ITV	9.5
2	This Is Your Life	ITV	9.4
3	Doctor On the Go	ITV	9.4
4	Coronation Street	ITV	9.1
5	World In Action	ITV	8.7
6	Tom O'Connor	ITV	8.4
7	Opportunity Knocks	ITV	8.4
8	Coronation Street	ITV	8.4
9	Dave Allen and Friends	ITV	8.2
10	Crossroads	ITV	8.0
11	Crossroads	ITV	8.0
12	Sale of the Century	ITV	7.8
13	Crossroads	ITV	7.7
14	Crossroads	ITV	7.7
15	Charlie's Angels	ITV	7.6
16	This Year, Next Year	ITV	7.6
17	Galton & Simpson Playhouse	ITV	7.5
18	The Six Million Dollar Man	ITV	7.5
19	Porridge	BBC	7.5
20	Are You Being Served?	BBC	7.2

APRIL

1	Oh No, It's Selwyn Frogitt	ITV	9.1
2	Coronation Street	ITV	8.9
3	This Is Your Life	ITV	8.5
4	Coronation Street	ITV	8.2
5	World In Action	ITV	8.1
6	Crossroads	ITV	7.8
7	Opportunity Knocks	ITV	7.8
8	Tom O'Connor	ITV	7.3
9	Galton & Simpson Playhouse	ITV	7.3
10	Are You Being Served?	BBC	7.3
11	Crossroads	ITV	7.2
12	Crossroads	ITV	7.2
13	Charlie's Angels	ITV	7.2
14	This Year, Next Year	ITV	7.1
15	Jesus of Nazareth	ITV	6.9
16	Romance	ITV	6.9
17	The Common Lot	ITV	6.7
18	Steptoe and Son	BBC	6.6
19	Roots	BBC	6.6
20	Roots	BBC	6.5

MAY

1	Eurovision Song Contest	BBC	9.1
2	Miss Jones and Son	ITV	8.3
3	Rising Damp	ITV	8.2
4	World In Action	ITV	8.1
5	Coronation Street	ITV	8.1
6	Coronation Street	ITV	8.1
7	Marti	ITV	7.9
8	Charlie's Angels	ITV	7.8
9	Crossroads	ITV	7.6
10	Crossroads	ITV	7.5
11	Bless This House	ITV	7.5
12	Crossroads	ITV	7.4
13	Little and Large	ITV	7.2
14	Crossroads	ITV	7.2
15	The Bionic Woman	ITV	7.0
16	Sale of the Century	ITV	6.7
17	Paradise Island	ITV	6.5
18	Rock Follies	ITV	6.2
19	Beryl's Lot	ITV	6.2
20	It's a Knockout	BBC	6.1

JUNE

1	Silver Jubilee	BBC	7.6
2	Starsky & Hutch	BBC	7.2
3	A Day of Celebration	BBC	7.2
4	Sale of the Century	ITV	7.0
5	General Hospital	ITV	6.9
6	Music of Morecambe & Wise	BBC	6.8
7	The Eric Sykes Show	ITV	6.6
8	Crossroads	ITV	6.6
9	Coronation Street	ITV	6.4
10	Coronation Street	ITV	6.4
11	Crossroads	ITV	6.4
12	Kojak	BBC	6.3
13	The Magnificent Showman	ITV	6.1
14	Crossroads	ITV	6.0
15	Silver Jubilee	BBC	6.0
16	News At Ten	ITV	6.0
17	Seaside Special	BBC	6.0
18	International Soccer	BBC	6.0
19	Nationwide Jubilee Fair	BBC	5.9
20	A Day of Celebration	BBC	5.8

JULY

1	Sale of the Century	ITV	7.3
2	General Hospital	ITV	7.1
3	Coronation Street	ITV	6.4
4	Man About the House	ITV	6.4
5	Winner Takes All	ITV	6.2
6	What's On Next?	ITV	6.1
7	The Sweeney	ITV	6.1
8	News At Ten	ITV	6.1
9	Crossroads	ITV	6.0
10	Crossroads	ITV	5.9
11	Crossroads	ITV	5.9
12	The XYY Man	ITV	5.8
13	News At Ten	ITV	5.7
14	Crossroads	ITV	5.7
15	News at Ten	ITV	5.6
16	The Foundation	ITV	5.6
17	Get Some In	ITV	5.5
18	Coronation Street	ITV	5.5
19	News At Ten	ITV	5.4
20	Roadrunner	ITV	5.4

AUGUST

1	Man About the House	ITV	12.6
2	Cottage To Let	ITV	12.5
3	Night Out At London Casino	ITV	11.7
4	General Hospital	ITV	11.5
5	Seaside Special	BBC	11.1
6	Winner Takes All	ITV	11.0
7	The Liver Birds	BBC	10.9
8	Coronation Street	ITV	10.9
9	News At Ten	ITV	10.8
10	Crossroads	ITV	10.7
11	Best Sellers	ITV	10.7
12	News At Ten	ITV	10.6
13	Cannon	BBC	10.5
14	Crossroads	ITV	10.5
15	Crossroads	ITV	10.4
16	Coronation Street	ITV	10.3
17	Crossroads	ITV	9.9
18	Mr and Mrs	ITV	9.9
19	Bless This House	ITV	9.7
20	The Firefighters	ITV	9.5

SEPTEMBER

1	Generation Game	BBC	15.9
2	Starsky and Hutch	BBC	14.9
3	Winner Takes All	ITV	14.5
4	The Benny Hill Show	ITV	14.4
5	Survival Special	ITV	13.8
6	The New Avengers	ITV	13.4
7	The World of Pam Ayres	ITV	13.3
8	Crossroads	ITV	13.0
9	The Dick Emery Show	BBC	13.0
10	Van der Valk	ITV	12.9
11	Crossroads	ITV	12.9
12	Crossroads	ITV	12.8
13	Coronation Street	ITV	12.8
14	Coronation Street	ITV	12.8
15	Crossroads	ITV	12.6
16	You're Only Young Twice	ITV	12.5
17	Whicker's World	ITV	12.5
18	Come Spy With Me	ITV	12.3
19	The Krypton Factor	ITV	11.9
20	The Duchess of Duke Street	BBC	11.8

OCTOBER

1	Generation Game	BBC	17.1
2	Coronation Street	ITV	14.7
3	Man From Atlantis	ITV	14.6
4	The Upchat Line	ITV	14.6
5	Crossroads	ITV	14.6
6	Crossroads	ITV	14.3
7	Van der Valk	ITV	14.3
8	You're Only Young Twice	ITV	14.2
9	Flight To Holocaust	ITV	14.2
10	Crossroads	ITV	14.2
11	The Muppet Show	ITV	14.0
12	Opportunity Knocks	ITV	13.8
13	The New Avengers	ITV	13.7
14	Crossroads	ITV	13.4
15	The World of Pam Ayres	ITV	13.2
16	Happy Ever After	BBC	13.0
17	Coronation Street	ITV	12.7
18	The Dick Emery Show	BBC	12.5
19	The Streets of San Francisco	ITV	12.4
20	Dave Allen At Large	BBC	12.4

NOVEMBER

1	Generation Game	BBC	18.9
2	The Two Ronnies	BBC	17.0
3	Coronation Street	ITV	16.1
4	Oh No, It's Selwyn Froggitt	ITV	15.3
5	Crossroads	ITV	14.9
6	Crossroads	ITV	14.8
7	The Muppet Show	ITV	14.7
8	Charlie's Angels	ITV	14.6
9	Crossroads	ITV	14.6
10	The Upchat Line	ITV	14.5
11	Crossroads	ITV	14.5
12	Sale of the Century	ITV	14.3
13	The World of Pam Ayres	ITV	14.3
14	The Duchess of Duke Street	BBC	14.0
15	Opportunity Knocks	ITV	13.6
16	The New Avengers	ITV	13.6
17	Dummy	ITV	13.5
18	Coronation Street	ITV	13.4
19	Gunfight At the OK Corral	ITV	13.2
20	The Rag Trade	ITV	13.2

DECEMBER

1	George and Mildred	ITV	19.5
2	Generation Game	BBC	19.5
3	Wednesday At Eight	ITV	18.0
4	This Is Your Life	ITV	17.2
5	Coronation Street	ITV	16.3
6	Crossroads	ITV	16.3
7	Coronation Street	ITV	16.2
8	Crossroads	ITV	16.0
9	Crossroads	ITV	16.0
10	Crossroads	ITV	15.9
11	The Two Ronnies	BBC	15.6
12	This England	ITV	15.5
13	Oh No, It's Selwyn Froggitt	ITV	15.2
14	Opportunity Knocks	ITV	14.7
15	Starsky and Hutch	BBC	14.6
16	Charlie's Angels	ITV	14.4
17	Sale of the Century	ITV	14.3
18	The Muppet Show	ITV	14.2
19	The Sweeney	ITV	14.1
20	The Duchess of Duke Street	BBC	13.9

1978

[Viewers in Millions]

JANUARY

1	Coronation Street	ITV	20.2
2	This Is Your Life	ITV	19.6
3	Coronation Street	ITV	17.8
4	Crossroads	ITV	17.6
5	Miss Jones and Son	ITV	17.5
6	Murphy's War	ITV	17.4
7	Crossroads	ITV	17.0
8	Crossroads	ITV	16.9
9	Mind Your Language	ITV	16.8
10	Maggie and Her	ITV	16.3
11	Crossroads	ITV	16.2
12	Sale of the Century	ITV	16.0
13	The Sweeney	ITV	15.8
14	Opportunity Knocks	ITV	15.8
15	Dave Allen	ITV	15.2
16	General Hospital	ITV	15.0
17	The Professionals	ITV	14.8
18	Carry On Camping	ITV	14.4
19	Starsky and Hutch	BBC	14.1
20	Emmerdale Farm	ITV	13.6

FEBRUARY

1	This Is Your Life	ITV	19.5
2	Mind Your Language	ITV	18.2
3	Miss Jones and Son	ITV	18.1
4	Coronation Street	ITV	18.0
5	Coronation Street	ITV	18.0
6	Maggie and Her	ITV	17.7
7	The Professionals	ITV	17.4
8	Crossroads	ITV	17.2
9	Crossroads	ITV	17.0
10	Crossroads	ITV	16.9
11	Crossroads	ITV	16.9
12	General Hospital	ITV	16.8
13	Mike Yarwood In Persons	BBC	16.7
14	Starsky and Hurtch	BBC	16.7
15	Wilde Alliance	ITV	16.6
16	Rising Damp	ITV	16.3
17	George and Mildred	ITV	16.2
18	Opportunity Knocks	ITV	16.1
19	Bernard Manning/Las Vegas	ITV	16.0
20	Dave Allen	ITV	15.5

MARCH

1	A Sharp Intake of Breath	ITV	17.8
2	Mind Your Language	ITV	17.5
3	Goldfinger	ITV	17.4
4	Mixed Blessings	ITV	17.4
5	Coronation Street	ITV	16.9
6	George and Mildred	ITV	16.8
7	Starsky and Hutch	BBC	16.6
8	The Professionals	ITV	16.6
9	Mike Yarwood In Persons	BBC	16.3
10	Dave Allen	ITV	16.2
11	Crossroads	ITV	16.0
12	Coronation Street	ITV	15.9
13	Robin's Nest	ITV	15.6
14	Armchair Thriller	ITV	15.3
15	Crossroads	ITV	15.1
16	Emmerdale Farm	ITV	15.0
17	Opportunity Knocks	ITV	14.9
18	Armchair Thriller	ITV	14.9
19	This Is Your Life	ITV	14.9
20	Wilde Alliance	ITV	14.8

APRIL

1	This Is Your Life	ITV	18.8
2	Rising Damp	ITV	18.2
3	Coronation Street	ITV	17.4
4	Mixed Blessings	ITV	16.7
5	Armchair Thriller	ITV	16.3
6	Whodunnit?	ITV	15.7
7	Wilde Alliance	ITV	15.2
8	Get Some In	ITV	15.0
9	Coronation Street	ITV	14.9
10	Ronnie Corbett's Special	BBC	14.7
11	Celebrity Squares	ITV	14.5
12	All Creatures Great & Small	BBC	14.5
13	Crossroads	ITV	14.5
14	Sale of the Century	ITV	14.5
15	Crossroads	ITV	14.2
16	Crossroads	ITV	13.9
17	Crossroads	ITV	13.6
18	Emmerdale Farm	ITV	13.5
19	Going Straight	BBC	13.3
20	Emmerdale Farm	ITV	12.9

MAY

1	Armchair Thriller	ITV	17.1
2	Rising Damp	ITV	16.9
3	This Is Your Life	ITV	16.4
4	Coronation Street	ITV	15.3
5	Winner Takes All	ITV	14.9
6	Ben Hur	ITV	14.9
7	Crossroads	ITV	14.5
8	Get Some In!	ITV	14.5
9	Crossroads	ITV	14.4
10	Crossroads	ITV	14.0
11	The Dick Emery Show	BBC	13.8
12	It's a Knockout	BBC	13.7
13	Kojak	BBC	13.5
14	Armchair Thriller	ITV	13.4
15	Crossroads	ITV	13.3
16	Celebrity Squares	ITV	12.9
17	Ronnie Corbett's Special	BBC	12.6
18	Emmerdale Farm	ITV	12.5
19	Dave Allen	ITV	12.4
20	Sale of the Century	ITV	12.3

JUNE

1	Winner Takes All	ITV	13.4
2	The Good Life Special	BBC	13.1
3	Coronation Street	ITV	12.3
4	Morecambe and Wise Show	BBC	12.3
5	World Cup Grandstand	BBC	12.2
6	Crossroads	ITV	12.1
7	Wheels	ITV	12.0
8	Coronation Street	ITV	11.9
9	Crossroads	ITV	11.5
10	You're Only Young Twice	ITV	11.5
11	Whodunnit?	ITV	11.4
12	World Cup	ITV	11.4
13	The Liberace Show	ITV	11.3
14	The Pink Medicine Show	ITV	11.1
15	World Cup Grandstand	BBC	11.0
16	The Incredible Hulk	ITV	10.8
17	Kojak	BBC	10.7
18	That's Life	BBC	10.5
19	Charlie's Angels	ITV	10.4
20	Celebrity Squares	ITV	10.1

JULY

1	That's Life	BBC	13.5
2	Coronation Street	ITV	13.0
3	Life Begins At Forty	ITV	12.8
4	The Incredible Hulk	ITV	12.5
5	London Night Out	ITV	12.4
6	Coronation Street	ITV	12.2
7	The Train Robbers	ITV	11.9
8	The Krypton Factor	ITV	11.5
9	The Pink Medicine Show	ITV	11.4
10	Don't Ask Me	ITV	11.2
11	Crossroads	ITV	11.2
12	Crossroads	ITV	11.1
13	Queen of Distant Country	ITV	11.0
14	You're Only Young Twice	ITV	10.9
15	Crossroads	ITV	10.8
16	Crossroads	ITV	10.6
17	News At Ten	ITV	10.5
18	Leave It To Charlie	ITV	10.2
19	The Last Day	BBC	9.8
20	Nine O'Clock News	BBC	9.8

AUGUST

1	London Night Out	ITV	12.9
2	Paul Daniel's Bonanza	ITV	12.7
3	Coronation Street	ITV	12.2
4	Coronation Street	ITV	11.8
5	What's On Next?	ITV	11.5
6	Crossroads	ITV	11.4
7	House In Nightmare Park	ITV	11.3
8	Crossroads	ITV	11.1
9	Nine O'Clock News	BBC	10.7
10	The Krypton Factor	ITV	10.7
11	3-2-1	ITV	10.7
12	Crossroads	ITV	10.6
13	Man Who Haunted Himself	BBC	10.5
14	Don't Ask Me	ITV	10.3
15	Crossroads	ITV	10.2
16	Commonwealth Games	BBC	10.2
17	Bass Player and the Blonde	ITV	10.1
18	Survival	ITV	10.0
19	Seaside Special	BBC	10.0
20	A Soft Touch	ITV	9.9

SEPTEMBER

1	Her Majesty's Secret Serviee	ITV	16.7
2	3-2-1	ITV	16.4
3	Freddie Starr Experience	ITV	16.1
4	Starsky and Hutch	BBC	14.0
5	The Rag Trade	ITV	13.9
6	The Return of the Saint	ITV	13.9
7	The Sweeney	ITV	13.8
8	George and Mildred	ITV	13.5
9	The Good Life	BBC	13.5
10	Seaside Special	BBC	13.3
11	Coronation Street	ITV	13.3
12	Star Games	ITV	13.2
13	Crossroads	ITV	13.1
14	Coronation Street	ITV	13.0
15	The Krypton Factor	ITV	12.9
16	Singalongamax	ITV	12.7
17	Mastermind	BBC	12.6
18	Main News & Weather	BBC	12.5
19	Crossroads	ITV	12.5
20	Z Cars	BBC	12.4

OCTOBER

1	Coronation Street	ITV	16.6
2	Robin's Nest	ITV	15.7
3	George and Mildred	ITV	15.5
4	3-2-1	ITV	14.8
5	The Professionals	ITV	14.6
6	Bruce Forsyth's Big Night	ITV	14.5
7	Mastermind	BBC	14.1
8	Mixed Blessings	ITV	14.1
9	The Sweeney	ITV	13.7
10	Coronation Street	ITV	13.7
11	The Rag Trade	ITV	13.4
12	Cooper – Just Like That!	ITV	13.2
13	Generation Game	BBC	13.2
14	Crossroads	ITV	13.0
15	Crossroads	ITV	13.0
16	Crossroads	ITV	12.9
17	Crossroads	ITV	12.8
18	The Return of the Saint	ITV	12.7
19	All Creatures Great & Small	BBC	12.6
20	Singalongamax	ITV	12.4

NOVEMBER

1	Some Mothers Do 'Ave 'Em	BBC	19.9
2	All Creatures Great & Small	BBC	18.0
3	Generation Game	BBC	17.5
4	The Sweeney	ITV	16.6
5	Coronation Street	ITV	16.5
6	Robin's Nest	ITV	16.0
7	Mastermind	BBC	15.2
8	Crossroads	ITV	15.2
9	Sale of the Century	ITV	15.1
10	Crossroads	ITV	15.0
11	This Is Your Life	ITV	15.0
12	Edward and Mrs Simpson	ITV	14.9
13	Coronation Street	ITV	14.8
14	Mixed Blessings	ITV	14.8
15	Crossroads	ITV	14.6
16	The Return of the Saint	ITV	14.6
17	Lillie	ITV	14.6
18	George and Mildred	ITV	14.0
19	The Professionals	ITV	13.9
20	Side By Side	ITV	13.9

DECEMBER

1	Coronation Street	ITV	18.6
2	Robin's Nest	ITV	17.8
3	Coronation Street	ITV	16.8
4	Wednesday At Eight	ITV	16.7
5	Some Mothers Do 'Ave 'Em	BBC	16.5
6	Generation Game	BBC	16.3
7	All Creatures Great & Small	BBC	16.2
8	George and Mildred	ITV	15.9
9	The Sweeney	ITV	15.8
10	This Is Your Life	ITV	15.4
11	Edward and Mrs Simpson	ITV	15.1
12	Crossroads	ITV	14.9
13	Crossroads	ITV	14.8
14	Crossroads	ITV	14.8
15	Bernie	ITV	14.1
16	Emmerdale Farm	ITV	14.1
17	Crossroads	ITV	13.9
18	Lillie	ITV	13.7
19	Mastermind	BBC	13.6
20	The Muppet Show	ITV	13.6

MONTH BY MONTH 1978

1979

[Viewers in Millions]

JANUARY

1	The Two Ronnies	BBC	18.4
2	It'll Be Alright On the Night	ITV	17.1
3	This Is Your Life	ITV	16.9
4	The Muppet Show	ITV	16.6
5	Carry On Henry	ITV	16.5
6	Coronation Street	ITV	16.4
7	Sale of the Century	ITV	16.2
8	The Two Ronnies	BBC	15.8
9	Charlie's Angels	ITV	15.7
10	Celebrity Squares	ITV	15.7
11	Bullitt	ITV	15.4
12	Room Service	ITV	15.4
13	Crossroads	ITV	15.4
14	Crossroads	ITV	15.3
15	Starsky and Hutch	BBC	15.2
16	Return of the Saint	ITV	15.0
17	Jim'll Fix It	BBC	14.6
18	Dick Turpin	ITV	14.5
19	General Hospital	ITV	14.4
20	The Aphrodite Inheritance	BBC	14.3

FEBRUARY

1	Coronation Street	ITV	17.9
2	The Two Ronnies	BBC	17.6
3	Mid-Week Sports Special	ITV	17.4
4	Coronation Street	ITV	16.3
5	Danger UXB	ITV	16.0
6	Crossroads	ITV	15.8
7	That's Life	BBC	15.7
8	Crossroads	ITV	15.5
9	Starsky and Hutch	BBC	15.2
10	This Is Your Life	ITV	15.1
11	Blankety Blank	BBC	15.1
12	Crossroads	ITV	15.0
13	Beasts Are On the Streets	BBC	14.9
14	Sale of the Century	ITV	14.9
15	Crossroads	ITV	14.7
16	Return of the Saint	ITV	14.6
17	Charlie's Angels	ITV	14.4
18	Jim'll Fix It	ITV	14.4
19	Sole Survivor	BBC	14.3
20	Emmerdale Farm	ITV	14.0

MARCH

1	This Is Your Life	ITV	18.1
2	Coronation Street	ITV	16.9
3	Coronation Street	ITV	16.8
4	Charlie's Angels	ITV	16.1
5	Crossroads	ITV	15.8
6	A Sharp Intake of Breath	ITV	15.6
7	Crossroads	ITV	15.3
8	Crossroads	ITV	15.3
9	Return of the Saint	ITV	15.2
10	Leave It To Charlie	ITV	15.1
11	Take My Wife	ITV	15.1
12	Sale of the Century	ITV	15.0
13	That's Life	BBC	15.0
14	Flambards	ITV	14.7
15	Emmerdale Farm	ITV	14.6
16	Jim'll Fix It	BBC	14.6
17	Crossroads	ITV	14.3
18	Hannibal Brooks	BBC	14.1
19	The Dick Emery Show	BBC	13.9
20	Danger UXB	ITV	13.7

APRIL

1	This Is Your Life	ITV	17.6
2	Coronation Street	ITV	17.4
3	Chalk and Cheese	ITV	16.7
4	Coronation Street	ITV	16.6
5	Danger UXB	ITV	16.0
6	Crossroads	ITV	15.5
7	Flambards	ITV	15.4
8	Crossroads	ITV	15.4
9	Blankety Blank	BBC	15.3
10	Thomas and Sarah	ITV	14.6
11	Winner Takes All	ITV	14.6
12	Crossroads	ITV	14.3
13	Crossroads	ITV	14.3
14	Jesus of Nazareth	ITV	14.0
15	Potter	BBC	13.9
16	Emmerdale Farm	ITV	13.6
17	Kenny Everett Video Show	ITV	13.5
18	Emmerdale Farm	ITV	13.5
19	Val Doonican Music Show	BBC	13.4
20	How's Your Father?	ITV	13.1

MAY

1	Blankety Blank	BBC	17.5
2	The TV Times Awards	ITV	16.7
3	Coronation Street	ITV	16.0
4	Crossroads	ITV	15.1
5	Crossroads	ITV	15.0
6	A Fire In the Sky	ITV	14.9
7	Crossroads	ITV	14.2
8	Top of the Pops	BBC	14.0
9	Holiday On the Buses	ITV	13.7
10	Coronation Street	ITV	13.6
11	The Dirty Dozen	BBC	13.4
12	Don't Just Sit There	ITV	13.2
13	Emmerdale Farm	ITV	13.1
14	Living Legends	BBC	13.0
15	That's Life	BBC	13.0
16	Crossroads	ITV	12.7
17	Chalk and Cheese	ITV	12.5
18	Emmerdale Farm	ITV	12.5
19	Hazel	ITV	12.5
20	News At Ten	ITV	12.0

JUNE

1	Dick Emery Comedy Hour	ITV	15.3
2	Coronation Street	ITV	15.3
3	In Loving Memory	ITV	14.8
4	Coronation Street	ITV	14.5
5	Crossroads	ITV	13.4
6	Crossroads	ITV	13.1
7	Crossroads	ITV	12.8
8	Crossroads	ITV	12.3
9	Lingalongamax	ITV	12.2
10	That's Life	BBC	12.2
11	World In Action	ITV	12.2
12	Hazel	ITV	11.9
13	Emmerdale Farm	ITV	11.7
14	Sword of Justice	BBC	11.6
15	Winner Takes All	ITV	11.2
16	The Mallens	ITV	11.2
17	Emmerdale Farm	ITV	11.1
18	Don't Just Sit There	ITV	11.0
19	The Kyrpton Factor	ITV	10.6
20	Paul Daniels Magic Show	BBC	10.6

JULY

1	Coronation Street	ITV	13.1
2	Coronation Street	ITV	12.7
3	In Loving Memory	ITV	12.1
4	The Mallens	ITV	11.9
5	Mr Horn	ITV	11.8
6	Winner Takes All	ITV	11.8
7	News At Ten	ITV	11.7
8	You're Only Young Twice	ITV	11.6
9	Crossroads	ITV	11.3
10	Oh Boy!	ITV	11.2
11	Crossroads	ITV	11.0
12	Crossroads	ITV	11.0
13	They Call Me Mr Tibbs	BBC	10.8
14	Crossroads	ITV	10.7
15	The Lovers	ITV	10.3
16	News At Ten	ITV	10.0
17	Celebrity Squares	ITV	10.0
18	George and Mildred	ITV	9.9
19	Don't Just Sit There	ITV	9.7
20	Mr Horn	ITV	9.7

AUGUST

1	Seaside Special	BBC	15.8
2	Des O'Connor Tonight	BBC	14.6
3	To Catch a Thief	BBC	14.5
4	Sword of Justice	BBC	14.3
5	It Ain't Half Hot Mum	BBC	13.8
6	Hunchback of Notre Dame	BBC	12.5
7	Return To Paradise	BBC	12.2
8	Star Trek	BBC	12.0
9	The Golden Fiddle Awards	BBC	11.9
10	Juke Box Jury	BBC	11.8
11	Nine O'Clock News	BBC	11.4
12	Coronation Street	ITV	11.4
13	Nine O'Clock News	BBC	11.0
14	Nine O'Clock News	BBC	10.8
15	Nine O'Clock News	BBC	10.7
16	Top of the Pops	BBC	10.5
17	Citizen Smith	BBC	10.5
18	The Onedin Line	BBC	10.0
19	Crossroads	ITV	9.9
20	The Hollywood Greats	BBC	9.8

SEPTEMBER

1	Seaside Special	BBC	20.0
2	Generation Game	BBC	19.3
3	Blankety Blank	BBC	19.2
4	The Belstone Fox	BBC	19.0
5	Mastermind	BBC	18.3
6	Carry On Screaming	BBC	18.1
7	Nine O'Clock News	BBC	17.9
8	Come Dancing Final	BBC	17.7
9	A Moment In Time	BBC	17.5
10	Earl Mountbatten's Funeral	BBC	17.3
11	Nine O'Clock News	BBC	17.2
12	Nine O'Clock News	BBC	17.0
13	Nine O'Clock News	BBC	17.0
14	Rings On Their Fingers	BBC	16.8
15	Avanti!	BBC	16.6
16	A Moment In Time	BBC	16.6
17	Some Mothers Do 'Ave 'Em	BBC	16.6
18	Angels	BBC	16.0
19	The Pirate	BBC	15.8
20	The Rockford Files	BBC	15.8

OCTOBER

1	To the Manor Born	BBC	24.0
2	Generation Game	BBC	23.6
3	Blankety Blank	BBC	23.3
4	Mike Yarwood In Persons	BBC	22.3
5	Last of the Summer Wine	BBC	21.9
6	Mastermind	BBC	21.9
7	Citizen Smith	BBC	21.8
8	Petrocelli	BBC	21.7
9	Secret Army	BBC	21.6
10	Sykes	BBC	21.2
11	Rings On Their Fingers	BBC	21.0
12	Some Mothers Do 'Ave 'Em	BBC	20.3
13	Shoestring	BBC	20.3
14	Star Trek	BBC	20.3
15	Nine O'Clock News	BBC	20.2
16	Angels	BBC	20.1
17	Dr Who	BBC	19.5
18	Top of the Pops	BBC	19.4
19	International Show Jumping	BBC	18.9
20	Roots	BBC	18.7

NOVEMBER

1	To the Manor Born	BBC	23.9
2	Shoestring	BBC	19.9
3	Blankety Blank	BBC	18.8
4	Roots	BBC	18.5
5	Generation Game	BBC	17.6
6	Top of the Pops	BBC	16.5
7	George and Mildred	ITV	15.9
8	Are You Being Served?	BBC	15.6
9	It's a Knockout	BBC	15.6
10	Kiss the Girls/Make Them Cry	BBC	15.4
11	Secret Army	BBC	15.3
12	The Professionals	ITV	14.9
13	Only When I Laugh	ITV	14.8
14	London Night Out	ITV	14.4
15	Coronation Street	ITV	13.9
16	Rising Stars	BBC	13.9
17	3-2-1	ITV	13.8
18	Crossroads	ITV	13.3
19	Go With Noakes	BBC	13.3
20	Coronation Street	ITV	13.2

DECEMBER

1	Coronation Street	ITV	18.1
2	Generation Game	BBC	17.7
3	Only When I Laugh	ITV	16.9
4	The Dawson Watch	BBC	16.3
5	Secret Army	BBC	16.1
6	Coronation Street	ITV	16.0
7	Blankety Blank	BBC	15.7
8	This Is Your Life	ITV	15.3
9	Nine O'Clock News	BBC	15.0
10	3-2-1	ITV	15.0
11	Give Us a Clue	ITV	14.4
12	Crossroads	ITV	14.0
13	The Big Top Variety Show	ITV	13.9
14	The Comedians	ITV	13.7
15	George and Mildred	ITV	13.7
16	Crossroads	ITV	13.5
17	Crossroads	ITV	13.4
18	Top of the Pops	BBC	13.2
19	Britain's Strongest Man	ITV	13.2
20	Porridge	BBC	13.1

1980

[Viewers in Millions]

JANUARY

1	This Is Your Life	ITV	18.2
2	Coronation Street	ITV	18.0
3	The Dick Emery Show	BBC	17.8
4	All Creatures Great & Small	BBC	17.4
5	Ryan's Daughter	ITV	16.9
6	Jim'll Fix It	BBC	16.4
7	Coronation Street	ITV	16.3
8	Keep It In the Family	ITV	16.0
9	London Night Out	ITV	15.9
10	Robin's Nest	ITV	15.6
11	Give Us a Clue	ITV	15.3
12	Crossroads	ITV	15.3
13	Dallas	BBC	15.1
14	3-2-1	ITV	15.0
15	Crossroads	ITV	14.4
16	Family Fortunes	ITB	14.3
17	Armchair Thriller	ITV	14.2
18	Crossroads	ITV	14.1
19	The Racing Game	ITV	13.8
20	Armchair Thriller	ITV	13.8

FEBRUARY

1	Jim'll Fix It	BBC	19.1
2	This Is Your Life	ITV	18.8
3	The Dick Emery Show	BBC	18.8
4	All Creatures Great & Small	BBC	18.4
5	Coronation Street	ITV	18.4
6	The Benny Hill Show	ITV	18.0
7	Coronation Street	ITV	17.3
8	Wonder Woman	BBC	16.0
9	Robin's Nest	ITV	16.0
10	Give Us a Clue	ITV	15.5
11	Keep It In the Family	ITV	15.1
12	Chief of Detectives	ITV	15.0
13	Crossroads	ITV	14.9
14	Crossroads	ITV	14.8
15	Armchair Thriller	ITV	14.7
16	Dallas	BBC	14.7
17	Crossroads	ITV	13.9
18	Crossroads	ITV	13.8
19	Watch This Space	BBC	13.8
20	Airport	BBC	13.8

MARCH

1	Jim'll Fix It	BBC	18.6
2	All Creatures Great & Small	BBC	18.3
3	The Benny Hill Show	ITV	18.0
4	This Is Your Life	ITV	17.2
5	Coronation Street	ITV	16.9
6	The Little & Large Show	BBC	16.6
7	Coronation Street	ITV	16.0
8	Dallas	BBC	16.0
9	Crossroads	ITV	15.1
10	Crossroads	ITV	15.0
11	Life Begins At Forty	ITV	14.6
12	Play Your Cards Right	ITV	14.4
13	Crossroads	ITV	14.3
14	Wonder Woman	BBC	14.3
15	Crossroads	ITV	13.9
16	The Jim Davidson Show	ITV	13.6
17	Hart To Hart	ITV	13.2
18	Kenny Everett Video Show	ITV	13.0
19	Leave It To Charlie	ITV	12.8
20	Emmerdale Farm	ITV	12.5

APRIL

1	Dallas	BBC	16.7
2	This Is Your Life	ITV	16.6
3	Coronation Street	ITV	16.3
4	Crossroads	ITV	15.5
5	Play Your Cards Right	ITV	15.4
6	The Val Doonican Show	BBC	14.4
7	The Great Waldo Pepper	BBC	14.2
8	Armchair Thriller	ITV	14.1
9	Potter	BBC	14.0
10	Generation Game	BBC	14.0
11	Cribb	ITV	13.9
12	Crossroads	ITV	13.6
13	Chief of Detectives	ITV	13.6
14	Nine O'Clock News	BBC	13.5
15	The Cannon & Ball Show	ITV	13.5
16	Family Fortunes	ITV	13.6
17	Armchair Thriller	ITV	12.9
18	Emmerdale Farm	ITV	12.5
19	The Risk Business	BBC	12.3
20	Hart To Hart	ITV	12.2

MAY

1	Only When I Laugh	ITV	17.0
2	This Is Your Life	ITV	15.0
3	Crossroads	ITV	14.3
4	Coronation Street	ITV	14.3
5	Whicker's World	ITV	14.3
6	Miss Great Britain	ITV	13.8
7	Emmerdale Farm	ITV	12.5
8	News At Ten	ITV	12.1
9	The Gentle Touch	ITV	12.0
10	Knots Landing	BBC	11.6
11	News At Ten	ITV	11.4
12	Val Doonican Music Show	BBC	11.4
13	News At Ten	ITV	11.3
14	Emmerdale Farm	ITV	11.2
15	The Nesbitts Are Coming	ITV	11.2
16	Play Your Cards Right	ITV	11.1
17	The Cannon & Ball Show	ITV	11.1
18	News Report	BBC	11.0
19	Streets of San Francisco	ITV	10.9
20	Shelley	ITV	10.8

JUNE

1	It'll Be Alright On the Night	ITV	16.3
2	Coronation Street	ITV	14.0
3	Coronation Street	ITV	13.9
4	Only When I Laugh	ITV	13.3
5	Crossroads	ITV	12.8
6	Crossroads	ITV	12.4
7	The Plank	ITV	12.3
8	Can We Get On Now, Please?	ITV	11.8
9	Adventures of Eliza Frazer	ITV	11.8
10	Winner Takes All	ITV	11.7
11	D-Day, the Sixth of June	BBC	10.8
12	Emmerdale Farm	ITV	10.7
13	The Mallens	ITV	10.7
14	The Other 'Arf	ITV	10.7
15	Nine O'Clock News	BBC	10.6
16	Knots Landing	BBC	10.4
17	Emmerdale Farm	ITV	10.3
18	That's Life Report	BBC	10.1
19	Tales of the Unexpected	ITV	9.8
20	Singalongamax	ITV	9.7

JULY

1	Coronation Street	ITV	13.8
2	Crossroads	ITV	12.6
3	The Guns of Navarone	ITV	12.4
4	Coronation Street	ITV	12.4
5	Chato's Land	BBC	11.8
6	The Pink Panther	BBC	11.6
7	Robin's Nest	ITV	11.4
8	Last of the Summer Wine	BBC	11.3
9	Starsky and Hutch	BBC	11.1
10	Nine O'Clock News	BBC	11.0
11	Crossroads	ITV	10.9
12	Family Fortunes	ITV	10.8
13	Return of the Saint	ITV	10.4
14	Miss Universe	ITV	9.9
15	The Cuckoo Waltz	ITV	9.9
16	The Nine O'Clock News	BBC	9.8
17	Emmerdale Farm	ITV	9.7
18	Don't Just Sit There	ITV	9.7
19	Winner Takes All	ITV	9.7
20	The Krypton Factor	ITV	9.6

AUGUST

1	Coronation Street	ITV	12.8
2	Hart To Hart	ITV	12.3
3	Coronation Street	ITV	11.9
4	Crossroads	ITV	11.7
5	Nine O'Clock News	BBC	11.5
6	Last of the Summer Wine	BBC	11.4
7	Starsky & Hutch	BBC	11.4
8	Robin's Next	ITV	11.1
9	International Athletics	BBC	11.0
10	ITV Playhouse	ITV	10.7
11	News At Ten	ITV	10.3
12	Main News	BBC	10.0
13	Lady Killers	ITV	10.0
14	Nine O'Clock News	BBC	9.8
15	Crossroads	ITV	9.8
16	Jeux Sans Frontieres	BBC	9.8
17	The Martian Chronicles	BBC	9.8
18	The Good Old Days	BBC	9.7
19	Winner Takes All	ITV	9.6
20	Grundy	ITV	9.5

MONTH BY MONTH 1980

SEPTEMBER

1	Morecambe and Wise Show	ITV	16.4
2	Coronation Street	ITV	15.6
3	Cowboys	ITV	15.3
4	Just Liz	ITV	14.7
5	The Professionals	ITV	14.1
6	Keep It In the Family	ITV	13.9
7	Generation Game	BBC	13.7
8	Coronation Street	ITV	13.5
9	Blankety Blank	BBC	13.3
10	Her Majesty's Secret Service	ITV	12.8
11	Crossroads	ITV	12.6
12	Hart of the Yard	ITV	12.2
13	Crossroads	ITV	11.7
14	Give Us a Clue	ITV	11.3
15	Yes Minister	BBC	11.3
16	That Lucky Touch	ITV	11.1
17	Terry and June	BBC	11.0
18	Arthur C Clarke	ITV	10.7
19	Play Your Cards Right	ITV	10.5
20	Crossroads	ITV	10.4

OCTOBER

1	Morecambe & Wise Show	ITV	18.6
2	To the Manor Born	BBC	18.5
3	Coronation Street	ITV	18.2
4	Coronation Street	ITV	17.0
5	Keep It In the Family	ITV	17.0
6	Cowboys	ITV	16.4
7	Give Us a Clue	ITV	16.2
8	Generation Game	BBC	15.4
9	Hart of the Yard	ITV	15.1
10	Just Liz	ITV	15.1
11	Crossroads	ITV	14.9
12	Crossroads	ITV	14.8
13	Blankety Blank	BBC	14.8
14	Mastermind	BBC	14.6
15	Juliet Bravo	BBC	14.2
16	Terry & June	BBC	13.8
17	Paul Daniels Magic Show	BBC	13.6
18	Play Your Cards Right	ITV	13.5
19	The Gentle Touch	ITV	13.4
20	Hammer House of Horror	ITV	13.3

NOVEMBER

1	To the Manor Born	BBC	21.5
2	Dallas	BBC	20.2
3	Mastermind	BBC	19.1
4	Coronation Street	ITV	17.5
5	This Is Your Life	ITV	17.3
6	The Two Ronnies	BBC	17.3
7	Coronation Street	ITV	17.1
8	London Night Out	ITV	17.1
9	Give Us a Clue	ITV	15.6
10	Blankety Blank	BBC	15.6
11	Rings On Their Fingers	BBC	15.6
12	Generation Game	BBC	15.4
13	Play Your Cards Right	ITV	15.2
14	Juliet Bravo	BBC	15.2
15	In Loving Memory	ITV	15.0
16	Crossroads	ITV	15.0
17	Survival Special	ITV	14.1
18	Hammer House of Horror	ITV	13.9
19	Arthur C Clarke	ITV	13.8
20	Crossroads	ITV	13.5

DECEMBER

1	Coronation Street	ITV	19.0
2	This Is Your Life	ITV	18.4
3	The Two Ronnies	BBC	18.3
4	Dick Emery Hour	BBC	18.3
5	Dallas	BBC	17.9
6	Generation Game	BBC	17.3
7	Coronation Street	ITV	17.3
8	Give Us a Clue	ITV	16.3
9	Juliet Bravo	BBC	16.1
10	Play Your Cards Right	ITV	15.7
11	Blankety Blank	BBC	15.6
12	Crossroads	ITV	15.5
13	In Loving Memory	ITV	14.8
14	Starsky and Hutch	BBC	14.4
15	Sink or Swim	BBC	14.2
16	Crossroads	ITV	13.8
17	Buck Rogers	ITV	13.5
18	The Professionals	ITV	13.4
19	Life for Christmas	ITV	13.3
20	Minder	ITV	13.3

Ratings compilers changed in July 1981. BARB calculated ITV & BBC positions for the last five months of the year but it did not publish viewing figures and no data has survived.

1981
[Viewers in Millions]

MONTH BY MONTH 1981

JANUARY

1	Benny Hill Show	ITV	20.0
2	Coronation Street	ITV	19.7
3	This Is Your Life	ITV	19.1
4	Coronation Street	ITV	18.3
5	Shelley	ITV	17.3
6	Crossroads	ITV	16.9
7	Holiday On the Buses	ITV	15.6
8	News At Ten	ITV	15.2
9	Family Fortunes	ITV	15.2
10	News At Ten	ITV	15.0
11	Crossroads	ITV	14.9
12	Jim'll Fix It	BBC	14.8
13	Beaulah Land	ITV	14.7
14	Nine O'Clock News	BBC	14.7
15	Starsky and Hutch	BBC	14.6
16	The Jim Davidson Show	ITV	14.5
17	The Professionals	ITV	14.3
18	The Gaffer	ITV	13.9
19	Sink Or Swim	BBC	13.9
20	3-2-1	ITV	13.9

FEBRUARY

1	This Is Your Life	ITV	18.3
2	Coronation Street	ITV	17.3
3	Coronation Street	ITV	17.1
4	Crossroads	ITV	15.9
5	The Gaffer	ITV	15.8
6	Starburst	ITV	15.5
7	Family Fortunes	ITV	15.1
8	Crossroads	ITV	14.9
9	The Golden Gate Murders	ITV	14.9
10	3-2-1	ITV	14.8
11	Solo	BBC	14.8
12	Wildlife On One	BBC	14.6
13	Jim'll Fix It	BBC	14.5
14	Wish You Were Here	ITV	14.3
15	That's Life	BBC	14.2
16	Shelley	ITV	13.9
17	Second Chance	ITV	13.6
18	The Professionals	ITV	13.6
19	The Jim Davidson Show	ITV	13.5
20	The Sweeney	ITV	13.3

MARCH

1	This Is Your Life	ITV	18.6
2	Coronation Street	ITV	18.4
3	Coronation Street	ITV	18.0
4	The Seven Dial's Mysteries	ITV	17.6
5	Holding the Fort	ITV	16.5
6	3-2-1	ITV	16.0
7	Crossroads	ITV	15.9
8	Family Fortunes	ITV	15.7
9	Crossroads	ITV	15.3
10	Open All Hours	BBC	15.0
11	Our Man Flint	ITV	14.7
12	Top of the Pops	BBC	13.9
13	Partners	BBC	13.9
14	Jim'll Fix It	BBC	13.7
15	Nature Watch	ITV	13.6
16	Hi-De-Hi	BBC	13.5
17	Starburst	ITV	12.9
18	Buck Rogers	ITV	12.9
19	Dallas	BBC	12.6
20	Janet and Company	ITV	12.5

APRIL

1	Coronation Street	ITV	16.8
2	Sorry!	BBC	16.8
3	Are You Being Served?	BBC	15.7
4	This Is Your Life	ITV	15.3
5	Coronation Street	ITV	15.2
6	Hart To Hart	ITV	15.1
7	Crossroads	ITV	13.9
8	Crossroads	ITV	13.8
9	Rising Damp	ITV	13.6
10	Family Fortunes	ITV	13.5
11	Val Doonican	BBC	13.3
12	Lena	BBC	13.2
13	Top of the Pops	BBC	13.1
14	Dallas	BBC	12.7
15	Nine O'Clock News	BBC	12.4
16	Terry and June	BBC	12.1
17	Nine O'Clock News	BBC	11.7
18	The Sweeney	ITV	11.7
19	West End Tales	ITV	11.6
20	Ask the Family	ITV	11.6

MAY

1	Coronation Street	ITV	15.7
2	Coronation Street	ITV	15.6
3	Are You Being Served?	BBC	15.2
4	Hart To Hart	ITV	15.0
5	The Professionals	ITV	14.8
6	The Benny Hill Show	ITV	14.8
7	Butterflies	BBC	14.5
8	Family Fortunes	ITV	14.5
9	Crossroads	ITV	14.3
10	Crossroads	ITV	14.1
11	Nine O'Clock News	BBC	14.1
12	Only When I Laugh	ITV	14.0
13	Avalanche Express	ITV	13.6
14	The Cannon and Ball Show	ITV	13.5
15	Diamonds	ITV	13.1
16	Top of the Pops	BBC	12.7
17	Where There's Life	ITV	12.6
18	FA Cup Final	BBC	12.5
19	Sale of the Century	ITV	12.4
20	The Other 'Arf	ITV	12.4

JUNE

1	Hart to Hart	ITV	16.3
2	Coronation Street	ITV	14.8
3	Shillingbury Tales	ITV	14.4
4	Coronation Street	ITV	13.7
5	The Professionals	ITV	13.7
6	World Cup Football	ITV	13.5
7	Crossroads	ITV	13.2
8	Crossroads	ITV	13.1
9	Magnum	ITV	12.6
10	Misfits	ITV	12.2
11	Nine O'Clock News	BBC	11.9
12	Butterflies	BBC	11.4
13	Top of the Pops	BBC	11.4
14	Tales of the Unexpected	ITV	11.3
15	Nine O'Clock News	BBC	11.1
16	Where There's Life	ITV	10.9
17	Young At Heart	ITV	10.9
18	That's Life	BBC	10.9
19	The Sweeney	ITV	10.8
20	Winner Takes All	ITV	10.8

JULY

1	Coronation Street	ITV	14.7
2	Coronation Street	ITV	14.5
3	Russ Abbott's Mad House	ITV	12.7
4	Lady In Danger	ITV	12.7
5	The Krypton Factor	ITV	12.6
6	I'm a Stranger Here Myself	ITV	11.9
7	Only When I Laugh	ITV	11.7
8	Crossroads	ITV	11.6
9	That's Life	BBC	11.6
10	Family Fortunes	ITV	11.6
11	Crossroads	ITV	11.4
12	The Video Entertainers	ITV	11.2
13	Quincy	ITV	10.7
14	Shoestring	BBC	10.6
15	Nine O'Clock News	BBC	10.5
16	Winner Takes All	ITV	10.2
17	Bless Me Father	ITV	10.2
18	Misfits	ITV	10.0
19	Crossroads	ITV	9.9
20	Crossroads	ITV	9.9

AUGUST

1	It Ain't Half Hot Mum	BBC
2	Nine O'Clock News	BBC
3	Gambit	BBC
4	Nine O'Clock News	BBC
5	Summertime Special	BBC
6	Top of the Pops	BBC
7	Citizen Smith	BBC
8	The Monday Film	BBC
9	The Good Old Days	BBC
10	News and Sport	BBC
1	Coronation Street	ITV
2	Coronation Street	ITV
3	Winner Takes All	ITV
4	A Sharp Intake of Breath	ITV
5	Seagull Island	ITV
6	Crossroads	ITV
7	The Big Top	ITV
8	The Krypton Factor	ITV
9	Crossroads	ITV
10	Quincy	ITV

SEPTEMBER

1	Generation Game	BBC
2	Blankety Blank	BBC
3	Juliet Bravo	BBC
4	Nine O'Clock News	BBC
5	Angela Rippon Meets	BBC
6	Salem's Lot	BBC
7	The Odessa File	BBC
8	Athletics	BBC
9	Only Fools and Horses	BBC
10	Summertime Special	BBC
1	Only When I Laugh	ITV
2	The Deep	ITV
3	Coronation Street	ITV
4	Coronation Street	ITV
5	Never the Twain	ITV
6	The Morecambe and Wise Show	ITV
7	The Flame Trees of Thika	ITV
8	Mc Q	ITV
9	The Amazing Spiderman	ITV
10	Keep It In the Family	ITV

OCTOBER

1	Paul Daniels Magic Show	BBC
2	Juliet Bravo	BBC
3	The Moving Target	BBC
4	Generation Game	BBC
5	Wildlife on One	BBC
6	Rosie	BBC
7	Mastermind	BBC
8	Flamingo Road	BBC
9	Tomorrow's World	BBC
10	It's a Knockout	BBC
1	Jaws	ITV
2	Coronation Street	ITV
3	Coronation Street	ITV
4	Benny Hill	ITV
5	Only When I Laugh	ITV
6	Never the Twain	ITV
7	Crossroads	ITV
8	The Morecambe and Wise Show	ITV
9	Bullseye	ITV
10	Play Your Cards Right	ITV

NOVEMBER

1	To the Manor Born	BBC
2	Bergerac	BBC
3	Mastermind	BBC
4	Paul Daniels Magic Show	BBC
5	Tenko	BBC
6	Juliet Bravo	BBC
7	Dallas	BBC
8	News and Sport	BBC
9	Generation Game	BBC
10	Festival of Remembrance	BBC
1	Coronation Street	ITV
2	This is Your Life	ITV
3	Crossroads	ITV
4	Coronation Street	ITV
5	Crossroads	ITV
6	Game For a Laugh	ITV
7	Give Us a Clue	ITV
8	That's My Boy	ITV
9	Bullseye	ITV
10	Play Your Cards Right	ITV

DECEMBER

1	The Two Ronnies	BBC
2	Bergerac	BBC
3	Hi-De-Hi!	BBC
4	Top of the Pops	BBC
5	Blankety Blank	BBC
6	Mastermind	BBC
7	News and Sport	BBC
8	Tenko	BBC
9	Sports Review of 1981	BBC
10	Dallas	BBC
1	Coronation Street	ITV
2	Coronation Street	ITV
3	Play Your Cards Right	ITV
4	This Is Your Life	ITV
5	London Night Out	ITV
6	Punchlines	ITV
7	Games For a Laugh	ITV
8	World's Strongest Man	ITV
9	Crossroads	ITV
10	Bullseye	ITV

1982
[Viewers in Millions]

JANUARY
1 Jim'll Fix It BBC 13.4
2 Last of the Summer Wine BBC 13.3
3 Top of the Pops BBC 12.5
4 Terry and June BBC 12.4
5 Goodbye Mr Kent BBC 12.3
6 Dallas BBC 12.3
7 Shoestring BBC 12.3
8 A Shot In the Dark BBC 11.9
9 The Les Dawson Show BBC 11.7
10 Holiday BBC 11.3

1 Coronation Street ITV 17.1
2 This Is Your Life ITV 16.9
3 Coronation Street ITV 16.8
4 Family Fortunes ITV 15.1
5 Wish You Were Here ITV 14.9
6 Shine On Harvey Moon ITV 14.5
7 The Fall Guy ITV 14.3
8 Hart To Hart ITV 14.3
9 Crossroads ITV 13.9
10 3-2-1 ITV 13.9

FEBRUARY
1 Last of the Summer Wine BBC 14.1
2 Jim'll Fix It BBC 13.6
3 Dallas BBC 12.6
4 Shoestring BBC 12.3
5 Terry and June BBC 11.8
6 The Black Windmill BBC 11.6
7 Holiday BBC 11.5
8 News And Sport BBC 11.5
9 Top of the Pops BBC 11.4
10 The Les Dawson Show BBC 11.1

1 This Is Your Life ITV 17.5
2 Coronation Street ITV 17.3
3 Coronation Street ITV 16.3
4 Family Fortunes ITV 14.9
5 Shine On Harvey Moon ITV 14.7
6 Hart To Hart ITV 14.6
7 Wish You Were Here ITV 14.5
8 The Fall Guy ITV 14.5
9 The Gentle Touch ITV 14.4
10 3-2-1 ITV 14.3

MARCH
1 Jim'll Fix It BBC 14.0
2 Top of the Pops BBC 13.3
3 Kenny Everett TV Show BBC 12.7
4 Shoestring BBC 12.7
5 Dallas BBC 12.7
6 The Dukes of Hazzard BBC 12.0
7 The McKenzie Break BBC 11.9
8 Nanny BBC 11.3
9 A Question of Sport BBC 10.8
10 The Les Dawson Show BBC 10.7

1 This Is Your Life ITV 17.3
2 Coronation Street ITV 17.1
3 Coronation Street ITV 17.0
4 Hart To Hart ITV 15.0
5 Family Fortunes ITV 14.7
6 3-2-1 ITV 14.4
7 Nature Watch ITV 14.2
8 Magnum Force ITV 14.2
9 Crossroads ITV 13.9
10 Minder ITV 13.9

APRIL
1 News and Sport BBC 13.8
2 Dallas BBC 13.2
3 Open All Hours BBC 12.4
4 World Superstars 1982 BBC 12.7
5 Top of the Pops BBC 12.0
6 Kenny Everett TV Show BBC 11.7
7 Chitty Chitty Bang Bang BBC 11.5
8 A Whale For the Killing BBC 10.5
9 Eleven Years of Parkinson BBC 10.3
10 The Scarlet Buccaneer BBC 10.2

1 Coronation Street ITV 16.9
2 The Benny Hill Show ITV 15.9
3 Coronation Street ITV 15.4
4 Minder ITV 15.0
5 3-2-1 ITV 13.8
6 Give Us a Clue ITV 13.3
7 Where There's Life ITV 12.8
8 Family Fortunes ITV 12.8
9 Crossroads ITV 12.6
10 Crossroads ITV 12.4

MAY
1 Top of the Pops BBC 12.6
2 Nine O'Clock News BBC 11.9
3 Nine O'Clock News BBC 11.8
4 Nine O'Clock News BBC 11.3
5 London's Marathon BBC 11.2
6 Taxi BBX 11.1
7 Evening News BBC 10.8
8 News and Sport (Sat) BBC 10.6
9 Merrill's Marauders BBC 9.8
10 Val Doonican Music Show BBC 9.4

1 Coronation Street ITV 16.1
2 Murder Is Easy ITV 14.2
3 Coronation Street ITV 13.9
4 Family Fortunes ITV 13.6
5 The Bounder ITV 13.3
6 We'll Meet Again ITV 13.2
7 Crossroads ITV 13.1
8 Give Us a Clue ITV 12.9
9 Where There's Life ITV 12.7
10 ITN News ITV 12.7

JUNE
1 Nine O'Clock News BBC 10.9
2 Nine O'Clock News BBC 10.7
3 Nine O'Clock News BBC 10.4
4 The Gumball Rally BBC 10.4
5 Visit of President Reagan BBC 10.1
6 News BBC 10.1
7 News BBC 10.0
8 Chicago Story BBC 9.3
9 Nine O'Clock News BBC 8.9
10 Batman BBC 8.9

1 Goliath Awaits ITV 13.4
2 Crossroads ITV 13.1
3 Coronation Street ITV 12.6
4 Coronation Street ITV 12.6
5 Goliath Awaits ITV 12.4
6 Family Fortunes ITV 11.9
7 Winner Takes All ITV 11.7
8 That Lucky Touch ITV 11.5
9 Crossroads ITV 10.6
10 The Cannon and Ball Show ITV 10.6

JULY
1 Nine O'Clock News BBC 10.5
2 Cagney and Lacey BBC 10.1
3 It's a Knockout BBC 7.9
4 Top of the Pops BBC 7.5
5 Chicago Story BBC 7.4
6 News and Sport BBC 7.2
7 World Cup Grandstand BBC 6.9
8 Legend/Walks Far Woman BBC 6.8
9 Fame BBC 6.7
10 News BBC 6.7

1 World Cup '82 ITV 13.6
2 Coronation Street ITV 13.4
3 Coronation Street ITV 11.3
4 Winner Takes All ITV 11.0
5 Crossroads ITV 11.0
6 Crossroads ITV 10.5
7 World Cup '82 ITV 10.4
8 News At Ten ITV 10.4
9 Give Us a Clue ITV 10.2
10 The Professionals ITV 10.1

AUGUST
1 Top of the Pops BBC 8.6
2 Nine O'Clock News BBC 8.5
3 Nine O'Clock News BBC 8.4
4 News and Sport BBC 8.4
5 Fame BBC 8.2
6 Cagney and Lacey BBC 8.1
7 Summertime Special BBC 8.1
8 Task Force South BBC 7.6
9 Nine O'Clock News BBC 7.6
10 Dynasty BBC 7.6

1 Coronation Street ITV 11.1
2 Coronation Street ITV 10.9
3 The Big Top Variety Show ITV 9.6
4 Crossroads ITV 9.6
5 Winner Takes All ITV 9.2
6 Family Fortunes ITV 9.1
7 Crossroads ITV 8.9
8 Crossroads ITV 8.9
9 Russ Abbot's Sat. Madhouse ITV 8.5
10 The Krypton Factor ITV 8.4

MONTH BY MONTH 1982

SEPTEMBER
1 Fame BBC 9.9
2 Dirty Harry BBC 9.3
3 That's Life BBC 8.9
4 Britain's Strongest Man BBC 8.7
5 To the Manor Born BBC 8.5
6 Blankety Blank BBC 8.5
7 The Eiger Sanction BBC 8.3
8 Nine O'Clock News BBC 8.3
9 Nine O'Clock News BBC 8.2
10 Solo BBC 8.2

1 Coronation Street ITV 12.9
2 Bridge Too Far ITV 12.2
3 Coronation Street ITV 12.0
4 Benny Hill ITV 11.9
5 The Agatha Christie Hour ITV 11.6
6 The Professionals ITV 10.8
7 The Eagle Has Landed ITV 10.3
8 Game For a Laugh ITV 10.1
9 Crossroads ITV 9.9
10 Crossroads ITV 9.9

OCTOBER
1 Dallas BBC 13.0
2 Claire BBC 11.0
3 Paul Daniels Magic Show BBC 10.8
4 Juliet Bravo BBC 10.4
5 Blankety Blank BBC 10.0
6 Top of the Pops BBC 9.9
7 News and Sport BBC 9.1
8 Angels BBC 8.6
9 XII Commonwealth Games BBC 8.6
10 To the Manor Born BBC 8.6

1 Coronation Street ITV 14.8
2 Coronation Street ITV 13.1
3 Tom, Dick and Harriet ITV 13.0
4 Benny Hill ITV 12.5
5 Crossroads ITV 12.5
6 Crossroads ITV 12.1
7 Game For a Laugh ITV 12.1
8 Shout At the Devil ITV 12.0
9 The Professionals ITV 11.8
10 Crossroads ITV 11.7

NOVEMBER
1 Paul Daniels Magic Show BBC 11.7
2 Juliet Bravo BBC 11.5
3 Tenko BBC 11.5
4 Blankety Blank BBC 11.2
5 Dallas BBC 11.0
6 Hi-De-Hi BBC 10.5
7 News and Sport BBC 10.2
8 Love and Bullets BBC 9.9
9 Top of the Pops BBC 8.7
10 With Six You Get Eggroll BBC 8.5

1 Coronation Street ITV 15.7
2 Coronation Street ITV 15.5
3 This Is Your Life ITV 14.0
4 The Professionals ITV 13.7
5 Hart To Hart ITV 13.3
6 Foxy Lady ITV 12.4
7 Give Us a Clue ITV 12.4
8 Game For a Laugh ITV 12.3
9 Crossroads ITV 11.7
10 Play Your Cards Right ITV 11.6

DECEMBER
1 Tenko BBC 13.5
2 The Little and Large Show BBC 12.5
3 Hi-De-Hi BBC 12.4
4 Three of a Kind BBC 12.1
5 World's Strongest Man BBC 11.6
6 Shogun BBC 10.7
7 Late Late Breakfast Show BBC 10.5
8 Dallas BBC 10.3
9 Top of the Pops BBC 10.1
10 Angels BBC 9.8

1 Coronation Street ITV 16.0
2 This Is Your Life ITV 15.6
3 Coronation Street ITV 14.0
4 The Professionals iTV 13.1
5 Crossroads ITV 12.4
6 Play Your Cards Right ITV 12.4
7 The Gentle Touch ITV 12.2
8 Crossroads ITV 12.1
9 Carry On Laughing ITV 12.1
10 Russian Roulette ITV 11.9

1983

[Viewers in Millions]

JANUARY

1	Holiday	BBC	11.3
2	Papillon	BBC	10.7
3	Hi-De-Hi	BBC	10.6
4	Main News	BBC	9.8
5	Top of the Pops	BBC	9.6
6	Nanny	BBC	9.5
7	Mastermind	BBC	9.5
8	Bergerac	BBC	9.4
9	Songs of Praise	BBC	9.4
10	Three of a Kind	BBC	9.1

1	Coronation Street	ITV	17.2
2	Superman	ITV	16.7
3	This Is Your Life	ITV	16.5
4	Coronation Street	ITV	15.8
5	Jaws 2	ITV	15.8
6	The Benny Hill Show	ITV	14.0
7	The Professionals	ITV	13.6
8	Crossroads	ITV	13.3
9	Family Fortunes	ITV	13.3
10	Return of the Pink Panther	ITV	13.2

FEBRUARY

1	Last of the Summer Wine	BBC	15.6
2	Bergerac	BBC	13.0
3	The Citadel	BBC	12.8
4	Holiday '83	BBC	12.8
5	Nanny	BBC	12.4
6	Wildlife On One	BBC	12.3
7	Jim'll Fix It	BBC	12.2
8	Dallas	BBC	11.7
9	Top of the Pops	BBC	11.7
10	Mastermind	BBC	11.6

1	Coronation Street	ITV	17.2
2	Coronation Street	ITV	16.6
3	This Is Your Life	ITV	14.7
4	3-2-1	ITV	14.4
5	Wish You Were Here	ITV	14.0
6	Mike Yarwood In Persons	ITV	13.3
7	Family Fortunes	ITV	13.3
8	Crossroads	ITV	13.1
9	That's My Boy	ITV	13.1
10	Crossroads	ITV	13.1

MARCH

1	Last of the Summer Wine	BBC	14.1
2	The Citadel	BBC	13.2
3	Bergerac	BBC	13.1
4	Dallas	BBC	11.7
5	Kenny Everett TV Show	BBC	11.7
6	Holiday '83	BBC	11.3
7	Nanny	BBC	11.1
8	Nine O'Clock News	BBC	11.1
9	Top of the Pops	BBC	10.9
10	Mastermind	BBC	10.8

1	Coronation Street	ITV	16.4
2	Coronation Street	ITV	15.8
3	This Is Your Life	ITV	14.4
4	3-2-1	ITV	13.9
5	Family Fortunes	ITV	13.7
6	Crossroads	ITV	13.4
7	Crossroads	ITV	12.5
8	Punchlines	ITV	12.4
9	Village Earth	ITV	12.2
10	Emmerdale Farm	ITV	11.6

APRIL

1	The Grand National	BBC	12.9
2	Kenny Everett TV Show	BBC	12.8
3	The Paras	BBC	12.5
4	Top of the Pops	BBC	11.4
5	Nine O'Clock News	BBC	11.4
6	Nine O'Clock News	BBC	10.3
7	Antiques Roadshow	BBC	9.7
8	That's Life	BBC	9.6
9	Wogan	BBC	9.1
10	Mastermind	BBC	9.0

1	Coronation Street	ITV	16.0
2	This Is Your Life	ITV	14.9
3	3-2-1	ITV	14.3
4	Coronation Street	ITV	13.8
5	Family Fortunes	ITV	13.3
6	Crossroads	ITV	13.2
7	Crossroads	ITV	13.2
8	T.J.Hooker	ITV	13.0
9	Only When I Laugh	ITV	12.9
10	Carry On Laughing	ITV	12.7

MAY

1	Dallas	BBC	12.7
2	That's Life	BBC	12.6
3	News and Weather	BBC	11.8
4	Some Mothers Do 'Ave 'Em	BBC	11.8
5	Top of the Pops	BBC	10.5
6	Mastermind	BBC	10.1
7	Three of a Kind	BBC	10.0
8	Fame	BBC	9.7
9	Rooster Cogburn	BBC	9.7
10	Nine O'Clock News	BBC	9.4

1	Coronation Street	ITV	16.5
2	Coronation Street	ITV	13.7
3	3-2-1	ITV	12.8
4	Crossroads	ITV	12.2
5	Family Fortunes	ITV	12.2
6	Where There's Life	ITV	12.1
7	Russ Abbot's Madhouse	ITV	12.0
8	Crossroads	ITV	11.9
9	Crossroads	ITV	11.8
10	T.J.Hooker	ITV	11.8

JUNE

1	That's Life	BBC	10.5
2	The War Wagon	BBC	9.2
3	News and Weather	BBC	8.4
4	The Visit	BBC	8.3
5	Carrott's Lib	BBC	8.0
6	Cagney and Lacey	BBC	8.0
7	News and Weather	BBC	7.9
8	The Visit	BBC	7.8
9	News and Sport	BBC	7.7
10	Pop Quiz	BBC	7.7

1	Coronation Street	ITV	12.1
2	Coronation Street	ITV	12.0
3	Crossroads	ITV	10.7
4	Crossroads	ITV	10.6
5	Crossroads	ITV	10.5
6	Family Fortunes	ITV	10.3
7	Jim Davidson's Special	ITV	10.2
8	Emmerdale Farm	ITV	9.7
9	Where There's Life	ITV	9.6
10	Tales of the Unexpected	ITV	9.3

JULY

1	Cagney and Lacey	BBC	7.6
2	Nine O'Clock News	BBC	7.6
3	Lady In Cement	BBC	7.5
4	Top of the Pops	BBC	7.3
5	Sports Special	BBC	7.0
6	Fame	BBC	6.9
7	Nine O'Clock News	BBC	6.6
8	Jury	BBC	6.5
9	The Black Adder	BBC	6.5
10	Odd One Out	BBC	6.2

1	Coronation Street	ITV	12.4
2	Coronation Street	ITV	12.0
3	Candid Camera Now & Then	ITV	10.4
4	Crossroads	ITV	10.0
5	Tales of the Unexpected	ITV	9.9
6	Crossroads	ITV	9.6
7	Crossroads	ITV	9.0
8	Where There's Life	ITV	9.0
9	Winner Takes All	ITV	8.7
10	T.J.Hooker	ITV	8.6

AUGUST

1	El Dorado	BBC	8.2
2	Nine O'Clock News	BBC	7.8
3	Only Fools and Horses	BBC	7.6
4	The Main Attraction	BBC	7.2
5	Nine O'Clock News	BBC	6.9
6	Top of the Pops	BBC	6.8
7	Fame	BBC	6.8
8	Oliver's Story	BBC	6.8
9	News and Weather	BBC	6.6
10	News and Sport	BBC	6.5

1	Coronation Steet	ITV	13.3
2	Coronation Street	ITV	12.2
3	Crossroads	ITV	10.1
4	The Krypton Factor	ITV	10.0
5	Crossroads	ITV	9.7
6	Crossroads	ITV	9.5
7	The A-Team	ITV	9.4
8	Where There's Life	ITV	9.3
9	Winner Takes All	ITV	9.2
10	The Happy Apple	ITV	9.1

SEPTEMBER

1	Nine O'Clock News	BBC	9.9
2	Blankety Blank	BBC	9.9
3	Athletics	BBC	9.8
4	Late Late Breakfast Show	BBC	9.2
5	Juliet Bravo	BBC	8.9
6	Three af a Kind	BBC	8.2
7	News And Sport	BBC	8.1
9	Britain's Strongest Man	BBC	8.1
9	Top of the Pops	BBC	8.0
10	Bergerac	BBC	7.9

1	Coronation Street	ITV	14.8
2	Coronation Street	ITV	14.3
3	The Sea Wolves	ITV	13.3
4	Morecambe and Wise Show	ITV	12.1
5	The Winds of War	ITV	12.1
6	The Benny Hill Show	ITV	12.0
7	Escape From Alcatraz	ITV	11.9
8	Crossroads	ITV	11.3
9	Crossroads	ITV	11.0
10	Keep It In the Family	ITV	10.9

OCTOBER

1	Just Good Friends	BBC	11.7
2	Blankety Blank	BBC	10.3
3	Late Late Breakfast Show	BBC	9.5
4	Juliet Bravo	BBC	9.4
5	Bergerac	BBC	9.4
6	Three of a Kind	BBC	9.1
7	News and Sport	BBC	8.4
8	Top of the Pops	BBC	8.1
9	Nine O'Clock News	BBC	8.1
10	Gone With the Wind	BBC	7.8

1	Coronation Street	ITV	15.0
2	Coronation Street	ITV	14.2
3	The Winds Of War	ITV	14.1
4	The A-Team	ITV	13.9
5	Winner Takes All	ITV	13.1
6	Give Us a Clue	ITV	11.9
7	Punchlines	ITV	11.8
8	The Krypton Factor	ITV	11.7
9	The Bounder	ITV	11.3
10	Morecambe and Wise Show	ITV	11.2

NOVEMBER

1	Blankety Blank	BBC	11.0
2	Paul Daniels Magic Show	BBC	10.6
3	Late Late Breakfast Show	BBC	10.4
4	News and Sport	BBC	10.1
5	Dallas	BBC	10.0
6	Juliet Bravo	BBC	9.9
7	Royal British Legion Festival	BBC	9.7
8	Top of the Pops	BBC	9.4
9	Only Fools and Horses	BBC	9.4
10	Wildlife On One	BBC	9.1

1	Coronation Street	ITV	15.7
2	Coronation Street	ITV	15.0
3	Give Us a Clue	ITV	14.1
4	Name That Tune	ITV	14.1
5	This Is Your Life	ITV	14.1
6	The A-Team	ITV	14.1
7	Family Fortunes	ITV	13.6
8	A Fine Romance	ITV	13.3
9	Never the Twain	ITV	13.2
10	The Benny Hill Show	ITV	13.2

DECEMBER

1	The Two Ronnies	BBC	13.8
2	Late Late Breakfast Show	BBC	12.1
3	Dallas	BBC	11.0
4	Wildcats of Saint Trinians	BBC	10.9
5	Only Fools and Horses	BBC	10.7
6	Top of the Pops	BBC	10.6
7	Bergerac	BBC	10.3
8	Sports Review of the Year	BBC	10.3
9	Cold Sweat	BBC	10.0
10	Terry and June	BBC	9.9

1	Coronation Street	ITV	16.9
2	Coronation Street	ITV	14.8
3	This Is Your Life	ITV	14.8
4	Name That Tune	ITV	14.3
5	Up the Elephant	ITV	14.2
6	In Loving Memory	ITV	13.9
7	Give Us a Clue	ITV	13.2
8	Crossroads	ITV	12.8
9	Cannon and Ball	ITV	12.6
10	Family Fortunes	ITV	12.3

1984

[Viewers in Millions]

JANUARY

1	Thunderball	ITV	16.6
2	Coronation Street	ITV	15.3
3	Name That Tune	ITV	13.9
4	The Two Ronnies	BBC	13.4
5	Give Us a Clue	ITV	13.0
6	This Is Your Life	ITV	12.9
7	Up the Elephant	ITV	12.7
8	The A-Team	ITV	12.4
9	3-2-1	ITV	12.1
10	The Thorn Birds	BBC	11.9
11	Bergerac	BBC	11.7
12	Crossroads	ITV	11.7
13	That's Life	BBC	11.4
14	Child's Play	ITV	11.3
15	A Fine Romance	ITV	11.2
16	Bronco Billy	ITV	11.0
17	Hi-De-Hi	BBC	10.7
18	Bullseye	ITV	10.4
19	You Only Live Twice	ITV	10.4
20	Auf Wiedersehen Pet	ITV	10.3

FEBRUARY

1	Coronation Street	ITV	17.6
2	Coronation Street	ITV	15.3
3	Name That Tune	ITV	15.1
4	This Is Your Life	ITV	14.9
5	A Fine Romance	ITV	14.7
6	Minder	ITV	14.7
7	Wish You Were Here	ITV	14.1
8	In Loving Memory	ITV	14.0
9	Auf Wiedersehen Pet	ITV	13.4
10	3-2-1	ITV	13.3
11	World In Action	ITV	12.3
12	Foxy Lady	ITV	12.2
13	Family Fortunes	ITV	12.2
14	T J Hooker	ITV	11.0
15	Telethon	ITV	10.9
16	News At Ten	ITV	10.7
17	Nine O'Clock News	BBC	10.5
18	More Than Murder	ITV	10.4
19	A Question of Sport	BBC	10.3
20	Quincy	ITV	10.2

MARCH

1	It'll Be Alright On the Night	ITV	16.8
2	Duty Free	ITV	15.4
3	Coronation Street	ITV	15.2
4	Minder	ITV	15.0
5	3-2-1	ITV	13.4
6	This Is Your Life	ITV	13.1
7	Wish You Were Here	ITV	12.8
8	Fresh Fields	ITV	12.6
9	T.J. Hooker	ITV	12.6
10	Live From Her Majesty's	ITV	12.4
11	Child's Play	ITV	12.0
12	Crossroads	ITV	11.9
13	Shroud For a Nightingale	ITV	11.7
14	Emmerdale Farm	ITV	11.3
15	The Other 'Arf	ITV	11.3
16	9 To 5	ITV	11.1
17	The Professionals	ITV	10.9
18	Dallas	BBC	10.7
19	A Question of Sport	BBC	10.1
20	Some Mothers Do 'Ave 'Em	BBC	9.9

APRIL

1	The Price Is Right	ITV	16.0
2	Coronation Street	ITV	15.5
3	Tribute To A. Tatlock	ITV	14.4
4	Smokey & Bandit Ride Again	ITV	14.0
5	Child's Play	ITV	13.9
6	Shroud For a Nightingale	ITV	13.6
7	This Is Your Life	ITV	13.1
8	Bear Island	ITV	13.1
9	Live From Her Majesty's	ITV	13.0
10	Fresh Fields	ITV	12.1
11	Crossroads	ITV	11.9
12	A Question of Sport	BBC	11.7
13	The Professionals	ITV	11.6
14	Family Fortunes	ITV	11.4
15	Emmerdale Farm	ITV	11.3
16	What's My Line	ITV	11.3
17	Dallas	BBC	10.8
18	Kit Curren Radio Show	ITV	10.5
19	TV Eye	ITV	10.4
20	Wogan	BBC	10.4

MAY

1	Missing From Home	BBC	12.8
2	Coronation Street	ITV	12.5
3	The Price Is Right	ITV	11.6
4	Dallas	BBC	11.6
5	Porridge	BBC	11.0
6	The Two Ronnies	BBC	11.0
7	That's Life	BBC	11.0
8	That's My Boy	ITV	10.8
9	It's Mike Yarwood	ITV	10.7
10	Just Amazing	ITV	10.6
11	A Question of Sport	BBC	10.4
12	Crossroads	ITV	10.3
13	Emmerdale Farm	ITV	10.2
14	Tales of the Unexpected	ITV	9.8
15	Top of the Pops	BBC	9.5
16	Give Us a Clue	ITV	9.4
17	The Pyramid Game	ITV	9.3
18	Surprise, Surprise	ITV	9.1
19	We Got It Made	BBC	8.9
20	World Snooker	BBC	8.8

JUNE

1	Jim Davidson Special	ITV	14.0
2	Coronation Street	ITV	13.3
3	Morecambe and Wise Show	ITV	12.2
4	The Price Is Right	ITV	11.6
5	Crossroads	ITV	11.2
6	Emmerdale Farm	ITV	10.2
7	Sorrell & Son	ITV	10.0
8	The Two Ronnies	BBC	9.9
9	That's Life	BBC	9.9
10	That's My Boy	ITV	9.8
11	Brazil v England	ITV	9.7
12	What's My Line	ITV	9.7
13	The Scarecrow & Mrs King	ITV	9.6
14	Dynasty	BBC	9.5
15	Just Amazing	ITV	9.4
16	Porridge	BBC	9.4
17	Crimewatch UK	BBC	9.2
18	Aspel & Company	ITV	9.1
19	Winner Takes All	ITV	8.9
20	Shine On Harvey Moon	ITV	8.9

JULY

1	Coronation Street	ITV	12.2
2	That's Life	BBC	12.0
3	Morecambe and Wise Show	ITV	9.5
4	Crossroads	ITV	9.2
5	What's My Line	ITV	9.1
6	Wimbledon: Mens Final	BBC	8.9
7	Sorrell & Son	ITV	8.7
8	Dynasty	BBC	8.4
9	A Cry In the Wilderness	ITV	8.4
10	Solo	BBC	8.3
11	Shine On Harvey Moon	ITV	8.2
12	Brass	ITV	8.1
13	Simon and Simon	ITV	8.1
14	The Bob Monkhouse Show	BBC	8.0
15	Wimbledon: Ladies Final	BBC	8.0
16	The Gentle Touch	ITV	7.8
17	Starsky and Hutch	BBC	7.8
18	Winner Takes All	ITV	7.5
19	Pull the Other One	ITV	7.5
20	The Brief	ITV	7.4

AUGUST

1	Coronation Street	ITV	12.8
2	Only Fools & Horses	BBC	11.6
3	A Town Like Alice	BBC	10.0
4	Crossroads	ITV	9.9
5	Killer By Night	BBC	9.5
6	Starsky and Hutch	BBC	8.6
7	Voyage of the Damned	ITV	8.4
8	Hi-De-Hi	BBC	8.1
9	The Krypton Factor	ITV	8.1
10	Dynasty	BBC	8.1
11	Ultra Quiz	ITV	7.9
12	Now and Then	ITV	7.8
13	Top of the Pops	BBC	7.8
14	Where There's Life	ITV	7.8
15	The Paras	BBC	7.5
16	Winner Takes All	ITV	7.5
17	The Pyramid Game	ITV	7.3
18	Best of Game For a Laugh	ITV	7.3
19	Entertainment Express	ITV	7.2
20	The Harding Trail	BBC	7.2

SEPTEMBER

1	Minder	ITV	15.4
2	Coronation Street	ITV	14.1
3	Coronation Street	ITV	13.7
4	Lace	ITV	13.7
5	News	ITV	13.4
6	Duty Free	ITV	12.9
7	Jim Davidson Special	ITV	12.7
8	Fresh Fields	ITV	12.7
9	Me & My Girl	ITV	11.6
10	Play Your Cards Right	ITV	11.1
11	News At Ten	ITV	11.1
12	Star Trek: The Movie	ITV	10.9
13	Give Us a Clue	ITV	10.8
14	Benny Hill Show	ITV	10.6
15	Paul Daniels Magic Show	BBC	10.5
16	Child's Play	ITV	10.5
17	Stunt Challenge '84	ITV	10.4
18	News At Ten	ITV	10.2
19	Nine O'Clock News	BBC	10.1
20	3-2-1	ITV	10.1

OCTOBER

1	Coronation Street	ITV	16.6
2	Fresh Fields	ITV	16.3
3	Duty Free	ITV	14.7
4	The Benny Hill Show	ITV	14.6
5	Just Good Friends	BBC	13.8
6	Tenko	BBC	13.7
7	Paul Daniels Magic Show	BBC	12.9
8	Play Your Cards Right	ITV	12.9
9	Glory Boys	ITV	12.8
10	Tripper's Day	ITV	12.8
11	Crossroads	ITV	12.6
12	Me and My Girl	ITV	12.5
13	Give Us a Clue	ITV	12.5
14	The A-Team	ITV	12.0
15	Juliet Bravo	BBC	11.9
16	The Krypton Factor	ITV	11.5
17	It'll Be Alright On the Night	ITV	11.3
18	Des O'Connor Tonight	ITV	11.3
19	We Love TV	ITV	11.1
20	Blankety Blank	BBC	11.1

NOVEMBER

1	Coronation Street	ITV	19.0
2	Give Us a Clue	ITV	15.5
3	Tenko	BBC	15.3
4	Just Good Friends	BBC	15.1
5	Crossroads	ITV	14.8
6	Name That Tune	ITV	14.6
7	Dallas	BBC	14.6
8	Hi-De-Hi	BBC	14.5
9	Play Your Cards Right	ITV	14.5
10	Surprise Surprise	ITV	13.7
11	Hallelujah	ITV	13.0
12	The A-Team	ITV	13.0
13	Child's Play	ITV	13.0
14	The Gentle Touch	ITV	12.7
15	Emmerdale Farm	ITV	12.5
16	Cannon & Ball	ITV	12.4
17	Bullseye	ITV	12.4
18	Juliet Bravo	BBC	12.2
19	Clive James On Television	ITV	12.2
20	Rising Damp	ITV	12.2

DECEMBER

1	Coronation Street	ITV	19.3
2	Name That Tune	ITV	15.6
3	Crossroads	ITV	15.2
4	Benny Hill Show	ITV	14.8
5	Child's Play	ITV	14.8
6	The A-Team	ITV	14.6
7	Tarby & Friends	ITV	14.5
8	Play Your Cards Right	ITV	14.1
9	Punchlines	ITV	14.0
10	Dallas	BBC	14.0
11	Emmerdale Farm	ITV	13.7
12	Tenko	BBC	13.6
13	Bullseye	ITV	13.1
14	Give Us a Clue	ITV	13.1
15	3-2-1	ITV	13.1
16	Hitchike	ITV	13.0
17	Quincy	ITV	12.9
18	News	ITV	12.9
19	Travelling Man	ITV	12.9
20	Hallelujah	ITV	12.7

MONTH BY MONTH 1984

1985

[Viewers in Millions]

From 1985 programmes with more than one episode a week begin to dominate the chart. As a result only one transmission has been included.

MONTH BY MONTH 1985

JANUARY

1	Coronation Street	ITV	20.3
2	It'll Be Alright On the Night	ITV	18.5
3	Wish You Were Here	ITV	17.6
4	Name That Tune	ITV	16.6
5	You'll Never See Me Again	ITV	15.8
6	Crossroads	ITV	15.7
7	That's Life	BBC	15.6
8	Dempsey and Makepeace	ITV	15.5
9	Full House	ITV	15.4
10	All Star Secrets	ITV	15.1
11	Emmerdale Farm	ITV	15.1
12	Bullseye	ITV	14.8
13	Dallas	BBC	14.7
14	This Is Your Life	ITV	14.4
15	News: Early Evening	ITV	13.8
16	Up the Elephant	ITV	13.6
17	The Beiderbecke Affair	ITV	13.3
18	Fresh Fields	ITV	13.2
19	The Price Is Right	ITV	12.8
20	Dynasty	BBC	12.7

FEBRUARY

1	Coronation Street	ITV	18.9
2	Last of the Summer Wine	BBC	18.8
3	Coronation Street	ITV	18.6
4	That's Life	BBC	16.4
5	Game For a Laugh	ITV	16.0
6	Wish You Were Here	ITV	15.6
7	Name That Tune	ITV	14.7
8	Family Fortunes	ITV	14.4
9	All Star Secrets	ITV	14.3
10	News and Weather	BBC	14.1
11	Dallas	BBC	14.0
12	This Is Your Life	ITV	13.9
13	Full House	ITV	13.9
14	One By One	BBC	13.2
15	Dynasty	BBC	12.6
16	Mastermind	BBC	12.6
17	News	ITV	12.4
18	That's My Boy	ITV	12.4
19	Fresh Fields	ITV	12.2
20	Dempsey and Makepeace	ITV	12.1

MARCH

1	Coronation Street	ITV	18.0
2	Coronation Street	ITV	17.9
3	Last of the Summer Wine	BBC	16.3
4	The Two Ronnies	BBC	16.0
5	Miss Marple – Pocket of Rye	BBC	15.6
6	QED	BBC	14.5
7	Miss Marple – Pocket of Rye	BBC	14.3
8	That's Life	BBC	14.3
9	One By One	BBC	14.1
10	Cover Her Face	ITV	14.1
11	Wish You Were Here	ITV	14.0
12	Are you Being Served?	BBC	14.0
13	EastEnders	BBC	13.8
14	That's My Boy	ITV	13.8
15	Dempsey and Makepeace	ITV	13.4
16	Only Fools and Horses	BBC	13.3
17	Quincy	ITV	13.3
18	Busman's Holiday	ITV	13.0
19	The Practice	ITV	13.0
20	Weekend News & Weather	BBC	12.8

APRIL

1	Coronation Street	ITV	18.0
2	Last of the Summer Wine	BBC	14.5
3	Only Fools and Horses	BBC	14.1
4	Dallas	BBC	14.1
5	Blazing Saddles	BBC	14.1
6	Emmerdale Farm	ITV	13.6
7	Best of Cannon and Ball	ITV	13.1
8	Minder	ITV	13.1
9	Are You Being Served?	BBC	13.0
10	Bird Brain of Britain	BBC	13.0
11	Up the Elephant	ITV	12.9
12	This Is Your Life	ITV	12.9
13	Busman's Holiday	ITV	12.9
14	Paul Daniels Easter Special	BBC	12.5
15	Noel Edmunds Egg Awards	BBC	12.4
16	Rollercoaster	ITV	12.4
17	Dynasty	BBC	12.3
18	Roll Over Beethoven	ITV	12.3
19	Chance In a Million	ITV	12.3
20	Crossroads	ITV	12.2

MAY

1	Coronation Street	ITV	15.8
2	Widows	ITV	13.1
3	Hawk the Slayer	ITV	13.0
4	Minder	ITV	12.7
5	EastEnders	BBC	12.5
6	Dallas	BBC	12.3
7	Emmerdale Farm	ITV	12.0
8	Dynasty	BBC	12.0
9	Home To Roost	ITV	11.9
10	Busman's Holiday	ITV	11.9
11	Crossroads	ITV	11.9
12	Bloodline	ITV	11.6
13	Operation Crossbow	BBC	11.6
14	Family Fortunes	ITV	11.5
15	That's Life	BBC	11.2
16	A Fine Romance	ITV	11.2
17	C.A.T.S.Eyes	ITV	11.2
18	Three Up, Two Down	BBC	11.1
19	The Price Is Right	ITV	10.9
20	Kenny Everett TV Show	BBC	10.8

JUNE

1	Championship Boxing	BBC	18.0
2	Coronation Street	ITV	15.0
3	Jenny's War	ITV	12.4
4	Bob Hope's Royal Birthday	ITV	12.3
5	EastEnders	BBC	11.9
6	Emmerdale Farm	ITV	11.9
7	The Price Is Right	ITV	11.9
8	Dynasty	BBC	11.7
9	Crossroads	ITV	11.5
10	That's Life	BBC	11.4
11	Dallas	BBC	11.2
12	Bulman	ITV	11.2
13	Murder She Wrote	ITV	11.0
14	Jim Davidson Special	ITV	10.9
15	The Comedians	ITV	10.9
16	Give Us a Clue	ITV	10.9
17	Hunter	ITV	10.6
18	That's My Boy	ITV	10.3
19	A.C.Clarke's Strange Powers	ITV	10.3
20	News (17.45)	ITV	10.1

JULY

1	Coronation Street	ITV	14.2
2	Royal Gala Performance	BBC	14.0
3	That's Life	BBC	12.2
4	Dallas	BBC	11.1
5	Emmerdale Farm	ITV	10.2
6	Shine On Harvey Moon	ITV	9.8
7	Crossroads	ITV	9.7
8	Paul Daniels Magic Show	BBC	9.2
9	Bulman	ITV	8.9
10	Give Us a Clue	ITV	8.8
11	Taggart	ITV	8.8
12	Points of View	BBC	8.6
13	Ultra Quiz 85	ITV	8.5
14	Duty Free	ITV	8.3
15	News At Ten	ITV	8.3
16	A.C.Clarke's Strange Powers	ITV	8.2
17	Des O'Connor Now	ITV	8.2
18	Morecambe and Wise Show	ITV	7.9
19	Murder She Wrote	ITV	7.8
20	EastEnders	BBC	7.7

AUGUST

1	EastEnders	BBC	15.8
2	Coronation Street	ITV	15.7
3	Duty Free	ITV	14.1
4	EastEnders	BBC	13.8
5	Murder She Wrote	ITV	12.5
6	Miami Vice	BBC	12.4
7	Funny Side	ITV	11.5
8	Bulman	ITV	11.4
9	Winner Takes All	ITV	11.3
10	Taggart	ITV	11.0
11	Never the Twain	ITV	10.7
12	Emmerdale Farm	ITV	10.6
13	Crossroads	ITV	10.6
14	International Athletics	ITV	10.2
15	The Two Ronnies	BBC	10.0
16	Beyond the Poseidon	ITV	9.9
17	Where There's Life	ITV	9.8
18	Are You Being Served?	BBC	9.7
19	Shine On Harvey Moon	ITV	9.5
20	Krypton Factor	ITV	9.3

SEPTEMBER

1	Fresh Fields	ITV	16.3
2	Open All Hours	BBC	16.1
3	Coronation Street	ITV	15.8
4	Superman 3	ITV	15.5
5	Brothers McGregor	ITV	15.1
6	In Sickness and In Health	BBC	14.7
7	Minder	ITV	14.4
8	EastEnders	BBC	13.2
9	Whicker's World	BBC	12.0
10	Crossroads	ITV	11.3
11	Russ Abbots's Mad House	ITV	11.0
12	Blankety Blank	BBC	10.9
13	3-2-1	ITV	10.9
14	Dempsey and Makepeace	ITV	10.8
15	Dynasty	BBC	10.7
16	Stunt Challenge '85	ITV	10.5
17	Emmerdale Farm	ITV	10.4
18	A-Team	ITV	10.4
19	Krypton Factor	ITV	10.3
20	Name That Tune	ITV	10.2

OCTOBER

1	Open All Hours	BBC	18.7
2	Fresh Fields	ITV	17.4
3	Coronation Street	ITV	16.4
4	EastEnders	BBC	16.2
5	In Sickness and In Health	BBC	15.4
6	Minder	ITV	14.5
7	Bergerac	BBC	14.3
8	Diary of Adrian Mole	ITV	13.9
9	Weekend Weather News	BBC	13.5
10	Brothers McGregor	ITV	13.4
11	Blankety Blank	BBC	13.2
12	Howard's Way	BBC	12.7
13	Just Good Friends	BBC	12.6
14	Ever Decreasing Circles	BBC	12.3
15	3-2-1	ITV	12.1
16	Crossroads	ITV	12.0
17	Dempsey and Makepeace	ITV	11.7
18	Live From Her Majesty's	ITV	11.7
19	Emmerdale Farm	ITV	11.6
20	Dynasty	BBC	11.3

NOVEMBER

1	EastEnders	BBC	19.3
2	Coronation Street	ITV	16.4
3	Last of the Summer Wine	BBC	15.2
4	'Allo 'Allo	BBC	14.7
5	Full House	ITV	14.6
6	Late Late Breakfast Show	BBC	13.0
7	Juliet Bravo	BBC	12.9
8	Girls On Top	ITV	12.9
9	Crossroads	ITV	12.8
10	A-Team	ITV	12.8
11	Howard's Way	BBC	12.7
12	Fawlty Towers	BBC	12.7
13	Crossroads Revisited	ITV	12.6
14	Bob's Full House	BBC	12.5
15	Live From Her Majesty's	ITV	12.4
16	Paul Daniel's Magic Show	BBC	12.3
17	Bergerac	BBC	12.2
18	Operation Julie	ITV	12.1
19	3-2-1	ITV	12.0
20	Emmerdale Farm	ITV	11.6

DECEMBER

1	EastEnders	BBC	19.6
2	From Russia With Love	ITV	17.2
3	Coronation Street	ITV	15.7
4	Just Good Friends	BBC	13.7
5	Minder	ITV	13.6
6	Porridge	BBC	12.9
7	Don't Wait Up	BBC	12.9
8	Blind Date	ITV	12.9
9	Only Fools and Horses	BBC	12.9
10	Play Your Cards Right	ITV	12.8
11	Copy Cats	ITV	12.8
12	Full House	ITV	12.8
13	Crossroads	ITV	12.7
14	Juliet Bravo	BBC	12.5
15	The Bill	ITV	12.0
16	Bullseye	ITV	12.0
17	The A-Team	ITV	11.9
18	Benny Hill Show	ITV	11.9
19	Blankety Blank	BBC	11.7
20	This Is Your Life	ITV	11.7

1986

[Viewers in Millions]

JANUARY

1	EastEnders	BBC	21.8
2	Coronation Street	ITV	17.9
3	People Do Funniest Things	ITV	17.8
4	Blind Date	ITV	17.6
5	Duty Free	ITV	17.3
6	You Only Live Twice	ITV	17.3
7	When Time Ran Out	ITV	15.1
8	This Is Your Life	ITV	14.7
9	Crossroads	ITV	14.0
10	Never the Twain	ITV	13.8
11	Don't Wait Up	BBC	13.7
12	All In Good Faith	ITV	13.4
13	Blankety Blank	BBC	13.2
14	Wish You Were Here	ITV	13.1
15	The Two Ronnies	BBC	12.7
16	Hi-De-Hi	BBC	12.6
17	Spitting Image	ITV	12.6
18	Emmerdale Farm	ITV	12.4
19	News	ITV	12.3
20	Copy Cats	ITV	12.2

FEBRUARY

1	EastEnders	BBC	22.4
2	Coronation Street	ITV	17.5
3	Late Late Breakfast Show	BBC	15.6
4	Surprise Surprise	ITV	14.8
5	Duty Free	ITV	14.7
6	That's Life	BBC	14.2
7	Don't Wait Up	BBC	13.9
8	Hi-De-Hi	BBC	13.6
9	Crossroads	ITV	13.3
10	The Bill	ITV	13.2
11	Every Second Counts	BBC	13.2
12	Crazy Like a Fox	ITV	13.2
13	Bullseye	ITV	13.1
14	Never the Twain	ITV	13.0
15	All In Good Faith	ITV	13.0
16	Wish You Were Here	ITV	12.6
17	Blankety Blank	BBC	12.6
18	This Is Your Life	ITV	12.5
19	A-Team	ITV	12.3
20	Emmerdale Farm	ITV	12.0

MARCH

1	EastEnders	BBC	23.0
2	Coronation Street	ITV	16.6
3	Surprise Surprise	ITV	15.2
4	Dallas	BBC	14.0
5	Taggart	ITV	13.6
6	All At Number 20	ITV	13.4
7	Crazy Like a Fox	ITV	13.3
8	Auf Wiedersehen Pet	ITV	13.3
9	French Connection	ITV	13.1
10	Crossroads	ITV	13.1
11	Dear John	BBC	13.0
12	Catchphrase	ITV	13.0
13	Bullseye	ITV	13.0
14	That's Life	BBC	12.9
15	Emmerdale Farm	ITV	12.7
16	Wish You Were Here	ITV	12.7
17	A-Team	ITV	12.0
18	Hancock's Half Hour	BBC	11.9
19	Price Is Right	ITV	11.7
20	Boon	ITV	11.7

APRIL

1	EastEnders	BBC	20.5
2	Coronation Street	ITV	16.5
3	Auf Wiedersehen Pet	ITV	15.1
4	Ashanti	ITV	15.0
5	Three Up Two Down	BBC	14.5
6	Question of Sport	BBC	13.3
7	Dallas	BBC	13.1
8	Antiques Roadshow	BBC	13.0
9	Catchphrase	ITV	12.9
10	Crossroads	ITV	12.8
11	Tomorrow's World	BBC	12.3
12	Bobby Davro On the Box	ITV	12.2
13	This Is Your Life	ITV	12.1
14	The Price Is Right	ITV	11.9
15	Emmerdale Farm	ITV	11.8
16	Holiday '86	BBC	11.4
17	What's My Line	ITV	11.3
18	That's Life	BBC	10.8
19	News	ITV	10.6
20	Every Second Counts	BBC	10.4

MAY

1	EastEnders	BBC	19.6
2	Auf Wiedersehen Pet	ITV	14.2
3	The Deep	ITV	13.8
4	Coronation Street	ITV	13.1
5	Bread	BBC	13.0
6	Dallas	BBC	11.8
7	Crossroads	ITV	11.3
8	That's Life	BBC	11.0
9	European Cup Final	ITV	10.5
10	Antiques Roadshow	BBC	10.5
11	Emmerdale Farm	ITV	10.4
12	Tomorrow's World	BBC	10.4
13	The Price Is Right	ITV	10.3
14	Catchphrase	ITV	10.0
15	Dynasty	BBC	9.9
16	Lame Ducks	BBC	9.8
17	Cannon and Ball	ITV	9.8
18	Battle of Midway	BBC	9.8
19	News	BBC	9.7
20	Sorry	BBC	9.6

JUNE

1	EastEnders	BBC	17.3
2	Coronation Street	ITV	13.4
3	Kane and Abel	BBC	12.6
4	Weekend Weather News	BBC	12.5
5	That's Life	BBC	11.9
6	Crossroads	ITV	10.4
7	Nine O'Clock News	BBC	10.0
8	Emmerdale Farm	ITV	10.0
9	Bread	BBC	9.7
10	Thirteen At Dinner	ITV	9.6
11	C.A.T.S.Eyes	ITV	9.5
12	Mastermind	BBC	9.3
13	Airport 77	BBC	9.3
14	Bob Monkhouse	BBC	9.0
15	Boys In Blue	ITV	8.9
16	Where There's Life	ITV	8.9
17	The Price Is Right	ITV	8.6
18	Laughter Show	BBC	8.6
19	News	ITV	8.4
20	To Catch a Thief	ITV	8.3

JULY

1	EastEnders	BBC	16.6
2	Coronation Street	ITV	13.2
3	Crimewatch UK	BBC	12.3
4	Return of Sherlock Holmes	ITV	10.3
5	All Star Secrets	ITV	10.3
6	Crossroads	ITV	10.1
7	Bullitt	ITV	9.8
8	Dynasty	BBC	9.6
9	Emmerdale Farm	ITV	9.5
10	'Allo 'Allo	BBC	9.5
11	The Benny Hill Show	ITV	9.2
12	Dallas	BBC	9.2
13	In Sickness and In Health	BBC	9.1
14	In Loving Memory	ITV	9.1
15	I Feel Fine	ITV	9.0
16	Return To Eden	ITV	9.0
17	No Place Like Home	BBC	8.7
18	Miami Vice	BBC	8.6
19	We Love TV	ITV	8.6
20	Winner Takes All	ITV	8.4

AUGUST

1	EastEnders	BBC	16.1
2	Coronation Street	ITV	14.2
3	Street Cop	BBC	11.2
4	Return To Eden	ITV	10.6
5	Crossroads	ITV	10.1
6	Winner Takes All	ITV	9.9
7	Emmerdale Farm	ITV	9.9
8	The Thorn Birds	BBC	9.6
9	Dallas	BBC	9.6
10	No Place Like Home	BBC	9.4
11	Dynasty	BBC	9.2
12	Des and the Best of Guests	ITV	8.8
13	Honkytonk Man	ITV	8.6
14	Return of Sherlock Holmes	ITV	8.5
15	Nine O'Clock News	BBC	8.2
16	Points of View	BBC	8.2
17	All Star Secrets	ITV	8.1
18	Summertime Special	ITV	8.0
19	We Love TV	ITV	7.8
20	News	ITV	7.7

MONTH BY MONTH 1986

SEPTEMBER

1	EastEnders	BBC	17.4
2	Coronation Street	ITV	14.8
3	Only Fools and Horses	BBC	14.2
4	Murder With Mirrors	ITV	13.4
5	Blind Date	ITV	12.6
6	Howards' Way	BBC	12.0
7	Ever Decreasing Circles	BBC	11.6
8	Taggart	ITV	11.1
9	3-2-1	ITV	10.9
10	Dempsey and Makepeace	ITV	10.9
11	We'll Think of Something	ITV	10.7
12	Open All Hours	BBC	10.6
13	Superman Two	ITV	10.6
14	Crossroads	ITV	10.6
15	Emmerdale Farm	ITV	10.5
16	Weekend Weather News	BBC	10.4
17	Play Your Cards Right	ITV	10.2
18	A-Team	ITV	9.8
19	Krypton Factor	ITV	9.8
20	The Jim Davidson Show	ITV	9.6

OCTOBER

1	EastEnders	BBC	21.2
2	Coronation Street	ITV	16.5
3	20 Years of the Two Ronnies	BBC	15.0
4	Open All Hours	BBC	13.4
5	Blind Date	ITV	13.0
6	Howards Way	BBC	12.7
7	Dallas	BBC	12.3
8	Runaway Train	ITV	11.8
9	In Sickness and In Health	BBC	11.8
10	Bullseye	ITV	11.7
11	Russ Abbot Show	BBC	11.7
12	Crossroads	ITV	11.6
13	Dempsey and Makepeace	ITV	11.2
14	3-2-1	ITV	11.2
15	New Faces of '86	ITV	10.9
16	Play Your Cards Right	ITV	10.8
17	Krypton Factor	ITV	10.7
18	Brush Strokes	BBC	10.7
19	Emmerdale Farm	ITV	10.7
20	A-Team	ITV	10.6

NOVEMBER

1	EastEnders	BBC	21.6
2	Coronation Street	ITV	15.7
3	Blind Date	ITV	15.1
4	20 Years of the Two Ronnies	BBC	15.1
5	Hi-De-Hi	BBC	14.2
6	Equalizer	ITV	13.6
7	Bullseye	ITV	13.2
8	Executive Stress	ITV	12.8
9	All the Best – Dave Allen	BBC	12.6
10	The A-Team	ITV	12.4
11	Howards Way	BBC	12.4
12	Every Second Counts	BBC	12.1
13	Crossroads	ITV	12.1
14	Cassandra Crossing	ITV	11.9
15	3-2-1	ITV	11.7
16	This Is Your Life	ITV	11.6
17	Krypton Factor	ITV	11.5
18	Unnatural Causes	ITV	11.2
19	Two of Us	ITV	11.1
20	Emmerdale Farm	ITV	10.9

DECEMBER

1	EastEnders	BBC	22.9
2	Coronation Street	ITV	16.4
3	Just Good Friends	BBC	15.5
4	2nd Alright On t]he Night	ITV	13.7
5	Bullseye	ITV	13.5
6	A-Team	ITV	13.4
7	This Is Your Life	ITV	12.9
8	Equalizer	ITV	12.9
9	'Allo 'Allo	BBC	12.5
10	London's Burning	ITV	12.5
11	Play Your Cards Right	ITV	12.4
12	Beadle's About	ITV	12.3
13	Executive Stress	ITV	12.2
14	The Benny Hill Show	ITV	12.1
15	Strike It Lucky	ITV	12.1
16	Paul Daniels Magic Show	BBC	11.7
17	Porridge	BBC	11.7
18	Crossroads	ITV	11.7
19	The Price Is Right	ITV	11.6
20	Three Up Two Down	BBC	11.2

1987

[Viewers in Millions]

MONTH BY MONTH 1987

JANUARY

1	EastEnders	BBC	25.3
2	Coronation Street	ITV	17.6
3	Bergerac	BBC	15.2
4	Joe Kidd	ITV	14.7
5	Wish You Were Here	ITV	14.4
6	Miss Marple	BBC	14.3
7	Paul Daniels Magic Show	BBC	14.2
8	Inspector Morse	ITV	13.8
9	Three Up Two Down	BBC	13.8
10	That's Life	BBC	13.6
11	Last of the Summer Wine	BBC	13.2
12	'Allo 'Allo	BBC	13.0
13	A-Team	ITV	12.9
14	Crossroads	ITV	12.9
15	Bob's Full House	BBC	12.9
16	Growing Pains/Adrian Mole	ITV	12.8
17	For a Few Dollars More	BBC	12.7
18	The Equalizer	ITV	12.6
19	This Is Your Life	ITV	12.6
20	Me and My Girl	ITV	12.5

FEBRUARY

1	EastEnders	BBC	23.4
2	Question of Sport	BBC	19.0
3	Coronation Street	ITV	18.1
4	Three Up Two Down	BBC	15.2
5	Bergerac	BBC	15.1
6	Wish You Were Here	ITV	13.7
7	Paul Daniels Magic Show	BBC	13.6
8	Surprise Surprise	ITV	13.0
9	Equalizer	ITV	13.0
10	This Is Your Life	ITV	12.9
11	Bread	BBC	12.9
12	Bob's Full House	BBC	12.8
13	That's Life	BBC	12.6
14	Any Which Way You Can	ITV	12.5
15	Crossroads	ITV	12.4
16	The A-Team	ITV	12.2
17	Miss Marple: Nemesis	BBC	12.2
18	Antiques Roadshow	BBC	11.9
19	Holiday '87	BBC	11.8
20	Tomorrow's World	BBC	11.8

MARCH

1	EastEnders	BBC	25.5
2	CoronationStreet	ITV	16.6
3	Aspel and Company	ITV	14.9
4	Don't Wait Up	BBC	14.8
5	Surprise Surprise	ITV	14.7
6	The A-Team	ITV	13.5
7	One By One	BBC	13.2
8	Bob's Full House	BBC	13.0
9	Question of Sport	BBC	12.9
10	Antiques Roadshow	BBC	12.6
11	This Is Your Life	ITV	12.4
12	Boon	ITV	12.3
13	TV Times Awards	ITV	12.1
14	Weekend Weather News	BBC	12.0
15	The Price Is Right	ITV	12.0
16	Tomorrow's World	BBC	12.0
17	Bobby Davro's TV Weekly	ITV	11.8
18	Catchphrase	ITV	11.7
19	Sporting Triangles	ITV	11.6
20	Emmerdale Farm	ITV	11.4

APRIL

1	EastEnders	BBC	22.2
2	EastEnders	BBC	22.1
3	Coronation Street	ITV	16.1
4	Coronation Street	ITV	15.6
5	Don't Wait Up	BBC	15.0
6	Live From the Palladium	ITV	14.0
7	Just Good Friends	BBC	13.4
8	This Is Your Life	ITV	13.2
9	Only Fools and Horses	BBC	13.0
10	Bergerac	BBC	12.9
11	Opportunity Knocks	BBC	12.8
12	News, Sport & Weather	BBC	11.8
13	Crossroads	ITV	11.7
14	Question of Sport	BBC	11.6
15	Crossroads	ITV	11.5
16	Crossroads	ITV	11.3
17	Tomorrow's World	BBC	11.1
18	Holiday '87	BBC	11.0
19	Emmerdale Farm	ITV	11.0
20	Cagney & Lacey	BBC	11.0

MAY

1	EastEnders	BBC	18.6
2	EastEnders	BBC	18.5
3	Escape From Sobibor	ITV	13.0
4	News	ITV	12.9
5	Live From the Palladium	ITV	12.5
6	Coronation Street	ITV	12.4
7	Coronation Street	ITV	11.9
8	News	ITV	11.3
9	Fields of Fire	ITV	11.1
10	C.A.T.S.Eyes	ITV	10.6
11	A Question of Sport	BBC	10.1
12	Emmerdale Farm	ITV	10.0
13	The Price Is Right	ITV	9.6
14	Strike It Lucky	ITV	9.5
15	Tomorrow's World	BBC	9.4
16	Catchphrase	ITV	9.1
17	Crossroads	ITV	9.1
18	News and Weather	BBC	8.8
19	That's Life	BBC	8.6
20	Emmerdale Farm	ITV	8.5

JUNE

1	EastEnders	BBC	19.4
2	EastEnders	BBC	19.1
3	Coronation Street	ITV	13.6
4	Coronation Street	ITV	13.4
5	Strike It Lucky	ITV	11.5
6	Emmerdale Farm	ITV	11.2
7	That's Life	BBC	10.7
8	Mastermind: The Final	BBC	10.7
9	If Tomorrow Comes	ITV	10.4
10	Crossroads	ITV	10.4
11	C.A.T.S Eyes	ITV	10.2
12	Me and My Girl	ITV	9.9
13	Taggart	ITV	9.8
14	News	ITV	9.6
15	Russ Abbot's Madhouse	ITV	9.6
16	Farrington	ITV	9.6
17	Crossroads	ITV	9.4
18	Emmerdale Farm	ITV	9.3
19	Tomorrow's World	BBC	9.2
20	Top of the Pops	BBC	9.2

JULY

1	EastEnders	BBC	17.3
2	EastEnders	BBC	16.7
3	Coronation Street	ITV	13.6
4	Coronation Street	ITV	12.5
5	What a Carry On	BBC	11.4
6	News	ITV	10.3
7	Bread	BBC	10.1
8	Summertime Special	ITV	9.5
9	Sorry	BBC	9.5
10	The Gauntlet	ITV	9.5
11	Home James	ITV	9.0
12	Cagney and Lacey	BBC	8.8
13	Family Fortunes	ITV	8.8
14	Don't Wait Up	BBC	8.7
15	Crossroads	ITV	8.6
16	Every Second Counts	BBC	8.6
17	Star Trek:The Wrath of Khan	ITV	8.5
18	Where There's Life	ITV	8.4
19	Crossroads	ITV	8.4
20	Crossroads	ITV	8.1

AUGUST

1	EastEnders	BBC	17.8
2	EastEnders	BBC	17.6
3	Coronation Street	ITV	14.1
4	Coronation Street	ITV	13.5
5	News	ITV	13.0
6	Summertime Special	ITV	10.4
7	The Equalizer	ITV	10.4
8	Bread	BBC	10.4
9	Carry On Cowboy	BBC	10.2
10	Bulman	ITV	10.2
11	Name That Tune	ITV	10.1
12	Home James	ITV	9.8
13	Minder	ITV	9.7
14	Terry and June	BBC	9.3
15	Tarby's Frame Game	ITV	9.3
16	Survival Team	BBC	9.2
17	Wolf To the Slaughter	ITV	9.2
18	The Bill	ITV	9.1
19	Snowbeast	ITV	9.0
20	Cook Report	ITV	8.5

SEPTEMBER

1	EastEnders	BBC	18.4
2	EastEnders	BBC	17.9
3	Romancing the Stone	ITV	14.2
4	Coronation Street	ITV	14.2
5	Coronation Street	ITV	14.1
6	Beyond Bermuda Triangle	ITV	13.4
7	News	ITV	12.9
8	Blind Date	ITV	12.5
9	Taggart	ITV	11.8
10	The Last Frontier	ITV	11.8
11	News	ITV	11.3
12	The Two of Us	ITV	11.2
13	Bread	BBC	11.1
14	Sins	ITV	10.9
15	New Faces of '87	ITV	10.8
16	Bust	ITV	10.6
17	Beadle's About	ITV	10.6
18	Three Up, Two Down	BBC	10.6
19	3-2-1	ITV	10.0
20	Russ Abbot Show	BBC	9.9

OCTOBER

1	EastEnders	BBC	20.7
2	EastEnders	BBC	17.8
3	Coronation Street	ITV	15.7
4	Coronation Street	ITV	15.4
5	Blind Date	ITV	14.6
6	Raiders of the Lost Ark	ITV	14.0
7	Bread	BBC	13.6
8	Only Fools and Horses	BBC	13.6
9	Dear John	BBC	12.5
10	Beadle's About	ITV	12.4
11	The Bill	ITV	12.1
12	Three Up, Two Down	BBC	11.8
13	News	ITV	11.8
14	Strike It Lucky	ITV	11.6
15	Howards Way	BBC	11.5
16	Russ Abbot Show	BBC	11.4
17	Bullseye	ITV	11.2
18	The Krypton Factor	ITV	11.2
19	Live From the Palladium	ITV	11.1
20	Clive James On TV	ITV	10.9

NOVEMBER

1	EastEnders	BBC	22.8
2	EastEnders	BBC	20.0
3	Coronation Street	ITV	16.3
4	Bread	BBC	15.8
5	Coronation Street	ITV	15.7
6	21 Years of the Two Ronnies	BBC	13.7
7	This Is Your Life	ITV	13.4
8	Blind Date	ITV	13.4
9	The Bill	ITV	13.1
10	The Charmer	ITV	12.9
11	Boon	ITV	12.5
12	Howards Way	BBC	12.3
13	News, Sport, Weather	BBC	12.0
14	Just Good Friends	BBC	11.6
15	Whatever Next	BBC	11.4
16	3-2-1	ITV	11.4
17	Home To Roost	ITV	11.3
18	Crossroads	ITV	11.2
19	In Sickness and In Health	BBC	11.2
20	The Krypton Factor	ITV	11.0

DECEMBER

1	EastEnders	BBC	21.4
2	EastEnders	BBC	21.3
3	Coronation Street	ITV	16.0
4	Coronation Street	ITV	16.0
5	Blind Date	ITV	15.5
6	The Bill	ITV	15.2
7	21 Years of the Two Ronnies	BBC	14.2
8	A Question of Sport	BBC	13.6
9	Bullseye	ITV	13.2
10	News, Sport, Weather	BBC	12.5
11	'Allo 'Allo	BBC	12.5
12	Strike It Lucky	ITV	12.4
13	The A-Team	ITV	11.8
14	North and South Book 2	BBC	11.4
15	Just Good Friends	BBC	11.3
16	Blood and Orchids	ITV	11.2
17	The Hostage Tower	ITV	11.1
18	Wish You Were Here	ITV	11.1
19	Whatever Next	BBC	11.0
20	Casualty	BBC	10.9

1988

From 1988, with the growing number of soap operas in the top 20 distorting chart entries, only the top scoring single episode of each soap is listed.

[Viewers in Millions]

JANUARY

1	EastEnders	BBC	24.5
2	Coronation Street	ITV	18.1
3	Surprise Surprise	ITV	13.9
4	After Henry	ITV	13.6
5	Wish You Were Here	ITV	13.3
6	Neighbours	BBC	13.3
7	Hi-De-Hi	BBC	13.3
8	Harem	ITV	13.2
9	Strike It Lucky	ITV	13.2
10	Supergirl	ITV	12.7
11	Bergerac	BBC	12.6
12	Bullseye	ITV	12.6
13	Holiday '88	BBC	12.5
14	Paul Daniels Magic Show	BBC	12.0
15	Bob's Full House	BBC	11.7
16	A Question of Sport	BBC	11.6
17	Hannay	ITV	11.5
18	This Is Your Life	ITV	11.3
19	Bless This House	ITV	11.3
20	Emmerdale Farm	ITV	11.2

FEBRUARY

1	EastEnders	BBC	23.6
2	Coronation Street	ITV	17.0
3	Wood,Walters and Wise	BBC	16.6
4	Question Sport/Spitting Image	BBC	16.4
5	Dad's Army	BBC	16.4
6	Jasper Carrott/Blackadder	BBC	15.9
7	Man With the Golden Gun	ITV	15.4
8	Lift Off	BBC	15.2
9	That's Life	BBC	15.0
10	Neighbours	BBC	14.3
11	Wish You Were Here	ITV	14.1
12	After Henry	ITV	13.9
13	Catchphrase	ITV	13.4
14	All Creatures Great & Small	BBC	13.4
15	News and Weather	BBC	12.8
16	Antiques Roadshow	BBC	12.8
17	Corbett,Palin,Garnett & Cool	BBC	12.8
18	Emmerdale Farm	ITV	12.7
19	Holiday '88	BBC	12.2
20	Wish Me Luck	ITV	12.0

MARCH

1	EastEnders	BBC	22.8
2	Coronation Street	ITV	16.1
3	Antiques Roadshow	BBC	14.2
4	Neighbours	BBC	13.8
5	Wish You Were Here	ITV	13.1
6	Holiday '88	BBC	12.8
7	News	ITV	12.8
8	London's Burning	ITV	12.6
9	Bobby Davro's TV Weekly	ITV	12.5
10	You Bet!	ITV	12.4
11	News and Weather	BBC	12.4
12	That's Life	BBC	12.3
13	Catchphrase	ITV	12.3
14	All Creatures Great & Small	BBC	11.9
15	Inspector Morse	ITV	11.9
16	Emmerdale Farm	ITV	11.8
17	Top of the Pops	BBC	11.7
18	The Price Is Right	ITV	10.8
19	Headliners	ITV	10.7
20	Crossroads	ITV	10.7

APRIL

1	EastEnders	BBC	18.9
2	For Your Eyes Only	ITV	17.8
3	Coronation Street	ITV	16.4
4	1988 Grand National	BBC	14.3
5	Neighbours	BBC	14.2
6	Crossroads	ITV	12.6
7	Steptoe and Son	BBC	12.3
8	Grand Larceny	ITV	12.3
9	Catchphrase	ITV	12.1
10	Holiday '88	BBC	12.1
11	The Two of Us	ITV	11.9
12	A Question of Sport	BBC	11.4
13	News	ITV	11.1
14	Every Breath You Take	ITV	11.1
15	Family Fortunes	ITV	10.7
16	The Price Is Right	ITV	10.5
17	Return of Sherlock Holmes	ITV	10.3
18	News and Weather	BBC	10.3
19	McGruder and Loud	ITV	10.3
20	Gentlemen and Players	ITV	10.2

MAY

1	EastEnders	BBC	18.0
2	Neighbours	BBC	13.3
3	Coronation Street	ITV	13.2
4	Steptoe and Son	BBC	13.2
5	That's Life	BBC	13.2
6	Diamonds Are Forever	ITV	12.7
7	News and Weather	BBC	11.9
8	News	ITV	11.2
9	Catchphrase	ITV	10.8
10	Brushstrokes	BBC	10.6
11	The Two of Us	ITV	10.5
12	One By One	BBC	10.0
13	Menace Unseen	ITV	10.0
14	Emmerdale Farm	ITV	9.8
15	Inspector Morse	ITV	9.8
16	Tales of the Unexpected	ITV	9.8
17	Benny Hill Show	ITV	9.8
18	Three Up, Two Down	BBC	9.8
19	News, Sport and Weather	BBC	9.0
20	Children Royal Performance	BBC	9.0

JUNE

1	EastEnders	BBC	15.4
2	Coronation Street	ITV	14.1
3	Neighbours	BBC	13.6
4	Steptoe and Son	BBC	11.9
5	The Equalizer	ITV	11.6
6	Dead Man's Folly	ITV	11.5
7	That's Life	BBC	11.3
8	Crimewatch UK	BBC	11.0
9	News and Weather	BBC	10.7
10	Queenie	ITV	10.3
11	Emmerdale Farm	ITV	10.3
12	In Sickness and In Health	BBC	10.0
13	Tomorrow's World	BBC	9.7
14	Brush Strokes	BBC	9.7
15	Every Second Counts	BBC	9.6
16	Don't Wait Up	BBC	9.3
17	Top of the Pops	BBC	9.1
18	Run the Gauntlet	ITV	8.9
19	Columbo	BBC	8.6
20	News, Sport, Weather	BBC	8.5

JULY

1	EastEnders	BBC	16.8
3	Coronation Street	ITV	13.7
3	Neighbours	BBC	13.5
4	In Sickness and In Health	BBC	12.2
5	Bread	BBC	11.8
6	Monte Carlo	ITV	10.3
7	'Allo'Allo	BBC	9.9
8	The Flying Doctors	BBC	9.8
9	Don't Wait Up	BBC	9.8
10	Emmerdale Farm	ITV	9.7
11	News and Weather	BBC	9.6
12	Anastasia	BBC	9.6
13	The Bill	ITV	9.2
14	The Two of Us	ITV	9.0
15	Me and My Girl	ITV	8.9
16	Time Bomb	ITV	8.8
17	News	ITV	8.8
18	Murder She Wrote	ITV	8.7
19	Through the Keyhole	ITV	8.7
20	Family Fortunes	ITV	8.6

AUGUST

1	EastEnders	BBC	15.0
2	Neighbours	BBC	13.3
3	Coronation Street	ITV	13.1
4	Bread	BBC	12.2
5	Private Benjamin	ITV	10.6
6	The Bill	ITV	10.2
7	Emmerdale Farm	ITV	9.3
8	Wheel of Fortune	ITV	9.0
9	News and Weather	BBC	8.9
10	Murder in Coweta County	BBC	8.8
11	The Eiger Sanction	ITV	8.8
12	Ever Decreasing Circles	BBC	8.8
13	News	ITV	8.8
14	Fun and Games	ITV	8.3
15	Top of the Pops	BBC	8.1
16	Three Days of the Condor	ITV	8.1
17	Wipe Out	ITV	8.1
18	News At Ten	ITV	8.0
19	In the Heat ff the Night	ITV	8.0
20	Survival	ITV	7.9

SEPTEMBER

1	EastEnders	BBC	17.0
2	Coronation Street	ITV	13.8
3	Neighbours	BBC	13.5
4	Bread	BBC	13.0
5	The Russ Abbot Show	BBC	12.2
6	The Bill	ITV	11.8
7	All Creatures Great & Small	BBC	11.8
8	Taggart	ITV	11.8
9	News, Sport and Weather	BBC	11.7
10	Blind Date	ITV	11.7
11	Howards Way	BBC	10.5
12	'Allo 'Allo	BBC	10.4
13	Wheel of Fortune	ITV	10.4
14	Casualty	BBC	10.0
15	Crimewatch UK	BBC	9.9
16	Witness	BBC	9.6
17	The Equalizer	ITV	9.6
18	Benny Hill Show	ITV	9.3
19	Telly Addicts	BBC	9.2
20	Emmerdale Farm	ITV	9.2

OCTOBER

1	EastEnders	BBC	18.8
2	Bread	BBC	16.4
3	Coronation Street	ITV	14.9
4	Neighbours	BBC	14.9
5	Blind Date	ITV	13.8
6	'Allo 'Allo	BBC	13.8
7	News, Sport and Weather	BBC	12.7
8	All Creatures Great & Small	BBC	12.6
9	Taggart	ITV	12.5
10	Bullseye	ITV	12.5
11	Piece of Cake	ITV	12.2
12	The Bill	ITV	12.2
13	Airplane	ITV	11.6
14	Howards' Way	BBC	11.3
15	Me and My Girl	ITV	11.0
16	Crimewatch Uk	BBC	11.0
17	Beauty and the Beast	ITV	10.8
18	Family Fortunes	ITV	10.7
19	Casualty	BBC	10.7
20	Concentration	ITV	10.5

NOVEMBER

1	EastEnders	BBC	20.1
2	Bread	BBC	17.0
3	Coronation Street	ITV	16.9
4	Neighbours	BBC	16.3
5	This Is Your Life	ITV	15.1
6	First Born	BBC	13.6
7	The Bill	ITV	13.2
8	Boon	ITV	12.7
9	Fawlty Towers	BBC	12.2
10	Blind Date	ITV	12.1
11	All Creatures Great & Small	BBC	11.8
12	Howards Way	BBC	11.8
13	Emmerdale Farm	ITV	11.7
14	Killer In the Mirror	ITV	11.5
15	Question of Sport	BBC	11.4
16	Casualty	BBC	11.4
17	The Krypton Factor	ITV	11.3
18	Live From the Palladium	ITV	11.2
19	Family Fortunes	ITV	11.2
20	Casualty	BBC	10.7

DECEMBER

1	EastEnders	BBC	21.5
2	Bread	BBC	21.0
3	Neighbours	BBC	17.7
4	Coronation Street	ITV	17.0
5	This Is Your Life	ITV	14.4
6	Blind Date	ITV	13.8
7	Supersense	BBC	13.4
8	Fawlty Towers	BBC	13.1
9	The Bill	ITV	12.8
10	Beadle's About	ITV	12.6
11	The Krypton Factor	ITV	12.6
12	Boon	ITV	12.5
13	Brush Strokes	BBC	12.2
14	'Allo 'Allo	BBC	11.6
15	Edmonds Sat. Roadshow	BBC	11.6
16	Emmerdale Farm	ITV	11.4
17	Murder She Wrote	ITV	11.3
18	The Rainbow	BBC	11.2
19	Top of the Pops	BBC	11.2
20	Question of Sport	BBC	11.1

MONTH BY MONTH 1988

1989
[Viewers in Millions]

JANUARY

1	EastEnders	BBC	21.6
2	Neighbours	BBC	18.9
3	Coronation Street	ITV	17.6
4	This Is Your Life	ITV	14.6
5	Minder	ITV	14.5
6	Inspector Morse	ITV	14.4
7	Poirot	ITV	14.1
8	News	ITV	14.0
9	Only Fools and Horses	BBC	13.9
10	Antiques Roadshow	BBC	13.8
11	The Bill	ITV	13.7
12	'Allo 'Allo	BBC	13.4
13	Raiders of the Lost Ark	ITV	13.1
14	Wish You Were Here	ITV	13.0
15	Thunderball	ITV	12.8
16	Strike It Lucky	ITV	12.4
17	Emmerdale Farm	ITV	12.3
18	Top of the Pops	BBC	11.9
19	Holiday '89	BBC	11.9
20	Boon	ITV	11.8

FEBRUARY

1	Coronation Street	ITV	23.2
2	EastEnders	BBC	20.0
3	Only Fools and Horses	BBC	18.9
4	Neighbours	BBC	18.0
5	The Bill	ITV	14.1
6	Bergerac	BBC	13.9
7	This Is Your Life	ITV	13.9
8	A Bit of a Do	ITV	13.6
9	'Allo 'Allo	BBC	13.4
10	Antiques Roadshow	BBC	13.2
11	Minder	ITV	13.2
12	Wish You Were Here	ITV	13.2
13	Paul Daniels Magic Show	BBC	13.0
14	The Bill	ITV	12.8
15	Flying Squad	ITV	12.6
16	Joint Account	BBC	12.4
17	The Two of Us	ITV	12.1
18	Crimewatch UK	BBC	12.0
19	That's Love	ITV	11.9
20	That's Life	BBC	11.8

MARCH

1	Coronation Street	ITV	23.4
2	EastEnders	BBC	21.1
3	Neighbours	BBC	18.6
4	Forever Green	ITV	15.7
5	News	ITV	13.9
6	Bergerac	BBC	13.7
7	Antiques Roadshow	BBC	13.5
8	Catchphrase	ITV	13.2
9	The Good Life	BBC	12.8
10	The Bill	ITV	12.1
11	Wish You Were Here	ITV	11.9
12	Busman's Holiday	ITV	11.4
13	News, Sport and Weather	BBC	11.4
14	Poirot	ITV	11.3
15	A Question of Sport	BBC	10.9
16	Opportunity Knocks	BBC	10.9
17	Flying Squad	ITV	10.8
18	Wildlife On One	BBC	10.8
19	You Bet	ITV	10.7
20	A Night of Comic Relief	BBC	10.6

APRIL

1	Coronation Street	ITV	23.2
2	Neighbours	BBC	20.1
3	EastEnders	BBC	19.5
4	The Good Life	BBC	14.7
5	Tanamera	ITV	14.5
6	The Heroes	ITV	14.4
7	The Bill	ITV	14.3
8	News	ITV	13.5
9	A Question of Sport	BBC	12.2
10	Busman's Holiday	ITV	12.1
11	Capstick's Law	ITV	11.8
12	Emmerdale Farm	ITV	11.7
13	Wildlife On One	BBC	11.3
14	Catchphrase	ITV	11.3
15	Family Fortunes	ITV	11.1
16	News, Sport and Weather	BBC	11.0
17	The Benny Hill Show	ITV	10.6
18	Columbo	BBC	10.5
19	Every Second Counts	BBC	10.4
20	Watching	ITV	10.4

MAY

1	Coronation Street	ITV	17.1
2	Neighbours	BBC	15.8
3	EastEnders	BBC	15.3
4	The Bill	ITV	12.4
5	Pale Rider	ITV	12.1
6	Children Royal Performance	BBC	11.9
7	Tanamera	ITV	10.8
8	Star Trek III	BBC	10.8
9	After Henry	ITV	10.6
10	Murder, She Wrote: Movie	ITV	10.3
11	News	ITV	9.8
12	The Match	ITV	9.8
13	News	ITV	9.7
14	The Benny Hill Show	ITV	9.6
15	Wildlife On One	BBC	9.6
16	Take Me Home	BBC	9.5
17	Eurovision Song Contest	BBC	9.5
18	That's Life	BBC	9.5
19	Every Second Counts	BBC	9.1
20	News, Sport and Weather	BBC	9.0

JUNE

1	Coronation Street	ITV	18.9
2	Neighbours	BBC	17.1
3	EastEnders	BBC	15.8
4	The Bill	ITV	14.6
5	Mastermind	BBC	12.1
6	The Russ Abbott Show	BBC	12.0
7	News and Weather	BBC	11.6
8	That's Life	BBC	11.4
9	Every Second Counts	BBC	10.6
10	The 19th Hole	ITV	10.3
11	Split Ends	ITV	10.2
12	Bread	BBC	10.1
13	Columbo	BBC	10.0
14	Emmerdale Farm	ITV	9.9
15	Everybody's Equal	ITV	9.9
16	Cook Report	ITV	9.8
17	Open All Hours	BBC	9.5
18	News, Sport & Weather	BBC	9.2
19	Top of the Pops	BBC	9.1
20	All Creatures Great & Small	BBC	9.0

JULY

1	Coronation Street	ITV	15.8
2	Neighbours	BBC	15.6
3	EastEnders	BBC	13.6
4	Wimbledon: Men's Final	BBC	11.7
5	The Bill	ITV	11.2
6	News, Sport and Weather	BBC	10.5
7	All Creatures Great & Small	BBC	10.4
8	News and Weather	BBC	10.4
9	Only Fools and Horses	BBC	10.1
10	Crimewatch UK	BBC	9.7
11	In Sickness and In Health	BBC	9.5
12	Wimbledon: Ladies Final	BBC	9.5
13	Airplane 2	ITV	9.4
14	Columbo	BBC	9.3
15	Supersense	BBC	9.3
16	The Gladiator	BBC	9.2
17	Supergirl	ITV	9.2
18	Casualty	BBC	9.1
19	Chelworth	BBC	8.9
20	Bread	BBC	8.8

AUGUST

1	Neighbours	BBC	16.3
2	Coronation Street	ITV	15.7
3	EastEnders	BBC	15.5
4	The Bill	ITV	12.0
5	News and Weather	BBC	10.8
6	Cassandra Crossing	BBC	10.7
7	News, Sport and Weather	BBC	10.1
8	Casualty	BBC	9.8
9	Columbo	BBC	9.5
10	Emmerdale Farm	ITV	9.3
11	The River	BBC	9.3
12	Barrymore's Saturday Night	BBC	9.3
13	The Joe Longthorne Show	ITV	9.1
14	Bread	BBC	9.0
15	Home and Away	ITV	8.1
16	All Creatures Great & Small	BBC	8.9
17	Nine O'Clock News	BBC	8.9
18	The Dirtwater Dynasty	BBC	8.9
19	Affair In Mind	BBC	8.2
20	Evergreen	ITV	7.8

MONTH BY MONTH 1989

SEPTEMBER

1	Coronation Street	ITV	18.3
2	EastEnders	BBC	16.0
3	Neighbours	BBC	15.7
4	Bread	BBC	14.1
5	Only Fools and Horses	BBC	12.8
6	Casualty	BBC	11.7
7	News, Sport and Weather	BBC	11.6
8	All Creatures Great & Small	BBC	11.3
9	In Sickness and In Health	BBC	11.2
10	Crimewath UK	BBC	11.1
11	Challenge Anneka	BBC	10.9
12	The Bill	ITV	10.8
13	Taggart	ITV	10.6
14	The Russ Abbott Show	BBC	10.3
15	French Fields	ITV	10.3
16	Howards' Way	BBC	10.0
17	The Krypton Factor	ITV	9.7
18	Emmerdale Farm	ITV	9.0
19	Home and Away	ITV	9.0
20	'Allo 'Allo	BBC	8.9

OCTOBER

1	Coronation Street	ITV	19.9
2	EastEnders	BBC	16.6
3	Neighbours	BBC	16.3
4	Jewel of the Nile	ITV	14.3
5	Only Fools and Horses	BBC	14.2
6	Blackadder Goes Forth	BBC	13.1
7	News, Sport and Weather	BBC	12.8
8	Blind Date	ITV	12.7
9	In Sickness and In Health	BBC	12.2
10	The Bill	ITV	11.7
11	All Creatures Great & Small	BBC	11.7
12	Casualty	BBC	11.6
13	Beadle's About	ITV	11.3
14	Challenge Anneka	BBC	11.1
15	Crimewatch UK	BBC	10.9
16	Brewster's Millions	BBC	10.9
17	News	ITV	10.9
18	The Russ Abbott Show	BBC	10.7
19	'Allo 'Allo	BBC	10.5
20	Boon	ITV	10.4

NOVEMBER

1	Coronation Street	ITV	20.9
2	Neighbours	BBC	18.2
3	EastEnders	BBC	17.5
4	Blind Date	ITV	14.4
5	Bread	BBC	14.0
6	Beadle's About	ITV	13.7
7	This Is Your Life	ITV	13.6
8	London's Burning	ITV	12.6
9	The Krypton Factor	ITV	12.5
10	Birds of a Feather	BBC	12.5
11	Some Mothers Do 'Ave 'Em	BBC	12.5
12	The Bill	ITV	12.3
13	Casualty	BBC	12.1
14	Crimewatch UK	BBC	12.0
15	News, Sport and Weather	BBC	11.9
16	Catchphrase	ITV	11.8
17	Home and Away	ITV	11.7
18	Family Fortunes	ITV	11.3
19	Around/World in 80 Days	BBC	11.3
20	Boon	ITV	11.1

DECEMBER

1	Coronation Street	ITV	21.4
2	Neighbours	BBC	19.1
3	EastEnders	BBC	18.1
4	Blind Date	ITV	16.0
5	Beadle's About	ITV	14.1
6	Victoria Wood	BBC	13.9
7	The Bill	ITV	13.8
8	Stay Lucky	ITV	13.1
9	News	ITV	13.0
10	Home and Away	ITV	12.8
11	London's Burning	ITV	12.8
12	This Is Your Life	ITV	12.6
13	Watching	ITV	12.6
14	Wish You Were Here	ITV	12.4
15	Caribbean Mystery	ITV	11.7
16	Family Fortunes	ITV	11.7
17	Question of Sport	BBC	11.4
18	Crimewatch UK	BBC	11.2
19	Top of the Pops	BBC	11.1
20	Dad's Army	BBC	11.0

1990

[Viewers in Millions]

JANUARY

1	Coronation Street	ITV	22.8
2	Neighbours	BBC	19.3
3	EastEnders	BBC	18.9
4	This is Your Life	ITV	15.7
5	For Your Eyes Only	ITV	15.2
6	Inspector Morse	ITV	15.1
7	The Bill	ITV	14.6
8	Blind Date	ITV	14.6
9	Watching	ITV	14.5
10	Strike It Lucky	ITV	14.0
11	Bergerac	BBC	13.8
12	Wish You Were Here	ITV	13.7
13	Home to Roost	ITV	13.6
14	Home and Away	ITV	12.7
15	Antiques Roadshow	BBC	12.2
16	Yellowthread Street	ITV	12.1
17	Poirot	ITV	12.1
18	A Question of Sport	BBC	12.0
19	Emmerdale	ITV	11.8
20	The Two of Us	ITV	10.8

FEBRUARY

1	Coronation Street	ITV	21.7
2	EastEnders	BBC	20.1
3	Neighbours	BBC	18.2
4	This Is Your Life	ITV	15.4
5	Blind Date	ITV	14.8
6	No Job For a Lady	ITV	14.4
7	Wish You Were Here	ITV	13.6
8	Bergerac	BBC	13.4
9	Strike It Lucky	ITV	12.9
10	Antiques Roadshow	BBC	12.8
11	Catchphrase	ITV	12.3
12	The Ronn Lucas Show	ITV	12.3
13	Poirot	ITV	12.2
14	Home and Away	ITV	12.2
15	Murder She Wrote	ITV	12.1
16	The Two of Us	ITV	12.0
17	May To December	BBC	12.0
18	Emmerdale	ITV	10.6
19	El Cid	ITV	10.4
20	Stolen	ITV	10.4

MARCH

1	Coronation Street	ITV	20.4
2	Neighbours	BBC	18.7
3	EastEnders	BBC	18.6
4	This Is Your Life	ITV	14.5
5	Strike It Lucky	ITV	13.6
6	The Bill	ITV	13.3
7	Surprise Surprise	ITV	13.2
8	Home and Away	ITV	13.0
9	Cook Report Special	ITV	12.4
10	Inspector Morse	iTV	12.0
11	Antiques Roadshow	BBC	11.8
12	Brush Strokes	BBC	11.4
13	The Two of Us	ITV	11.4
14	Little and Large	BBC	11.2
15	A Question of Sport	BBC	10.8
16	You Bet!	ITV	10.7
17	No Job For a Lday	ITV	10.7
18	Jaws	BBC	10.6
19	El Cid	ITV	10.6
20	Bergerac	BBC	10.6

APRIL

1	EastEnders	BBC	19.8
2	Coronation Street	ITV	19.4
3	Neighbours	BBC	16.9
4	Wish You Were Here	ITV	13.8
5	This Is Your Life	ITV	12.7
6	Home and Away	ITV	12.7
7	Strike It Lucky	ITV	12.7
8	Inspector Morse	ITV	12.7
9	Surprise Surprise	ITV	12.6
10	The Bill	ITV	12.2
11	You Bet!	ITV	11.8
12	News	ITV	11.3
13	Emmerdale	ITV	11.1
14	Through the Keyhole	ITV	10.7
15	Joint Account	BBC	10.7
16	News, Sport And Weather	BBC	10.5
17	Grand National	BBC	10.3
18	A Question of Sport	BBC	10.3
19	To the Manor Born	BBC	9.9
20	Baywatch	ITV	9.6

MAY

1	Coronation Street	ITV	18.7
2	EastEnders	BBC	16.0
3	Neighbours	BBC	15.7
4	This Is Your Life	ITV	14.0
5	Strike It Lucky	ITV	12.5
6	The Bill	ITV	11.6
7	Home and Away	ITV	11.6
8	Through the Keyhole	ITV	11.2
9	F.A.Cup Final	BBC	11.2
10	Crimewatch UK	BBC	10.9
11	Emmerdale	ITV	10.7
12	Upper Hand	ITV	10.4
13	Taggart – The Movie	ITV	10.4
14	Trading Places	ITV	10.4
15	Busman's Holiday	ITV	10.2
16	Mistress of Suspense	ITV	10.1
17	The Two of Us	ITV	9.9
18	Kind Of Magic	ITV	9.7
19	Children's Variety	BBC	9.6
20	Surgical Spirit	ITV	9.2

JUNE

1	Coronation Street	ITV	18.5
2	Neighbours	BBC	16.0
3	EastEnders	BBC	15.4
4	Survival Special	ITV	12.2
5	Home and Away	ITV	12.1
6	News and Weather	BBC	11.6
7	$64,000 Question	ITV	10.9
8	The Bill	ITV	10.9
9	Strike It Lucky	ITV	10.7
10	Upper Hand	ITV	10.6
11	Emmerdale	iTV	10.5
12	Busman's Holiday	ITV	10.3
13	Island Son	ITV	9.9
14	World Cup:Brazil v Sweden	BBC	9.9
15	Surgical Spirit	ITV	9.6
16	Crimewatch UK	BBC	9.5
17	Ronn Lucas Show	ITV	9.4
18	World Cup:Italy v Austria	ITV	9.3
19	Takeover Bid	BBC	9.1
20	Two of Us	ITV	9.0

JULY

1	Coronation Street	ITV	17.4
2	W.Germany v England	BBC	16.7
3	Neighbours	BBC	15.0
4	EastEnders	BBC	14.8
5	World Cup Final	BBC	13.1
6	World Cup: Italy v England	BBC	12.5
7	Argentina v Italy	BBC	11.9
8	Home And Away	ITV	11.2
9	News, Sports and Weather	BBC	11.1
10	Gremlins	ITV	10.7
11	The Bill	ITV	10.6
12	Bergerac	BBC	10.0
13	Emmerdale	ITV	9.1
14	$64,000 Question	ITV	9.0
15	The Cook Report	ITV	8.7
16	Victoria Wood	BBC	8.6
17	W Germany v England	ITV	8.5
18	Prescription:Murder	ITV	8.4
19	Murder At the Vicarage	BBC	8.4
20	Island Sun	ITV	8.1

AUGUST

1	Coronation Street	ITV	16.1
2	EastEnders	BBC	15.8
3	Neighbours	BBC	14.3
4	Home and Away	ITV	10.6
5	The Bill	ITV	10.3
6	The Upper Hand	ITV	10.2
7	News, Sport and Weather	BBC	9.9
8	BabyM	BBC	9.4
9	Blackadder the Third	BBC	9.2
10	Emmerdale	ITV	9.1
11	The Cook Report	ITV	9.1
12	News and Weather	BBC	8.8
13	Agatha Christie:Bertram's	BBC	8.7
14	Murder She Wrote	ITV	8.5
15	Nine O'Clock News	BBC	8.3
16	Stars In Their Eyes	ITV	8.3
17	It's Beadle	ITV	8.2
18	$64,000 Question	ITV	7.8
19	Six O'Clock News	BBC	7.8
20	There Must be a Pony	BBC	7.8

MONTH BY MONTH 1990

SEPTEMBER

1	Coronation Street	ITV	16.1
2	EastEnders	BBC	14.9
3	Neighbours	BBC	14.5
4	The Bill	ITV	11.7
5	Bread	BBC	11.4
6	News and Weather	BBC	10.8
7	Taggart	ITV	10.7
8	Home and Away	ITV	10.4
9	Casualty	BBC	10.3
10	On the Up	BBC	10.0
11	Never the Twain	ITV	9.9
12	Diamonds Are Forever	ITV	9.6
13	'Allo 'Allo	BBC	9.6
14	The Krypton Factor	ITV	9.5
15	Generation Game	BBC	9.4
16	Crimewatch UK	BBC	9.2
17	Emmerdale	ITV	9.0
18	Family Fortunes	ITV	9.1
19	Blind Faith	ITV	8.9
20	Howard's Way	BBC	8.8

OCTOBER

1	Coronation Street	ITV	15.2
2	Beadle's About	ITB	13.0
3	Blind Date	ITV	13.0
4	EastEnders	BBC	12.7
5	Bread	BBC	12.3
6	Top Gun	ITV	12.2
7	'Allo 'Allo	BBC	12.0
8	London's Burning	ITV	11.6
9	The Bill	ITV	11.3
10	Casualty	BBC	11.3
11	The Generation Game	BBC	11.2
12	Stay Lucky	ITV	11.1
13	Ruth Rendell Mysteries	ITV	10.6
14	Birds of a Feather	BBC	10.6
15	The Krypton Factor	ITV	10.5
16	Last of the Summer Wine	BBC	10.3
17	Boon	ITV	10.3
18	Nine O'Clock News	BBC	10.2
19	Never the Twain	ITV	10.1
20	Neighbours	BBC	10.1

NOVEMBER

1	Coronation Street	ITV	17.3
2	EastEnders	BBC	17.3
3	Neighbours	BBC	17.2
4	Blind Date	ITV	14.4
5	Beadle's About	ITV	13.2
6	London's Burning	ITV	13.1
7	Birds of a Feather	BBC	13.0
8	Casualty	BBC	12.7
9	News	ITV	12.1
10	Family Fortunes	ITV	12.1
11	The Trials of Life	BBC	12.1
12	Keeping Up Appearances	BBC	12.1
13	The Generation Game	BBC	11.9
14	Home and Away	ITV	11.8
15	The Bill	ITV	11.6
16	Ruth Rendell Mysteries	ITV	11.2
17	Stay Lucky	ITV	11.1
18	Strike It Lucky	ITV	10.7
19	Emmerdale	ITV	10.4
20	The Krypton Factor	ITV	10.3

DECEMBER

1	Coronation Street	ITV	19.6
2	Neighbours	BBC	19.0
3	Eastenders	BBC	18.4
4	Blind Date	ITV	13.9
5	Keeping Up Appearances	BBC	13.6
6	Wish You Were Here	ITV	13.5
7	Casualty	BBC	13.4
8	Happy B/day Coronation St	ITV	13.1
9	Birds of a Feather	BBC	12.9
10	Taggart	ITV	12.8
11	This Is Your Life	BBC	12.8
12	Home and Away	ITV	12.6
13	Beadles About	ITV	12.1
14	The Generation Game	BBC	11.7
15	Only Fools and Horses	BBC	11.6
16	Family Fortunes	ITV	11.4
17	Star Trek III	BBC	11.3
18	Nine O'Clock News	BBC	11.2
19	News At Ten	ITV	11.1
20	The Bill	ITV	10.8

1991

[Viewers in Millions]

MONTH BY MONTH 1991

JANUARY

1	EastEnders	BBC	19.9
2	Coronation Street	ITV	19.5
3	Neighbours	BBC	18.3
4	Only Fools and Horses	BBC	16.6
5	You've Been Framed	ITV	15.2
6	Home and Away	ITV	14.6
7	Curse of Mr Bean	BBC	13.8
8	Blind Date	ITV	13.7
9	Watching	ITV	13.4
10	Poirot	ITV	13.3
11	Antiques Roadshow	BBC	13.2
12	This Is Your Life	ITV	13.1
13	Des O'Connor Tonight	ITV	12.3
14	'Allo 'Allo	BBC	12.2
15	The Bill	ITV	12.1
16	News	ITV	11.5
17	Lovejoy	BBC	11.4
18	P D James: Desires	ITV	11.4
19	Surgical Spirit	ITV	11.2
20	News, Sport/Weather	BBC	11.2

FEBRUARY

1	EastEnders	BBC	19.8
2	Coronation Street	ITV	19.0
3	Neighbours	BBC	19.3
4	You've Been Framed	ITV	17.8
5	Watching	ITV	16.4
6	Best of Blind Date	ITV	14.6
7	The Bill	ITV	14.5
8	Man/Golden Gun	ITV	14.4
9	Antiques Roadshow	BBC	14.5
10	Home and Away	ITV	13.6
11	News	ITV	13.5
12	Surgical Spirit	ITV	13.0
13	P D James: Desires	ITV	12.6
14	Wish You Were Here	ITV	12.6
15	News and Weather	BBC	12.5
16	Poirot	ITV	12.4
17	This Is Your Life	ITV	12.4
18	News	ITV	12.3
19	Catchphrase	ITV	12.2
20	The Bill	ITV	12.2

MARCH

1	EastEnders	BBC	17.6
2	Coronation Street	ITV	16.8
3	Neighbours	BBC	16.1
4	Antiques Roadshow	BBC	13.6
5	This Is Your Life	ITV	12.2
6	Lovejoy	BBC	12.2
7	The Bill	ITV	12.0
8	Home and Away	ITV	11.6
9	Upper Hand	ITV	11.2
10	Brush Strokes	BBC	11.1
11	You Bet	ITV	11.0
12	$64,000 Question	ITV	11.0
13	Surprise Surprise	ITV	10.8
14	Butterflies	BBC	10.8
15	Question of Sport	BBC	10.7
16	Poirot	ITV	10.7
17	Emmerdale	ITV	10.3
18	9 O'Clock News	BBC	10.2
19	Columbo	ITV	10.1
20	'Allo 'Allo	BBC	10.0

APRIL

1	EastEnders	BBC	17.1
2	Darling Buds of May	ITV	16.6
3	Neighbours	BBC	16.6
4	Coronation Street	ITV	16.4
5	Prime Suspect	ITV	13.9
6	Goonies	ITV	12.9
7	Live and Let Die	ITV	12.9
8	Home and Away	ITV	12.7
9	The Bill	ITV	12.3
10	Open All hours	BBC	12.0
11	You Bet	ITV	12.0
12	Batteries Not Included	BBC	11.7
13	Overboard	BBC	11.6
14	This Is Your Life	ITV	11.6
15	Question of Sport	BBC	11.6
16	Surprise Surprise	ITV	11.3
17	Taggart the Movie	ITV	10.9
18	Chief	ITV	10.6
19	Through the Keyhole	ITV	10.4
20	Emmerdale	ITV	10.0

MAY

1	Darling Buds of May	ITV	17.2
2	EastEnders	BBC	15.6
3	Neighbours	BBC	13.9
4	Coronation Street	ITV	15.3
5	Home and Away	ITV	12.1
6	Untouchables	BBC	12.1
7	News and Weather	BBC	11.7
8	Big Break	BBC	11.2
9	The Bill	ITV	10.9
10	Crimewatch UK	BBC	10.6
11	Home and Away	ITV	10.5
12	Dragonslayer	ITV	9.8
13	Second Thoughs	ITV	9.6
14	Emmerdale	ITV	9.5
15	Through the Keyhole	ITV	9.4
16	Upper Hand	ITV	9.4
17	9 O'Clock News	BBC	9.1
18	Cluedo	ITV	8.9
19	Dad's Army	BBC	8.8
20	Jeeves and Wooster	ITV	8.6

JUNE

1	Coronation Street	ITV	15.6
2	EastEnders	BBC	14.9
3	Neighbours	BBC	14.0
4	Fifteen Streets	ITV	12.0
5	Home and Away	ITV	11.5
6	Birds of a Feather	BBC	10.6
7	The Bill	ITV	9.9
8	Open All Hours	BBC	9.6
9	In Suspicious Circumstances	ITV	9.6
10	Second Thoughts	ITV	9.5
11	Perfect Hero	ITV	9.4
12	Big Break	BBC	9.3
13	Emmerdale	ITV	9.2
14	Bob's Your Uncle	ITV	9.2
15	Stars In Their Eyes	ITV	9.2
16	Through the Keyhole	ITV	9.1
17	Night Walk	ITV	9.0
18	News	ITV	9.0
19	Cluedo	ITV	9.0
20	Chancer	ITV	8.9

JULY

1	Coronation Street	ITV	13.6
2	EastEnders	BBC	13.0
3	Neighbours	BBC	12.4
4	Home and Away	ITV	10.4
5	Big Break	BBC	10.1
6	The Bill	ITV	10.1
7	Emmerdale	ITV	9.5
8	9 O'Clock News	BBC	9.4
9	Chimera	ITV	9.4
10	Open All Hours	BBC	9.4
11	Birds of a Feather	BBC	9.2
12	Dad's Army	BBC	9.1
13	May To December	BBC	9.1
14	Rich Tea and Sympathy	ITV	8.7
15	News	ITV	8.2
16	News	BBC	7.8
17	Father Dowling	ITV	7.4
18	Stars In Their Eyes	ITV	7.4
19	On the Up	BBC	7.3
20	Busman's Holiday	ITV	7.3

AUGUST

1	Coronation Street	ITV	16.9
2	Neighbours	BBC	15.5
3	EastEnders	BBC	15.4
4	Deliberate Stranger	BBC	14.7
5	Home and Away	ITV	13.4
6	Deliberate Stranger	BBC	12.5
7	The Bill	ITV	12.5
8	Emmerdale	ITV	10.7
9	Private Benjamin	BBC	10.0
10	News At Ten	ITV	10.0
11	Best of Tommy Cooper	ITV	9.7
12	Busman's Holiday	ITV	9.5
13	The Bill	ITV	9.4
14	Just For Laughs	ITV	9.3
15	Open All Hours	BBC	9.3
16	Wheel of Fortune	ITV	9.2
17	New Life	BBC	9.2
18	L.A. Law	ITV	8.7
19	To Each His Own	ITV	8.6
20	Brush Strokes	BBC	8.6

SEPTEMBER

1	Coronation Street	ITV	17.6
2	EastEnders	BBC	15.6
3	Neighbours	BBC	14.9
4	Big Trouble In Little China	ITV	14.3
5	Casualty	BBC	12.2
6	Home and Away	ITV	12.0
7	Crocodile Dundee	BBC	12.0
8	The Bill	ITV	11.7
9	Birds of a Feather	BBC	11.3
10	Minder	ITV	11.2
11	Specially Canned Carrot	BBC	9.9
12	Crimewatch File	BBC	9.8
13	Hospital Watch	BBC	9.6
14	French Fields	ITV	9.6
15	Achille Lauro Affair	ITV	9.4
16	Bread	BBC	9.4
17	On H. M. Secret Service	ITV	9.2
18	You've Been Framed	ITV	9.1
19	Emmerdale	ITV	9.1
20	You Bet	ITV	9.0

OCTOBER

1	EastEnders	BBC	19.3
2	Coronation Street	ITV	18.7
3	Neighbours	BBC	16.6
4	Ruth Rendell Mysteries	ITV	14.3
5	London's Burning	ITV	14.1
6	The Bill	ITV	13.9
7	Blind Date	ITV	13.2
8	Casualty	BBC	13.1
9	Home and Away	ITV	13.1
10	Krypton Factor	ITV	12.6
11	Birds of a Feather	BBC	12.4
12	Minder	ITV	12.2
13	Strike It Lucky	ITV	12.1
14	Wilt	ITV	11.0
15	Never the Twain	ITV	10.9
16	Beadle's About	ITV	10.8
17	Emmerdale	ITV	10.8
18	French Fields	ITV	10.8
19	You Bet	ITV	10.7
20	Crimewatch UK	BBC	10.4

NOVEMBER

1	EastEnders	BBC	22.4
2	Coronation Street	ITV	21.0
3	London's Burning	ITV	17.2
4	Neighbours	BBC	16.9
5	Casualty	BBC	15.7
6	Ruth Rendell Mysteries	ITV	15.4
7	Blind Date	ITV	14.3
8	Strike It Lucky	ITV	14.1
9	The Karate Kid	ITV	14.1
10	The Bill	ITV	14.1
11	Home and Away	ITV	13.8
12	The Krypton Factor	ITV	13.7
13	Beadle's About	ITV	13.2
14	Birds of a Feather	BBC	12.3
15	Emmerdale	ITV	11.9
16	This Is Your Life	ITV	11.9
17	Minder	ITV	11.8
18	Bullseye	ITV	11.6
19	You Bet!	ITV	11.6
20	$64,000 Question	ITV	11.5

DECEMBER

1	Coronation Street	ITV	21.4
2	EastEnders	BBC	20.5
3	Neighbours	BBC	18.1
4	You've Been Framed	ITV	17.2
5	Big	ITV	16.4
6	Casualty	BBC	15.1
7	The Bill	ITV	15.1
8	Home and Away	ITV	14.6
9	The Is Your Life	ITV	14.5
10	Blind Date	ITV	13.9
11	Strike It Lucky	ITV	13.5
12	Wish You Were Here	ITV	13.5
13	Only Fools and Horses	BBC	13.2
14	Canned Carrot	BBC	12.4
15	Bullseye	ITV	12.2
16	Emmerdale	ITV	12.1
17	Ruth Rendell Mysteries	ITV	12.1
18	Family Fortunes	ITV	12.1
19	Upper Hand	ITV	11.5
20	Boon	ITV	11.3

1992
[Viewers in Millions]

JANUARY

1	EastEnders	BBC	22.9
2	Coronation Street	ITV	21.5
3	Neighbours	BBC	18.4
4	You've Been Framed	ITV	18.1
5	The Bill	ITV	16.3
6	This Is Your Life	ITV	15.8
7	Taggart	ITV	14.8
8	Family Fortunes	ITV	14.8
9	Home and Away	ITV	14.6
10	Watching	ITV	13.9
11	The Bill	ITV	13.5
12	Barrymore	ITV	13.4
13	Caught In the Act	BBC	13.3
14	Lovejoy	BBC	13.2
15	Antiques Roadshow	BBC	12.7
16	Time To Dance	BBC	12.7
17	As Time Goes By	BBC	12.7
18	Wish You Were Here	ITV	12.6
19	Upper Hand	ITV	12.5
20	Emmerdale	ITV	12.2

FEBRUARY

1	EastEnders	BBC	22.2
2	Coronation Street	ITV	20.4
3	You've Been Framed	ITV	19.0
4	Elizabeth R	BBC	17.8
5	Darling Buds of May	ITV	17.8
6	Neighbours	BBC	17.6
7	Wish You Were Here	ITV	16.2
8	Family Fortunes	ITV	15.0
9	Watching	ITV	14.8
10	This Is Your Life	ITV	14.8
11	One Foot In the Grave	BBC	14.4
12	Home and Away	ITV	14.3
13	The Bill	ITV	14.2
14	Best of Blind Date	ITV	14.7
15	Antiques Roadshow	BBC	14.4
16	Murder Squad	ITV	13.3
17	As Time Goes By	BBC	12.6
18	Big Break	BBC	12.0
19	Inspector Morse	ITV	11.8
20	Upper Hand	ITV	11.8

MARCH

1	EastEnders	BBC	22.0
2	Coronation Street	ITV	19.5
3	Neighbours	BBC	16.9
4	One Foot In the Grave	BBC	16.2
5	Wish You Were Here	ITV	15.2
6	You've Been Framed	ITV	15.1
7	Take Your Pick	ITV	14.4
8	So Haunt Me	BBC	14.2
9	The Bill	ITV	13.6
10	Home and Away	ITV	13.3
11	The Murder Squad	ITV	12.9
12	Noel's House Party	BBC	12.7
13	Antiques Roadshow	BBC	12.6
14	Forever Green	ITV	12.5
15	Lovejoy	BBC	12.0
17	Stars In Their Eyes	ITV	11.9
17	News and Weather	BBC	11.7
18	Emmerdale	ITV	11.5
19	The Brian Conley Show	ITV	11.5
20	Murder She Wrote	ITV	11.1

APRIL

1	Coronation Street	ITV	19.2
2	EastEnders	BBC	18.7
3	Inspector Morse	ITV	15.7
4	Neighbours	BBC	15.2
5	The Bill	ITV	14.1
6	Home and Away	ITV	12.9
7	A Question of Sport	BBC	12.7
8	In Suspicious Circumstances	ITV	12.6
9	Taggart	ITV	12.3
10	Opening of Euro Disney	ITV	12.3
11	This Is Your Life	ITV	12.3
12	Heartbeat	ITV	12.3
13	Man's Best Friends	BBC	12.2
14	Television's Greatest Hits	BBC	12.2
15	The Benny Hill Show	ITV	11.1
16	Emmerdale	ITV	11.0
17	Surprise Surprise	ITV	10.4
18	Medics	ITV	10.3
19	A Masculine Ending	BBC	10.0
20	Back To the Future	BBC	10.0

MAY

1	Coronation Street	ITV	19.2
2	EastEnders	BBC	18.1
3	Neighbours	BBC	15.8
4	Heartbeat	ITV	13.1
5	Only Fools and Horses	BBC	12.6
6	Through the Keyhhole	ITV	12.6
7	Home and Away	ITV	12.4
8	FA Cup Final 1992	BBC	12.3
9	A Fatal Inversion	BBC	12.1
10	The Bill	ITV	12.1
11	Grandstand	BBC	12.1
12	King Solomon's Mines	ITV	11.5
13	Eurovision Song Contest	BBC	11.4
14	Emmerdale	ITV	11.0
15	The Cook Report	ITV	10.7
16	Surprise, Surprise	ITV	10.3
17	The Benny Hill Show	ITV	10.2
18	Roses Are For the Rich	BBC	10.1
19	A Prince Among Islands	ITV	10.0
20	Diamonds Are Forever	ITV	9.9

JUNE

1	Coronation Street	ITV	19.3
2	EastEnders	BBC	17.0
3	Neighbours	BBC	14.9
4	Home and Away	ITV	13.4
5	The Bill	ITV	12.5
6	Through the Keyhole	ITV	12.0
7	Heartbeat	ITV	11.8
8	Wheel of Fortune	ITV	11.2
9	A Small Dance	ITV	11.1
10	Cluedo	ITV	11.0
11	Watching	ITV	11.0
12	Emmerdale	ITV	10.7
13	Porridge	BBC	9.8
14	Airplane	BBC	9.6
15	Birds of a Feather	BBC	9.4
16	Side By Side	BBC	9.4
17	The Cook Report	ITV	9.2
18	Mastermind: The Final	BBC	9.1
19	Root Into Europe	ITV	8.9
20	Keeping Up Appearances	BBC	8.7

JULY

1	Coronation Street	ITV	16.5
2	999	BBC	12.7
3	EastEnders	BBC	12.3
4	The Bill	ITV	11.8
5	Emmerdale	ITV	10.5
6	Crocodile Dundee	BBC	10.5
7	Neighbours	BBC	9.9
8	Catchphrase	ITV	9.8
9	Shadows of the Heart	BBC	9.4
10	Family Fortunes	ITV	9.4
11	News and Weather	BBC	9.3
12	Firm Friends	ITV	9.2
13	Keeping Up Appearances	BBC	9.2
14	Three Men and a Baby	ITV	9.1
15	Casualty	BBC	9.0
16	Home and Away	ITV	8.8
17	Father Dowling Investigates	ITV	8.6
18	News and Weather	BBC	8.6
19	Birds of a Feather	BBC	8.6
20	Growing Pains	BBC	8.4

MONTH BY MONTH 1992

Picture Credits

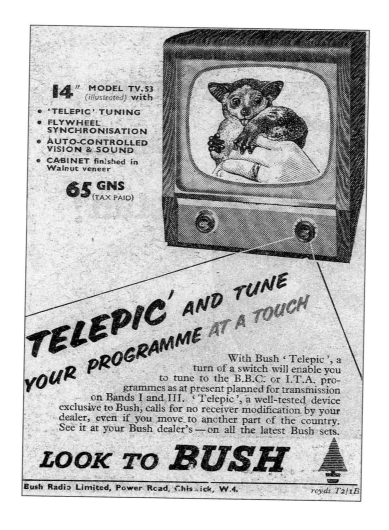